PT Boat
Odyssey

PT Boat Odyssey

*In the Pacific War with Motor Torpedo
Boat Squadron 16, 1943–1945*

ROBERT P. GELZHEISER

McFarland & Company, Inc., Publishers
Jefferson, North Carolina

ALSO BY ROBERT P. GELZHEISER

Labor and Capital in 19th Century Baseball
(McFarland, 2006)

LIBRARY OF CONGRESS CATALOGUING-IN-PUBLICATION DATA

Names: Gelzheiser, Robert P., 1955– author.
Title: PT boat odyssey : in the Pacific war with Motor Torpedo Boat Squadron 16, 1943–1945 / Robert P. Gelzheiser.
Other titles: In the Pacific war with Motor Torpedo Boat Squadron 16, 1943–1945
Description: Jefferson, North Carolina : McFarland & Company, Inc., Publishers, 2019 | Includes bibliographical references and index.
Identifiers: LCCN 2019014945 | ISBN 9781476662640 (paperback : acid free paper) ∞
Subjects: LCSH: Gelzheiser, Francis, 1921–2011. | United States. Navy. Motor Torpedo Boat Squadron 16—Biography. | Sailors—United States—Biography. | Torpedo-boats—United States—History—20th century. | World War, 1939–1945—Pacific Area. | World War, 1939–1945—Naval operations, American.
Classification: LCC D774.M67 G45 2019 | DDC 940.54/5973—dc23
LC record available at https://lccn.loc.gov/2019014945

BRITISH LIBRARY CATALOGUING DATA ARE AVAILABLE

**ISBN (print) 978-1-4766-6264-0
ISBN (ebook) 978-1-4766-3389-3**

© 2019 Robert Gelzheiser. All rights reserved

No part of this book may be reproduced or transmitted in any form or by any means, electronic or mechanical, including photocopying or recording, or by any information storage and retrieval system, without permission in writing from the publisher.

Front cover: PT *221* underway
(World War II PT Boats Museum and Archives, Germantown, Tennessee)

Printed in the United States of America

*McFarland & Company, Inc., Publishers
Box 611, Jefferson, North Carolina 28640
www.mcfarlandpub.com*

To Electrician's Mate Second Class
Francis L. Gelzheiser
and his
Motor Torpedo Boat Squadron 16 squadron mates

Near the snow, near the sun, in the highest fields,
See how these names are fêted by the waving grass
And by the streamers of white cloud
And whispers of wind in the listening sky.
The names of those who in their lives fought for life,
Who wore at their hearts the fire's centre.
Born of the sun, they travelled a short while toward the sun
And left the vivid air signed with their honour.
—From "The Truly Great" by Stephen Spender

Table of Contents

Acknowledgments	ix
Introduction	1
1. A Father's Workshop	5
2. December 7, 1941	9
3. The Motor Patrol Torpedo Boat	18
4. The Grand Adventure: The Voyage to Panama	35
5. PT Boat Squadron 16 and the War in Alaska	55
6. The Battle for New Guinea and the Motor Torpedo Boat Returns to the Philippines	88
7. American Production Versus the Japanese Spirit Warrior in World War II	120
8. Mindoro	142
9. The Battle for Manila and a Sailor's Journey into the Darkness	234
10. Father and Son, Confessions and a Sailor's Last Voyage	247
Afterword: Killing	261
Appendix A. Motor Torpedo Boat Squadron 16 Honor Roll: Awards and Citations	267
Appendix B. Memorandum and Suggested Unit Citation Sent by Lieutenant Commander Davis to Rear Admiral Bowling	269
Chapter Notes	271
Bibliographic Note	281
Bibliography	284
Index	287

Acknowledgments

Numerous individuals assisted me in the writing of *PT Boat Odyssey*, and I am grateful to all of them. Without the efforts made by James M. "Boats" Newberry to preserve the history of World War II patrol torpedo (PT) boats, I do not believe it would have been possible to write this book. "Boats" served as a chief boatswain's mate in Squadron 9 on PT boat *155*. Chief Newberry and his shipmates participated in some of the most dangerous and successful PT boat operations of the war, and he is a man who certainly deserves to be called "war hero."

After the war, "Boats" started a successful business, raised a family, and hunted big game. However, he never lost his love of PT boats and the men who served on them. In 1967 he founded PT Boats, Inc., and when he retired, he devoted himself full-time to this organization. He located thousands of World War II PT boat veterans and encouraged them to join this organization. He located and then raised hundreds of thousands of dollars to acquire and refurbish PTs *617* and *796*. These Elco and Higgins boats are today displayed at Battleship Cove in Fall River, Massachusetts, and thousands of individuals see these boats each year.

Just as important, PT Boats, Inc., collected thousands of documents related to PT boats in World War II. Photos, models, artifacts, and first hand narratives are all housed in Fall River and the PT Boats, Inc., headquarters in Germantown, Tennessee. He also helped to organize the annual PT boat reunions that my father and his squadron mates faithfully attended. After the passing of "Boats" in 1985, his wife, Alyce Forster "Mrs. Boats" Newberry, who had worked tirelessly by her husband's side since the founding of PT Boats, Inc., continued his work until her passing in 2005. Beginning in 1982, their daughter Alyce worked for PT Boats, Inc. She became instrumental in the ongoing operation and success of PT Boats, Inc., and she was eventually joined by her daughter Allyson. Both Alyce and Allyson helped me to locate primary sources and photographs for this book, and they answered numerous questions about PT boats and PT Boat Squadron 16. Their efforts to keep the story of World War II PT boats alive would make Chief Newberry proud.

Donald Shannon is employed by PT Boats, Inc., and is the PT Boat Curator at Battleship Cove. Don oversees PTs *617* and *796*, and he also maintains the extensive archive collection at the museum. He is one of the foremost experts on the construction and operation of World War II PT boats. And when I visited him at Fall River, Don was generous with his time, and he helped me to locate many materials that were valuable in writing this book. He also answered numerous questions I had on the construction and armaments of the boats, and he graciously gave me a private tour of the Higgins boat at Battleship Cove.

Nancy Manning is a published novelist and teaches English at Woodland Regional High School in Beacon Falls, Connecticut. She and I worked together for many years. She read an early draft of this book, made many valuable and insightful comments and suggestions, and encouraged me to continue my research and complete the book. Susan Cinoman teaches English and drama at Woodland Regional High School. Susan is a successful writer, and she and her husband Doug patiently listened as I told them the story of my father and encouraged me to write this book. Coach Tim Phipps and Ben Palladino taught history with me at Woodland Regional High School. Coach Phipps is a fine military historian, and Ben Palladino is a serious student of George Washington and the Colonial Period in American history. Both of these men listened patiently as I told them Squadron 16's story, helped me to better understand this in the context of World War II, and gave me encouragement and sound advice while I was in the process of writing this book. My wife, Lynn Gelzheiser, spent many hours proofreading my manuscript and helped me with numerous technological problems, and I am sure she knows more about World War II PT boats than she ever wished to know.

I am also grateful to all of the sailors who served in Squadron 16 who took the time to record their stories. Some of these men, like Tom Hart, I was fortunate enough to get to know. Others, I learned about through my father, and others I only got to know through the written accounts they left behind. It would have been very difficult to write this book without the accounts of their experiences in Squadron 16.

Finally I want to thank my father, Francis Gelzheiser. Late in his life I came to understand that my dad wanted the story of PT Boat Squadron 16 to be told. I believe that ego had little to do with this. Instead I believe he had a desire to record the story of these small boats, to remind future generations of the sacrifices that were made by the men who crewed them in the defense of liberty, and to also remind future generations that war is horrible, that all citizens should carefully ponder whether or not the nation should go to war, and that war should be avoided whenever possible.

Introduction

Only a virtuous people are capable of freedom.—Ben Franklin

Virtuous Men

Growing up in the decades following World War II, the public face of the war was everywhere. On weekends we would go to the movies and for fifty cents watch Gregory Peck, David Niven, and Anthony Quinn destroy the *Guns of Navarone*, John Wayne and an all-star cast endure *The Longest Day* as America fought to liberate Western Europe, or Ernest Borgnine, Charles Bronson, Lee Marvin and the rest of the *Dirty Dozen* fight to earn their freedom by going on a "suicide mission." My good friend Joe Delco's father had fought with General George Patton during the war, and when the movie *Patton*, starring George C. Scott, came out in 1970, Joe memorized the speech delivered by Scott during the film's opening scene. At our request, Joe would tack an American flag to a wall, stand in front of it, and recite the speech much to our delight. From our small black and white television sets, we would spend evenings enthralled by the exploits of the bomber crews in *Twelve O'Clock High* or the soldiers who endeavored to defeat Field Marshal Erwin Rommel and the Germans in *The Rat Patrol*. If it was laughter we wanted, we could tune in and watch Colonel Robert Hogan and his men make fools of the Germans in *Hogan's Heroes* or Quinton McHale and his PT boat crew have a grand time in the Pacific. Before beginning our dirt bomb fights, we would first argue about who would be the Germans or "Japs" and who would get to be the Americans. Our world was simple, and there was a clear delineation between the United States, the force of good, and the Japanese and Germans, the forces of evil.

There was another face to the war that was more ubiquitous and at the same time almost invisible. The real heroes of the war resided on most blocks in America, and Fairfield, Connecticut, the town of my youth, was no different. The post–World War II period was perhaps the Golden Age of the American sandlot. After school or on summer mornings we would gather at friends' houses and then set out on our bikes to play baseball. As we peddled to the various fields on which we played, we often passed these men, but we never saw them in the same light as the heroes we viewed on movie screens or television sets. We would roll past Mr. Delco working on his car, and we never thought of him as a hero … I now realize that he was. He had fought with the 9th Infantry Division or "Old Reliables" in North Africa and then at Normandy and across France and in the Battle of the Bulge. What had he endured so that we could experience the freedom of our youth? At Doug's house we would encounter Mr. Williams. He was a successful Yale-educated lawyer who helped many of us out when the foolish acts of our youth caused us to have issues with the law. It was only when he died and I read his obituary, that I learned he was a Marine Corps fighter pilot at the Battle of Okinawa. The Dobyns boys' dad flew fighters in both World War II and Korea, but I never heard him say a word of his experiences; and Mark's father, Mr. Kalinowski, was an aerial photographer in the Pacific. When he died and I helped his family move, we found thousands of the photographs he took. What risks did he take to get these photographs, and what stories did he have to tell that we never heard?

My parents had numerous friends and family members who also fought in World War II. Mr. Josselyn taught middle school science and helped me with my chemistry. He had stormed the beaches of Normandy. Mr. Dreese was always kind to me, and he was a loyal friend to my parents. He spoke with a funny accent because he had migrated from Holland soon after the Germans were defeated. His story was fascinating and mysterious. He had joined the Dutch Underground early in the war and fought with them until the Germans were defeated. His entire family was killed by the Nazis.

My uncle, Glenn Koach, who is now in his mid-nineties, is thoughtful, wise, and blessed with a wonderfully dry sense of humor. He also served as a turret gunner on a B-24 Liberator Bomber during World War II. Despite the fact that bomber crews in World War II had the most dangerous job in the American military, he has told me little of his experiences during the war. He did share with me at my father's wake that he lamented that the United States continued to drop thousands of tons of bombs on the Germans during the last weeks of the war. I think it haunted him that we continued to kill so many when he believed Germany was already defeated.[1]

Not since children grew up in the shadow of the Civil War had heroes been so prevalent in America; and yet although we interacted with these men every day, their past heroism went unacknowledged. These men taught school, raked and burned leaves on cool fall afternoons, coached youth sports, cooked hotdogs and hamburgers at elementary school fairs, took us fishing, and played catch with us on summer evenings after they had come home from work. But they said almost nothing about their war, and we asked little about what they had experienced. We knew they had served, but we did not view them as men who had helped to win World War II.

I believe there are several reasons why we did not see these men as heroes. When I was in the fifth and sixth grades, my teachers, Mrs. Jones and Mrs. Cope, both taught lengthy units on World War II, and both examined the Holocaust. They did not spare us from the brutal truth of this event. I can still remember the films they showed with mounds of emaciated bodies being bulldozed into trenches and near dead, blank eyed, starving people staring into the camera. These people had clearly endured something beyond my comprehension, and in an attempt to understand this industrialized slaughter of innocents, I conjured up an image of an enemy so brutal and evil that they had to be some kind of super humans. Since normal people could not commit such horrendous acts, normal people, like the men I encountered every day, could not have defeated them or their allies.

In addition, the World War II veterans of my youth possessed a modesty and decency that precluded them from talking about their war in any detail, and I am sure many did not talk about their war because it was too difficult to do so or because what they had done and witnessed could never really be understood by people who had never been to war. I do not know how many of these men suffered from post-traumatic stress disorder, possibly they all did, but if they did, they suffered in silence. Perhaps they had nightmares or turned to drink when the demons were too haunting or quietly cried in the night, but they always kept the real war from us.

If there was a common denominator to boyhood during this era it was freedom. In summers we would be gone from dawn until dusk, fishing, playing baseball, or just hanging out. We were living a boyhood our fathers could have only dreamed of as they suffered through the Great Depression. Perhaps they believed that if they burdened us with the truths of their war that somehow the innocence of our boyhood would be shattered. I feel guilty writing this, but their silence was a gift to us.

In 1998 Tom Brokaw wrote a book titled *The Greatest Generation* about the people who survived the Great Depression and then fought World War II. Despite the huge success of this book, I am doubtful if most of the modest, quiet heroes of my youth would have been comfortable with the title; and although there is no doubt of the greatness of this generation, I choose to use a different term to define them.

When America was being created, our founders disagreed on much. Some wanted two chief executives, others none, and some wanted to create an American monarchy. Some embraced the weakness of the Articles of Confederation, and others wanted a stronger central government than the one that was eventually created. What they all agreed on was that if a republic of America's size was to survive, it had to be populated by virtuous citizens. There was even some disagreement about what constituted virtue, but all agreed that a central component of virtue was the willingness to put aside one's self-interest for the interests of the republic.

Virtue is rarely talked about today, and my guess is that few of the men of my youth thought of themselves as virtuous or even used the word in any context. I do not know if this was America's greatest generation, but I have no doubt that it was a virtuous one. Today narcissism is so prevalent that millions tweet to the world or publish on their Facebook page what kind of breakfast burrito they ate in the morning and somehow they think we should care. It is strange to think of this in the context of the men I passed on my way to play baseball, who when young had risked everything and helped to save the world from a grave evil and who said almost nothing of their exploits. They would never say or probably even think this, but these men exemplified what it means to be a virtuous citizen.

PT Boat Odyssey is the story of one of these men, my father, Francis Gelzheiser. A child of the Depression, he spent the war as a member of Motor Torpedo Boat Squadron 16. He and his shipmates would motor their small wooden craft through the Gulf of Mexico and then south until they reached the Panama Canal. After advanced training in Panama they were taken back to Seattle, Washington, and then they journeyed under their own power north to Alaska and faced the dangers of the Bering Sea as they motored to the desolate island of Attu at the far end of the Aleutian Islands. After returning to Seattle, they were sent to New Guinea and then the Philippine islands of Leyte and Mindoro. It was in the Philippines that a desperate Japan unleashed a new weapon, the kamikaze, and while at Mindoro the sailors of Squadron 16 would face these horrifying manned bombs. After the island of Luzon was invaded, a grim battle for the capital city of Manila was waged. Some of the worst urban fighting of the war occurred in the Philippine capital, and in the process, most of the city was leveled and 100,000 Filipino civilians were killed. Shortly after the city had been liberated, my father and a friend journeyed into it. What he witnessed haunted him for the rest of his life.

The central figures in this story, my father and his squadron mates, were far from the warrior super heroes that so often fill American movie screens. In fact, most of these sailors were ordinary men of average physical stature who spent their post-war lives doing average things: raising families, doing their best at their chosen professions, and being good, reliable members of their communities. However, their very ordinariness makes their story even more compelling. They had all grown up during the Great Depression and known poverty, real poverty. They had volunteered for the Navy when their country had been attacked, and then volunteered to serve on tiny wooden PT boats. These vessels often engaged much larger ships, endured ferocious seas, and regularly motored into harm's way. The John Ford film made about these boats was titled *They Were Expendable*, and I believe this title was appropriate.

World War II was a conflict fought by tens of millions of people in all corners of the globe, and often when the war is examined the focus is on huge armies and navies and the officers who commanded them. However, war is the most human of stories, and to understand it one must examine it at its most individual level. As ordinary as they may have been, my father and his squadron mates were almost all men who possessed an innate decency and quiet courage, and they understood that history had dictated that their generation had been called to combat evil. Many today might find this trite, but they all believed that they had to do their duty, and in doing so, they displayed the best attributes of the American citizen warrior.

My father's story is worth telling for a variety of reasons. The PT boat was a small craft that saw an inordinate amount of action during World War II, but most students of the war know little about these small vessels. In addition, the actions in which my father and the sailors of Squadron 16 participated—Alaska, New Guinea, and the Philippine island of Mindoro—are often under-examined in traditional World War II histories. In order to put my father's story in context, I will examine these campaigns in a larger perspective and then explore the role played by the PT boats of Squadron 16. In the last part of the book I will examine how my father came to terms with the war as he grew older.

The quiet heroes of my youth are almost all gone now, but I still want to take this opportunity to thank them. I want to thank them for their courage, decency, and for the respect they showed all of us as we were growing up. I want to thank them for helping to defeat the great forces of evil that descended upon the world in the 1930s and 40s and then for coming home and helping to build a post-war world that for us was carefree and wonderful. Most of all, I want to thank them for their virtue. We should all be grateful for their sacrifices, and we can all still learn much from their example.

1

A Father's Workshop

To men who have been long in battle and have thought about it deeply, there comes at last the awareness of this ultimate responsibility—that one man must go ahead so that a nation may live.... At the time one accepts it simply as the rule of life and death.—Colonel Samuel Lyman Atwood Marshall, Men Against Fire

For most of my father's adult life, if you descended into the basement of his house, you would have found a cluttered workshop. A table saw, lathe, drill press, chop saw, and numerous other power tools were haphazardly placed throughout the shop; and on and around each was multi-colored sawdust and other detritus that blended together from the various projects he had worked on over the years. Against the wall was an old, sturdy workbench my father built shortly after he married my mother in 1952. On the back, sides, and front of the workbench, well-worn hand tools that had assisted him in countless ways were stored on shelves and hung on various nails and hooks, and on the bench's front right was a vice. Although constructed of hardened steel, it was lined with wood so as not to damage whatever was placed in it.

When I was a little boy, one of the first skills my father taught me was how to cut wood with a crosscut saw. He showed me how to mark a straight line with a T-square where I wanted to cut, and then how to put the wood in the vice, making sure that the portion to be cut off did not protrude too far out. If it did, the board would vibrate when cutting it. He explained how to grip the handle of the saw with my right hand and steady it on the top with my left. He then gently guided me as I pulled the saw backward to start the cut. When this cut was sufficiently deep to keep the saw in the groove, he showed me how to push the saw forward in a slow, even motion. "Let the saw do the cutting," he quietly directed, and like magic, with each push, the saw cut deeper into the wood. As the saw neared the end of the four- to five-inch-wide board, he urged me to slow down and ease into the final cut, so as not to tear the wood. Finally, with one last gentle push of the saw, the piece that was hanging outside the vice fell to the floor. As it hit the ground, I felt a quiet sense of satisfaction. I had followed his directions, cut only on the forward thrust, gently pulled back ... cut ... pulled back ... and cut all the while following the line to ensure straightness.

I was about seven at the time, but when that piece fell to the floor, I felt in some mysterious way like I had entered the world of men. In the 1950s and 1960s, this world was filled with men who had fought a great war, come home, perhaps gone to college on the G.I. Bill, started families, worked, and spent much of their free time in basement and garage workshops. They had vices, saws, workbenches, and numerous other hand and power tools, and they took great pride in knowing how to use them. They could build furniture, fix almost anything, and maintain their cars, and they were always willing to lend a hand when a neighbor had a project that was too big for one man. I wonder though, in the hundreds of hours they spent alone in their workshops repairing, tinkering, building, painting, and sanding, where did their minds drift? As the boys of America played baseball on neighborhood sandlots or watched *Superman* or baseball or the latest epic film that would inspire them or ignite their imaginations, in a world with little fear or blood or real pain, where were their fathers?

Underneath my father's workbench, he kept a plane. This tool was always placed on its side when not in use, and it was stored in a well-worn brown box. The plane was about nine inches long, and at its rear was a smooth, S-shaped wooden handle that the user could comfortably wrap his hand around. Much of the varnish was worn off this handle, and this was replaced by the patina created by the sweat and hand oils that had rubbed off after hours of use. Toward the front of the plane, underneath the smooth, polished, shiny steel base was the blade. For the tool to work properly, this blade had to have a razor-like edge, and this was why my father insisted that the tool be stored on its side. When I was a boy, my father encouraged me to look at the plane carefully. He pointed out the wheel on the top of the plane in front of the handle. This allowed the user to adjust the blade. He instructed me to turn the wheel clockwise, and I watched as the blade would protrude slightly more downward and be more exposed with each turn. He then had me turn it counterclockwise, and slowly the blade would be pulled back closer to the tool's smooth base.

The plane was a tool my father valued greatly, and although I am not sure he understood this, the rules of the plane were his rules of life. The plane was Fran Gelzheiser's survival guide. Used properly, the plane could create great beauty in wood. The user firmly gripped his right hand around the wooden S-shaped rear handle that rose vertically from the tool's metal base, and the palm of the left hand would rest on the smooth, rounded wooden knob secured to the tool's front. The metal base of the tool would be kept flat on the wood, and rhythmically the user would push the tool forward at a slight leftward angle, always following the grain. Special care had to be taken if knots or other blemishes were found in the wood; however, wood that held these could be especially beautiful, but only if it was planed in a gentle, deliberate way. Many times I watched my father plane. As the tool was guided forward, the blade would slice a thin veneer off the surface of the wood. This would curl up and exit through a thin slot in back of the blade and gently fall to the floor. With each thrust of the plane, a new curled strip would float to the basement floor and deposit itself around my dad's feet. Slowly the wood would take on a new texture. From rough hewn to smooth to glasslike, the wood's character, grain, and beauty would become more visible. No tool could transform a piece of wood like the plane. The key to using the plane and finding this beauty was to expose only as little of the blade as possible, to place just the slightest pressure on the top front of the tool, and to gently push and never drive the tool from the rear. My father would never have used this term, but there was a Zen to proper planing.

Placed in the wrong hands, the plane was an instrument of destruction. The user who wanted to complete the job too quickly, who did not understand that finding beauty took time, would expose too much of the blade, put too much downward pressure on the tool's front, and drive the plane forward in an unyielding way. The result would be disastrous. Instead of removing long, beautifully curled, smooth strips, the blade would gouge into the wood, scarring and potentially ruining it. To my father, a piece of wood was living. It housed great beauty, and at the same time it could be put to important uses. It was the perfect mix of the practical and aesthetic, and for a man who was equal parts artist, naturalist, and engineer, such a material warranted our respect. Wood deserved to be planed properly.

Not surprisingly, my father was a master with the plane. With patience and gentleness, the wood would surrender her beauty to his plane, but always on her terms. To rush the process, to demand that the rules be different, was to destroy. Acceptance of the realities of the tool, the wood, and the man were everything when planing.

On the left side of the tool rack mounted on the rear of my father's workbench was a sheathed knife. It was an official United States Navy–issue knife stamped U.S.N. M.K.1. It was issued to my father shortly after he entered the Navy, and he was told always to take care of it. Although well worn, the blade is still sharp today, and other than the broken snap on the sheath, it looks much as it did when he first received it. Unlike the vice, saw, plane, and numerous other tools on his workbench, I do not recall my father teaching me how to use this knife. Looking back, I do not recall him ever using this tool in my presence. He had numerous other knives, and he showed me how to sharpen and use them safely, and I can still hear him gently reminding me to "always cut away from your body so that if the knife slips it will not cut you." Often, when camping, we would strip the bark off slim branches to make sticks suitable for roasting hot dogs and marshmallows on the campfires he loved to make, and once we even made a working wooden pocket knife that I still have. When I was still a very young boy, he gave me my first pocket knife, a tool I still use today. Still, in the countless hours we spent together in his shop as he taught me skills that I still utilize today, as we repaired bicycles, built and refinished furniture, or worked on our fishing tackle, I never recall the Navy knife leaving its sheath.

Knives were useful tools, but I do not believe that using them gave my father much joy. Compared to the plane, knives were crude, blunt, imprecise instruments. They were necessary, but unlike the plane, their rhythmic use would not unlock the hidden beauty of wood. The plane could teach a man about life … not the knife.

For decades, the Navy knife rested in its designated spot on the workbench. I was already well into middle age when my father finally unsheathed it and directed me to look carefully at the knife's bolster. Here, easily visible, were three small grooves, and if you angled them toward the light, each of them glistened as they did more than seventy years ago when they were first etched. It is these small grooves that tell part of a great untold story, for each of these was put there to represent a man that my father shot

My father's Navy knife. Notice the three grooves on the bolster. Bob Gelzheiser collection.

and killed at close range on a little known Philippine island in the final year of World War II. Looking back, I am not sure if he was just keeping the secret of the knife from me. Now I believe it was the worst kind of secret, one that he was trying to keep from others and more importantly from himself. Thus begins the story of my father and his war as a member of Motor Torpedo Boat Squadron 16.

2

December 7, 1941

Thousands of our men will soon be returning to you. They have been gone a long time and they have seen and done and felt things you cannot know. They will be changed.—Ernie Pyle, *Brave Men*

On October 13, 1921, Art Nehf, the skilled left-handed pitcher for the New York Giants, threw a four-hit shutout against the New York Yankees and future Hall of Fame pitcher Waite Hoyt at the Giants' home park, the Polo Grounds, to win the fifth and deciding game of that year's World Series by a score of 1–0. Hoyt pitched 27 innings in the series and did not give up an earned run, and the only run scored in the deciding game occurred when Yankee shortstop Roger Peckinpaugh allowed a ground ball to skip through his legs which allowed Giants shortstop Dave Bancroft to score from second base.[1]

Four hundred and four miles to the west, as the Giants' fans were celebrating, 26-year-old, German-born Josephine Theresa Gelzheiser gave birth to my father, Francis Leo Gelzheiser. Ironically, on my father's 39th birthday, a gritty, slick fielding second baseman from the coal country of West Virginia named Bill Mazeroski came to the plate for the Pittsburgh Pirates in the bottom half of the ninth inning against the New York Yankees in game seven of the World Series. With the score tied 9–9, "Maz" hit the next pitch over left fielder Yogi Berra and the left field wall at Pittsburgh's Forbes Field to defeat the mighty Yankees and win the World Series for Pittsburgh. My father remembered this home run and victory well, and often on his birthday I would wish him a happy anniversary to the "Maz" home run, and also "Happy Birthday."

On the day of Nehf's pitching gem and my father's birth, Warren G. Harding, a man always on the bottom tier of presidential historians' rankings, occupied the White House. That same year the Washington Disarmament Conference was held, an event that would play an important role in America's troubled relationship with Japan leading up to the attack on Pearl Harbor. Japan's Crown Prince Hirohito would be named Prince Regent, Takashi Hara, the Premier of Japan, would be assassinated, and Hitler's Storm Troopers, the SA, would terrorize the fledgling Nazi Party's opponents two years prior to Hitler's failed Beer Hall Putsch.[2]

I have almost no knowledge of my father's first six years. I know that his mother was born in Germany, and she became a naturalized citizen. She had a seventh-grade education, never held a full-time job, and in 1939 her reported income was zero dollars. She also loved her two children very much. His father, Joseph Ignatius Gelzheiser, is a kind of ghost in the Gelzheiser family history, and growing up we almost never asked about him. I do know that he was unable or unwilling to care for his wife and two young children. One of the few times my father ever mentioned him occurred when one of my friends asked my dad about his father and my father acted as if he did not hear the question. After the question was asked again, my dad responded tersely, "My father was a plumber and he made good potato pancakes." It was clear that this was a subject that he did not want to talk about and a moment or two of silence followed. Then out of the blue he quipped, "But he was a good guy." I have since learned that my grandfather was almost forty when my dad was born, and that he intermittently worked as a plumber, cooper, laborer in a steel mill, and bartender. This last occupation was a poor career choice since he was also an alcoholic. He died before my father graduated from high school.

My father's older sister Marie shared with me that during my father's first six years their parents fought often, and then one day, with no explanation, strange people came to their small apartment and removed my father and Marie. They were taken to Saint Joseph Orphan Asylum, a German-Catholic orphanage on Troy Hill Road in Pittsburgh, where they would spend almost the next eight years of their lives. Once he arrived at "The Home" my father's relationship with his father ended, and he only saw his mother on visiting days.[3] However, despite the fact that he was abandoned by his father at six, I was not surprised when my father remarked that his father was a "good guy." He was displaying an essential survival skill that he would continue to employ many decades later while on his deathbed. No matter what the situation, my father almost always found a way to view it positively.

My father talked freely about his time in "The Home," and if you believed that he told the entire story, you would think spending more than seven years of your youth in a Catholic orphanage during the Great Depression was a wonderful way to grow up. The Saint Joseph Orphanage was a fortress-like structure that segregated boys from girls. This separation was so rigidly enforced that when my father's sister Marie had a serious medical problem, most likely a ruptured appendix, my father was not allowed to visit her for the months she was convalescing, and when they did finally see each other from the opposite sides of a chain link fence, they were both reprimanded for touching each other's hands through the fence.

In a corner of the orphanage's yard next to the exterior fence were a number of chickens and their coops. "The Home" would use the eggs to supplement the meager rations that were available to each child, and my father and a friend got the job of tending the chickens. In this secluded area, the two boys spent much time trying to carve out some normalcy in their otherwise difficult childhoods. Once after completing their chores at the chicken coops, they starting playing with matches they had found. Dry hay and grass quickly caught fire, and soon the fence and other nearby detritus were on fire. When their efforts to extinguish the flames failed, the two boys panicked and fled.

The nuns' response to this was quick and decisive, but the conclusion they reached was wrong. "The Home" had its share of bullies, and one of them regularly tormented and beat my dad. Ironically, this was the young man the nuns determined had started the fire. My father never believed they had any evidence, but instead the nuns were looking for a reason to punish a young man they did not trust or like, and this provided them with such an opportunity. My father was already terrified, but his fear only grew when he went to the Mother Superior's office and heard the bully screaming and then witnessed the Head Nun beating my father's nemesis.

My dad now felt guilty over the fire he had ignited and the suffering his actions had caused another boy to endure. This guilt was mixed with fear over what would happen if the bully and Mother Superior found out my father had started the fire. As the Mother Superior continued to hit the innocent boy and his screams echoed through the hallway, my father meekly knocked on her door. Mid-wallop he told her that he had started the fire, and her response was to become angrier. However, her anger was not directed at my dad, but at the realization that she now could no longer continue paddling a boy she viewed as a trouble maker and seemed happy to be hitting.

My father always smiled when he then explained that not only did the Mother Superior not punish him, but the bully was so grateful to my father for rescuing him from the beating that he never harassed my dad again and on several occasions even protected him from other bullies.[4]

Despite the funny stories my father told of his time in "The Home," it was a very difficult place to grow up. He never fully explained this reality to me, but over time his sister Marie and her friend, who was there at the same time, told me the truth that my dad refused to tell or buried so deep that he hid it even from himself. The Saint Joseph Orphan Asylum had the look and feel of a nineteenth-century prison. Its walls were high, dark and foreboding. Behind them food and clothing were scarce, and the orphans who lived there were required to spend long hours doing arduous chores, such as waxing the facility's floors by hand, working in the kitchen, and keeping the bunk area where they lived spotless. The nuns were strict, and corporal punishment was administered freely. They did work hard to provide a safe environment for the children, but they were almost never maternal or loving. Buildings were cold in the winters and hot in the summers.

Although the orphans were under-loved and poorly fed and clothed, they were well educated. My father's keen mind responded well to the rigid structure that was employed by the nuns who served as teachers, and by the time he left at fourteen he had mastered English grammar and arithmetic, and he was a skilled reader. I never heard him complain about his time in the orphanage, and in fact he told me on several occasions that in "The Home" he received a good education and had a roof over his head, and in many ways his

My father and his sister Marie on the day they arrived at the Saint Joseph Orphan Asylum. Notice the look of bewilderment on his face. Bob Gelzheiser collection.

childhood was better than countless other children whose parents did not abandon them. I am not sure if he believed this or if this is another example of his insistence of always seeing things in a positive light.

My father and his sister were not released from "The Home" because their mother had remarried or gotten a job, or because their father was now a better breadwinner. Their release was made possible because Josephine Gelzheiser had started to receive a small monthly relief check from the government. In addition, while attending Avalon High School, my father got a job at the school through Roosevelt's National Youth Administration Program, and he also worked additional odd jobs. During the summer he would wash neighbors' houses, and during the school year he worked as a pin boy at the local bowling alley.[5]

Money was always tight; and on a tour of his old neighborhood when I asked him why he had lived in so many different places, he responded that often they would flee an apartment in the middle of the night because the family was unable to pay the rent. It is always difficult to assess the impact that a person's upbringing has on them, but the one result of the poverty he faced in his youth that my father always acknowledged was that he never forgot the shame he felt because his family had received "charity" from the government. He made no secret that he vowed to never again need "relief," and for all of his adult life he took great pride in providing a good life for his family. Another byproduct of being abandoned as a small boy was that my father needed to be needed.

Despite being fatherless and poor, the years between my dad's release from "The Home" and the war were good to my father. Always keenly observant, he started to draw. At 14, he passed a beautiful German Shepherd named Bozo on his way home from school each day. He befriended the dog, carefully examined his features each day, and went home and drew what he remembered. Today the drawing of Bozo hangs on my office wall, a beautiful rendering of a handsome dog. His drawings and paintings were often used on posters to advertise school events and regularly were displayed on the hallway walls at Avalon High School or in the pages of the school yearbook, the *Avalon Annual*.

It was also during these years that my dad developed the love of nature that he retained for the rest of his life and that I believe helped to sustain him during the war. On summer days and on weekends when he was not working, he and his buddies would take from their homes or purchase some canned food and head out on camping trips. Sometimes a friend's dad would drive them to their destination, but more often they would simply walk for miles until they had left the city and entered a woods or meadow. They would camp by streams, take long hikes, swim, capture butterflies, and enjoy evening campfires.

Several of the apartments where my dad spent his middle school and high school years were within walking distance of the Ohio River, and he and his friends spent summer days swimming in the river; and as a result, my father developed into the best underwater swimmer I have ever known. The reason he developed this skill was various factories deposited their waste into the river and the surface of the water was often covered by scum. This scum tended to congregate near the shore, so the boys would heave a large stone as far as they could and then quickly swim under water until they reached the hole in the scum. From here, they would catch their breath and then descend below the scum and try to make it to the less polluted center of the river. When returning, they would often stay on the water's surface and would swim to shore using a modified breaststroke that they referred to as the "Ohio River Crawl." Instead of driving their arms forward and then pulling them back and to the side, they would instead hold their palms open and facing forward and up and out of the water. As they kicked themselves to shore, they would push the surface scum and debris ahead of them until they reached the shore.

My father became adept at capturing, identifying, and mounting insects, and he often displayed his mounted insects in frames that he made in his high school woodshop. On occasion, he would meet with entomologists at the University of Pittsburgh to get help identifying and mounting the insects he had captured, and once some insects were so rare and well displayed that the University accepted them as a gift from my father. One frame of his butterflies and one of his moths still survive, and they look as good today as the day the insects were mounted. The specimens in the frames are huge, and most are species that I have never seen. My brother Ed, who shared my father's keen observation skills and love of nature, still proudly displays these beautiful framed creatures on a wall in his apartment.

My father's high school experience was a happy one. He was the vice president of Mr. Floyd's Motor Club, and he helped to organize the Gym Hop that the club put on in September of his senior year. He also "lent his artistic touches to the organization by displaying posters," and he worked on the school's yearbook as an artist, salesman, and co-business manager. His senior comment proclaims, "The attractive and delightful artwork which distinguished our dance decorations were developed through the labor of obliging Francis Gelzheiser. 'Gelch' was also well learned in entomology. His many social functions around the school earned him a spotlight in the Avalon High School Hall of Fame."[6]

When my father graduated from high school in June 1940, he had grown to a height of five feet and eight inches. He was wiry and rail thin, the result of an active youth and a scarcity of food. He had wonderful thick, wavy dark hair that turned gray in late middle age and white as an old man. Although he maintained a certain vanity about his hair, he almost never washed it with anything but a bar of soap, and his idea of styling it was to wet his comb and comb it straight back. He had a large nose and a thick full face that always looked younger than its years, and he smiled and laughed easily. He had keen, deep blue eyes, and these retained their sparkle until his death. When he graduated from high school, his dreams were simple and his goals for the remainder of his life poorly defined.

Because of the improving American economy, he was able to get a job working as a brakeman on the railroad. He loved this job, and late in life he still smiled when he told me of riding through the forests and over the hills of western Pennsylvania in his small room at the end of the train or on top of one of the loaded boxcars. His career on the railroad came to an abrupt end when he fell off a moving train, split his head open, and laid unconscious next to the tracks for an undetermined amount of time. Doctors

My father's high school graduation photo. Francis Gelzheiser collection.

told him he would have bled to death by the time he was found, but the temperature that night was freezing and this slowed the bleeding. For three days he remained unconscious in the hospital, and when he suddenly regained consciousness he almost instantly had a smile on his face, and he then proceeded to help the hospital staff with their chores until his release.

Like most men and women of his generation, my father's life changed forever on December 7, 1941. When he learned of the attack on Pearl Harbor he was "dumbfounded." I am sure he had little understanding of the geopolitics of the world at that time, but he understood the awesome military power that would result when American industry was fully harnessed, and he did not see how Japan could ever defeat the United States. At the time of the Japanese attack, he was working in the plating and welding rooms of the Curtiss-Wright Company, located in Beaver, Pennsylvania, manufacturing hollow steel airplane propellers for American warplanes. Because his job was considered "essential to the war effort," he was exempt from military service, and he could have sat out the war in relative safety. However, patriotism, the fire of youth, and anger over the Japanese attack swept over him, and he enlisted in the United States Navy. My father was very honest about why he chose the Navy. He accepted that killing and the risk of death were part of war, but he did not want to have to kill people at close range as many of his counterparts in the Army and Marines would be required to do. In addition, as a result of his youth spent hiking, camping, and swimming, he had grown to love the rivers of Pittsburgh, and after high school he and a friend had purchased an old wooden Chris Craft named *Dixie IV* that he had plied on the waters of the Ohio River in the years leading up to World War II.[7]

My father camping on the banks of the Allegheny River and enjoying a river cruise on his beloved *Dixie IV* shortly before he enlisted in the Navy. Francis Gelzheiser collection.

He entered the service on December 3, 1942, and eight days later he was taken by train to the Naval Training Center at Sampson, New York, and then to the Great Lakes Naval Training Center in North Chicago. At the end of this course, he was given his choice of schools, and he volunteered to serve on Motor Torpedo Boats. Because these boats were small, service on them was selective. He was deemed to be qualified and was sent to the Motor Torpedo Boat Squadrons Training Center on Narragansett Bay in Melville, Rhode Island.[8] It was on these boats that he would spend the war.

The Training Center at Melville was opened in March of 1942. The man most instrumental in creating the facility was Lieutenant Commander William C. Specht, who had commanded Motor Torpedo Boat Squadron 1 at Pearl Harbor, and most of the men who trained there referred to the facility as "Specht Tech."[9]

A number of the instructors at the facility were combat veterans, and the training was physically rigorous and mentally challenging. The trainees lived in crude quonset huts that were cold in the winter and hot in the summer.[10] Because of their diminutive size, PT boats would spend much of their time near shore. The crews would often operate them at night in uncharted waters, and it was even expected that these crews might find themselves on land engaged in fighting generally reserved for their counterparts in other branches of the service. Thus, during their two to three months of training at Melville, recruits were instructed in the use of small arms and hand-to-hand combat, and it was appropriate that the PT boat forces were often referred to as a naval "guerrilla force."[11] Although each member of the crew was expected to learn a specific skill, all members of the crew were required to be able to execute all of the duties on the boats. My father was trained as an electrician, and he was responsible for maintaining the electrical systems of six to twelve boats in his squadron. He often performed additional duties, and on more than one occasion, he manned the twin .50 caliber machine guns or assisted on the 20 mm or other guns during combat.

Electrician's Mate Second Class Francis Gelzheiser. Francis Gelzheiser collection.

At Melville, the PT boat crews spent a great deal of time honing their skills as sailors and warriors. My father's fondest memory of his time at Melville was night gunfire training. As an old man, he still smiled when he talked of the glowing ordnance streaking across the sky above quiet Narragansett Bay, and he seemed to forget that in the not too distant future, these same glowing shells and their Japanese counterparts would mean death to the Japanese and his fellow Americans.[12]

PT boat sailors relied on their boats and each other, and success in combat and survival was often determined by how well the boats' crews could work together. Perhaps this aspect of the PT boat experience was best summed up by Captain Robert J. Bulkley, Jr., in his definitive book on the boats *At Close Quarters: PT Boats in the United States Navy*, when he wrote, "It must be remembered that the best PT is no better than its crew. The success of the PTs depended and always will depend on the ability and valor of their officers and men, on their eagerness to seek out the enemy and engage him at close quarters."[13]

When his two months of training at Melville was completed, my father was sent to New Orleans, Louisiana. Here he was assigned to Squadron 16, Patrol Torpedo Boat *221*, which her new crew would soon name *Omen of the Seas*.[14] The initial Squadron Commander was Lieutenant Commander Russell H. Smith; and as a result, the Squadron

Top: PT Boat Squadron 16 being commissioned, February 26, 1943, New Orleans, Louisiana. *Bottom:* PT Boat Squadron 16 Base Force. My father is in the front row and is the third man in from the right side. Both photographs, World War II PT Boats Museum and Archives, Germantown, Tennessee.

insignia became the popular cartoon character "Snuffy Smith" riding a torpedo. Two months after he was given this command, Lieutenant Commander Smith turned over leadership of the Squadron to Lieutenant Commander Almer P. Colvin, but the squadron insignia remained.[15] After a series of training exercises and breakdown cruises in the Gulf of Mexico, they began the almost 2,500-mile cruise to the Patrol Torpedo Boat Advanced Training Base on Taboga Island, Panama.[16]

PT Boat Squadron 16 insignia. World War II PT Boats Museum and Archives, Germantown, Tennessee.

3

The Motor Patrol Torpedo Boat

You've taken me out of the jaws of death ... and I won't forget it. The PT boats have earned their keep a thousand times over.—General Douglas MacArthur

What were these Motor Torpedo Boats that would take the men of Squadron 16 to the far corners of the globe and into harm's way? When the Japanese attacked Pearl Harbor in December 1941, PT boats were a minute component of the American naval fleet. However, from the war's onset, they played a vital role in the fight against Imperial Japan, and they would eventually play an important role in the war against the Axis powers in Europe. At the time of the Japanese attack, there were only three squadrons of PT boats. Lieutenant Commander Specht commanded the twelve boats of Motor Torpedo Boat Squadron 1 berthed in Pearl Harbor. The eleven boats of Motor Torpedo Boat Squadron 2 were led by Lieutenant Commander Earl S. Caldwell and stationed in the New York Navy Yard, and Lieutenant Commander John D. "Buck" Bulkeley commanded the six boats of Motor Torpedo Boat Squadron 3 which was based in the Philippines.[1]

Many in the American Navy questioned the value of the Motor Torpedo Boat and the role that it would play in the war.[2] However, the small boats quickly showed their worth and in short order became a vital cog in the American war machine. As hundreds of planes from Japanese aircraft carriers unleashed their ordnances on the poorly defended ships at Pearl Harbor, six PT boats of Squadron 1 that were docked at a submarine base near Battleship Row worked heroically to fend off the Japanese attack. The PT boat crews in these boats were some of the first to fire at the Japanese planes, and the gunners on PT 23 hit a low flying Japanese plane carrying a torpedo and shot the plane down before it could unleash its explosive. It is believed that this was the first Japanese plane shot down by an American in World War II.[3]

Less than 12 hours after the strike on Pearl Harbor, the Japanese bombed Clark Field and devastated American air power in the Philippines. Shortly after this attack, the Japanese invaded the American held Philippine Islands more than 5,000 miles from Pearl Harbor. With the fall of Wake Island on December 12, the United States could not reinforce the Philippines, which insured the success of the Japanese invasion. The Philippines fell on May 8, 1942. The Japanese success in the Philippines was in many ways even more devastating to the United States than the attack on Pearl Harbor.[4]

When the Japanese invaded the Philippines, they had the most powerful navy in the

Pacific, and the only American naval presence defending the islands were the six old and leaking PT boats of Squadron 3. It was inevitable that this tiny American naval force would be defeated, but this did not prevent the PT boat crews from fighting valiantly.

Lieutenant Commander Bulkeley, the officer in charge of the tiny PT boat fleet, was often referred to as "The Wild Man of the Philippines." The handsome, bearded, and green-eyed Lieutenant Commander Bulkeley was well suited to lead this ragtag naval force. He was bold, fearless, energetic, and adept at navigating uncharted waters. More than any other combatant, he would prove the worth of PT boats and insure they played an important role in the naval war in the Pacific.[5]

As the greatest military disaster in American history was unfolding, Lieutenant Commander Bulkeley and his men shot down Japanese planes and harassed the Japanese Navy at sea and her Army on land. Simply keeping his boats operational was an enormous achievement. There was a chronic shortage of parts, the gasoline supply was limited, and often it was of such poor quality that it caused the engines to run poorly or not at all.[6] The boats' wooden hulls were leaky from overuse and lack of maintenance, and with each patrol they became slower and less reliable. While on patrol Lieutenant Commander Bulkeley's crews had to worry about hitting mines, fire from shore batteries, attack from planes, and encountering more powerful and often faster Japanese ships.[7] The PT boat crews could expect no assistance from American aviators in fending off the numerous Japanese planes that roamed the skies over the Philippines. Cavite Navy Yard and Nichols Field in the Philippines were no longer operational, and many of the American planes stationed in the Philippines had been destroyed by the Japanese early in the conflict.[8]

As the exhausted, poorly trained and equipped 15,000 Americans and 60,000 Filipino "Battered Bastards of Bataan" neared starvation and readied to surrender, President Franklin Roosevelt concluded that General MacArthur was too valuable to the war effort to be captured by the Japanese. Several rescue scenarios were discussed, but it was finally determined that Lieutenant Commander Bulkeley and his four remaining operational PT boats provided the best chance for a successful escape. On March 11, General MacArthur, his family, and a few key aides were loaded on to PT *41* to begin the almost 600-mile journey to the island of Mindanao. The escape plan then called for him to be flown to Australia where he would lead the American war effort against Japan.[9]

From the beginning it was doubtful whether the PT boats would make it. By the time of the rescue attempt, all of the boats' engines had at least four times the recommended hours on them. Because of the difficult circumstances under which the crews had been operating, the boats had been poorly maintained and this resulted in leaky hulls, and bottoms that needed cleaning and painting. Consequently, none of the boats had a top speed above 27 miles per hour. They were heading into uncharted waters, patrolled by the most powerful navy in the Pacific, and the compasses they used for navigation were little better than the ones a 1940s-era Boy Scout would use to earn a merit badge in orienteering. They traveled mostly at night, so dead reckoning was a key to navigating. They had no sonar or radar, and the waters they would navigate were filled with reefs. In addition, the Japanese knew the Americans would try to rescue General MacArthur, so all of The Rising Sun's ships were on the lookout for the American vessels and their valuable cargo.[10]

The escape plan was simple. The four boats would try to stay together. If discovered by the Japanese, Lieutenant Commander Bulkeley's PT *41*, which was transporting General MacArthur and his family, would flee, and PTs *32, 34,* and *35* would engage the enemy in an attempt to allow PT *41* to escape.[11] As the voyage proceeded, all of the passengers got violently seasick, storms raged, lightening struck frequently and often close to the small boats, seas swelled to make travel slower and more difficult and uncomfortable, and there was the constant fear that they would be located by the Japanese.[12] Miraculously, on March 13, at 6:30 a.m., PTs *41* and *34* arrived at their destination. Four days later two B-17 Flying Fortresses took MacArthur and his family and entourage to Australia.[13]

Lieutenant Commander Bulkeley's exploits in the Philippines and safe delivery of General MacArthur and his family did much to enhance the reputation of PT boats in the United States Navy; and for all that Lieutenant Commander Bulkeley had done during the desperate early months of the war, he was awarded the Congressional Medal of Honor by President Roosevelt. More importantly, General MacArthur, the senior American soldier in the Pacific, was now a believer in the small boats that had taken him and his family to safety. Shortly after his rescue from the Philippines as he was helping to develop America's strategy for defeating Japan, MacArthur told Lieutenant Commander Bulkeley that when he met with the president to receive his Medal of Honor he should tell the president that the general believed the PT boat fleet had to be expanded dramatically. When he met with President Roosevelt, Lieutenant Commander Bulkeley explained: "Motor Torpedo Boats should be the basis of a separate branch of the service for specialists.... There is no other location such as the Philippine Islands and the islands south of the Philippines where they can be so effectively used."[14]

Bulkeley's exploits also occurred at a time when morale in America was at its lowest point in the war. Allied losses in the Pacific were occurring with frightening regularity, and Japan seemed invincible. Shortly after his delivery of General MacArthur, Lieutenant Commander Bulkeley and some of the other officers on the now-famous PT boats were interviewed by the journalist William L. White. White then wrote the book, *They Were Expendable*, which was published in 1942 and quickly became a national bestseller; and in 1945 John Ford directed the film *They Were Expendable*, based on the exploits of Lieutenant Commander Bulkeley and his men.[15] The tiny boats that almost no one had heard of and fewer had believed in at the war's onset were now deemed to be a vital part of the American war effort; and the PT boat sailors, who had overcome such difficult odds, were the underdog heroes that Americans needed in the desperate early days of the war.[16] By the time the war ended, Motor Torpedo Boats would participate in actions in New Georgia, Bougainville, New Guinea, the Aleutian Islands, Saipan, Guam, the Philippines, Solomon Islands, the English Channel, and Mediterranean Sea.

The Motor Torpedo Boat was first conceived after the American Civil War. With the development of the mechanized mobile torpedo, naval leaders determined that a craft was necessary from which these weapons could be launched. In 1890 the 140-foot USS *Cushing*, America's first Motor Torpedo Boat, was launched, and this ship saw action in the Spanish American War. By the late 1890s the United States Navy had lost much interest in this type of craft, and it was not until the 1930s when interest in the Motor Torpedo Boat was revived.[17] The British had developed a fleet of fast torpedo boats, and American rum runners, appreciating the speed of these craft, had modified the boats during Prohibition in order to avoid authorities as they transported their illegal cargo.[18] With renewed interest in developing a fleet of Motor Torpedo Boats, the United States purchased a 70-foot boat from Scott-Pine in England on September 5, 1939. This craft was to become PT *9*, and it would serve as a prototype for all of American Motor Torpedo Boats that would follow.[19]

In 1937 President Roosevelt advocated for the construction of a small fleet of Motor Torpedo Boats, and $13 million was allocated for their development. Three years later, the first operational PT boat was delivered to the United States Navy.[20] These boats would continue to evolve throughout the war, and the boats that took the sailors of Squadron 16 to the Philippines in late 1944 had changed much from the craft that took General MacArthur out of harm's way in early 1942.

Initially, there were a number of different PT boat designs. The size of the early craft ranged from 58 to 81 feet, and some were constructed of wood and others aluminum.[21] A wartime shortage of aluminum determined that the PT boat fleet would ultimately be constructed of wood; and because of the size of the torpedoes and the weight of the guns the boats would carry, it was determined that the newly constructed fleet should consist of boats of at least 77 feet in length.[22]

There was much competition to determine which boats would become part of the American PT boat fleet, including the two famous "Plywood Derbies" in which prospective boats competed with each other in 190-mile races in Connecticut and New York waters near Block Island, Fire Island, and Montauk Point.[23] During the races, seas reached heights of eight to fifteen feet, and although the crews took a pounding, the boats performed well. The top average speed attained was almost 40 knots by one of the Elco boats, but speed was not the only attribute being measured in the races.[24] In addition, boats were rated for traits such as: structural efficiency, habitability, sea-keeping qualities, maneuverability and fuel consumption.

After the testing, the government awarded contracts to three companies: Electric Launch Corporation or Elco, Higgins Industries, and Huckins Yacht Works.[25] Ultimately, only eighteen Huckins boats were built, and none of these saw combat. These craft, along with Elco and Higgins boats, were used as training boats at the Motor Torpedo Boat Training Center in Melville, Rhode Island.[26] Elco would manufacture a 77-foot boat that was used early in the war and an 80-foot model that became the most common American PT boat. Higgins manufactured a 78-foot craft.[27] These boats would make up the United States Motor Torpedo Boat fleet during World War II. In total 212 PT boats would serve in the Pacific during World War II.[28]

To the layman, Elco and Higgins PT boats look similar, but to the men who crewed these craft, there were important differences. Elco boats were constructed in Bayonne, New Jersey. These boats had three screws and three rudders and were generally deemed more comfortable and slightly faster than the Higgins boats. They had a "Day Room" above deck amidship, and in rough water the boats were generally dryer because of the greater outward flare of the hull. In total, 320 80-foot Elco boats were manufactured, but many of these found their way to other navies as a result of the American Lend Lease Program.[29]

Higgins boats were manufactured in New Orleans. They also had three screws, but only two rudders that were larger than the three used in the Elco boats, and this made the Higgins boats more maneuverable. Their flush deck provided a superior gun platform, but it also tended to make the boats wetter in rough seas, and when the boats were moving slowly, the bow tended to nose under and flood the deck and the sailors on it. In total 205 of these boats were manufactured at a cost of approximately $120,000 to $150,000 each without armament, but as a result of Lend Lease, they not only flew the American flag but also sailed with the fleets of our British and Soviet Allies.[30] Higgins boats that were fully armed and in good repair had a maximum speed of approximately 39 knots.

Top: Higgins PT boat underway. *Bottom:* Higgins PT boat under construction, New Orleans, Louisiana. Both photographs, World War II PT Boats Museum and Archives, Germantown, Tennessee.

This made them slightly slower than the 80-foot Elco boats, but they had a tighter turn radius, which could be extremely important, especially when trying to outmaneuver an attacking kamikaze late in the war.[31]

Almost all of the officers and crew on PT boats were under the age of 30, and on many boats the oldest sailor was not yet 25. Although lack of experience created problems, it is probably best that the men who manned these vessels were so young. The Higgins PT boat was designed to be fast and maneuverable, and thus it had a very stiff ride. Even in seas with just a small chop, the boats would constantly pound; and as waves grew, this pounding would only become more violent, and sore knees and damaged backs were common, especially when novice sailors had not acquired sea legs. One PT boat sailor said the ride, "jarred the fillings out of your teeth," and violent bounces often did result in cracked teeth. In addition, the compartments below deck had low ceilings and door hatches, so sailors in rough seas had to guard against being bounced upwards and banging their heads.

In a September 1944 story on the boats, the *San Francisco Chronicle* described them as "part merry-go-round and part bronco," and the *San Francisco News* in a story written the same week called the vessels, "TNT in an eggshell." Even seasoned navy men who rode on the boats commented on how much they pounded, but because the PT boat sailors were so young, and the majority had never served on a vessel other than a PT boat, they almost never complained about the ride, and most spent all of their war years on the vessels and did not consider transferring to a larger craft with a smoother ride.[32]

All of the boats of Squadron 16 were Higgins Motor Torpedo Boats, and thus my father and his shipmates referred to themselves as "Higgins Men" when talking with other PT boat sailors. These 78-foot boats had a beam of approximately 20 feet, a draft of five to six feet, and they displaced between 43 and 60 tons of water depending on the boat's load and armaments.[33] The boats' hulls were usually constructed of two layers of lightweight, splinter resistant, five-eighth-inch-thick and six-inch-wide mahogany planking laid over laminated wood frames, usually constructed of spruce but occasionally of white oak. Some boats also had an additional one or two layers of planking in the sections of the hull that would be under the most stress. On some vessels, the two layers of mahogany planking were laid in the same direction, and on other craft the exterior planks were put down in the opposite direction as the interior planks in an attempt to increase the strength of the hull. In between the two sections of planking were marine glue and a layer of airplane fabric, and approximately 400,000 screws were also used to hold each boat together. The boats' keels were made of spruce, and the deckhouses were framed with spruce and then covered with plywood. The space between the frames and superstructure was filled with cork for insulation. The boats' decks were also constructed of two layers of mahogany boards with marine glue and airplane fabric sandwiched in between.[34]

The boat bottoms were primed with a water-repellant preservative and then painted with three coats of copperoid bottom enamel.[35] During the course of the war it was the bane of many a PT boat sailor to be tasked with scraping and then repainting his boat's bottom.[36] The bridge or cockpit was the only area of the boat to be protected by armor, and some believed that this negatively impacted the morale on some boats since this would primarily protect officers. Consequently, this plating was removed from some of the vessels.[37]

In the bow of the boat was a rope locker in which line, shackles, and other equipment were stored. Behind this were the crew's quarters and a small head used by the enlisted men. On most boats there were four lower and four upper bunks, and the crew used the lower bunks as seats during the day.[38] The officers' quarters were to the rear of the crew's. There was a small head in this section, and the two forward gas tanks were also housed here. Behind this was the engine room, which also contained the auxiliary generator and heater. This room was almost one half of the hull length. This relatively large space made it easier to work on and maintain the engines, but it also reduced the available space for the crew's quarters and storage.[39] To the stern was the tank room in which there were tanks that could hold up to 3,000 gallons of 100-octane gasoline and approximately 200 gallons of fresh water. Finally near the boat's stern was the lazaret, which was used for storage and occasionally for sleeping when additional crew were on board, and the rudder room that contained the steering apparatus and when needed could also accommodate two men for sleeping.[40]

Crews generally worked hard to keep boats clean, but many vessels still had to deal with rats taking up residence in the bilges; and cockroaches were common on many boats, especially in more tropical climates. Boats could only hold enough supplies to last approximately five days, and the simple refrigerators on the boats were small. Thus PT boat squadrons were usually accompanied by PT boat tenders, which supplied the boats with food, fuel, ordnance, and most of the other provisions required to operate the vessels.[41]

The boats were powered by three 2,950-pound, fresh-water-cooled Packard engines manufactured specifically for Motor Torpedo Boats by the Packard Motor Company of Detroit, Michigan.[42] Each engine initially produced 1200 horsepower; but as the war progressed and armaments were added to the boats, the added weight made it necessary to increase the horsepower of the engines. By the war's end, a supercharged engine could produce 1500 horsepower. The boat's aluminum-manganese-bronze propellers were attached to shafts made of the nickel/copper alloy Monel, and each propeller spun at 1,350–2,400 revolutions per minute. All three of the boat's propellers turned in a counterclockwise direction when viewed from the stern; and since the vessels lacked bow thrusters, it took a skilled boat operator to dock the boats and maneuver them at slow speeds.

Boat transmissions were hand controlled from the engine room. When the sailor operating the boat from the bridge wanted to change gears, he would ask for the gear change through a telegraph annunciator, and a sailor—known as the "Motor Mac"—who straddled two large levers below, would initiate the gear change. Officially, a Higgins boat with its hull and upgraded motors in excellent condition could travel with a full load at up to 40 knots and had a cruising range of approximately 550 miles. In reality, most crews deemed only 2,500 of the 3,000 gallons of fuel to be usable. Since boats running at near full speed would burn approximately 300 gallons of fuel per hour, boats could run for eight hours and cover approximately 300–330 miles. If they traveled at slower speeds, this distance could be increased significantly. However, the condition of the boat's hull and engine would greatly affect its speed and range, and it was the job of each boat crew to determine the distance a boat could travel on any particular day.[43]

The boats had six mufflers on their sides, and exhaust could be sent into the air or water. Closing the butterflies on the exhaust pipes sent the exhaust gases into the water. This quieted the motors a great deal, and the noise they did make resembled the sound of the surf and would thus be less likely to alarm the enemy. However, it also slowed the speed at which the boats could travel considerably, and a boat exhausting its gases into the water could only travel at 6–12 knots per hour.[44]

When properly maintained, the engines were generally reliable. However, they did require changing or overhaul after only 600 hours of operation, and this was often impossible when in a war zone. Thus, engine problems could be frequent and serious.[45]

There was no sonar or other modern method to detect water depth on the boats. Therefore in a war that would be brought to its end with the explosion of an atom bomb, the PT boat crews would determine water depth by dropping marked, lead-weighted lines into the water, much the way mariners had done for millennium. It is not surprising that grounding was one of the most common and serious problems the sailors faced in the Mosquito Fleet, especially for boats in the Pacific.[46]

Early in the war, none of the boats were equipped with radar. However, as the war progressed, Bell Labs developed and Westinghouse manufactured radar that was appropriate for PT boats. Eventually, all boats were equipped with this essential navigation aid, and radar was generally considered the most important improvement made to Motor Torpedo Boats during World War II. Often boats patrolled at night, and radar enabled them to locate enemy ships and navigate out of harm's way. Fortunately for PT boat crews, because the boats generally operated close to shore and were low to the water, it was often difficult for enemy ships to locate them on their radar. This was especially true when they were navigating in heavy seas.[47]

Compass technology also improved as the war progressed. Initially, boats were equipped with liquid magnetic compasses. As any mariner who has used such devices knows, these compasses could bounce 20 degrees to either side in rough water, thus making it difficult to follow a course. PT boat sailors became adept at picking a point in the distance, such as a star, cloud, or point of land, and then navigating using this as a reference point instead of trying to follow the bouncing compass. Later in the war, these primitive compasses were replaced with gyro-controlled Fluxgate compasses. These showed true north in all seas and, coupled with radar, made navigation in all conditions easier.

VHF radios were also added later to the boats, and in much of the Pacific the radio code for a PT boat was "Martini." These radios improved the communication between PT boats and planes and other ships. However, communication between PT boats and Allied ships and planes was far from perfect even as the war drew to a close. PT boats received friendly fire from the sea and air with surprising frequency, and there continued to be instances when PT boats fired on American planes and occasionally Allied ships. Often when boats were underway and in close proximity to each other they would communicate using semaphore, and the radios were only used sparingly.[48]

PT boat officers and crew took great pride in their boats, and most believed that the small boats on which they served were fine looking craft. In reality, when not moving the Higgins boats appeared squat and bow heavy. However, while underway, the boats looked magnificent. The bow would flare up, a great wave would fly off it, and a rooster tail wake would arch off the stern as the boat glided forward. Ironically, this rooster tail would be illuminated at night by phosphorescence, and this would make it easy for planes to locate the boats and then strafe, bomb, or crash into them. Prior to getting up on plane, the boats would displace an enormous amount of water and throw up a huge wake, and generally at speeds between 7 and 26 miles per hour the boats produced a huge wake and ran inefficiently.

Perhaps what PT boats were best known for was their speed. However, a variety of

Unidentified Higgins PT boats underway. World War II PT Boats Museum and Archives, Germantown, Tennessee.

factors affected this, and it was not uncommon for the boats to be slower than some of the much larger craft they would encounter. For example, torpedo boat destroyers, or TBDs, were at least ten times the size of a Motor Torpedo Boat, and yet they were often faster. The myth of the speed of these small boats that emerged in the early years of the war was certainly an exaggeration believed by many Americans desperate for positive news about America's military.[49]

Stripped down, the PT boats were extremely fast, with one recording a speed in excess of 60 miles per hour. However, the PT boat was pound for pound the most heavily armed craft in the United States Navy. The boats also carried a crew of two to three officers and 9 to 13 enlisted men and up to 3,000 gallons of fuel, and more than 2,000 pounds of water. All of this added enormous weight, and a battle ready boat in excellent condition could only achieve speeds of approximately 37–40 miles per hour. Over time, as the hulls started to leak or be pocked with barnacles and other marine growth, and the engines began to wear out, the maximum speed of the boats was often significantly reduced.[50]

Even with its speed reduced, the PT boat had some advantages over its larger adversaries. Because it was small and wooden, it drew less than six feet of water. This meant that it was not low enough in the water to be hit by most torpedoes. However, the boats lacked almost any protective armor, so if hit by any ordnance the crews and boats were extremely vulnerable. One of the best illustrations of this vulnerability occurred when a

Two sailors and an officer on the deck of a Higgins PT boat. World War II PT Boats Museum and Archives, Germantown, Tennessee.

torpedo dropped by a Japanese torpedo bomber in New Guinea passed through both sides of PT *167*'s bow above the water line leaving a gaping hole and a crew who was terrified but thankful that the torpedo did not explode as it passed through the boat.[51]

In addition, the boats could escape larger vessels by running to shallow water, or fleeing into rivers and small coves. They were highly maneuverable, especially as the crews became more skilled, and boats would escape larger vessels by running a zigzag course until they reached a shallow water cove that was often far from where their adversaries could venture. Usually when fleeing enemy ships or planes, PT boats would unleash a smoke screen from the smoke generators that were on the stern of all boats. These generators contained titanium tetrachloride, and when released into the air it produced a thick cloud of smoke. However, this also produced hydrochloric acid, which could be toxic. Consequently, boat decks had to be carefully washed after the smoke generators were used. During the course of the war, there were numerous occasions in which PT boats avoided destruction at the hands of enemy ships or planes as a result of their smoke screens and evasive maneuvers.[52]

Above all, the PT boat was designed for offense, and the torpedo was one of its most important weapons. Unfortunately, early in the war, American torpedoes unleashed from planes, ships, and boats proved to be ineffective and sometimes dangerous for those who launched them. During the decades preceding the war, military budgets were low, so practice with live ordnance was kept to a minimum. Live torpedo training was particularly expensive; as a result, the United States designed and built significant numbers of torpedoes in the years prior to the war, but it did little to test the effectiveness of this ordnance or train the crews on how to best use it.[53] Early torpedoes used by PT boats were generally Mark XIV or Mark VIII of World War I vintage. They often ran too shallow or too deep, were slow and unreliable, inaccurate to the point that fired torpedoes often traced erratically, and more than 60 percent of these torpedoes were defective. On some occasions these weapons turned mid-course and headed back toward the vessel that fired them. Much to the frustration of the men who launched them, when the torpedos did hit their targets, they frequently did not detonate, and they were more likely to explode if they hit their target at an angle instead of head on.[54]

With the replacement of Mark XIV and Mark VIII torpedoes midway through the war with Mark XIII torpedoes, the PT Boat became a more lethal war machine. These torpedoes were designed for aircraft, and although they still could be unreliable, they were far superior to the torpedoes they replaced. They were capable of speeds of 45 knots, and they had a range of 6,300 yards. They carried a 600-pound warhead, were slightly larger in diameter than earlier torpedoes and shorter, with a length of 161 inches. Perhaps the biggest advantage to the Mark XIII torpedo was that they were equipped with non-tumbling gyros. This meant that they did not have to be launched from an even keel to achieve accurate runs. As a result, torpedo tubes could be removed from PT Boats, and replaced with racks. These racks were designed by Lieutenant George Springel, Jr., and Lieutenant (junior grade) James Costigan, who were both serving on PT *188*. The two officers sketched a torpedo rack system on a pocket notebook and then fabricated a prototype from scrap metal found in the New York Navy Yard. Their design was eventually used on most of the boats in the Mosquito Fleet.[55]

There were many advantages gained by removing these tubes. Early torpedoes were fired from Higgins Boats with compressed air. Too often torpedoes got stuck in the tubes after the firing sequence had been initiated, and this was potentially cata-

Men standing on deck of a Higgins PT boat near the torpedo tubes. World War II PT Boats Museum and Archives, Germantown, Tennessee.

Men relaxing near forward torpedo tubes on a Higgins PT boat. World War II PT Boats Museum and Archives, Germantown, Tennessee.

strophic. Prior to firing a torpedo from the tube, the propeller motor was started, and after the propeller spun a prescribed number of times, it would explode when it hit a solid object. Unfortunately, if a torpedo got stuck in a tube, the terrified crew would be forced to remove the live ordnance and stop the torpedo propeller from spinning before the armament was jolted by a wave or sharp turn resulting in the charged torpedo exploding and destroying the boat.[56] In addition, keeping torpedo tubes clean was the bane of many a torpedo man, and tasks such as greasing the interior of the tubes and keeping the tube caps clean and secure were no longer necessary when the tubes were removed.

Removing the tubes lightened the boats considerably, and this resulted in most boats replacing the 20 mm stern gun with a more lethal 40 mm cannon. This more powerful weapon proved to be extremely effective against Japanese barges in New Guinea and the Philippines. As the war progressed, the Motor Torpedo Boat evolved from being primarily a torpedo boat to a gunboat, and the addition of more powerful guns was important to this development.[57]

Two to four depth charges were also mounted on each boat, and these were used to harass enemy submarines, and they were sometimes dropped to deter ships that were pursuing the PT boats. These were kept in racks on the boat's stern, and they would fall into the water when their restraining straps were removed. Because the PT boats lacked sonar, the depth charges were generally not employed effectively, and there were few occasions during World War II when a PT boat sunk an enemy submarine or ship with a depth charge.[58]

There were a variety of guns on PT boats, and the number, size, and placement of these weapons changed during the course of the war. Generally, as the war wore on, and it was less likely the boats would encounter an enemy destroyer, their primary task changed, and they became a coastal gunboat. This meant that more guns were added, and PT boats ultimately had the offensive capability of a destroyer. This was one of the reasons that the total horsepower of the three Packard engines was increased by 750 horsepower per boat by the war's end, but this increased horsepower was more than offset by the additional 20,000 pounds added to most boats, and generally the speed of PT boats in the Pacific was reduced as the war progressed.[59]

By the summer of 1943, most PT boats in the Pacific had a 20 mm Oerlikon cannon or a 37 mm cannon on the bow or both. These could fire 450 and 120 rounds per minute, respectively. One twin .50 caliber turret-mounted machine gun was mounted amidship on each side of the boat, and these had a firing rate of 6,000 rounds per minute. Two-thirds of the rounds were black tipped and armor piercing, and the remainder were red tipped tracer rounds designed to improve firing accuracy. However, each boat was allowed some discretion in determining how rounds would be belted. A 40 mm Bofors Cannon

Men behind a 37 mm gun. World War II PT Boats Museum and Archives, Germantown, Tennessee.

Higgins PT boat chart house with single .50 caliber gun. World War II PT Boats Museum and Archives, Germantown, Tennessee.

was mounted on the boat's stern, and this very effective weapon could fire a variety of rounds at 130 cartridges per minute. Late in the war rocket launchers and 80 mm mortars were installed on some boats. In addition, the boats carried small arms, hand grenades, automatic shotguns, and even Thompson machine guns. One observer remarked, "the boats had the strength of a Goliath crammed into the frame of a David," and this was certainly an apt description, especially after the additional armaments were added during the last two years of the war.[60]

While in combat, it was sometimes necessary to fire most of the mounted guns at once, and the noise could be deafening. My father, like many of his shipmates, suffered some permanent hearing loss as a result of this thunderous noise, and on more than one occasion men in his Squadron had their eardrums punctured by the concussion of the firing guns.[61]

While on patrol, near shore, in shallow, calm waters and moving slowly, PT Boats could unleash accurate deadly fire on enemy boats and shore installations. However, when operating at high speeds and in rougher water, the small boats were constantly moving and this resulted in a gun platform that was very unsteady, and often under these conditions boats would have great difficulty hitting their targets.[62]

The Motor Torpedo Boat fleet was organized by squadron. Most squadrons were made up of all Elco or all Higgins boats, but a small number did have boats from both manufacturers.[63] Squadrons were comprised of approximately 12 boats, and there were

PT Boat Squadron 16 sailors brandishing small arms. Such weapons were often kept on PT boats during World War II. World War II PT Boats Museum and Archives, Germantown, Tennessee.

45 commissioned squadrons during the war, including Squadrons 2(2) and 3(2). The size of boat crews tended to grow as armament was added to the boats. Early boats had two machinist's mates, two to four gunner's mates, two torpedomen, one radioman, one quartermaster, one cook, and sometimes a boatswain's mate. In addition to the crew, each boat also had three to four officers. By the war's end most boats had added an additional officer and one to three crew members.[64]

Squadrons and boats were also supported by PT boat tenders and a base force, and there was no clear delineation between the men who crewed and the men who supported the PT boats. For example, my father was an electrician's mate, and thus he was technically part of the base force. However, he was also considered part of the crew of PT *221*, and at one point was even listed as the boat's cook. He generally traveled on this boat, and frequently went on patrols. It was also not unusual for a crew member to leave the boat for a period of time and work as part of the base force. PT boats had one of the least rigid organizational structures in the United States Navy, and since most of the men on the boats and base force could perform many of the boat and base jobs, movement from base to boat and boat to base on any given day was common.[65]

The Motor Torpedo Boat had many functions, and these continually evolved depending on where the boats were operating and what the needs of the Navy and Army were at a given place and time. Boats were sent on search-and-destroy missions. Larger ships were attacked with torpedoes, submarines were occasionally confronted with torpedoes and depth charges, and harbors were blockaded to prevent the Japanese from leaving or receiving supplies. They transported Allied scouts, raiding parties, and guerrillas; resupplied these men; and collected and delivered intelligence. They defended coastlines, screened invasion forces during beach landings, and laid smoke screens to help friendly vessels avoid enemy fire. They fought off enemy planes and kamikazes, rescued men who had been forced to abandon ship after their vessel had been hit, and rescued pilots after their planes were shot down. They laid mines, and motored dangerously close to shore to draw enemy fire so shore batteries could be located and destroyed. In the Pacific, one of the primary functions of the boats was to locate and destroy the ubiquitous Japanese barges and luggers that ferried men and supplies from different locations on an island or from island to island. Based on the tens of thousands of Japanese troops left stranded and starving until the war's end, cut off by PT boats from escaping or being resupplied, the small crafts did their job well.[66]

The tactics and doctrines used in combat were initially developed at the Melville Rhode Island Training Center under the leadership of Lieutenant Commander Specht.[67] Officers and crew were instructed to use different formations and tactics depending on the enemy they were engaging. An enemy submarine, traditional aircraft, kamikaze, large surface ship, or coastal barge would each require a different response from the boats, and as experience was gained throughout the course of the war, these tactics often changed.[68]

PT boat crews paid careful attention to wind direction. Wind blowing in the proper direction would reduce the amount of noise from the PT boats that the enemy could hear. In addition, boats escaping enemy ship fire would remain better hidden under the cloud of smoke created by the smoke generators if the wind was blowing in the same direction in which the boats were running. These generators could produce a smoke screen for up to three miles when the boats were traveling at full speed. When attacking a ship with torpedoes, the lead boat in the formation would generally fire first, and then the remaining boats in the formation would move up and release their "fish."[69] Since PT boats tended to plane better and run faster when they had more weight in the forward section of the craft, torpedomen generally fired the two rear torpedoes first and then launch those closer to the bow of the boat if necessary.[70]

Some tactics could only be developed in battle conditions. PT boats learned that when under attack by dive-bombers it was best to wait until the last minute, when the bomber had released its ordnance, to make a quick turn to avoid being hit. Late in the war when the kamikaze were the most terrifying weapon the boats faced, crews learned to run a zigzag course and try to wait until the plane was so close to the water that it could no longer turn to make a last minute course change so that the plane crashed into the water without hitting the boats. This tactic proved to be effective in avoiding the manned bombs but was terrifying for PT boat crews.[71]

Obviously stealth was important to the sailors on PT boats. In the Pacific, most boats were painted navy or tropical green to blend in with the jungles found on most of the islands. Some boats were painted with traditional camouflage patterns and a few were painted with zebra stripes to make it difficult for enemy ships to identify the boats.[72]

When Walt Disney was tasked with designing a logo for the new PT boat fleet, he drew a mosquito wearing a sailor's hat holding on to a torpedo. The point of the image was clear: these boats were small, but they could still sting. At the war's inception, there was some disagreement as to what the role of the boats should be, although generally

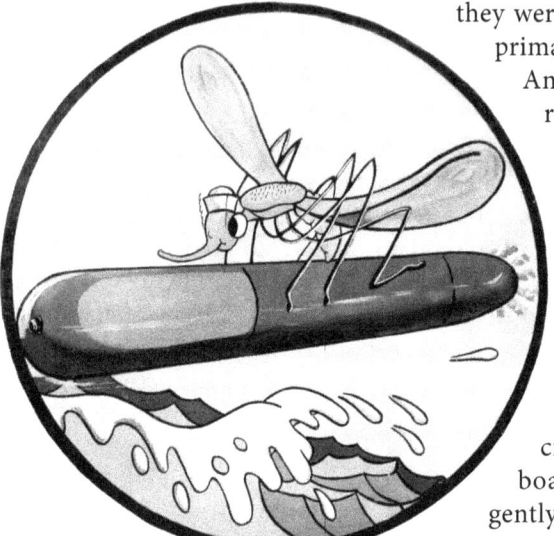

Motor Torpedo Boat insignia designed by Walt Disney. World War II PT Boats Museum and Archives, Germantown, Tennessee.

they were viewed as an anti-shipping craft whose primary weapon would be the torpedo. By 1943 American strategy had evolved, and as a result the mission of the PT boats had changed. The primary function of the boats was now to destroy near-shore Japanese shipping with the boats' deck guns, and trap Japanese warriors on islands throughout the Pacific. As a result, the basic design of the boats stayed the same, but significant changes to the boats' weaponry were made at the factory, in boatyards, and even by the crews in combat zones. The Navy and PT boat officers and enlisted men worked diligently to determine which weapons were best suited for the conditions under which the boats were operating, and sometimes different conclusions were reached. Consequently, by the war's end, it was not uncommon for boats within the same Squadron to have different armaments. This is a testament to the ingenuity of the officers and men of the PT boat force. Ultimately PT boats would destroy 250,000 tons of enemy shipping during the war, and trap tens of thousands of Japanese soldiers on islands scattered through the Pacific. This at least partially illustrates the lethality of the Mosquito Boats' sting and the important role they played in helping the Allies win World War II.[73]

4

The Grand Adventure: The Voyage to Panama

I've sailed every type of ship in the Navy except one of these PTs, and this is the worst bridge I have ever been on. I wouldn't do duty on one of these God damned PTs for anything in the world. —Rear Admiral Francis W. Rockwell on board a PT boat with General MacArthur

On the morning of April 16, 1943, six boats from Motor Torpedo Boat Squadron 16: *219, 220, 221, 222, 223*, and *224* left the West End Yacht Club in New Orleans bound for Taboga Island, Panama. PT *221*, the boat my father was on, had been placed into service on March 12, and the five boats it sailed with had also only recently been built. The six other boats that made up the original Squadron 16 had been transferred to Squadron 15, and the six boats that would eventually be added to Squadron 16 had yet to be constructed. As a result, the six older boats would be referred to as Squadron 16A, and after they were constructed, the six newer boats would be called Squadron 16B. Later in the war the two squadrons would merge, creating Squadron 16. My father, eager to begin his war, had volunteered for immediate sea duty, and was a last minute addition to PT *221*. In addition to their normal complement of three officers and nine to ten men, each boat also carried ten to twelve members of the base force, so men had to bunk wherever they could on their journey to Panama.[1]

Officially, the Squadron's departure time and destination had been a secret, but somehow a few of the crew's girlfriends found their way to the dock as the boats departed and waved their white handkerchiefs to the appreciative crew. Even some of the young women who worked at "Moms," a popular hangout for the men of the Mosquito Fleet, joined the crowd. Some of the crew were happy to be finally going to sea, but others were sad to be leaving New Orleans and all of its numerous attractions. For my father, I believe his emotions were mixed. He always talked fondly of his time in the "The Big Easy," but he was also eager to make his contribution to the war effort.[2]

Shortly after their 7:00 a.m. departure, the six boats were stopped by a drawbridge that spanned the narrow swamp-lined waterway they were navigating. Nearby were a man and a mule, and the boats were told that the animal would be commanded to open the bridge after a fee was paid to the bridge operator. Such payment had not been authorized by the United States Navy, and rather than digging into their own pockets to pay the fee, the gunner on the lead boat lowered his .50 caliber weapon and slowly turned it toward the toll collector. In short order, the mule was opening the bridge, and the six boats were continuing on their way.[3]

Not all of the men who were required to be on PT *221* when it departed were aboard the craft that morning. One of the officers, who had already lost favor with the crew, had failed to arrive at the boat by its departure time. The officer was tall and fastidious, and he expected the crew to behave in the more formal manner that was required on larger naval ships. He came from an affluent family and often made condescending jokes or remarks that angered the crew. In addition, he was always criticizing the men for the condition of the boat or their personal appearance, and yet he kept the officer's quarters a mess and expected members of the crew to pick up after him. Almost all of the crew came from humble backgrounds, and they had been raised to respect authority. However, they were also smart and proud, and loathe to be treated as servants and not Navy men.[4]

Tension had grown between the officer and the crew, and to a man they were happy when he failed to show up on time and was left behind as the boats pulled out of the dock. What had transpired was that a day or two prior to their departure, the officer's wife had arrived in New Orleans for a visit. Like many a navy man before him, he became over zealous in his pre-voyage revelry and then broke the cardinal rule of all navies, he failed to show up prior to the departure of his boat. Such a slip-up would have a serious impact on the young officer's career, and it could even have landed him in the brig. Luckily for him, he had been apprised of the route the Squadron would be traveling, and he managed to get a ride to a bridge the boats would have to pass under in order to reach the Gulf of Mexico. Fortunately for him, he arrived at the bridge before the boats. Unfortunately, he had alienated the crew to the extent that they would make no effort to pull the boat over to shore so that he could board PT *221*. While the officer stood on the bridge and waved, the boat's crew ignored him and motored forward. Realizing he was about to miss his last chance to board his boat in time to avoid disciplinary action, the young officer threw his sea bag onto the vessel and then leaped off the bridge onto the deck of the moving PT *221*. Nothing was said, but all on board were smiling at the arrogant officer who had been forced to act so desperately. His treatment of the crew improved after the incident.[5]

What must this journey have been like for the young man from Pittsburgh? Long after the war, my dad and I plied the waters of Long Island Sound on various crafts for almost 50 years, and the one constant was that he loved to stand either next to or behind the boat's wheel and gaze out at the horizon. Quietly he would take in the never-changing, yet ever-changing water around him. The hum of the motor would merge with the silence to become silence; and his thoughts could drift so far that they were not thoughts; and sight, feeling, and sound would merge to form a new sense that was both numb and acute. Now I imagine him standing watch at the beginning of a great crusade, silently looking out at the horizon. Tens of thousands of miles would pass before his sojourn was over, and I am sure on a great many of these miles he quietly surveyed the horizon much the way he would still do as an old man. All of the men on the small boat with my father were young, full of the courage that seems to leave us with age. They were inexperienced but proud and cocky and undoubtedly confident that their cause was righteous. How many of them, like my father, found a kind of meditative peace by staring into the horizon; and how many, like my dad, would remember this peace for the remainder of their lives?

As the boats entered the Gulf of Mexico, the sky was still bright and the seas calm. However, early in the afternoon the sky darkened, winds picked up considerably, and the increasingly large swells made the voyage more uncomfortable. One unfortunate sailor on the *221* boat was bounced up in the air by a large wave. He violently landed on a cap-

4. The Grand Adventure: The Voyage to Panama

PT *221* underway. World War II PT Boats Museum and Archives, Germantown, Tennessee.

stan and fractured his ankle.⁶ The executive officer was at the boat's wheel, got seasick, and fell asleep. Slowly the boat started to creep out of formation. Fortunately, the boat's lookout noticed that the man at the wheel was standing, but he had his chin on his chest and was sleeping. Quickly, Lieutenant (jg.) James C. "Pete" Rock, the captain of PT *221*, ordered the officer below and took the wheel. Shortly after this incident, the leader of the Squadron, Lieutenant Commander Colvin, ordered the six boats to make a course for the calmer waters of the Intracoastal Waterway.⁷

Lieutenant (jg.) Rock was a full-blooded Chippewa Indian from Cass Lake, Minnesota. He stood six feet tall, weighed well over 200 pounds and was quick minded and athletic. More importantly, he was patient, a good teacher, and always willing to help a member of his crew. He was respectful of all of the men on his boat, and they in turn respected and had great affection for him. Lieutenant (jg.) Rock also loved to have a good time, and on more than one occasion he had to convince the shore patrol to not take him and the enlisted men he was with to jail for transgressions they had committed while on liberty.⁸

The first stop for the Squadron was Pensacola, Florida. The crew was divided into two groups. One would be required to stay on the boats, and the other was given liberty. Radioman Second Class MacIntyre "Tex" Henderson was one of the more colorful members of the crew of PT *221*. At 29, the five-foot-nine-inch MacIntyre was one of the oldest men in the Squadron. He had been married and divorced three times, had little formal education, and a great fondness for liquor and women. In the vernacular of World War II Navy men, he was a "liberty hound." Unfortunately, he was also an aggressive drunk, and his shipmates often had to step in and break up brawls that he had started. Not a man to be taken lightly, he had spent time prior to the war in the Texas State penitentiary for clubbing a man on the head during a fight.[9]

Although many of the sailors found Pensacola to be a "dead town," Tex soon met some civilians who had whiskey, the address of a nearby all-night bar, and a car to get them there. Henderson jumped into the car; and soon after they sped off toward the bar, the driver, who had already been drinking for some time, smashed the car into an immovable object. Henderson's head violently hit the windshield smashing his face and cutting a long gash under his eye. Not surprisingly, he presented a "sorry spectacle" the next day on the boat.[10]

The following evening, the second half of the crew of PT *221* were given liberty, and more trouble was found. Lieutenant (jg.) Rock and three of the boat's crew were out drinking, and at 11:30 p.m. they were stopped by the shore patrol. The four were about to be locked up when one of the shore patrol officers realized that Lieutenant (jg.) Rock was an officer. They agreed to let the men go, but first they confiscated the almost full bottle of whiskey the sailors had recently purchased. As the members of the shore patrol entered their car and started up the engine, Lieutenant (jg.) Rock barked, "Get that quart." One of his enlisted accomplices, Quartermaster First Class Lester P. Ellis, pulled open the rear door of the car and grabbed the bottle. As he was grabbing it, men who had previously been picked up and were sitting in the back seat of the patrol vehicle frantically jumped out and started running for their freedom. All of the sailors fled with the shore patrol officers in pursuit. In short order they scattered in every direction. Realizing that capturing any of the men was now unlikely, the shore patrol returned to their vehicle and drove off looking for other military lawbreakers.[11]

From Pensacola the boats motored to St. Petersburg and Tampa. The stops were short and uneventful because none of the sailors were given liberty. From Tampa, the boats journeyed to Key West, and my father remembered this portion of the voyage as pleasant and beautiful. The sea was calm, the sun bright, and the water clear and cobalt blue. Most of the sailors relaxed on the deck of the boats and enjoyed the beauty that surrounded them and the gentle breeze provided by the boats' forward movement. They arrived in Key West late in the afternoon. Surprisingly, several of the Squadron's petty officers were ordered to do shore patrol duty for the night. They were given leggings and billy clubs, and although they may have looked the part, they proceeded to carry out this duty by discreetly drinking beer and walking in the opposite direction whenever they encountered trouble. While they spent only a short time in Key West, my father remembered his time there fondly for the rest of his life. The town was vibrant and full of packed bars and excellent ice cream. Trouble was avoided, and the men had one question on their minds when they returned to their boats: Where are we going next?[12]

As they pulled out of the dock at Key West, excitement spread through the Squadron as the men were told they were going to Cuba. As the boats motored southward, the water temperature warmed, lone and schooled flying fish leaped from the water, Portuguese man-of-war drifted near the water's surface, and gulls, ducks, and black geese filled the sky.

My father's favorite shipmate was Gunner's Mate First Class Tom Hart, and they would remain close friends for the rest of their lives.[13] Hart was wiry, stood five feet six inches, and had reddish brown hair. He was raised on a farm in southeastern Ohio; and like my father, he was keenly observant, loved nature and exploration, and was smart but not well suited to thrive in a rigid, strict, traditional military environment. He was thus very well suited to serve on PT boats. He was a fine sailor, hard worker, and a man who would prove on numerous occasions to have great courage, although his quiet, modest nature would prevent him from talking at any length about his war exploits. He was also a fine shot, and when the men of PT *221* finally faced the Japanese in combat, Tom Hart was a man that the crew could count on.

Tom Hart and his wife Cecelia would periodically visit our family, and I always enjoyed talking with him, although he rarely spoke about his exploits in the war with me. He had a quiet confidence and a gentle demeanor; and thinking about him now, decades removed from the war, I realize that he was a perfect example of the citizen sailor who served the United States so well during World War II. When he returned home from the war, he earned a bachelor's degree in agriculture, operated a small farm, taught at several different universities, faithfully attended PT boat reunions, and I believe like my father, worked hard to not think about some of what he had seen and done in the war.[14]

When they entered the waters off the small town of La Fe on the western end of Cuba, most of the men in the Squadron found themselves outside of the United States for the first time. It was already dark, and the water near shore was dangerously shallow. There was no port with available docks, so the boats were anchored in a small bay. The men who were granted liberty were ferried to shore on small whaleboats through the barracuda infested waters. Machinist's Mate First Class Ormand O. Fowler, already a seasoned navy veteran of 16 years, served as the coxswain on the boat that took my father and Tom Hart to shore. Immediately Fowler started to bark out orders using the colorful language he had acquired over the years. "Get the hell off the gunnel.... This water is full of barracuda. Do you want one to take a chunk out of your ass? Get your dumb hands out of the water. Mother of Christ do you want to lose a finger? I hope one does bite one of you. If it does, don't come whining to me."[15]

The town that greeted the sailors when their small boat landed was like nothing any of them had ever seen. The buildings were small, and many had only one room. They were only five to six feet high, and the conical shaped roofs were made of thatch. The majority of the inhabitants were Indians, but small numbers of blacks and whites also mingled around as the boat unloaded.

The sailors quickly found a small saloon, and soon the cerveza and rum were flowing. A kind of friendly chaos emerged. None of the sailors spoke Spanish well, and the Cubans' mastery of English was limited, but despite this language barrier, both groups seemed to enjoy the other's company. The Americans quickly got drunk, and perhaps endeared themselves to the Cubans with their willingness to buy them drinks. Not surprisingly, as the beer and rum flowed and the revelry grew, one word was being uttered over and over by the sailors: "señorita."

Nearby, Lieutenant (jg.) Rock and Tex Henderson spotted a more substantial looking building. Inside, men were drinking, laughing, and carrying on; and the two men proceeded to walk over and attempt to join the revelry. As they started to enter the building, a short, heavy-set man wearing khaki pants and a white undershirt barked, "You can't come in here." Henderson, never one to back down, replied, "Who the hell are you?" The heavy man replied, "I am the captain of the base. This is an officers' recreational hut. You can prepare for a court martial tomorrow." Henderson tried to talk his way out of trouble by explaining he thought the man was a chief, but this did little good. Fortunately Lieutenant (jg.) Rock was able to smooth over the incident and the court martial never occurred.[16]

At 2:30 a.m. their liberty was about over, and the more responsible men of PT *221* tried to round up the drunken sailors and lead them back to the whaleboat. Some were dragged, others coaxed, and still others had to be threatened to get them to leave. In one of the more memorable events of the evening, Lieutenant (jg.) Rock found one of his young officers on the roof of one of the few multistoried buildings in town. The young man had his penis in hand waiting for the squadron commander to pass by so he could urinate on him. Fortunately for the young officer, Lieutenant (jg.) Rock convinced him to put his penis back in his pants and return to the boat.[17]

In short order, drunken men stepped and half fell into the whaleboat. One young officer took an awkward step and fell face first into the water. Alcohol had paralyzed him to the point where he could not or would not help himself, and if Tex Henderson and another sailor had not grabbed him by the feet and pulled him into the whaleboat he would have drowned.[18]

The next day the crew of PT *221* explored the town and its surrounding area. What struck them was the pervasive poverty they encountered. They found a crude road and walked inland and found the conditions under which the people lived only got worse.

Higgins PT boats docked in La Fe, Cuba. World War II PT Boats Museum and Archives, Germantown, Tennessee.

Opposite, top: **Young boys playing in La Fe, Cuba. World War II PT Boats Museum and Archives, Germantown, Tennessee.** ***Bottom:*** **Village in the interior of Cuba. Francis Gelzheiser collection.**

The farmland appeared to be of poor quality. The huts in which the people lived were approximately nine feet in diameter and thatched from the ground up. Floors were dirt, and often seven or eight people lived in each of these crude dwellings.

After their exploration, they found their way back to the village, and by 2:00 p.m. they had begun drinking again in the small tavern. Later they would learn that the Cuban beer had an alcohol content as high as 14 percent, which was much higher than the beer they had enjoyed in the United States. Since they did not know or perhaps care about the additional alcohol, they became intoxicated quickly. In short order, Motor Machinist's Mate Second Class Francis Clougherty proceeded to untie a horse from a tree, mount it, and ride the animal up and down the dirt road freely using a lash he had improvised to convince the animal to run at full speed. Shortly after he was persuaded to get off the horse, he jumped into a truck that had recently been driven into the village. He then succeeded in starting the engine and proceeded to race the vehicle up and down the same dirt road terrifying all he came near and angering the vehicle's owner and numerous town residents. The sailors feared trouble, especially when they discovered that the truck's owner had a knife and seemed determined to use it. Finally, after nearly wrecking the vehicle two or three times, he stopped, got out of the truck, and before he could cause any more trouble, Yeoman Jack Mayerhardt approached him, knocked him out with a blow to the face, and then with the help of other sailors the unconscious Clougherty was dragged back to his boat.

Sailors were getting into fights and even resisting officers who attempted to break them up. Several others, in perhaps the most ridiculous display of the day, got down on all fours. Some took on the role of a dog and proceeded to chase others, who played the part of rabbits. They raced through the doors, between the legs of their drunken squadron mates, and then through the flimsy walls of the crude saloon. The evening's revelry continued. Some of the sailors seemed "happy," others "silly," some "quarrelsome," and some "stupid," and there were even a few who were not drinking at all.[19]

The next day a group of sailors heard that there was going to be a dance in the town of Cayuco, which was approximately six miles inland. A number of the men got cleaned up, put on their best clothing, and began to hike toward the town. After a long walk down an old dirt road, they were finally picked up by a Cuban man in an old Ford pickup truck and delivered to the dance. Immediately two things surprised them. One was that the large barn structure in which the dance was taking place was roped into two sections with one for blacks and one for everyone else. One of the American sailors, whose chestnut complexion had been made even darker by the days he had spent in the sun, was identified as black by men manning the door and told he would have to stay in the section of the dancehall cordoned off for blacks. It took much persuading by his shipmates to get the doorkeeper to relent and allow him to enter the non-black section with them.

More importantly, in the eyes of the sailors, the dance hall was filled with numerous young, well-dressed, beautiful, Cuban women. Over the next few hours, the sailors danced the "Fast Jitterbug" and did their best to communicate with their dance partners. Great fun was had by all of the sailors, and it is doubtful that any of them regretted their journey to Cayuco when they returned to their boats over two hours after their liberty was officially over. Fortunately, all of the officers were asleep, and none of the exhausted sailors faced any consequences for being absent without leave.[20]

The next day Lieutenant (jg.) Rock approached my father and threw a dead rooster on the deck in front of my dad. The Lieutenant inquired, "Can you cook a chicken Gelch?"

My dad, who I am sure had never cooked a chicken in his life, responded, "Sure Mr. Rock, I'll cook it." Why was my father, an electrician's mate, being asked to cook a chicken? Because of their small crew and limited galley space, many of the PT boats did not have a trained cook on board. PT *221* had set out with a cook, but he had gotten "banged up" early in the voyage. My father, who had been a short-order cook for a brief time prior to the war and always liked to be helpful, volunteered to be the boat's cook. The problem with this was that although my father had a variety of talents, cooking was not one of them.

After much effort my father had removed most of the bird's feathers and entrails and placed the sorry looking creature into the oven. Two hours later, Lieutenant (jg.) Rock walked into the crew's quarters and jabbed a fork into the sizzling bird. He turned and looked at my dad and remarked, "That bird is tough as hell." My father, acting as if he knew what he was doing replied, "It takes awhile for older chickens." An hour later the boat's captain returned and again stabbed the cooking chicken and again found the bird to be tough. At this point my father was becoming nervous but he responded, "It shouldn't take much longer." When Lieutenant (jg.) Rock made his third and final examination of the chicken, there had been no improvement. Annoyed, the boat's skipper entered the crew's quarters and awoke Machinist's Mate Second Class Francis X. Lerz, the sailor who had given him the chicken, and sharply asked, "Where did you get that rooster, Lerz?" The startled sailor responded, "At the cockfight. You know, you were there." Lieutenant (jg.) Rock inquired, "Who gave it to you?" The nervous Lerz replied, "No one did. Don't you remember that fight where the favored cock, the one brought in from somewhere else by professional cockfighters was going against a local bird? The favored cock was winning. The local product was down and everyone thought the fight was over. Don't you remember? The local cock rose up, gave one desperate shuffle, and dropped dead at the same time that the other cock ran away. Each side claimed its cock had won. The referees were arguing and people were starting to fight. That's when I went over, picked up the dead rooster, and took off."

After learning the truth, Lieutenant (jg.) Rock brought an end to my father's first, and I am sure final, attempt at cooking a chicken on the *Omen of the Seas*. The rooster found its way overboard, and sometime later, a new sailor was cooking for the crew. My father would go through life only reluctantly admitting that he had failed as a cook on PT *221*, and he periodically made attempts at cooking as I was growing up. Ironically, the one dish he prepared that everyone loved was his chicken soup.[21]

As the sun rose on April 26th, the sailors of Squadron 16A raised their boats' anchors and bid goodbye to Cuba. They did not know their next destination. The seas were calm as the boats motored in a V-formation south. All of the sailors stayed on the deck enjoying the sun, "sparkling blue water," and the abundant sea life and birds. Late that afternoon, they arrived at Cozumel Island off the coast of the Yucatan Peninsula of Mexico. My father would remember his time here fondly and talked of it often for the rest of his life. As in Cuba, the docking facilities were limited, so the boats had to anchor in a small bay. Although the water was over 30 feet deep, it was easy to see fish and turtles swimming or resting on the bottom, and my dad had a particularly keen memory of a giant turtle that slowly swam by, unbothered by the sailors. How exotic must the waters of Cozumel have seemed when compared to the Ohio River? A line was tied to the stern and the swift current caused it to drift backward and dangle on the water's surface. Sailors would then leap off the bow, drift past the boat, grab onto the stern line and then pull themselves to the boat and then climb up the stern ladder back into the boat.

Liberty was granted, but no boat was available to take the men to shore. Eventually my dad and a few of the other more powerful swimmers swam the 500 yards to shore through the "grass green" water. The current was swift, but his years swimming in the rivers of Pittsburgh had helped him to develop a strong and efficient swimming stroke. After a short time they reached the shore where they saw little, cut their feet on the sharp shells and barnacles, and then had a brief talk with a group of Indians they encountered. They were told that the waters were infested with sharks and barracuda and that "no one swims here." Soon after, with their feet still bleeding, they swam back to the boat, and upon returning they were again admonished for being fools for swimming in the shark infested waters with bleeding feet. My father always smiled when he told this story.[22]

The good fortune that had followed Squadron 16A from Cuba to Cozumel was no longer evident as they departed for Honduras in late April. The seas were rough, and most of the men became seasick. To compound these difficulties, the food supply was limited to a small amount of fruit and salami. The latter was in ample supply, but it was not the sort of fare a man wrenching from seasickness would find appetizing. To make matters worse, the boats got lost, fuel supplies grew dangerously low, the waters were too deep to anchor the boats, and vicious lightening storms exploded on the horizon.

Finally, as night fell and they still had little idea of where they were, the decision was made to put out a sea anchor. Immediately, the greenness of the officers and crew became evident. Not only did no one know where the sea anchor was stored, but an argument ensued as to how to properly use the device. At one point after the sea anchor had been located, crew members were about to drop it off the bow of the boat only to be told by Torpedoman's Mate John A. Novak, one of the few sailors on the boat who seemed to know how to use the device, that sea anchors had to be dropped off the stern of the boat. More than an hour after the order had been given to deploy the anchor, the device was properly positioned.[23]

Fortunately, the sea anchors did their jobs, and the boats of Squadron 16A drifted little during the night. The next day, the boats soon came to within sight of land, and the men eagerly took turns looking at the mountains and heavily forested shoreline through binoculars. They later learned that they had missed their destination by more than 60 miles; but by day's end, the boats had located the small town of La Ceiba, on the northern coast of Honduras, and they were able to find crude docks on which they could tie up. Soon after their arrival, modesty was forgotten, and a large hose was mounted to one of the poles on the dock, and men stripped and enjoyed the first shower they had had in days.[24]

After completion of their showers, the sailors were divided into two groups. One was required to stay behind with their boat, and the other sailors were allowed to journey into the town. La Ceiba was more substantial than it originally appeared, and despite the fact that it was isolated, the sailors found it charming and beautiful. Large trees grew everywhere and provided shade and made it difficult to determine how large the town was. Numerous dogs walked the streets unattended, and although many of the townspeople were so poor they lacked shoes, they were still gracious and friendly. The sailors were surprised that most of the people they encountered spoke English, and when they inquired why, they were told that English was taught to all Honduran students in the primary grades.

La Ceiba had numerous well-maintained buildings, two small movie theaters, and the Hollywood Hotel, which was the sailors initial stop. The hotel catered primarily to

Americans, most of whom were employed by the United Fruit Company of Boston, and it was surprisingly cool and comfortable. All of the PT boat men were appreciative of the meal that was provided. Leaving the hotel, the sailors watched men on horseback pull carts full of fruit, cars of recent vintage drive by, men leading packhorses carrying burgeoning packs down the street, and boys and women with baskets of fruit on their heads walk by. Boys appeared at the dock selling fruit that many of the sailors had never seen before. The boys sold coconuts, plantains, and small bananas that were about two to three inches long and were called bird bananas; and all were purchased. In the distance were forested mountains that provided a wonderful backdrop to the town they were exploring.

While most of the sailors spent their precious liberty exploring the town, two sailors spent their time searching for the town's house of prostitution. After making several inquiries, the men located a small brothel. One sailor was quickly ushered upstairs by the only available woman, and the other was left waiting in a room below. The police soon arrived, and the woman who was with the sailor upstairs panicked and cried out, "My God, the police," and then jumped out of the window. The young sailor, completely naked, grabbed his clothes, leapt out of the window, and landed on a pineapple patch. The prickly leaves punctured the man's skin in a number of places, but this did not prevent him from fleeing, clothes still in hand, to a patch of nearby vegetation where he promptly put on his clothes and headed back to his boat. His partner in crime, who had been apprehended by the police when they came through the front door, was given a warning and released. He immediately returned to his boat.[25]

Unfortunately, La Ceiba could not provide Squadron 16A with fuel, and at the end of the day the six boats motored out of the pleasant town bound for Puerto Castilla, Honduras. The late afternoon sun was hanging in the horizon as the boats left the harbor of La Ceiba in column formation. Soon it grew dark, but the seas were calm, and a slight breeze helped to make the conditions near perfect for the men who lingered on the boats' decks. Years later Tom Hart would say, "On that night we understood the phrase, the magic of the tropics."

As the boats neared the port at Puerto Castilla, PT *219*, the lead boat in the formation, was challenged by a blinker from one of the American warships in the port. For an unknown reason, the *219* boat did not respond in a timely manner, and soon shore lights were aimed at the boats. Numerous ships and shore installations began to challenge the boats simultaneously, and the small boats furiously responded to the challenges with blinkers and signaling messages. Things got so tense that the gunners on PT *219* manned their guns, and there was a real fear that soon the shore batteries would open fire on the six small vessels. Fortunately, searchlights finally got a clear view of the boats, the challenges were satisfactorily answered, and the boats were allowed to proceed to the dock at Puerto Castilla. It was only then that the Squadron learned that they had been mistaken for enemy submarines and that disaster had only narrowly been averted.[26]

The exhausted men soon tried to sleep, but this was prevented by the ubiquitous tiny sand fleas that proceeded to mercilessly bite the tired sailors. The next day, as the boats took on fuel, the men fished, cleaned the guns, and took care of various repairs on the boats. By this point in the voyage it was evident that an interesting transformation was occurring in Squadron 16A. With each day, the sailors were becoming more proficient at their jobs. The novice seamen who left New Orleans were starting to understand the numerous intricacies of operating a small warship. They better comprehended weather, how the boats would best handle different sea conditions, the engines, electrical systems, and numerous other aspects of their boats. However, while they were honing their skills as sailors, officers and crew were also "going native" and in all outward appearances, they looked less and less like members of the United States Navy and more and more like castaways. The men rarely wore shirts, and they all had dark tans. Pants were rarely worn, and instead cut off dungarees were worn while on shore and when underway. Broad brimmed straw hats were donned by almost all, and many sported beards and mustaches. In deference to the Spanish that most of the natives they encountered spoke, names were even modified. Donald became Donaldo; Carlson, Carlsono; Rucker, Ruckero, etc.

Enlisted men took great pride in their work, and they resented officers—especially new ones who had yet to prove themselves—who entered their world and tried to tell them what to do. This was especially true in the small engine rooms where motor machinist's mates toiled in hot, oily, and cramped conditions to keep the Packard engines running. On many boats when officers entered this tiny world and attempted to tell the sailors at work what to do, they were told by the sailors to get lost. Officers who complained of this insubordination to boat captains were usually told to leave the men in the engine room alone and to avoid entering this domain unless it was absolutely necessary, and some officers were instructed not to enter the engine room without asking for and receiving permission from the motor machinist's mates who were at work.

Enlisted men would never again embrace the formal Navy practices that they had learned during their stateside training, and periodically this would create problems when they were loaded on to ships or based in ports in the United States where more traditional Navy behavior was expected or when they encountered officers who were less accepting of the squadron's ragtag appearance or unwillingness to embrace the traditional culture of the United States Navy.[27]

Although they were able to fill their fuel tanks in Puerto Castilla, they were not able to take on much food. Meals continued to consist of salami, a small amount of fruit and crackers, and all of the sailors hoped that the next port would provide a greater variety of food.

After an uneventful voyage, Squadron 16A arrived at the coastal village of Cabezas, Nicaragua. The boats tied up on a small dock, and the crews were required to do extensive cleaning and maintenance on the boats. Late in the afternoon, my father and some of his shipmates were given liberty. The town was pleasant and well kept. Most of the homes were wood framed, had three to five rooms, and sat on wooded posts that raised the dwellings two to four feet off the ground. The streets were clean, and there were numerous shops, many of which were owned by people of Chinese ancestry. The majority of the citizens were black, and almost all of them spoke some English. Many of the sailors eventually located a small tavern, and they spent the remainder of the day drinking and singing.

As nightfall set in, the men were ordered to return to their boats. Most were granted liberty; but for unexplained reasons, they were required to stay within sight of the boats. A few local women showed up, and sailors went ashore to talk and flirt with them.[28] Some of the sailors conversed with the women's brothers who had escorted them. The young men talked of the injustice that was common in their country. Indians and blacks were treated as second-class citizens, and they had no chance if they found themselves in a court of law confronting a Spanish man. Americans and the Spanish residents owned much of the local industry, including a nearby sawmill. Local laborers were paid only 63 cents per day, and workers who were injured on the job were fired with no compensation.²⁹

The following morning, Squadron 16A motored out of Cabezas bound for Port Lemon, Costa Rica. The voyage was pleasant, and after tying the boats up to a dock, most of the sailors were given time to go into town so they could get a good meal. Although Port Lemon was populated by people who were racially and ethnically diverse, there were more Caucasians on the streets than there were in any of the other ports they had visited. The sailors spent the day walking the town's palm-tree-lined streets, resting in its public parks, or having drinks in one of the numerous bars. Many of the homes in town were well kept and substantial, and locals who were not at work spent the day fishing and enjoying the cool ocean breeze.³⁰

There were a number of excellent athletes in Squadron 16A, and while in Port Lemon a group of them formed a baseball team that challenged the local nine to a game. The final score of the contest has long been forgotten, but the sailors won decisively. The most memorable moment of the contest occurred late in the game when Lieutenant (jg.) Rock hit a ball that flew over the outfield fence and past the boxcars that were on the rail tracks outside of the park. The locals were so impressed with this prodigious home run that they picked up the 200-plus-pound boat captain and paraded him around town like a conquering hero.³¹

On the morning of May 7, the six boats started out for Panama, the final leg of their

Lieutenant (jg.) Rock slugging a baseball. Francis Gelzheiser collection.

journey. The seas were calm, and various activities were undertaken while underway. Sailors worked to modify their quarters to make them more livable. On PT boat *224*, Ensign Earl Benton made the mistake of trying to make the boat's crew "more navy" despite the fact that the men had gone more "native" with each day of their journey. There was no question that the officers were in charge, and generally orders were followed without questions; but saluting and overt rank distinctions were now kept to a minimum. Often, on board the boats and on shore, officers and crew ate, socialized, and went out on the town carousing together. I also believe that many of my father's squadron mates shared his disdain for equating rank with expertise. The goal was to get the job done, and he and his shipmates were most willing to listen to and follow the man who was most capable of leading them to achieving their goal. Ensign Benton's desire to make his men "more navy" was not likely to go over well.

Up to this point in their voyage, lookouts who saw land would report, "I see land ahead, Sir" or "There's a buoy off to port." They were instructed by the Ensign to instead sing out "Land-ho" or "Buoy-ho." The officer in charge would then respond "Where away," and the lookout in charge would respond with the direction. Sailors were not used to this formality, and most found it silly. Things came to a head when lookout Fireman First Class John Klemanski called out "Land-ho." Ensign Benton responded, "Where away" and Klemanski responded, "Far, far, away." Klemanski was admonished by his superior officer, but attempts at making the PT boat crews "more navy" were largely forgotten for the remainder of the war.[32]

If the sailors' confidence and skill had been honed by their training and the voyage to Panama, their remaining limitations as seamen would be made evident as they approached their destination. Lacking all the navigational aids that modern mariners rely on, the men on the PT boats had to navigate using basic nautical charts and a crude compass. Onboard the lead boat was a quartermaster named Elmer Sander who had been a commercial fisherman in western Washington prior to the war, and of all of the sailors making their way on this voyage, he was the most adept navigator. Using only a compass for navigation, Sander had regularly journeyed hundreds of miles out into the Pacific on his small fishing boat and then returned safely to port days or weeks later.

Up to this point, Sander had employed his considerable navigation skills to plot a course for Squadron 16A. However, the officer in command of the lead boat refused to listen to his advice, and instead the 90-day-wonder plotted his own course. This course caused the boats to miss the Panama Canal by more than 90 miles and travel as far south as northern Columbia. To make the situation worse, while lost, PT *221* hit a 20-to-30-foot log. The crew had spotted the object in the water, but the man at the wheel had been unable to turn the boat sharp enough to avoid it, and the boat rammed into it damaging all three of her screws. This caused the engines to vibrate a great deal and dramatically reduced the speed at which the boat could travel.

Late at night and dangerously low on fuel, the boats put out sea anchors and waited. As the sun rose the next morning they realized their error, but now they also had to navigate to the canal through a mine field; and to accentuate further just how inexperienced they still were, my father, who was taking his turn at the wheel, proceeded to almost hit a whale as they motored toward the canal.[33]

The six boats of Squadron 16A finally made it to the small naval base of Cocasola, Panama. The sailors were immediately assigned tasks on the boats. Numerous small repairs were made, guns and bilges were cleaned, and all of the compartments were scrubbed. At night groups of men were given liberty. Most sailors journeyed to the nearby towns of Cristobal and Colon. Sections of Cristobal and Colon were "beautiful," but the majority of these towns were bleak. Streets were narrow, dark, and dirty, and most of their inhabitants were poor. Many earned a meager living selling inexpensive trinkets to sailors and tourists. None of the sailors were unhappy when the time came to leave.

On the second day after their arrival, PT *221* was taken up a "narrow, filthy" waterway to a small boatyard where they hoped to get the boat's screws repaired. The equipment at the boatyard was crude; and in order to get the harness around the boat to lift it out of the water, an old man had to enter the excrement-filled water and swim the harness under the boat. The acidic water burned his face, and the onlooking crew felt sorry for the old man, especially when he returned to shore pushing the feces out of his way and rubbing his bloodshot eyes from the pain caused by the polluted water. In short order the boat was raised out of the water, and the bent screws and shafts were at least temporarily repaired.[34]

The day after the repair, the squadron motored to the Panama Canal to begin the much-anticipated journey across the Isthmus of Panama. While in the canal's famous locks, two boats were tied together, and most of the sailors found the crossing to the Pacific fascinating. My father talked often of his passage through the canal; and later in life he and Tom Hart went back with their wives to see it again, only this time on a modern cruise ship. Gatun Lake, which is at the highest elevation of the canal, was especially beautiful. Its water was deep blue, and on its shore grew exotic tropical vegetation. After ten hours in the canal, the squadron reached Balboa on the Pacific side of the Isthmus, and from here they journeyed to Taboga Island.[35]

The United States Naval Training Station on Taboga Island was established in August 1942, and it served as a training base for PT boat squadrons that were to be sent to the Pacific Theater. The training station's buildings had been quickly constructed, and then two small marine railways, overhaul shops, a power plant, water storage tanks, a radio building, mess hall, barracks, fuel storage tanks, munitions storage facilities, a torpedo workshop, and numerous other facilities were hastily installed or built.[36]

The island overlooked the Pacific entrance to the Panama Canal. In the mid–19th century, it had been a base for the British South Pacific Steamship Company, and until the early decades of the twentieth century it was an important region for fruit production. Prior to the war, the island had gained modest popularity as a health resort. On the eve of World War II, the island's economy was suffering; its fruit production had declined dramatically, its population was decreasing, and many of its inhabitants lived in poverty.

There was a small village constructed on the eastern side of the island. Simple dwellings were built just above the high tide mark, and these extended inland and a short distance up the hills that began at the end of the pleasant, crescent-shaped beach. Some of the hillside was covered with low-growing tropical vegetation, but there were also large areas in which the vegetation had been burned off or cleared using other means. There were small patches on the hillside where pineapples, mangoes, limes, lemons, oranges, bananas, coconuts and papayas were grown; but many of these orchards were not well tended and were badly overgrown. The people of the island appeared to be an ethnic mix of Indian, black, and white, and a number of the people that the sailors encountered spoke English and Spanish and appeared to be well educated.[37]

It had become evident during the brief voyage to Taboga Island that the recent

Taboga Island, Republic of Panama, December 1944. World War II PT Boats Museum and Archives, Germantown, Tennessee.

repairs done to PT *221* had not been done correctly, and shortly after its arrival the boat was again put in dry dock. While the screws and shafts were being repaired, the crew did extensive maintenance on the boat. The interior was painted, and the bottom was scraped with wire brushes; and the dust from the removed copperoid bottom paint soon got into the eyes and covered the hair, skin and clothing of the sailors doing the work. Sweaty, dust-covered PT men, in an attempt to remove the grime and cool off, jumped into the water, only to later learn that wetting the bottom paint dust would make it harder to get off. As a result, a number of the sailors who did the scraping were a golden brown for several days after the work was finished. The maintenance on the boat was soon completed, and advanced training began almost as soon as PT *221* was returned to the water.

Crews had to be prepared to man their boats 24 hours a day, and much of the training took place at night, often exhausting the crews. Torpedo firing, boat handling, depth charge deployment, barge hunting, and combat formation and tactics were all practiced. Crews learned to work with airplanes, lay smoke screens, and operate with other boats at high speeds and with limited visibility. Sham attacks on larger ships were made, and gunners learned how to fight off enemy aircraft. Most of all, crews learned how to work as a team, both on their own boats and with other boats in the squadron. The relentless training, difficult conditions, and lack of sleep caused nerves to fray and boats to almost collide on numerous occasions.[38]

Although the daily training after sunset was exhausting, many of the men in

4. The Grand Adventure: The Voyage to Panama

PT boat training exercise off of Taboga Island, Republic of Panama. World War II PT Boats Museum and Archives, Germantown, Tennessee.

Squadron 16A fondly remembered the beauty of the nights on the water off the coast of Panama. The air was warm, and the cloudless southern sky was full of stars that the sailors—all of whom came from much further north—had never seen, and the water thrown off to each side of the boats' bows while underway was full of bright and beautiful phosphorescence.

PT boat training maneuvers in the Panama Canal Zone, Taboga Island, Republic of Panama. An unknown PT boat is laying a smoke screen while PT *223* or *225* watches. World War II PT Boats Museum and Archives, Germantown, Tennessee.

When not training during the day, boats had to be carefully cleaned. The salt spray and air caused numerous problems with motors and generators, and these had to be attended to by the crew. In addition guns had to be taken apart and cleaned and polished to remove the rust that seemed to return almost immediately after cleaning. It was always hot, and the sun was almost always bright. As a result, sailors doing gun maintenance had to handle gun parts with pieces of cloth or they would blister their hands simply by touching the heated parts. Even ammunition became corroded and had to be cleaned daily. Some sailors looked for ways to avoid the difficult and tiring work, and one took the extreme step of jumping into the water, swimming to shore, and never returning to his boat. His shipmates never learned if he drowned or spent the war in the warmth and quiet of Panama.[39]

During their limited free time, sailors would erect canvas tents on the boats' decks and relax, fish, swim, watch dolphins glide by, walk the nearby beach, and collect beautiful seashells that seemed to be everywhere. During one free afternoon, my father and several shipmates journeyed to the Casco Viejo district, in Panama City, to see the golden altar of the Church of San Jose. He long remembered the elaborately carved wooden altar that was plated with gold and was impressed to learn that when pirates landed and threatened the beloved altar, residents painted it black to hide the gold coating, and thus saved it from the marauders. On occasion sailors would take the boats out and race them, much the way American teenagers raced their cars on summer nights in small American towns; and periodically members of the squadron schemed to concoct pranks to add some levity to difficult days.[40]

On June 4, 1943, PT Boats *219*, *220*, *221*, and *222* were loaded by crane onto the heavily armed tanker USS *Schuylkill*. The ship had been camouflaged to look like a cargo ship, but in reality it was one of the newest and largest tankers in the United States Navy. PTs *223* and *224* waited several days, and then were loaded onto a different tanker for their voyage north. Initially, *Schuylkill's* destination was New Caledonia; but after one day at sea they were ordered to head for Pearl Harbor; and finally on their third day, the crews were informed that they were going to Bremerton, Washington. Generally, the voyage was unpleasant. The sailors lived in their PT boats. They got up at 5:30 a.m. and then spent the day doing work that most of the PT boat men believed was not necessary. They were ordered to scrape the copper paint off the boats' bottoms and then repaint them even though this task had been performed only two weeks earlier. The captain of the ship was "Old Navy," and he insisted that the PT sailors dress properly and rigidly adhere to Navy rules. This angered the men who had become less and less willing to embrace Navy formalities during their journey to Panama.

When not working, many sailors wagered on dice and cards, and often there was tension between the PT boat men and the crew of *Schuylkill*. These were not games with small stakes. In Panama there had been little on which the men could spend their paychecks, so many of the PT sailors had a significant amount of money in their possession. Sailors would often bet 40 to 50 dollars on a single throw of the dice or hand of poker, and such high stakes created a great deal of tension. Shouting matches and fights broke out periodically. During one dice game, a sailor insisted on talking to and bothering the gamblers, and he continued to do this even when he was told to be quiet. Without warning another man jumped up and hit the man who was irritating the gamblers in the stomach. When hit, the man made a feeble attempt to fight back, but a blow soon landed on his mouth and this knocked him unconscious. He fell to the deck face down, and the game continued as his blood flowed across the deck of the boat toward where the dice were being thrown. Annoyed that the man's blood was about to disrupt their game, a sailor got up, filled a hat with water, and hurled it on to the face of the unconscious man. Slowly the man got up and staggered away to his bunk. My father was not a brawler; but he did have a keen calculating mind, self-control, and excellent observation skills. These helped to make him a skilled poker player, and he won a significant amount of money on this voyage.[41]

Traveling at 16–18 knots, the ship steadily made its way north, and each day the air became cooler. Gun practice was held daily, and the gun crews became adept at hitting the floating balloons that were unleashed into the air as targets. Porpoises followed the boat, and albatrosses and gulls were frequent and popular visitors. Finally, after 13 days, *Schuylkill* entered Puget Sound; and on the night of their arrival, the PT boats were unloaded.[42] For the next month, repairs and modifications were made to the boats. Some of the boats were equipped with Mark XIII torpedoes, one or two boats were equipped with radar, and more accurate Sperry Fluxgate gyrocompasses were added to the vessels to improve navigation.[43]

Many of the married men got a last chance to visit with their wives before they shipped out again, and two sailors in the squadron got married. After three weeks in Bremerton they moved to Seattle. Leave was granted on most nights, and this resulted in some sailors finding trouble. Several got into fights, others were arrested for various transgressions, and John Klemanski was sentenced to five days in the brig with nothing to consume but bread and water for returning from leave 12 hours late. One night when returning to their boat after a night on the town, my father and a shipmate noticed an officer staggering down the dock so drunk that they were afraid he would fall into the water and drown. They went up to the officer and each sailor took one of his arms and placed it around the back of his neck. Slowly they ushered the officer toward his boat and safety. Along the way, the officer continued to speak, although most of what he said made no sense. However, my dad and his friend heard something familiar in his voice; and as a result they took a careful look at the man they were helping and realized it was the film legend Henry Fonda. Mr. Fonda would serve with distinction during World War II and win the Bronze Star for his bravery. However, on this night he needed the help of two PT boat sailors to safely make his way back to his ship.[44]

Although MacIntyre Henderson usually went out on leave on his own, he did ask Tom Hart to join him on one occasion. Not surprisingly, their night on the town did not go as planned. They stopped at a tavern that was only a few hundred yards from the Bremerton Naval Yard gate. They enjoyed two beers and then got up to leave only to be separated when a large crowd of people entered the establishment. A few minutes later, Tom Hart spotted Henderson being escorted out the tavern door by two policemen and into a police car. Henderson spent the night and part of the next day in jail, and he was only let out when Lieutenant (jg.) Rock came in and persuaded the police to free the sailor. Henderson had made the mistake of grabbing a young woman in the buttocks. She did not seem to mind; but her boyfriend, who was also one of the policemen who arrested Henderson, did, and this was the reason Tom Hart's night of liberty with MacIntyre Henderson was prematurely brought to an end.

The PT boat sailors enjoyed their time in Seattle, but soon their evenings filled with revelry and their days with American normalcy would be a distant memory. On the morning of July 20, 1943, PT boats *219, 220, 221,* and *222* left the west coast city bound for the desolate Aleutian Islands on the turbulent Bering Sea. Their final destination would be the tiny island of Attu, and it would be more than nine long months before they would enjoy civilization again.[45]

5

PT Boat Squadron 16 and the War in Alaska

Those guys had a lot of fun, but service on those boats was awfully dangerous.—Armand Vigeant who served on the battleship USS *Massachusetts* during World War II

By the time Japan bombed Pearl Harbor, in December 1941, her leaders had formulated their grand vision of Japan's place in the world and developed a plan to make this vision a reality. Put simply, Japan, a resource starved island, wanted to insure national self-sufficiency by acquiring a huge colonial empire in the Pacific; and to achieve this goal, the United States and the European nations that had long controlled much of this region had to be removed.

Like her German ally in Europe, the Japanese realized that quick, decisive victories were necessary to counteract the overwhelming industrial superiority and military potential of her enemies. To achieve this, she needed a large navy and superior naval air power; and in the early phase of the Pacific war, Japan had attained naval and naval-air supremacy. At the time of the Pearl Harbor attack, she had 10 aircraft carriers to America's 4, 10 battleships to America's 4, 35 cruisers to America's 24, and 110 destroyers to America's 90. Each side had 44 submarines; but as in the PT boat fleet, the torpedoes on the American submarines were inferior to Japan's Type 93 or Long Lance torpedoes, which were faster and more powerful, accurate, and reliable than any torpedo in America's arsenal at the war's inception. As she prepared to engage the American Navy in the months following Pearl Harbor, Japan's naval commanders led a force that had not lost a naval battle in more than 100 years, and most Japanese officers and enlisted men were supremely confident in Japan's ultimate victory.

In addition, the Imperial Japanese Navy Air Service had 3,300 planes, which was more than America possessed. The Mitsubishi A6M1 "Zero" or "Zeke" fighter plane was perhaps the best in the world; and in the early months of the war, the land based Mitsubishi G4M attack bomber also proved to be a formidable aircraft.[1] In addition to superior aircraft early in the war, Japan's Navy had 5,000 pilots, and these men were better trained and more experienced than their American counterparts. All of these advantages caused Japan's military leaders to believe they were well positioned to win the air war against the United States.[2]

Japan used her military superiority to achieve astonishing success early in the war. In short order, French Indochina, Thailand, Hong Kong, British New Guinea and Rabaul, the Gilbert Islands, Wake Island, Guam, the Dutch East Indies, Portuguese Timor, Malaya, the Andaman Islands, Singapore—which British Prime Minister Winston Churchill called the "greatest disaster to British arms which our history records"—Brunei, Borneo, Nauru, Burma, and the Philippines, all fell, and many feared that Australia would soon follow.[3]

These stunning early victories should have satisfied Japan's desire for territory, and she ought to have turned her attention to fortifying her newly acquired empire. However, in April 1942 when Lieutenant Colonel James "Jimmy" Doolittle and his courageous Raiders took off from USS *Hornet* and unleashed their bombs over numerous targets on mainland Japan, the perception that Japan was beyond the reach of enemy bombers and essentially invincible was shattered. Little damage was done by the bombs, but the raid inspired millions of Americans to raise a defiant fist in the air at finally striking back at their hated enemy, and it forced Japanese military leaders to expand their Empire even more to insulate the homeland from future attacks.

Admiral Isoroku Yamamoto, who had brilliantly orchestrated the attack on Pearl Harbor, now initiated a plan to expand Japan's forward line of defense to include the Aleutian Islands in Alaska and Midway Island far to the south. These new acquisitions, in addition to controlling Wake Island, the Marshall and Gilbert Islands, and the Southern Solomons to Port Moresby, would allow Japanese air patrols to insure that American planes did not pass into Japanese territory unimpeded by Japan's naval and air forces. In addition, the Japanese believed that the United States might eventually invade Japan from the west, and planes and ships based in the Aleutians could be used to help repel this invasion.[4]

Although some in the Japanese High Command argued that their quick advance in the Pacific had left Japan overextended, most still believed that a decisive victory or A-Go over the United States Navy was possible. Japan had lost fewer ships than expected in the early months of the war, and Japanese leaders still trusted their Navy to defeat America's Pacific Fleet if Japan could find a way to lure it into a confrontation with Japan's superior naval forces. This would enable Japan to add Midway and the Aleutian Islands to its defensive perimeter and would make Japan's Pacific wall so formidable that they believed America would lose the will to resist, and the Pacific would be conceded to Japan.[5]

Soon, both the Japanese and the Americans would find out that the Aleutian Islands and the Alaskan mainland were not places well suited for war. On the mainland there were few roads, and the weather in Alaska was extreme and unforgiving. From May through August there were 18 to 24 hours of daylight per day, but during the long winter, each day was one endless night. Fog hung low to the ground almost daily, and when war came to the region it was not uncommon for B-17 pilots to fly at an altitude of 25 feet so that pilots could see and follow the sea wakes caused by the air blast of the plane flying in front of them.[6]

At approximately 1,200 miles long, the 69 Aleutian Islands made up the longest archipelago in the world, and were the location of some of the most extreme weather on earth..[7] As it moved in from the south, the tropical Japanese or Kuroshio Current collided with the cold, dry, Siberian air mass. This resulted in a low-pressure system that hung over the islands and helped create weather that was almost impossible to predict. The Aleutians were one of the few places on earth where high winds, often reaching speeds from 50 to 140 miles per hour, and fog existed at the same time. Rain often blew sideways, and on occasion upside down. There was no calm or dry season, and only 8 to 10 days per year could be described as clear in the region. Williwaws would sweep out of the mountains without warning, and within one-half-hour achieve speeds in excess of 100 miles per hour. Large waves, unpredictable currents, narrow channels, and a poorly charted coastline all made ship and boat navigation nerve wracking and dangerous.[8]

The air was constantly damp, and for many months of the year, mosquitoes were large, hungry, and ubiquitous. Because of the constant winds, almost no trees grew on the islands, and instead vegetation consisted of weeds, firewood, wildflowers, and muskeg, which was a mixture of matted dry grasses and topsoil that was composed of volcanic ash. When wet, which was most of the time, this mixture became quicksand like, and often soldiers and sailors would sink to their knees in this mess and have their boots sucked off when they walked through it.[9] Surprisingly, extreme cold was uncommon on the Aleutian Islands, so this was one problem with which the warriors on both sides did not have to regularly contend.

Much of America's war against the Japanese in Alaska would be fought from the air, and there were numerous natural impediments to a successful air campaign in Alaska and the Aleutians. Pilots had to take off from crude runways, often covered with mud. Plane wings were often coated in ice; oil became lumpy; and winds would loosen rivets, bend wings, and clog carburetors. The crew of a B-17 flying at 35,000 feet would have to endure temperatures as low as 85 degrees below zero; and as temperatures cooled and warmed as planes ascended and descended, metals in the planes would contract, expand and weaken. All of these difficulties took an enormous physical and psychological toll on airplane pilots and crews.[10]

What strategic value did the Aleutian Islands and the Alaskan mainland have for the United States? The western Aleutian Islands were only 650 miles from the large Japanese naval and army base at Paramushiro in the Kuril Islands, and some military planners believed that airstrips could be built in the western Aleutians from which bombers could fly missions against this important base.[11] In addition, America's ally, the Soviet Union, was fighting for its existence against Germany, and some in the American government believed that Alaska could be used as a staging ground from which much needed lend-lease material could be sent to the Soviet Union. The United States also hoped that the Soviet Union would eventually join America in its fight against Japan and that military planners could coordinate attacks on the Rising Sun from the eastern Soviet Union and Alaska. Most importantly in the view of many Americans, it was simply unacceptable to allow Japan, the hated attacker of Pearl Harbor, to control even a square foot of American territory.[12]

In the spring of 1942, Admiral Yamamoto developed a plan designed to lure America's Pacific Fleet into a trap, destroy its remaining aircraft carriers, and expand Japan's Empire to include part of Alaska and Midway Island. It was believed that this would provide Japan and her Greater East Asia Co-Prosperity Sphere with an impregnable defensive perimeter, and force the United States to agree to a negotiated peace.[13]

The plan developed by Admiral Yamamoto to occupy islands on the Aleutians, destroy the American forces at Dutch Harbor, capture Midway Island, and destroy America's Pacific aircraft carrier fleet was bold and complex. The Admiral decided to divide his massive naval force. The smaller portion would attack Dutch Harbor in Alaska and occupy the Aleutian Islands of Adak, Kiska, and Attu. He believed that this would force the American Pacific Fleet to leave Pearl Harbor and steam northwest to protect the homeland. This would allow the bulk of Yamamoto's fleet to conquer and occupy Midway

Island and then use the airfields on the island and the four aircraft carriers attached to this fleet to destroy the American carriers when they sailed from Alaska to protect Midway. With the implementation of this plan, the United States' carrier fleet would be destroyed, and Midway and the Aleutian Islands would be part of Imperial Japan.[14]

In hindsight, many have been critical of Admiral Yamamoto's plan. They argue it was too bold and complicated or simply unnecessary. However, the plan was well conceived, and when the vast superiority of his naval force is considered, success clearly favored the Japanese. What Admiral Yamamoto did not know was that a brilliant, eccentric, pajama-and-slipper-wearing American Naval Commander named Joseph J. Rockefort and his team identified as JN 25 had worked round the clock to decipher the Japanese code; and in one of the more well-known episodes of the war, American Naval Commanders were able to trick the Japanese into telling them their plans. As Victor Davis Hanson remarked in his excellent account of the Battle of Midway in his brilliant book *Carnage and Culture: Landmark Battles in the Rise of Western Powers*, "Hundreds of brave Japanese sailors would be cremated at Midway because of an officer working in his slippers knew they were coming."[15]

The Japanese armada that set sail to destroy the American fleet and take Midway and the Aleutians in late May and early June 1942 was the most powerful naval force ever assembled up to that point in history. In total almost 200 ships, and 100,000 sailors and pilots were involved in the campaign, and it is likely that all had great confidence that they would achieve victory.[16] Although breaking the Japanese code gave the United States Navy an enormous advantage, Admiral Chester Nimitz would confront the Japanese with a much smaller fleet, inexperienced pilots and crew, and antiquated planes often armed with defective torpedoes that almost never worked.[17]

If it was American genius and ingenuity that enabled the United States to break the Japanese code and foil Admiral Yamamoto's plan for a surprise invasion of Midway and attack on the American fleet, it was American luck, pluck, and raw courage that enabled the much weaker United States Navy to win the battle. Once the Japanese carriers had been located, the initial attacks on them by American planes were a disaster. Experienced Japanese pilots and deck gunners shot down slow, outdated, American Devastator torpedo bombers with ease. When the planes did get close enough to release their ordnance, their torpedoes never worked; and tragically of the 82 men who flew in these planes on the day of the battle, only 13 made it back to their ships alive. In total, of the 102 planes in the first eight waves of American aircraft that attacked the four Japanese carriers, none did any real damage. However, these men did not fight and die in vain. As the confidence of Japanese airmen and carrier crews grew as a result of their astonishing early success, a final wave of 50 American planes arrived. These were flying at an altitude of 15,000 to 20,000 feet, and as the Japanese wreaked havoc below, the dive-bombers above went unnoticed. In four to six minutes they would alter the course of world history.[18]

As the American dive-bombers readied for their descent, the decks of the Japanese carriers below had been unwittingly turned into bombs waiting to be ignited. Planes lined the decks, and deck crews frantically worked to remove the bombs from the planes that were to be used in the attack on Midway Island and replace them with torpedoes that were better suited to attack the American aircraft carriers. Airplane fuel was in the planes' tanks and in fuel trucks on the decks, doors to hanger lockers were open, and below were additional ammunition, bombs and torpedoes. The flight decks were made of wood, and tools and other debris were scattered everywhere waiting to become shrapnel when the bombs from the undetected enemy above found their mark.[19]

At 10:22 a.m., twenty-five Scout Bomber Douglas (SBD) Dauntless dive-bombers of squadrons VB6 and VS6 led by Lieutenant Commander Clarence "Wade" McClusky from the American carrier USS *Enterprise* dove at 250 miles per hour toward the Japanese aircraft carrier *Kaga*. Four to six of the released bombs hit their target and set off a chain reaction of explosions on and below the deck of the ship. In minutes 800 men were burned alive and the ship was destroyed. At almost the same moment, Lieutenant Commander Richard Halsey "Dick" Best and five SBD dive-bombers who had also taken off from *Enterprise* landed one to three bombs on *Kaga's* sister ship, *Akagi*. It too was doomed.[20] The United States was now able to reap the rewards for its miraculous repair of *Yorktown* after the Battle of the Coral Sea. Flying from the newly repaired ship was Bomber Squadron 3, composed of 17 planes led by Lieutenant Commander Maxwell Franklin "Max" Leslie. As an inferno raged on and in *Akagi* and *Kaga*, bombs from Bomber Squadron 3 found their mark on *Soryu*, and it also found its way to the bottom of the Pacific.[21]

Later that day, planes flying from the remaining Japanese aircraft carrier *Hiryu* located and hit *Yorktown*, and the proud ship would eventually sink. However, 24 SBDs from *Enterprise* and *Yorktown* led by Lieutenants Earl Gallagher, Dick Best, and Dewitt W. Shumway found their way to the last of the four Japanese aircraft carriers at Midway. The pilots fearlessly flew through horrid anti-aircraft fire, landed four bombs on the deck of *Hiryu*, and sent the enormous ship to the ocean's bottom. As a final indicator of the courage of the men who flew that day, many pilots only located their targets after their fuel gauges registered less than one-half full. This meant that they continued flying toward the enemy knowing that even if they survived the fire from the ships and attacking planes they were likely to run out of fuel on the return to their mothership and crash into the Pacific. After they crashed it was possible they never would be found and would be consumed by the sea or the creatures that lived in it.[22]

The Japanese losses at Midway were staggering. In addition to the four irreplaceable aircraft carriers, she lost a heavy cruiser and another was damaged. Half of Japan's best carrier pilots, considered by many the finest combat pilots in the world, were gone; and experienced flight crews, 2,155 seamen, and 332 aircraft were lost. Perhaps most importantly, the sense of invincibility that had permeated the Japanese military since their stunning victory in the Russo-Japanese War in 1905 was shattered.

Prior to Midway many believed that after the small island and the Aleutians were taken, Japan could turn her sights on New Caledonia, Fiji, and then even Hawaii as early as August. Many in Japan dreamed that after this Australia and even ports in the western United States could be next. These dreams came to an end at Midway, and for the remainder of the war the Japanese would be on the defensive. The goal of an impenetrable defensive perimeter stretching from Midway to the Aleutians would never be a reality. However, despite the fact that without Midway the Aleutians had much less strategic importance for Japan, the plan to control the Aleutians remained intact; and when the Japanese occupied Attu and Kiska the people of Japan were told of a great victory in the Aleutians. The disaster at Midway was kept a secret.[23]

Unlike the Battle of Midway, which resulted in a quick, pivotal victory for the United States, the fight for Dutch Harbor and the Aleutians was much more drawn out and less decisive. A poor communications system, lack of experience, and an unwillingness to believe the available intelligence hindered the Americans. Japanese efforts were handicapped by weather and the inability to resupply troops when they achieved control of Attu and Kiska. In addition they underestimated the ability of America's military forces to adapt to the challenges of fighting in this difficult environment and how determined the United States was to drive them out of Alaska.

As the largest portion of the Japanese fleet motored toward Midway Island, a smaller naval force steamed for the American base at Dutch Harbor on the island of Unalaska. The fleet was made up of light aircraft carriers *Ryujo* and *Junyo,* heavy cruisers, destroyers, submarines, three transports, 2,500 invasion troops, and 82 carrier-based planes.[24]

The American fleet in the region was under the command of Rear Admiral Robert "Fuzzy" Theobald and consisted of two heavy cruisers, three light cruisers, and ten destroyers. Rear Admiral Theobald had been warned of the impending Japanese attack, but he was not a believer in the code breakers back at Pearl Harbor, and thus did not use their intelligence when he formulated his plan. Rather than forming a defensive perimeter off the coast of Unalaska and wait for the Japanese to come, Rear Admiral Theobald sent his small fleet miles from the island to form a "picket line" that would intercept the enemy long before they arrived at Dutch Harbor. The small number of American ships, weather, and the vast area to be patrolled made it unlikely that the plan would succeed, and the Japanese fleet motored undetected past the "picket line" on its way to Dutch Harbor.[25]

On the night of June 2–3, 1942, the planes from the Japanese light carriers took off to attack Dutch Harbor. Unlike at Pearl Harbor, the Japanese planes were spotted by American patrol planes, so the attack was not a surprise. As the Japanese planes approached Dutch Harbor, outdated planes operated by inexperienced pilots took off to intercept them. They proved to be no match for the Zeros and their experienced pilots. But inadequate planning by the Japanese resulted in pilots dropping their bombs as they saw fit, and although the scene at Dutch Harbor appeared disastrous, in reality, only minor damage was done to installations on the ground. Twenty-five Americans were killed. The second wave of Japanese planes was impeded by the weather and achieved little success, and a number of the returning planes fell victim to the harsh weather in the region and missed the carrier decks when landing and crashed into the sea.[26]

On the afternoon of June 4, the Japanese attacked again. The Americans were waiting, but despite the lack of surprise the Japanese scored hits on an oil storage tank, the base hospital, a warehouse, and four fuel storage tanks containing 750,000 gallons of fuel.[27] None of these hits did serious damage to the United States war effort, and clearly these Japanese planes would have had a much greater impact on the war had they been used at Midway instead of Dutch Harbor.

Ironically, as the disaster at Midway was unfolding for the Japanese, Admiral Yamamoto had radioed task-force commander Rear Admiral Kakuji Kakuta and told him to abort the attack on Dutch Harbor and steam to Midway to participate in this much more important battle. Unfortunately for Admiral Yamamoto, the planes had already left the carrier flight decks when the message was received, and this made it impossible for the ships at Dutch Harbor to immediately leave to assist the fleet at Midway.[28]

Having seen his grand plan result in failure, Admiral Yamamoto pondered his next move. Without Midway, the Aleutians had lost much of their worth; however, they were still considered important for the defense of northern Japan, and the occupation of islands that were part of the United States would be an enormous propaganda victory. Admiral Yamamoto ordered his forces to invade and occupy the poorly defended Aleutian Islands of Adak, Kiska and Attu. Plans to take Adak were soon cancelled when the Japanese learned of a previously unknown American airbase on the nearby island of Umnak. On the night of June 6–7, 1,250 Japanese troops landed on the island of Kiska. The only people on the island were there to operate the island's meteorological station, and eventually all 10 were captured by the Japanese. On the afternoon of June 7, the Japanese entered Massacre Bay on the island of Attu. In short order 1,200 men occupied the island. There was no American resistance.[29]

The Americans and Japanese now played a cat-and-mouse game with each other on Kiska and Attu. To give the islands military value, the Japanese had to construct airfields, and to build these they needed heavy equipment and supplies. This would require ships from Japan to penetrate the American naval and air blockade and deliver the needed goods. Initially, Japanese attempts at supplying the islands were haphazard, and showed a real aversion to risk on their part. Transport ships would be sent from the base on the Japanese island of Paramushiro, on the northernmost end of the Kurile Island Chain, with little support. If they encountered American warships, they would turn around, if not they would take their supplies to the islands. On March 10, 1943, the last Japanese transport reached the Japanese on Attu. All attempts after this failed, and the Japanese realized that if they wanted to properly supply the islands they would need to provide the transports with naval support ships; and if American ships were encountered, a battle would be necessary to break the blockade.[30]

On March 22, 1943, three transports overflowing with supplies left Paramushiro bound for the Japanese-held islands in the Aleutians. Escorting the transports were two heavy cruisers, two light cruisers, and four destroyers. Additional supplies had also been loaded onto the destroyers. On the morning of March 26, the American Northern Pacific Fleet—composed of four destroyers, a light cruiser, and heavy cruiser USS *Salt Lake City*, under the command of Vice Admiral Charles "Soc" McMorris—spotted Japanese ships 200 miles west of Attu. Vice Admiral McMorris soon realized that his ships were not facing unescorted Japanese transports but loaded transports and a Japanese fleet that was significantly larger than the one under his command. In addition, the Japanese ships were newer, larger, and faster, and had guns that were superior to those on the American vessels.

Although facing a vastly superior force, the vice admiral quickly decided to try and sink the three transports and then flee to avoid a protracted battle with a superior foe. At 8:42 a.m. under unusually clear skies, the Battle of Komandorskis began. The Japanese were the first to fire; but it was the Americans who scored the first hit, landing several shells on heavy cruiser *Nachi*. The ship was not seriously damaged. At 9:10 a.m. the Japanese hit and badly damaged cruiser *Salt Lake City*. The ship lost power, and icy water flooded the lower compartments. Men ran below and waded through waist deep water to try and contain the damage. On the ship's deck, frantic gunners continued to fire, ammunition supplies grew low, and terrified sailors watched as Japanese ships moved closer to their ship, which was dead in the water. The ship's skipper, Captain Bertram Rodgers, was asked if he wanted to abandon ship, and he replied, "No." To protect the wounded ship, the small destroyers circled around her laying smoke. Finally, in desperation, the command was given to the destroyers to attack.

What must have gone through the minds of the young men on those small ships as they motored toward the Japanese fleet? The combined weight of the destroyers was 5,000 tons, and the fleet they now attacked had a gross tonnage of about 10 times this weight. One shell from one of the large Japanese guns could have sunk any one of the small American ships, but in an attempt to save the severely damaged *Salt Lake City* they continued to motor rapidly toward the enemy. Destroyer USS *Bailey* was hit and lost speed, but destroyers USS *Monaghan* and USS *Coghlan* continued toward their targets and got to within 9,000 yards of the large cruiser *Nachi*. Much to the relief of the terribly outgunned Americans, and in one of the more shocking developments of the war in the northern Pacific, the Japanese fleet then turned and steamed homeward.

Why did the Japanese fleet, which was clearly on the verge of victory, prematurely end the battle? When the order to withdraw was made, the Battle of Komandorskis had lasted three and one-half hours and was the longest continuous gunnery duel in modern naval history. It was also a rarity in World War II because planes had played virtually no role in the battle. The Japanese commanders were afraid that American planes would soon arrive; and when the Japanese realized they would not get air support for their ships, they feared being vulnerable to attack from above. Some in the Japanese fleet mistakenly believed that American planes had already arrived. In addition, almost all of the Japanese ships were low on fuel and ammunition.

The Battle of Komandorskis was important for a number of reasons. It was the last time the Japanese would try to penetrate the American blockade in the Aleutians with surface ships in an attempt to resupply Attu and Kiska. They would continue to use submarines to supply the two islands, but these vessels could only carry limited supplies. Thus the heavy equipment necessary to build airfields would never arrive, and the bases on the two islands would serve little purpose other than preventing the United States from using them. It also marked the end of Japanese naval supremacy in the northern Pacific. As in most of the rest of their vast Empire, they would now try to defend the territory they had acquired, often sacrificing thousands of lives to a cause that was doomed to fail. The weak American Navy that was charged with holding the line as much as possible during the war's first year had largely done its job, and the full might of America's productive capability would soon be brought to bear. Japan's long, slow, brutal, and deadly retreat was about to begin, and PT boats would play an important role in America's march to victory.[31]

Initially, there was some disagreement among American civilian and military leaders about what to do with the Japanese on Attu and Kiska. Some believed that their lack of planes and airstrips made them an impotent enemy, and thus they should be left alone. Others believed that the United States should invade both of the islands after a prolonged bombing campaign. Eventually, orders came from Washington to drive the Japanese from the Aleutians and American soil.[32]

On August 30, 1942, the Army occupied Adak, an island 200 miles east of Kiska, without resistance, and soon 4,500 soldiers were garrisoned on the island. Miraculously, a serviceable airstrip was built in 12 days, and from here bomber missions were launched against Attu and Kiska whenever possible, and America's planes, submarines, and surface fleet made further Japanese improvements on Attu and Kiska almost impossible. The island would also prove to be a valuable staging ground for the future invasions of Attu and Kiska.[33]

The Americans faced enormous obstacles to their goal of driving the Japanese out of Alaska. Although the Japanese could muster little air or naval resistance to American attacks, they had been ordered by the Japanese high command to "hold the Western Aleutians at all cost." They were well dug in, and as was discovered by the United States so often in World War II, massive aerial bombing often did much less damage to the Japanese than was expected.

After the Battle of Komandorskis, the weather was the real arbitrator of what happened in the Aleutians. When possible, American pilots would take off from Dutch Harbor, Adak, and eventually Amchitka and fight through the clouds, wind, cold, the vastness of the Aleutians, and enemy flack to bomb the Japanese on Attu and Kiska. The Japanese would hunker down and absorb the onslaught and endure. Their rations and everything else were limited, and there was little hope they would ever be able to construct air bases and take the offensive. Instead, the Japanese who suffered on Attu and Kiska were there to be a thorn in the side of the Americans, to serve as a tool for the Japanese propaganda machine, and to prevent the United States from controlling these islands and building bases on them from which America could initiate bombing missions against Japan.[34]

The weather did much to protect the Japanese. Each day American pilots would awake thinking they were going to fly only to often find out that their missions were cancelled due to weather. When they did fly, weather conditions were never ideal. In the fall of 1942, the United States lost nine planes in combat and 63 to weather and mechanical problems.[35]

Despite the numerous obstacles they faced, the small United States fleet was able to blockade the Japanese-held islands and prevent vital supplies from reaching the Japanese; and the Army Air Corps continued to bomb whenever weather permitted. However, after nine months of bombing, the American military planners came to the conclusion that if the Japanese were to be removed from the Aleutians, it would require ground forces to drive them out.[36] As a precursor to the invasion of Attu and Kiska, the Americans landed on the unoccupied island of Amchitka on January 12, 1943. The island was only 70 miles east of Kiska, and after the rapid construction of an airfield, bombing raids against the Japanese commenced.[37]

Initially, American military strategists had planned to invade Kiska first, but after they realized that Attu was less well defended, the decision was made to "island hop" past Kiska and invade Attu. In reality, Attu did have fewer Japanese defenders than Kiska. However, American intelligence had wrongly estimated that the island was only protected by 500 Japanese soldiers, when in fact 2,650 of the enemy had dug in and were waiting to defend the island.[38]

On May 11, 1943, Operation Landcrab, the invasion of Attu, was initiated. Prior to the Army's 7th Division landing on the island's beaches, a naval fleet that consisted of three battleships, one escort carrier, three heavy and three light carriers, and 19 destroyers and transports bombarded the tiny island.[39] Not surprisingly, the Army's 7th Division, which had little experience with amphibious landings, encountered numerous problems almost immediately after they hit the beaches. Soldiers found it difficult to move, and artillery quickly became bogged down in the sand. Infantrymen found it impossible to stay dry, initially lacked shelter, and from the first day of the invasion trench foot and gangrene were serious problems. However, the Japanese plan to defend the island did not include engaging the Americans at the landing zones; and by the end of the first day, the three American invading forces had landed 2,000, 1,500, and 400 men respectively on different parts of the island. The mission of these forces was to drive into Attu's interior and then trap and destroy the Japanese occupiers.[40]

As would happen on numerous other islands held by the Japanese during World War II, once the Americans landed, Attu's defenders would be left to fend for themselves. Supplies would not be sent, and each Japanese soldier knew he had one duty: to fight until all hope was lost, and then die for the Emperor either by being killed by the Americans or committing suicide. Eventually, the United States landed 14,000 men on the tiny island. Fighting both the island's harsh environment and a fanatical and courageous enemy, the American forces slowly drove the Japanese back.[41]

On May 28, American forces surrounded what remained of the Japanese forces and put them in a hopeless military position. The defenders of Attu were dramatically outnumbered and outgunned, their backs were to the water, and resupply or rescue was impossible. Surrender was never an option for Japanese commander Colonel Yasuyo Yamasaki, and in a move that was a harbinger of what would tragically happen on numerous islands in the future, he prepared his men for one final suicidal attack. At this point he had approximately 800 men in fighting shape and 600 wounded to counter the 14,000 Americans that now opposed him.

Most of the 600 wounded were killed with morphine or grenades, and then in the early morning of May 29 the remaining Japanese soldiers were ordered to make a fanatical charge directly into the American lines. Colonel Yamasaki hoped that the surprised front line of the American troops could be overrun and that his soldiers could then gain control of the American artillery and direct these guns on their enemy.[42]

Colonel Yamasaki was correct when he surmised that the attack would shock the Americans and cause some soldiers to abandon their positions. The charging Japanese continued to move rapidly forward until they encountered the Army's 50th Engineers. Refusing to yield their ground, the Engineers engaged the charging Japanese in some of the worst hand-to-hand combat of the war. The heroic men of the 50th Engineers broke the momentum of the assault, and realizing that their mission would not achieve its goal, 500 Japanese soldiers then committed mass suicide. The battle for Attu was over. To win back the tiny island that most Americans had never heard of, the United States lost 600 men and 1,200 more were wounded. Only 28 Japanese, or approximately 1 percent of the men garrisoned on the island were taken prisoner, and many of these had been wounded prior to the final assault and were spared only because attempts to kill them had failed.[43]

Since the American victory on Attu, some have argued that it was an unnecessary battle and that the American and Japanese lives lost on the island died in vain. In reality, the desolate island played an important role in America's war against Imperial Japan. From Attu, the United States flew approximately 1,500 missions against the Japanese on the Kuril Islands and their Paramushiro Base. These were some of the longest and most dangerous bomber missions of the war, and the direct impact they had on the Japanese war effort was negligible. However, as a result of these missions, the Japanese were required to keep 500 planes and 41,000 troops in the Kuril Islands to defend against an American invasion that never came. Had Attu not been taken and the raids not occurred, these forces would have been used against the United States in other parts of the Japanese Empire and certainly would have resulted in the deaths of numerous American and Japanese servicemen.[44]

Opposite, top: Approximately 40 dead Japanese on Attu. United States Army Signal Corps. *Bottom:* Japanese guns captured by the Americans on the island of Attu. World War II PT Boats Museum and Archives, Germantown, Tennessee.

The war in Alaska presented a unique set of problems for American military leaders. Weather, distance, geography, sea conditions, topography, and an enigmatic enemy made planning difficult; and all branches of the American military had to employ an arduous process of trial and error to determine what equipment and tactics could best be employed to survive in this difficult environment, defeat the Japanese, and then ensure American control of this vast territory.

On August 20, 1942, PT Boat Squadron 1, composed of PTs *22, 24, 27,* and *28*, motored out of Seattle under the command of Lieutenant Clinton McKellar, Jr., bound for Dutch Harbor, Alaska, 2,500 miles to the north.[45] Twelve days later these four Elco boats arrived at their destination; and not surprisingly, these vessels and the PT boats that followed them had numerous problems while stationed in Alaska. These boats had almost no heat, and during their time in Alaska, frost, which sometimes reached two inches in thickness, often formed on the boats' bulkheads. Salt spray froze on the boats' decks, guns, and torpedo tubes adding much extra weight and making the boats less seaworthy. Heavy seas put tremendous strain on the boats' hulls. Strong winds caused boat cleats to be pulled out when the boats were tied to docks and anchor lines to break or anchors to pull free when boats were at anchor. Hail and snow were common, and they made navigation difficult. Props were damaged when rocks were hit, and repair facilities were few and often inadequately provisioned. None of the four boats was equipped with radar when they left Seattle, and only PT *28* was outfitted with this vital navigation aid after the boats arrived at Dutch Harbor.[46]

The four PT boats of Squadron 1 had limited success during their time in Alaska. Naval leaders had hoped the small boats could unleash their torpedoes on Japanese war ships, but opportunities to do this never occurred. They did lay mines and carry out reconnaissance and supply missions for the Army.[47] By the time winter arrived, all four boats in Squadron 1 needed numerous repairs, and they were sent to King Cove on the western end of the Alaskan peninsula to get overhauled. On January 5, the work was completed, and the boats set out for Dutch Harbor. Problems would continue to plague the boats for the remainder of their time in Alaska. Only PTs *24* and *27* made the return voyage from America's most northern state, and it is surprising that the Navy did not end the experiment of using PT boats in Alaska then.[48]

The difficulties encountered by the four boats of Squadron 1 and the report filed by Lieutenant McKellar stating that PT boats were not well suited for the northern Pacific did not convince the Navy that the Aleutians were an unsuitable place for PT boats. Shortly after the two boats returned, the 12 boats of Squadron 13, under the leadership of Lieutenant James B. Denny, prepared to motor north. On March 31, 1943, the first group of four boats completed the journey from Seattle to Adak. They were followed by four more, and the final four boats arrived on May 27. These 12 vessels were newer Higgins boats, and they were better suited for the harsh conditions of Alaska. They had stronger hulls, motor driven hot air heaters, and a number of the boats were equipped with radar.[49]

The boats were based on the island of Adak, and while there they were tasked with protecting Amchitka from possible Japanese attack during the American invasion of Attu and preventing the Japanese from sending reinforcements to Kiska. They also were used as water taxis, mail boats, tugs, troop transports, and crash boats. After the successful American invasion of Attu, a PT boat base was installed there in Massacre Bay. While based in Attu, the PT boats would escort larger ships through the notorious fog, and

Top and bottom: PT boat base, Adak, Alaska. World War II PT Boats Museum and Archives, Germantown, Tennessee.

PT Boat Squadron 13 Higgins PT boats moored in Attu, July 1943. United States Navy.

ferry officers to other parts of the island. Like the boats in Squadron 1, they never engaged the Japanese in combat.[50]

On July 20, 1943, Motor Torpedo Boat Squadron 16A, made up of PT boats *219*, *220*, *221*, *222*, *223*, and *224* left Seattle bound for Attu. The voyage to Alaska was a journey that my father would remember for the rest of his life, and he was fortunate to travel part of the same route later in life with my mother on a small cruise ship.[51] By now the boats of Squadron 16A had been outfitted with radar and this would prove its worth over and over again for the remainder of the war. Unfortunately, the charts of the waters they were motoring through were limited, and generally the boats found their way by using a compass to navigate to a buoy. They would then set a new course for the next one. This proved to be a hit or miss process, and sailors had to constantly be on the lookout for shallow water, rocks, logs and other debris. However, the scenery was magnificent, and I suspect most of the sailors in Squadron 16A enjoyed this voyage as much as my father.[52]

The Squadron's first stop on its journey north was Patricia Bay on the southern end of Vancouver Island. Although the water was cold, several sailors went swimming. Some of the men journeyed to the beautiful city of Victoria when liberty was granted, but most stayed in close proximity to where the boats were docked. Some sailors did not travel to Victoria because they did not wish to spend the time in transit to the city, but the more common reason for not making the journey was that the sailors soon learned that the women of the Canadian Women's Auxiliary Air Force (WAAF) were based near the berthing place of the PT boats. And for most of the men in Squadron 16A, this would be one of their last opportunities to interact with women for the next nine months. Several of the women were convinced to take a tour of PT *221*, and Tex Henderson, always the ladies' man, managed to get one of the women to spend the night with him on the beach.[53]

The next day, the boats stopped at Port Hardy on the Northern end of Vancouver Island. This was a drab town dominated by its cannery. Liberty was given to some of the men, and they did manage to find a store where a generous American bought them beer; but when morning came, none of the sailors was sad to leave.

As they motored north early the next morning, the sailors were greeted with some of the most beautiful scenery in North America. At this point the passage was narrow, often less than one-half mile wide; and on all sides the sailors gazed at rolling, forest-covered hills, snow-covered mountains, huge rock outcroppings, and a blue, white cloud-filled sky. Islands of various sizes protruded from the water, and these insured that the waters on this part of the voyage would be calm. If any sailor forgot their destination, he was constantly reminded by the air, which grew cooler with each passing mile.[54]

The next stop was the Canadian Army camp of Shearwater. There was little to do here, and after fueling and getting a good night's rest, the boats moved on early the next morning. They passed an abandoned, nameless village, and then stopped at the small hamlet of Butedale. The majority of the buildings here were run down, and the sailors learned that most of them were owned by the local cannery and rented out to the cannery workers for thirty dollars per month. The majority of the town's residents were members of the Kittemath Indian tribe. Most of the women in the town worked in the cannery, and the men spent their days fishing on small boats.[55]

That evening, some of the PT boat sailors persuaded the townspeople to have a dance, and as local Indian boys played guitar, sailors danced with Indian girls. The revelry ended when Lieutenant (jg.) Rock arrived and ordered the men back to the boats. Not surprisingly, three of the sailors from PT *221* snuck into the woods with three Indian girls undetected by Lieutenant (jg.) Rock. They did not return to their boat until early the next morning, but either the boat's captain did not realize they had spent the night absent without leave or he chose to ignore it. The men never found out, and nothing was said to the sailors when the boat motored northward.[56]

In one of the small villages that the squadron stopped at prior to Ketchikan, some of the sailors told the townspeople that they were running low on food. The townspeople could only provide the boats with limited supplies, but they did advise the men that the salmon were running and that with some hard work and pluck they could make themselves an excellent salmon dinner. Hearing this, the men headed inland armed with bailing hooks, nets, and carbine rifles. In short order they located a waterfall with hundreds of fish trying to leap up it. Some men tried to impale the fish with bailing hooks, others netted them when they fell back into the water below the falls after their failed attempt at leaping over it, and others shot the fish, and then grabbed them as they floated downstream. It did not take long to attain enough salmon to feed the squadron, and the sailors headed back to their boats.

While they were cleaning their catch, Lieutenant (jg.) Lewis Hindley, PT *222*'s executive officer, baited a hook on a fishing rod he found on his PT boat and sent the bait to the bottom. Soon, a powerful fish was hooked, and with much effort, a large halibut was brought to the surface. At this point it became evident that the fisherman had not figured out how the massive fish would be lifted out of the water and brought into the boat. Quickly it was decided that the fish should be shot. The first bullet found its mark, but instead of killing the fish, it caused it to swim frantically away from the boat. After great effort the fish was again reeled boat-side and then shot again. The second bullet killed the fish, but now the crew had to find a way to get the fish into the boat. Again, using less than traditional angling tactics, the crew convinced one of the more diminutive members of the squadron to let them hold his feet, lower him to the water, and then after he grabbed the massive fish, they pulled him and the fish into the boat. The plan worked splendidly, and the halibut provided the squadron with a fine meal the next day.[57]

The first stop for the PT boats in Alaska was the town of Ketchikan. Although it only had a population of approximately 5,000, the sailors still found much to do. It had numerous bars and a roller skating rink. Totem poles dotted the street corners, and souvenirs were for sale almost everywhere. The boat departed early the next morning motoring through Alaska's famous Inside Passage, and soon they arrived at the beautiful Wrangell Narrows. Here there was a tremendous current and powerful tides that made navigating the boats difficult. Water cascaded down the sides of the steep cliffs on the sides of the channel, and pine trees grew to the edge of the water. Many of the sailors marveled at the beauty that surrounded them.[58]

Not long after they had passed through the Narrows, the waters became rough. Tom Hart was proud of the fact that he never got seasick; and when he found himself about to lose his breakfast while on the boat's deck, he sheepishly slipped behind a torpedo so he could get sick undetected. He returned to the wheelhouse smiling to himself that no

Higgins PT Boat motoring in the Inside Passage. World War II PT Boats Museum and Archives, Germantown, Tennessee.

Higgins PT boat underway in the Inside Passage. World War II PT Boats Museum and Archives, Germantown, Tennessee.

one had seen him. Boat Captain Rock, holding the boat's wheel with a slight smile on his face greeted Hart by saying, "Kind of lost your pancakes, didn't you, Tom." Fortunately for Tom Hart, Lieutenant (jg.) Rock kept this embarrassing bout of seasickness from the rest of the crew.[59]

Casual observers might not realize how much seasickness impacted the crews of the Mosquito Fleet. It was an ongoing problem, and although the crew's normal response to a sailor getting seasick was to make fun of the man, it could be debilitating and impact the ability of the boats to carry out their assigned tasks. There were numerous occasions during the course of the war when more than half the officers and crew of PT *221* were seasick to the point where they could not perform their duties. On one occasion when my father was on the *Omen of the Seas,* more than 10 of the men on the boat were so sick that the remaining three men, which included my father, had to carry out all of the boat's functions, and on at least one occasion a man jumped overboard in an attempt to kill himself rather than endure the excruciating pain caused by the seasickness.

My father spent thousands of hours on boats of all sizes and in all kinds of sea and weather conditions before, during, and after the war, and he never got seasick. This made him a valuable man in the PT boat fleet, and it was one of the reasons that even though he was officially a member of the base force he regularly patrolled as a crew member on PT *221*.[60] Seasickness was not the only ailment that befell the sailors of Squadron 16A as they motored north. Lieutenant (jg.) Chet Bell, skipper of PT *223*, suffered an attack of appendicitis, and the almost constant pounding as the boats motored through rough seas caused many sailors to suffer numerous bruises, cuts, and even broken bones.[61]

At darkness, the squadron tied up at the nearly deserted village of Baranof, which was located on the eastern side of Baranof Island. Most of the men of Squadron 16A were surprised to learn that despite its small population, there were several attractions in the town to be enjoyed. A small store run by a local woman sold beer, hard liquor, and a variety of other items. In addition, on her property there were hot mineral springs. Wooden tubs were filled with this water, and for a small fee sailors could take a hot mineral bath. Many sailors took advantage of this and found it invigorating. Others hiked inland and found a beautiful pristine stream, several sailors were able to catch some trout, and others hunted unsuccessfully for black bear.

In the evening many of the men returned to the store where the liquor flowed freely, and the elderly woman proprietor proceeded to step up, remove most of her clothes, and dance for the sailors. Some found this amusing; others felt pity for the old, lonely woman. After her dance she babbled on to all who would listen about her life. She had been married and loved her husband, but lost him when he robbed a bank in Kansas City and was sent to jail. She smiled when she explained that the authorities never recovered the money. She had generously bought alcohol for the PT boat sailors that night, and many believed that this was paid for with the proceeds from the bank robbery. Finally, as the evening came to an end, she started to cry because she was so sad to see "young boys sent off to war and slaughter."[62]

After departing Baranof, the squadron made brief, uneventful stops at Port Althorp on the northern tip of Chichagof Island and then the Port of Yakutat. The sailors were denied any liberty in this tiny town. Almost all of the town's men were out fishing, and consequently servicemen were barred from entering the community.

The boats then motored to the town of Seward. Here the sailors were granted liberty and Tex Henderson and two others proceeded to ignore the city's 11:00 PM curfew for servicemen; and before they could return to their boats they were arrested along with some soldiers they had met while out on the town. Fortunately, the authorities released the sailors before their boats departed, but the soldiers were kept in jail after the sailors were released. Seward was the last town on their journey that would have much semblance of civilization, and as they motored away from the town the next morning, many sailors wondered how long it would be before they would again enjoy modern comforts.[63]

The seas were calm as the boats motored out of Seward; but as was often the case in this part of the world, they quickly grew rough, and eventually waves reached heights in excess of 30 feet. Many in the crew became seasick, and a huge wave crashed into the chart house of PT *221* causing several of the electrical devices to begin to smoke. General quarters was sounded, and nerves were put to the test when a port forward torpedo came partway out of its tube. The crew realized a potential crisis was on their hands when the torpedo's impeller started to spin. They frantically tried to fire the ordnance, but this failed. After 200 rotations the torpedo would have been armed, and once this occurred a bump could have caused it to go off, destroying the boat and killing most of the crew. Fearing fire from the electrical system and terrified that the torpedo would explode, the crew of PT *221* shut down their engines. As the rest of the squadron's boats motored north, the crew stabilized the torpedo and did all they could to extinguish the burning in the boat's electronics. By the time this was done, the other boats in the squadron were out of sight. Fortunately when these boats realized that PT *221* was no longer with them, they were able to reverse their course using their new compasses, locate PT *221*, and escort the damaged vessel to Kodiak Island. Here the torpedo was replaced and the damaged electronics were repaired.[64]

5. PT Boat Squadron 16 and the War in Alaska

Conditions on Kodiak Island were primitive, but a number of the sailors were excited because they hoped to hunt Kodiak bear. They were soon disappointed when Army authorities informed them that the bears had already killed two soldiers and that American servicemen were banned from hunting them. From Kodiak Island the squadron went to Chignik Island and anchored in Chignik Bay. Much of the island was covered with the offal of the fish from the large cannery that operated on the island, and a number of the men got sick from the smell. After pulling up the anchors that were draped with decaying fish remains, they motored to Sand Point, the last stop before the Aleutian Islands.[65] The first stop for Squadron 16A in the Aleutians was Dutch Harbor. Here the men spent their days cleaning, scraping, and painting their boats in preparation for the long voyage to Attu.[66]

Up until this point, decent weather and the protection offered by the Inside Passage had largely spared the sailors from rough sea conditions. This changed almost immediately. After leaving Dutch Harbor, rain, gale force winds, and waves that grew in height by the hour greeted the tiny boats. Sailors who tried to rest were bounced out of their bunks. Pots, pans, and anything else that was not tied down was sent flying, and most of the men became seasick. The driving rain and huge waves made it almost impossible for the men at the helm to see ahead of them, and finally the boats were ordered to head for Inanudak Bay on the northern coast of Umnak Island. Here they anchored and hoped that the weather would improve.[67]

Squadron 16A PT boat underway somewhere in Alaska. Francis Gelzheiser collection.

The next morning the winds had subsided some, and the boats set out for Chernofski on Unalaska Island. After refueling, the boats motored through Umnak Pass and into the Bering Sea. From here they motored to Atka Island. There was a stark beauty to this barren island. The ground was covered with reindeer moss, which was rich in color but also made walking difficult. In the island's interior were a number of small lakes, and animal paths made walking easier. While on a walk, two sailors found a large set of reindeer antlers that measured over four feet in diameter, and these were proudly mounted on the bow of PT 221.[68]

From Atka Island they sailed to Adak Island. Although thick fog made the early part of this voyage difficult, by late morning the fog had lifted and an unusually clear sky and calm seas made the voyage quite pleasant.[69]

In early August 1943, PT Boat Squadron 16A arrived at Attu. Their journey from Seattle had covered approximately 4,500 miles, and more than 1,100 of these were on the unprotected and unpredictable waters of the Bering Sea. Shortly after their arrival, PT Boat Squadron 13 departed Attu for Adak Island, and from there they would continue the long voyage to Seattle.

Base 5 or 13 in the Aleutians, Squadron 13 or 16A. World War II PT Boats Museum and Archives, Germantown, Tennessee.

Top: PT Boat Base 13, located in Casco Cove, Attu, Alaska. PT boat squadrons 13 and 16A operated from here during the Aleutian Campaign. The base was only 650 miles from Japan's Kuril Islands and more than 1,000 miles from the Alaskan mainland. *Bottom:* PT boat base camp on Attu. Both photographs, World War II PT Boats Museum and Archives, Germantown, Tennessee.

Attu Island is approximately 20 miles wide and 35 miles long. The small naval base on the island was on a peninsula at Massacre Bay, and the boats would be based there for most of the eight months they spent in the Aleutians.[70] Although the men of Squadron 16A would never engage the Japanese while in the Aleutians, there were numerous other challenges that made service on Attu difficult. For much of the year there was little sunlight, and fog was common which added to the bleakness of most days. To fend off medical problems that could be caused by lack of sunlight, the United States Navy and Army made sure that apples, oranges, and vitamins were constantly available on mess tables.[71]

The area around Attu was almost a permanent low-pressure zone, so bad weather was the norm. While on patrol, the PT boat crews had to fear the williwaws that would sweep down from the mountains, and in less than a half-hour winds could reach speeds in excess of 100 miles per hour. One williwaw was so violent that it broke the wind gauge meter at the PT boat base, but before doing so it registered a speed of 135 knots per hour. Winds would whip up seawater, freeze it, and violently blow it into men's faces. Heavy seas, sometimes in excess of 35 feet, strong currents, a jagged and poorly charted shoreline, submerged rock formations, hail, and occasional snow all made even routine sorties dangerous. My father reported that on more than one occasion while on patrol, the waves were so large that while in the trough of a wave, the wall of water in front of the boat made it impossible to see the next vessel in the formation. Even while boats were at anchor or docked, sailors had to be on guard for winds breaking anchor or dock lines and driving boats onto jagged rocks. Despite the fact that sailors were far from the combat that they would soon face, the eight months that the squadron spent in the Aleutians were cold, wet, lonely, and dangerous.[72]

Many normally routine tasks were made more difficult as a result of the conditions that existed in the Aleutians. Painting boat bottoms, always a hated job by seamen, often required sailors to heat the paint before it could be applied. Because the waters were generally uncharted, boats periodically hit rocks or went aground, and bent screws and shafts regularly had to be repaired.[73] As was true on other islands in the Aleutians, the ground was covered with reindeer moss, and this made walking wet and difficult.

In January violent winds picked up a hatch on PT *220* while John Klemanski was working and drove it down on his hand severing two fingers. Many men got ill while serving on Attu. Ailments like colds were common, and more serious illnesses like pneumonia and even yellow jaundice inflicted sailors and soldiers.[74]

Surprisingly, my father said that the sailors often listened to Tokyo Rose, called "The Voice of Truth" by the Japanese, because "she played the best music." Often she would begin her broadcast with the greeting, "Hello you fighting orphans in the Pacific." On October 16, the sailors of Squadron 16A were amused to hear the most famous Japanese propagandists tell them that 18,000 Japanese troops had been landed on Attu, and two days later Ms. Rose warned them to get off the island by October 19 or they would be bombed off. None of this bothered the sailors, but my father admitted that when Tokyo Rose played songs like *White Christmas* or Frank Sinatra's *I'll Be Seeing You* and talked of how all the girls at home were with men who had avoided serving in the military and how lonely it must be for the sailors on Attu many of the sailors did become homesick.[75]

When possible, the boats were sent on training runs to practice torpedo firing, unleashing smokescreens, using the radar, and maneuvering in formation. Many men got seasick, and everyone got beat up by the constant pounding of the boats in the almost-always-turbulent seas.[76] Periodically, the Japanese would bomb the island, and although no real damage was ever done, it reminded the men that a Japanese attack was a real possibility. As a result of this threat, during one 10-day period, there was a standing condition in which sailors were ordered to stand watch two out of every four hours in full battle gear. Planes would periodically fly night missions, and when they did, PT boats and their crews had to be ready to head into the dark Bering Sea at a moment's notice to assist a plane that had crash landed.[77]

Many of the sailors had difficulties with boredom, loneliness, and the complete lack of any female presence on the island. Men spent hours in cramped PT boats or in bleak 20-by-40-foot Quonset huts heated by oil-burning pot-bellied heaters. One officer, obviously affected by the bleak conditions, was lying on his cot in his Quonset hut and asked a friend, "Lew, do you see that spot on the ceiling?" His friend responded, "Yeah." With that the officer pulled out his .45 and shot a hole in the ceiling where the spot had been, and then said, "Now there isn't one."[78]

On September 14, PT *219* was moored to a buoy on Cosco Cove approximately 350 yards from shore. The wind was blowing 40 to 55 knots per hour, and the constant strain on the line caused it to break. The crew quickly started the boat's engines, but before they could gain control of the vessel, the wind had crashed it into the rocks. The crash punctured a hole in its bottom, and water began to gush in. Five hours later seaplane tender USS *Casco* was summoned, and it pulled the boat from the rocks. Unfortunately,

Sailors working on a small skiff off the coast of Attu. World War II PT Boats Museum and Archives, Germantown, Tennessee.

the hole in the stern was quite large, and the engine compartment quickly filled with water. Despite frantic efforts to pump the water out of the boat, the stern continued to take on water faster than it could be removed. As the PT boat slowly began to sink, *Casco* was forced to release her, and the boat went to the bottom in 25 feet of water. Later a diver was sent down to do some basic repairs, and after these were complete, seaplane-wrecking derrick YSD *26* raised PT *219*. The boat was placed on a dry dock but was later scrapped when the boat and dry dock were destroyed by severe winds.[79]

Tom Hart described his time on Attu as, "interesting, exasperating, unpleasant, and painful;" and I believe my father and most members of the squadron would have agreed with him. On most days it was damp, cold, and windy, and the sky was gray. Operating the boats was difficult, and most of the men got knocked around and banged up when they were on the boats. Winds would periodically break the boats free from their docks or anchorage, and sailors would have to scramble to save them. The food was generally not good, there was little social life, and homesickness was an almost constant companion.[80]

In the winter it rained or snowed almost every day. Men would spend 24 hours on the boats and then 24 in the Quonset huts, and both places were uncomfortable. When not training or on patrol, men would eat, sleep, play cards, write letters that were censored by officers, talk, and argue. Nerves sometimes frayed and men occasionally fought.

My father and I spoke often about his time in Alaska; and it says much about his nature that in all of our conversations, I never once heard him complain about any aspect of his experience there. I believe there were three reasons for this. First, he was orphaned in the Depression and thus was used to depravity. Second, he had the most positive outlook on life of anyone I have ever known, and thus almost never complained about anything. And third, he knew that in many parts of the world American servicemen were fighting and dying, and in his judgment to complain about the difficult conditions on Alaska, even decades after the war was over, would have been unseemly.[81]

My father on the island of Attu. Francis Gelzheiser collection.

There were also happy, funny, and even exhilarating moments for the men on Attu. There was a stark natural beauty to the island, and despite the wet sponge-like ground conditions that made hiking difficult, many of the men explored the island's interior. There were numerous small lakes on Attu, and these were connected to dozens of small streams. Many of these contained large salmon fighting their way upstream, and their journey was fascinating to observe. Once the fish made it to their destination, they laid their eggs and then died. Hundreds of salmon carcasses lined the lake shores, and these attracted ravens, ptarmigan, and other consumers of carrion. Blue foxes were common and almost tame. They did not fear the sailors, and on a number of occasions they followed the men back to the PT boat base.[82]

On December 31, 1943, after working all day and into the night repairing boat struts, props, and shafts, a generous officer produced several bottles of Walker's Deluxe Bourbon; and as the men of Squadron 16A shared a toast to the coming New Year, tracer bullets were fired into the sky above Attu. In March of the New Year, USO Show 128 came to the base, and the sailors were entertained by some of the first women they had seen in months. Bonnie Holland sang seven songs, although this portion of the show took longer than expected because the sailors were required to head back to their boats three times because of reports of Japanese submarines. Vivian Francis did an acrobatic dance, and Roberta Carney did her comedy routine.[83]

One of the ubiquitous blue foxes found on Attu during the war. My father talked often and fondly of these creatures. World War II PT Boats Museum and Archives, Germantown, Tennessee.

One event displayed the extraordinary ingenuity of the sailors on PT *221* and also still brought a smile to my father's face decades after it occurred. While on Attu, one of the three engines on the *Omen of the Seas* was damaged beyond repair. It was near the end of their time on the island, they had to ship out in a few days, and operating without the third engine would leave the boat vulnerable. In addition, they had been ordered to "maintain full ability," so in the opinion of the boat's crew, they were under orders to keep all three of the boat's motors running. Desperate, the men concocted a scheme to steal the needed third engine. Berthed in the same harbor was a "crash boat" or tender boat, which was smaller than a PT boat and powered by two engines, one of which was similar to the Packards in the PT boats. Since the tender was used little, and in the view of the *221* boat's crew was not really a combat craft, the crew of the *221* boat decided to exchange their broken motor with the good one in the tender. Such an exchange would be no small feat. The motors were huge and weighed 2,950 pounds. In addition, the tender's crew was charged with guarding their boat, and they certainly would not willingly give up a good engine for a broken one, especially in a far-off berth in the Aleutians.[84]

The plan was simple enough, and it worked flawlessly. The tender crew was told that a film was being shown at the base. The crew of the *Omen of the Seas* had already seen it, and they would be willing to watch the tender if its crew wanted to see the movie. Happily, the unsuspecting crew of the tender went off to see the film. Acting quickly, the *221* crew boarded the vessel. One group had been instructed to unhook the tender's motor, another brought in a crane to remove it, another motored the *221* boat to the tender's stern. Quickly, the motors were exchanged. One team installed the bad motor into the tender, and another installed the new one into PT *221*. My dad and his team worked feverishly to hook up the new engine's electrical system. Before the tender's crew returned from the movie, the exchange had been completed, and *The Omen of the Seas* motored off with three operating engines.[85]

A medium-size, dark-furred mongrel dog appeared at the base one day, and the squadron immediately adopted it. They named the dog Duchess, and although she was officially a part of the "crew" of PT *222*, she spent time on all of the boats and even learned to climb up and down the steep steps that descended from the deck to the lower quarters of the boats. Even when I was a little boy, my father talked often of Duchess, and I believe the dog was not only a good friend to the sailors but a simple reminder of the dogs and the life they had left behind and would hopefully return to soon.[86]

On one occasion, sailors absconded with five gallons of the pure grain alcohol that was used to power the torpedoes. Most of the men had had nothing to drink for some time, failed to adequately dilute the 200-proof beverage, and proceeded to get very sick. One man almost died when he passed out on a snow bank.[87]

While in the chow line one day, sailors were surprised to see several men of Japanese ancestry standing near the end of the line. Although the men were wearing American issued parkas and other attire, they were not recognized by any sailor and were soon confronted. None of the men could speak English, and it was quickly determined that the three had survived the battle for Attu and had avoided the self- or officer-inflicted "suicide" that befell many of their comrades and escaped to Attu's interior. Starving, they acquired clothing from dead Americans, and quietly walked into the Navy base and then joined the sailors in the chow line. Fortunately they were not fanatical supporters of their cause determined to kill the enemy and then themselves. Instead, they were taken prisoner without incident.[88]

For many sailors the most popular activity they pursued during their free time was searching for Indian artifacts. The Naval base at Massacre Bay was within walking distance of an ancient Aleut village site where there were several mounds. Many sailors would spend hours digging through these in search of arrow and spear heads, lance and dart points, knives, scrappers, and fish hooks. On occasion, the skeletal remains of a long dead Aleut would be found, but these generally did not find their way back to the men's collections on the boats. Although my father observed these excavations into the mounds, I do not believe he ever joined the searchers. He always had a quiet and deep respect for other cultures, and whether alive or dead, he was reluctant to interfere with how they lived or to disturb their forgotten world long after they were gone. Collectors spent countless hours searching through the mounds and competed with other scavengers to see who could find the best artifacts and create the best collection.[89]

There was another more sinister kind of artifact collection that took place on Attu. In many ways World War II in the Pacific was a race war. Although Japan's leaders argued that they wanted to drive the Europeans and Americans from the Pacific so that Asia could be ruled by Asians, the Japanese believed that they were superior to the racially "inferior" subject peoples that populated their Empire. Japanese genocidal barbarism in China and Korea are the most brutal examples of the Japanese treatment of "inferior" Asian peoples, but similar cruelty was also unleashed on the people of the Philippines. The Japanese also viewed people of European ancestry to be racially inferior. Their European and American enemies were viewed as corrupt, barbaric, decadent, ugly, smelly, self-centered, spoiled, pampered, soft, lazy, and cowardly. White was inferior to yellow, and one of the reasons the Japanese were so brutal to those they defeated or captured was the contempt they had for those of non–Japanese racial stock.[90]

Unfortunately, there was also a racist element to the way the United States conducted its war and how individual warriors responded to the different enemies that confronted them. In the guise of national security, thousands of Japanese, many of whom were American citizens, were rounded up in California during the war and sent to detainment camps in California and other western states. During the war, lifeboats containing Japanese sailors were strafed by American pilots and machine gunned by American sailors and PT boat crews. Prisoners were shot, the dead were mutilated, gold teeth were extracted and turned into necklaces, and Japanese ears adorned American military vehicles.[91] "Kill Japs, kill Japs, kill Japs" was written by American servicemen all over the Pacific. Admiral William Frederick "Bull" Halsey, the eventual Naval Commander of the South Pacific Theater, while viewing the destruction at Pearl Harbor uttered, "Before we're through with 'em, the Japanese language will be spoken only in Hell." He often referred to the Japanese as "Monkey Meat," and he would close both official and personal correspondence by writing, "Kill Japs."[92]

To some extent these actions are an understandable reaction to what happened at Pearl Harbor, but they are also an indication of the insidious racism that existed in America at the time of World War II and the tendency of people to develop an almost tribal identity with individuals who are of the same race and ethnicity and to find it easier to confront those who are not. In a study done during the war to determine how American servicemen identified with the vanquished, it was discovered that after American servicemen viewed Japanese prisoners they felt like killing more Japanese. After viewing German prisoners the sentiment of the observers was that they were sad they had to kill them because they are "like us."[93]

The PT boat men were not immune from these sentiments. Unburied Japanese bodies were littered throughout the interior of Attu, and they could be found by searching for the swarms of flies hovering over the decaying corpses. Sailors would search the bodies for souvenirs much as military trophy hunters had done for centuries. However, if a sailor was not the first to come across a body he would almost always find the dead man's jaw shattered and most of his teeth extracted. These were used to make bracelets and necklaces. Often American soldiers in the days following the battle had been the ones to make these extractions. However, there were men of Squadron 16A who also succumbed to this vile kind of hatred and adorned themselves with this "jewelry." I believe that my father would grow to hate the Japanese, but I do not believe his hatred was grounded in racism; and he did not manifest his hatred by extracting the teeth of dead men. During the many occasions when I discussed the war with my father and his squadron mates, I often got the sense that they continued to be perplexed by the Japanese and their culture, but I never heard any man from the squadron make a derogatory comment on his former enemy based on race.[94]

Winter came early on Attu, and during this season life on the island became even more boring and dangerous. A williwaw picked up the corner of the Quonset hut that served as the mess hall and rolled it away. On October 31, after the mess hall had been repaired, it caught fire and burned down. An officer lost a finger while working on an engine, and shortly after caught pneumonia.[95] Men would periodically fall into the water; and if they were not removed quickly, they would be rendered helpless by hypothermia.[96] On one training mission, PT *220* crashed into net tender USS *Citrus*. On another occasion PTs *221* and *222* were returning from target practice. As they approached the base, PT *221* realized she was heading for nets that were strung across the water to protect the base from enemy submarines. The boat quickly slowed and put its engines in reverse. It was almost dark, and PT *222* did not realize the lead boat had slowed up, and she proceeded to ram *The Omen of the Seas* so hard that PT *221*'s 20 mm gun was broken loose. Both boats needed extensive repairs, and the transom on the *221* boat was so badly damaged that it had to be replaced.[97]

In mid–November, a williwaw ripped a crash boat from its mooring, and frantic sailors had to scramble to save the craft. A whaleboat was ripped from its dock and smashed into the rocks, and the roof on one of the Quonset huts was ripped off.

In January a particularly violent storm washed out parts of the jetty that were protecting several of the squadron's boats. Waves crashed over the exposed boats and a terrified sailor was washed overboard. Fortunately, a fellow sailor in foul-weather-gear jumped into the water and helped to remove the man from the water. It is likely he saved the man's life.[98]

The boats of Squadron 16A performed a variety of important tasks while in the Aleutians. If seas allowed, boats patrolled in search of enemy submarines that the United States Navy still believed plied the waters near Attu. Whenever planes of the Eleventh Air Force were sent off on bombing missions, PT boats stood at the ready in case a plane could not make it back. Actual rescues were rare, but knowing the boats were available to save downed pilots if necessary gave the pilots a welcomed sense of security and increased their confidence.[99] This sentiment was communicated to the PT boat sailors when General William O. Butler, commander of the North Pacific Force, wrote:

> I desire to express the appreciation of the officers and men of the combat elements of the Eleventh Air Force for the fine work being done by the PT Boat Squadron engaged in rescue work in the Western Aleutians. A marked increase in the spirit of daring that is so essential to effective air operations has been noted in all combat crews as a result of their knowledge that such courageous and able comrades are constantly "on alert" to lend them aid in case of accident. The loyalty and efficiency of this organization is highly commendable.[100]

On most days, at least two boats were kept fully manned at the dock at all times in case a rescue was necessary. Often, motors were kept running, and crews were expected to initiate a search for a downed pilot at a moment's notice and in almost any sea condition. On one occasion, PT *221* went in search of a man only to find him dead from exposure.[101] On another mission, the *Omen of the Seas* was sent with a medical officer to rescue an American soldier who had a broken leg. After motoring thirty miles, the boat arrived in the late afternoon at Stellar Cove, where the wounded man was believed to be, and dropped anchor. Torpedoman's Mate First Class Robert C. Carlson, Quartermaster First Class Dan G. Saunders and the medical officer got into a small boat and rowed to shore. When the crew of PT *221* did not hear from them for two hours, it was believed their boat had smashed into rocks, and the sailors had drowned. Finally, a light flashed from the shoreline, but the sailors would not return to the *Omen of the Seas* until the next day. On the way into shore, their small wooden boat had smashed on the rocks, and the wet and exhausted men had spent the night in a small tent. The next day, they set out looking for the wounded soldier, found him four miles from where they had landed, and tended to the soldier's leg as best they could. They signaled for PT *221*, and eventually the boat arrived. Tom Hart and Motor Machinist's Mate First Class James Donald rowed a small collapsible rubber raft to shore. The wounded sailor was loaded into the small craft, and Carlson and Saunders began to row the wounded man to PT *221* through seas that had grown much more rough. Although the poor soldier was in great pain and his leg had to hang over the side of the tiny rescue craft and get wet, the three men safely returned to PT *221*. Saunders then rowed the rubber raft back to shore and picked up Tom Hart, Donald, and the medical officer.[102]

On most mornings float planes would be sent out to determine if weather was suitable for American planes to make their bombing runs on Japan. On occasion, these planes would fly into severe weather and not be able to get back to their base. They would be forced to make emergency landings in the water, and PT boats would be sent to assist them.[103]

On one occasion a sailor on an American destroyer had an inflamed appendix. Motoring through six-foot seas, a PT boat made its way to the larger ship, and the skills of the sailors on both vessels were put to the test. Both boats were moving up and down at different rates; and if the wooden PT boat got too close to the steel destroyer and the vessels collided, it could have been disastrous for the smaller craft. Skillfully keeping the boats as close together as possible without colliding, a cable was passed from the destroyer to the PT boat and a wire basket was attached to it. The sailor was then placed in the basket, which was then slid down to the PT boat. The destroyer continued on its patrol, and the sailor was quickly brought to the small medical center that had been set up on Attu where he received the needed surgery and eventually recovered.[104]

Prior to the invasion of Kiska, American planes bombed the island whenever the weather permitted. To assist the bombers, two PT boats were sent to Bird Cape on Amchitka. Each day a weather plane would fly to Kiska. When it returned, it would fly in a northward direction over the PT boats if the weather was suitable for flying and southward if it was not. If the weather was suitable for flying, the PT boats would then motor to where they could see the skies over Kiska and prepare to depart quickly if they were needed to rescue a downed pilot.[105]

In March 1944 boats were sent to locate and rescue five men in a life raft. High seas hindered the search, and the men were never found. The next month, PT *221* was sent to search for pilots from two P-38s that had collided. Unfortunately, all the boat could locate was plane wreckage and an oil slick.[106]

Almost immediately after the Japanese were defeated on Attu, American military planners turned their attention to driving the Japanese from Kiska. Most believed this would be a more difficult undertaking than removing the Japanese from Attu, and initially this proved to be true. The Japanese defenders of Kiska had 100 rapid-fire antiaircraft guns making the island one of the most well-defended places in the Japanese Empire. It was believed that fewer Japanese were on Attu when the Americans landed and the fighting on this tiny island had been brutal and costly. The Americans did not know the number of enemy troops on Kiska, but the best estimate was that there were approximately 7,000, which was significantly more than had been faced on Attu. Prior to the invasion, American planes and ships relentlessly bombed and shelled the small island in the hope that the Japanese could be significantly weakened. But most American military leaders feared that despite the wet terrain, most of the Japanese were well dug in and would survive the onslaught and fanatically fight to defend the island when the Allied forces arrived.[107]

On August 13, 1943, 100 ships under the command of Vice Admiral Francis "Skinny" Rockwell sailed from the American-held Aleutian Island of Adak bound for Kiska. Two days later, after a massive bombardment of the island, Operation Cottage, the invasion of Kiska, began. Following a strategy that would be perfected as the war progressed, a massive force of 29,000 American and 5,300 Canadian troops awaited the command to hit the beaches of the 107-square-mile island and then overwhelm and defeat the Japanese defenders. The main landing took place on the northern part of the island; and in an attempt to confuse the Japanese on Kiska, five PT boats were sent to the southern portion of the island near Gertrude Cove. Each boat had a number of circle-shaped pieces of plywood attached to the top of the sides of the boats to make the boats resemble landing craft. The boats were ordered to motor 100 yards from shore and strafe the shoreline. The hope was that the Japanese would return fire and expose the positions of their shore batteries and draw some of the defending troops from the northern to southern side of the island, thus reducing the number of defenders the invading force would have to face. In addition, the boats would also be used as rescue boats if needed.[108]

Sometimes the gods of war are humane and they smile on both sides in a conflict. As thousands of troops landed on Kiska, and the PT boats unleashed the full firepower of their weapons, all were shocked when the only response was silence. As ground troops poured onto the island, they feared some kind of Japanese trap as they moved inland. Booby traps, mines, and friendly fire did kill 21 and wound 50 soldiers; but no matter where they searched, no Japanese troops could be located. Often the only sign of the enemy were the insults they had written mocking the Americans that were found all over the island. Finally, after searching for more than a week, the American command reached the embarrassing conclusion that the invasion was unnecessary, and that despite the best efforts of the United States Navy and America's overwhelming air superiority and constant monitoring of the island, all of the Japanese on Kiska had escaped.[109]

Many in the United States military were furious that somehow the Japanese had eluded the American forces. Training, equipping, and transporting the large invasion force was expensive. When the American public found out about the Japanese escape, it was embarrassing for the military brass. Some Americans viewed the Japanese escape as comical.

How the Japanese orchestrated this escape was one of the great mysteries of the war, and it was a puzzle that was not solved until many years after the conflict ended. On July 21, 1943, three cruisers, one oiler, and 11 destroyers left Paramushiro bound for Kiska. Their mission was to pick up all of the Japanese troops on the island, but many in the small fleet doubted they could avoid detection by American planes and ships.[110] The United States Navy had a large fleet patrolling the waters near Kiska. Military leaders believed that Japan might try to evacuate the island, and the American forces were determined to prevent this.

At approximately 1:00 a.m. on July 26, the American fleet located seven ships eight to twelve miles away on their radar screens, and it was believed that this was the Japanese fleet sailing for Kiska. What ensued after this discovery was the little known Battle of the Pips. The American ships unleashed a massive barrage of ordnance at what they believed was the Japanese fleet. In the process of pursuing and firing on the perceived fleet, many American ships grew low on fuel and ammunition. As the American ships continued to fire at the Japanese vessels, they became increasingly surprised at not receiving return fire; and no matter how hard they looked, they could not see any Japanese ships except on their radar screens.

At the onset of the Battle of the Pips, the Japanese radar operator on Kiska observed the American fleet turning to engage its perceived enemy. Realizing that this created an unexpected opportunity, the order was given to send the Japanese ships into the large harbor at Kiska, load all of the Japanese troops, and quickly steam away. An additional stroke of luck also benefited the Japanese. Prior to when the soldiers were loaded and after the ships departed on July 28, the skies over Kiska were overcast, and this prevented American planes from flying and observing the fleet and the evacuation.

After pursuing and firing on the seven radar blips for more than an hour, the American fleet faced an additional dilemma. They had planned on rendezvousing with an oiler to refuel; but when the enemy was sited, this was delayed, and now they were low on fuel. Finally, they realized that the perceived enemy was not the Japanese fleet, and they met with the oiler and began to refuel. This process was begun on the night of July 27, and it took 24 hours before all of the ships were refueled. On the afternoon of July 28, the Japanese fleet had entered Kiska, quickly loaded the Japanese troops who were waiting on the beach on to the ships and then escaped undetected and unengaged by American ships and planes. Four days later the Japanese fleet arrived at Paramushiro having achieved one of the boldest and least bloody victories of the war.[111]

For years it was debated what American radar operators saw on their screens. Some argued it was clusters of balloons planted by the Japanese, others claimed it was Japanese submarines mistaken for surface ships, and some claimed that rare atmospheric conditions temporarily bent the radar beam creating blips that looked like ships. This latter explanation was generally given as the official cause of the confusion, and it was not until 1991 when a more plausible and most likely accurate explanation was given. During that time of year thousands of birds called Dusky Shearwaters flock together at night and then disperse during the day in that part of the Aleutians. These birds are members of the Albatross family, and they often fly low over the water and then sleep on the water in large masses. Fishermen in the region familiar with the birds and World War II–era radar have surmised that the seven blips on American radar were large clusters of the birds hovering and sleeping. On numerous occasions their own radar has displayed blips that looked like ships but in fact were huge flocks of the same birds that most likely confused the United States Navy at the Battle of the Pips and allowed the Japanese to escape from Kiska.[112]

I smile as I write this. I do not believe my father ever knew the truth about how the Japanese were able to escape from Kiska, thus saving many lives on both sides and possibly even his own. I know if he had seen them he would have marveled at the sight of thousands of the large birds clustered together, and I am sure he would have been grateful for the confusion they caused and for the lack of fatalities on both sides that resulted from the Battle of the Pips.

In early May 1944, the sailors of Squadron 16A were informed that in three days they would leave Alaska and motor to Seattle. Quietly the men readied their boats for the long voyage. Only personal items that could fit in their Navy issued sea bags were allowed on the boats, so much gear had to be discarded. Many of the sailors were forced to leave their prized artifact collections behind.[113]

On the morning of May 5, under a rare bright sky, Squadron 16A motored out of Massacre Bay headed for Amchitka. Slowly Attu vanished in the distance, and as the men in the squadron gazed at this strange and desolate place they had called home for more than eight months, most knew they would never see this small island in the western Aleutians again.[114]

On the return voyage, the boats stopped at most of the same ports that they visited on the voyage north. For most of the journey to Dutch Harbor the seas were rough, but the exhausted sailors did get a pleasant surprise after they reached Dutch Harbor. A USO show with Errol Flynn and Martha O'Driscoll had recently arrived, and the PT boat men

Quonset hut attached to a wooden building, PT boat base, Amchitka, Alaska. World War II PT Boats Museum and Archives, Germantown, Tennessee.

were able to attend it. Needless to say, the sailors were happier to see Ms. O'Driscoll than Mr. Flynn.

On May 31, the squadron motored into Bremerton Navy Yard, 10 months and 11 days after they had departed. The Higgins boats and the seamen who operated them had performed well. However, after having motored almost 9,000 miles since their departure, the boats were in need of repair and the men rest and the comforts of civilization.[115]

My father did not make the journey to Seattle on PT *221*. Because of his skills as an electrician and gunner and uncanny ability to never get seasick, he had spent much time on PT *221* while in Alaska, and he would continue to do so for the remainder of the war. However, as an electrician's mate he was still technically part of the base force, so he and several other men from Squadron 16A were left behind on Attu to secure all of the gear. Five days after the PT boats departed, my father boarded a plane that took him to Seattle.[116]

Although there were numerous hardships, I believe my father enjoyed his time in Alaska. He was a brilliant man, and he had a marvelous ability to find practical solutions to problems; and I am sure this proved to be a valuable asset in the harsh environment of the Aleutians. He also enjoyed working with and helping others, which was also a daily occurrence in Alaska. In addition, my father was always able to remain calm under pressure. In the difficult conditions faced by the PT boat crews in the Aleutians, this trait would also have served him and his squadron mates well.

My father was extremely observant, and he loved nature. He was fascinated by the beauty and unique creatures that he observed in the Aleutians. When possible, he would journey inland to wild rivers and watch as the abundant salmon fought their way upstream in rivers both large and small. Wildflowers bloomed magnificently during the short summer, and he often told me of the numerous blue foxes that he would observe on his walks. In addition, the Aleutian Islands are the home of numerous bird species, and more than 10 million nest here each summer. I am sure he had never seen most of these species before, and I smile when I imagine him gazing at Puffins, Auklets, numerous Gulls, and Kittiwakes, marveling at their grace and beauty and reveling in life. He never said this to me, but I wonder if he hoped he could spend his war in Alaska, doing his duty, enduring hardships that would legitimize his service, but still far away from the killing. He would not be so lucky.

6

The Battle for New Guinea and the Motor Torpedo Boat Returns to the Philippines

The enemy has used PT boats aggressively.... On their account our naval ships have had a bitter pill to swallow.—Japanese World War II Tactical Manual

When the boats of Squadron 16A motored into Bremerton Navy Yard in late May 1944, none of the sailors knew where they would be sent next, and it is doubtful if many of them thought much about this. Although pay for World War II sailors was low—my father used to joke that he earned 30 dollars per day one day per month—the sailors who went out on liberty after their return from Alaska felt like rich men with money in their pockets to burn. For more than nine months there were few things they could buy, so the majority of the sailors had saved most of their paychecks. This frugality ended in Bremerton. Most of the sailors were granted leave and many soon found trouble.[1]

Within a few days, a number of sailors had been arrested, and four would eventually be court-martialed. Men gambled, drank, chased women, and got into fights. PT *222*'s Gunner's Mate William "Hank" Pierotti beat up a Chinese man and was arrested for assault, battery and robbery. He was eventually turned over to the Navy, court-martialed before Squadron Commander Colvin, and then reduced in rank. Four got married, and many of the men who were married prior to leaving for Alaska had their wives join them, and this caused them to burn through their money even faster. In short order many of the sailors ran out of cash. This resulted in some sailors curtailing their times on the town and others sent their wives home. However some, in an attempt to keep the good times rolling, sold their clothes and other belongings, and a few of the more nefarious members of the squadron stole things from the boats that they hoped would not be missed and then sold these items.[2]

The composition of the boats' crews also changed. Some men had applied to Officer Training School, been accepted, and now left to become officers. Others had had enough of life on the small boats and transferred to larger ships, and some sailors left to join different PT boat squadrons.

My father's situation was unique, and although I am sure he enjoyed himself, I am doubtful if he spent his money as frivolously as his shipmates. Since my father had left the orphanage at age fourteen, he had helped to support his mother and sister. His mother suffered from "Chronic Cardio Vascular Renal Disease." She was now an invalid and her condition was getting worse. She was unable to work and depended on my dad for support. Prior to joining the Navy, he had been able to provide his mother and sister with $100 per month, but the meagerness of his Navy pay meant that his monthly contribution to his mother and sister had to be reduced considerably. He even applied for and received a small increase in pay through the Servicemen's Dependent Allowance Act of 1942 because he was the sole supporter of dependents back home. Since both his mother and sister were dependent on his support, I am sure the majority of the little money he earned while in the Navy was sent home to them and not spent in bars and nightclubs.[3]

Excitement found the PT boat sailors almost as soon as they arrived in Bremerton. Not wanting to be denied liberty because of a dirty bilge, Motor Machinist's Mate Third Class Wallis "Red" Felde decided to expedite the cleaning of the bilge of PT *222* by using gasoline. Unfortunately, a spark from an auxiliary generator ignited the gasoline, and flames and smoke quickly poured out of the boat's hatch. Some sailors, fearing a massive explosion if the fuel tanks ignited, ran for their lives. Others including PT *221*'s James Donald and Lieutenant (jg.) Bell bravely grabbed a fire extinguisher, went below and into the flames, and put out the fire. In the confusion, Duchess, the beloved dog companion of the squadron who had made the voyage from Alaska on PT *222*, was now found dangling between PTs *221* and *222* still tethered to her lead. Shocked and choking, she was pulled out of the water. Soon after this unfortunate incident the crew decided their canine friend was probably better off in a more conventional home, and one of the sailors had the dog shipped to his family back east.[4]

Initially, the Motor Torpedo Boat was designed to be a small, fast, inexpensive craft that could seek out larger ships and damage or destroy them with torpedoes. This would continue to be one of the functions of the PT boat for the remainder of the war. However, as the war progressed it became apparent that the boats could contribute even more to the war effort as coastal gun ships. As a result significant alterations were made to some of the boats of Squadron 16A in Bremerton. Then more were made after they arrived in New Guinea, and thus within the squadron, boats had different armaments. Some of these changes were ordered by superiors outside of the squadron, and others were made because the crews on specific boats believed that the addition or subtraction of particular weapons would enable the boats to better carry out their assigned duties.

On some boats, the stern 20 mm gun was removed and replaced with a 40 mm "barge buster" gun. The 20 mm gun was then paired with the 20 mm gun that was already mounted on the bow. Often a second ammunition box was also added. On other boats, space was cleared on the bow and on the starboard side amidships for 60 mm mortars and two .50 caliber machine guns. Adding so much additional weight to the boats, especially on their bows, caused the bow to ride lower in the water and caused even more water to come over the bow of the already wet Higgins boats. One sailor on PT *221* remarked after the additional armaments were installed, "Every wave it crossed came over the bridge in a green sheet." Improved torpedo guidance and launch systems made it possible to remove the torpedo tubes and replace them with racks, and this reduced the weight of the boats significantly. In spite of the reduced weight achieved by the removal of the torpedo tubes, the added weight of the additional armaments and extra one or two crew members that were now needed to operate them caused the overall weight of the boats to increase significantly. One addition that was universally appreciated was the installation of Fluxgate gyro-stabilized compasses on all boats. These could keep a true course in the roughest seas and made navigation much easier and more accurate.[5]

After a short time in Bremerton, the boats were sent to Seattle. In July PTs *221, 222, 223,* and *224* and their crews were loaded on to the deck of the Texaco Oil Company tanker SS *Shenandoah* and taken to San Francisco. The ship was old, rusty, and slow, but the seas were generally calm, the food was good, regulations were few, and there was little required work and ample time to relax. As a result, most of the PT boat sailors enjoyed this voyage.[6] On July 23 the tanker motored under the Golden Gate Bridge and into San Francisco Bay. The boats were unloaded and docked at Treasure Island, and while here the engines were modified. This increased each engine's output to about 1,500 horsepower; but even with this additional power, the boats gained little speed due to the dramatic increase in the weight of each boat.

One calm morning after the engine work had been completed, my father crewed PT *221* as it went on a series of test runs in San Francisco Bay. Most of the boat's armaments had been removed, the crew was small, and little fuel was in the gas tanks. Although no official speed was recorded, my father believed that as a result of the pristine condition of the boat's newly sanded and painted hull, lightened weight, and upgraded engines, the boat achieved a speed well in excess of 50 miles per hour. He also believed that this may have been the fastest a boat had ever run under the Golden Gate Bridge up to that point. Of course this last claim was only conjecture on his part. Under similar conditions the San Francisco press was given a ride on the boats and an article was written about the PT boats and their crews. In a gesture to show their support for the war effort, most of the sailors in the squadron traveled to a blood bank together and donated blood to the local Red Cross.[7]

PT *224, Tail End,* in San Francisco Bay, September 1944. World War II PT Boats Museum and Archives, Germantown, Tennessee.

6. The Battle for New Guinea and Return to the Philippines

PT *223* in San Francisco Bay. World War II PT Boats Museum and Archives, Germantown, Tennessee.

In September 1944, the officers, crew, and boats of Squadron 16A were loaded on to several different ships in Oakland, CA. In Richmond they loaded munitions, and then while underway they learned that their new destination would be about as far from the small island of Attu as possible. They were bound for Mios Woendi, New Guinea, where they would finally be reunited with the five boats that comprised Squadron 16B.[8]

For the sailors on all of the boats, the voyage was long, tedious, and fascinating. For most of the officers and crew, the most memorable part of the voyage occurred when they passed over the equator. When this occurred, an age-old ritual commenced. That morning the Jolly Roger was raised, rank was temporarily forgotten, and all sailors who had never crossed the equator were deemed Pollywogs and thus they had to be humiliated in a variety of ways as part of an initiation ceremony. All Pollywogs were required to strip and then crawl or run on all fours between lines of Shellbacks—or sailors who had previously made the crossing—who were dressed as pirates. Almost none of the PT boat officers and crew had made the crossing previously, so the Shellbacks were composed largely of the officers and crews of the ships transporting the PT boats and crews.

As the Pollywogs crawled through the gauntlet of Shellbacks, the Shellbacks hit them with paddles on their bare behinds. After this part of the ceremony was completed, Pollywogs then met with a ridiculously costumed King Neptune, his Queen, and their baby who was a large bellied sailor with mustard smeared all over his stomach. Pollywogs, whose buttocks were red from the paddling, were now required to kiss the baby's rear end. Pollywogs were then ordered to drink a vile beverage consisting of vinegar, quinine,

Top: Mios Woendi, New Guinea, 1943. *Bottom:* Base 21, Mios Woendi, New Guinea, January 1945. Both photographs, World War II PT Boats Museum and Archives, Germantown, Tennessee.

Top: PT boats at Base 21, Mios Woendi, New Guinea, circa 1944. *Bottom:* Mios Woendi, New Guinea, PT boat base. Both photographs, World War II PT Boats Museum and Archives, Germantown, Tennessee.

red pepper, and fish oil. After consuming the drink, the victim stood at attention before the Royal Judge who was Squadron Commander Colvin, one of the few members of Squadron 16A who had previously passed over the equator, and learned what charges were being brought against him. Guilty was always the verdict, and the sailor's punishment was then determined. The guilty sailor was then escorted to the Royal Barber. His bench was wired, and when the Pollywog sat down a shock wave was sent through his buttocks. One merchant marine sailor was knocked out by the shock, and as a result the voltage was reduced. After this the Royal Barber proceeded to shave off large patches of the sailor's hair. Next, the sailor had to lie on the royal operating table on his back, and while still naked an electric brush was run over his body, and his testicles were touched with a wooden sword that had an electrified wire attached to the end. They were then painted with some kind of dirty oil, and then fish oil was poured on the victim's head and body. Finally, each Pollywog was led to the edge of a platform near the side of the ship. The ocean could be heard below, and the seated sailor was then pushed backwards. Some screamed, fearing they had been pushed into the ocean, and all were relieved when they fell four to five feet and landed in a tub of water. The Pollywog was now a Shellback, and at this point he could contribute to the initiation of those who had not completed the ceremony. Since officers went last, they faced the largest number of Shellback paddlers; and when a few officers resisted, they were rewarded by being paddled harder as they crawled through the gauntlet of Shellback paddlers.[9]

Although the boats were on the deck of SS *Lawson*, SS *Santa Isabel*, and the other transport ships, the PT boat sailors still had numerous tasks to perform while on their way to New Guinea. Boat bottoms were scraped and painted; bilges were scrubbed; guns were taken apart, oiled, and cleaned; and all of the equipment on the boats was inspected and repaired as needed. Generally there was a slight breeze, the temperature was mild, and most of the men slept on the ship's deck instead of on the bunks below. One night the sailors were told they were passing Guadalcanal. I can only guess what my father and the other PT boat men were thinking as they peered at the moonlit island where so many had died in the horrific battle that had taken place there.[10]

On October 9, *Lawson* began to pass numerous small islands and then it motored into Milne Bay, New Guinea. Here the ship anchored, but the men were not allowed to go ashore. Most were able to enjoy a swim in the bay's warm waters. Two days later, *Lawson* pulled up its anchor and motored to the harbor at Manus Island, which was located between the islands of Manus and Los Negros. *Lawson* arrived at night and surprisingly there were no blackout restrictions on the island. This meant that all of the ships in the enormous fleet of American warships that were anchored in the port were lit up, and the sight was not only beautiful but also a testament to the enormous naval firepower that was now at the disposal of the American war machine. Soon most of these ships would set sail for the Philippines, where they would take part in the historic Battle of Leyte Gulf. On October 16, the PT boats were lifted off of *Lawson* and the PT boats' sailors soon set foot on land for the first time in a month.[11]

Most of the sailors found Manus and Los Negros fascinating. Natives plied through the water in outrigger canoes carved from a single large tree that measured approximately 30 feet long and 18 inches wide. Each canoe was paddled by 8 to 10 men, and often a platform extended off the side of the boats on the outriggers loaded with goods for trade. Interesting and beautiful shells dotted the beaches, and sailors enjoyed collecting them. Coconut trees were abundant, and my father and other wiry sailors in the squadron commenced to climb the trees and pick the fruit. For many sailors their coconut consumption was quickly curtailed when they began to suffer from diarrhea; but my father and Tom Hart had no such problems, and continued to eat the tasty fruit.

After several days, the boats of Squadron 16A pulled out of the harbor bound for Tanah Merah Bay 440 miles to the west. To insure the boats had enough fuel for the voyage, additional rubber fuel tanks were filled with gasoline and placed on the deck of each boat; but boats still had to conserve fuel, so they had to travel at slow speeds, and the voyage took 30 hours.[12]

Tanah Merah Bay was near Hollandia on the north coast of Netherlands, New Guinea. Soon after the boats motored in, curious natives paddled their canoes up to the PT boats. These vessels were only about 15 feet long and had interesting figureheads carved in their bows. The natives were small, and most of the men were afflicted with a scaly and scabby skin condition that was unsightly and caused by one of the many fungi that were prevalent on the island.

After a short stay at Tanah Merah Bay the boats set out for Mios Woendi, their ultimate destination in New Guinea. Mios Woendi was the largest PT boat base in New Guinea, and it was here that the PT boats of Squadron 16A and 16B would finally be joined together to form Squadron 16. Mios Woendi was a tiny island approximately one mile by one-half mile located about 10 miles from the island of Biak. It was only a few feet above sea level and was surrounded by coral reefs.

Generally, PT boat service in New Guinea was difficult. It was hot, humid, and bug infested; it rained often; and there were numerous jungle ailments that sailors and soldiers could catch such as "New Guinea Jungle Rot." However, by the standards of New Guinea, the conditions on Mios Woendi were more tolerable. There was almost no potable water on the island; so to insure an adequate supply of drinking water, sea water had to be distilled. On the edge of the island were sandy beaches, and the interior was planted with coconut trees. The native males were powerful and well built, and they generally liked the Americans and hated the Japanese. Often these men would travel to the mainland to trade and to hunt, kill, and capture the Japanese. When they did capture them, they almost always brought them back to Mios Woendi and turned them over to the Americans.[13]

Shortly after Squadron 16A's arrival, a boatload of Javanese men and women arrived. All had been abused by the Japanese and were malnourished. Some of the women were pregnant as a result of being raped by the Japanese, and two of the pregnant women died shortly after arrival. Many had to be taken to the island of Biak to receive proper medical care.[14]

The Japanese had taken New Guinea in March 1942, and some Allied leaders believed they intended to use the island as a stepping stone in a planned future invasion of Australia.[15] At 300,000 square miles and almost 1,500 miles long on a northwest–southeast line, New Guinea is approximately the size of California and is the second-largest island in the world. The interior of the island is rugged jungle, steep gorges, and mountains. Vines grow across the dense treetops, reducing sunlight and causing the air to become steamy and often smelly after one of the numerous rain showers. There were numerous other difficulties for warriors on the island during World War II. Mosquitoes, venomous spiders and other dangerous insects, rats, pythons, and man-eating crocodiles, which grew to more than 20 feet, were all common; and anyone trying to navigate the island's interior would have to also battle the quicksand and bogs that were found throughout.

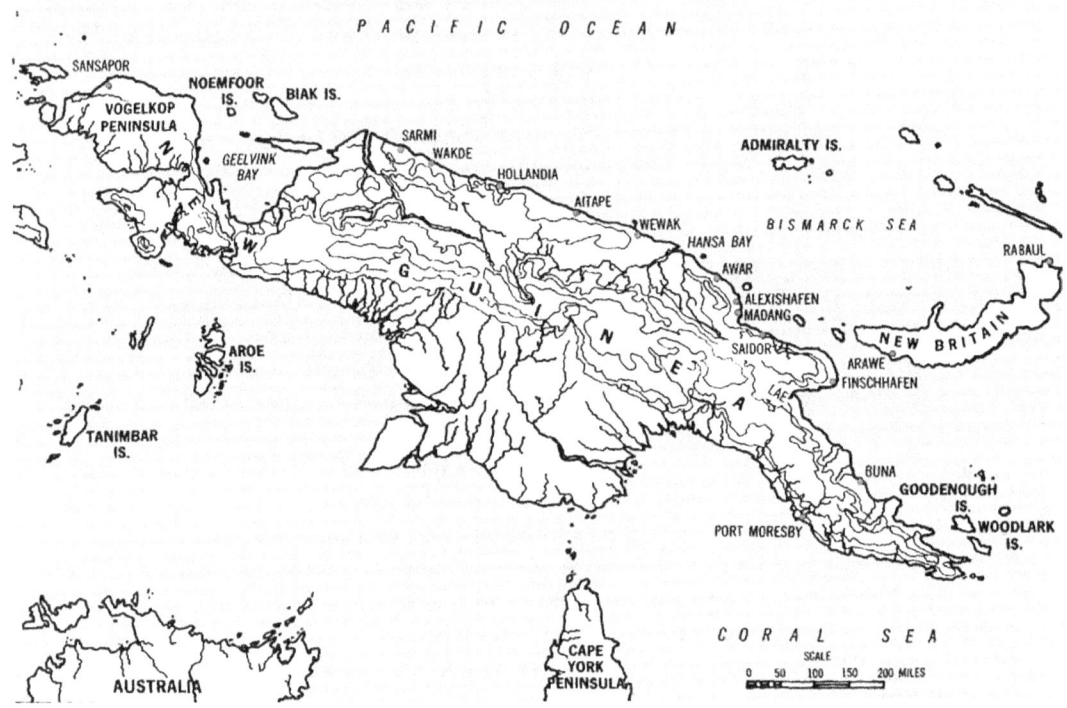

New Guinea. United States Army.

The Japanese soldiers occupying New Guinea were tough, battle-hardened warriors, but even they found it impossible to live off the land in New Guinea. Only a few mammals that could be hunted and consumed lived on the island, and there was little agriculture.

Because it was almost impossible to travel in the interior of New Guinea, the Japanese were largely concentrated along the island's shoreline. However, even along the coast there were almost no roads; consequently, coastal vessels had to be used to transport men and supplies. This form of transportation was also difficult and dangerous because the waters were shark infested, contained numerous navigational hazards, and were some of the least charted in the world. Although the environment of New Guinea was extremely hostile, the Japanese believed that maintaining control of the island was essential to their empire. Prior to and during the American advance on it, the Japanese poured enormous resources into the island in an attempt to prevent the United States from gaining control of it.[16]

General MacArthur's goal from the time he had landed in Australia was to go on the offensive. He determined that the best way to defend Australia, erode Japanese confidence, and force them to extend their supply lines was to invade New Guinea. He planned to methodically advance America's growing land, sea, and air forces westward along the island's coast and then use it as a base from which the invasion of the Philippines could be launched. Airstrips could be built from which bombers and fighter planes could take off, and these land-based aircraft, coupled with America's growing aircraft carrier fleet, would ensure that the Allies dominated the skies. To reduce American casualties, huge sections of the island would be bypassed, and American landings would often take place on portions of New Guinea where there were very few if any Japanese to oppose the Allies.[17]

6. The Battle for New Guinea and Return to the Philippines 97

PT boats played an important role in MacArthur's strategy in New Guinea. They participated in the battle for the island from the campaign's beginning, and for much of the campaign they were America's sole naval presence in New Guinea. For most of these PT boat sailors it was difficult and dangerous duty. The boats followed MacArthur's advance, and often the vessels were tasked with picking up survivors of the brutal battles the Americans waged with the Japanese.

Early PT boat bases were small, primitive, and often hidden in the jungle. Heat, humidity, mosquitoes and other bugs, venomous snakes, rain, mud, various skin ailments, frequent fevers, violent and unpredictable rivers, and lack of decent housing were constant problems. Malaria was common in the region; and to prevent it, sailors were required to take Atabrine tablets, which often made their skin turn yellow and shrivel. In addition, there were few roads and airstrips on the island, and building this essential infrastructure was always difficult and often deadly for the men charged with completing these construction projects.[18]

Boats patrolled often, and they quickly became worn out or damaged when hulls and props collided with floating objects and reefs. The supply line to New Guinea was long and difficult. Spare parts, supplies, tools, and even gasoline were hard to come by;

Disbursal dock at PT Boat Base 8, Morobe Island, New Guinea, July or August 1944. Most of the PT boat bases in New Guinea were primitive, and sailors had to contend with heat, humidity, rain, insects, disease, and the Japanese. World War II PT Boats Museum and Archives, Germantown, Tennessee.

PT boats in New Guinea. World War II PT Boats Museum and Archives, Germantown, Tennessee.

and repair facilities were often poor. Rank and ratings meant little, men often performed jobs that they were not trained to do, and sailors never wore uniforms.[19]

When not on patrol, boats were in constant need of repair. As any mariner knows, it is much more difficult to keep boat bottoms free of marine growth in warmer waters. Thus, in New Guinea and the Philippines, even if fresh copperoid bottom paint was applied, sailors still had to regularly scrape off the long green "beard" that grew on the water lines of boats and the barnacles that attached themselves to boat bottoms. It was common for bottom growth to reduce the maximum speed of the boats by six to fifteen miles per hour. This was obviously a huge concern for sailors and their officers, which only intensified the efforts to keep hulls as clean and smooth as possible.[20]

Gunner's mates had to strip and clean the salt water from guns and then grease the weapons almost daily. Radar and radios had to be checked and repaired, and mechanics worked in engine rooms where temperatures often reached 120 degrees Fahrenheit and extremely loud engines roared and damaged ears. Galleys and bilges had to be cleaned, and even refueling the boats was difficult because of the crude conditions in which early PT boats operated in New Guinea. Tanks held 3,000 gallons of fuel, and there were very few fuel pumps. As a result, men had to lift the extremely heavy barrels of fuel and slowly pour the gasoline through chamois cloth filters and into the tanks. Filling tanks could take hours, all spent in hot, humid air, while the sailors were ravished by bugs.[21]

PT boat at Tufi, New Guinea. World War II PT Boats Museum and Archives, Germantown, Tennessee.

Although PT boats were employed in numerous places and in many capacities in both the European and Pacific theaters of the war, New Guinea and the Philippines were two of the locations where they proved to be the most effective. After the Battle of the Bismarck Sea in early March 1943, the Japanese Navy was devastated. Japan still had hundreds of thousands of troops garrisoned throughout the Pacific, but when the Americans came in force they could not or would not risk using their conventional fleet to resupply troops and protect supply lines.[22] A shortage of non-military supply craft, and a growing reluctance to use their Navy to escort supply vessels, resulted in using coastal barges called daihatsus in New Guinea and then in the Philippines to resupply troops.[23] Initially the barges were approximately 46 feet in length and weighed about 20 tons. They could hold 35 to 60 men and were constructed of steel or wood. As the war against the barges progressed, the size of vessels grew to 60 to 100 feet in length; and each craft could carry between 4 to 10 tons of supplies. They continued to be constructed out of the same materials.

Early barges had little armor and instead relied on sandbags on the gunnels for protection; but over time, most boats had their sides armor plated. The majority moved under their own power, usually diesel engines, and reached speeds of seven to eight miles per hour; but some were towed by other vessels. They had a shallow draft, generally less

Top: PT boat gas dump on the Moroba River, New Guinea, 1943. Motor Machinist's Mate 1st Class Andy "Chop Chop" Pierman from PT *128* is standing. Refueling PT boats berthed at the numerous primitive bases in the Pacific was a difficult, time consuming, and exhausting job. *Bottom:* Crewmen roll drums of fuel off the ramp of an LCM at a PT boat base in New Guinea. Both photographs, World War II PT Boats Museum and Archives, Germantown, Tennessee.

than five feet, so they could navigate close to shore; and they could not be hit by most torpedoes. In addition, they were often camouflaged and rode low in the water; and their crews rarely stood. This made the barges difficult to see or locate on radar. They were usually armed with 40 mm or 75 mm cannons mounted on the deck or sides of the barge, and the soldiers and sailors on board could also defend the craft with small arms and various other guns. Furthermore, heavy caliber shore batteries could often protect barges when they were operating in areas controlled by the Japanese. The number of these deadly guns increased during the battle for New Guinea in a desperate effort to protect the barges as the Allies destroyed the vessels faster than the Japanese could produce them.[24]

Since the barges almost always operated close to shore in waters that were poorly charted, they were also protected by the numerous reefs and shallows that were common in the waters surrounding New Guinea and the Philippines. In New Guinea, the barges often originated from the Japanese stronghold of Rabaul, but the numerous rivers and inlets along the shore of New Guinea and the Philippines—and the jungle canopy that cloaked much of the shoreline—created a perfect environment to hide hundreds of tiny barge bases in these areas.[25]

Another component to the war against the barges in New Guinea was MacArthur's island-hopping strategy for winning the war in the Pacific. After the disaster at Pearl Harbor and the humiliating defeat in the Philippines, many American military planners believed it would take eight years or more, and millions of Allied casualties, to defeat the Japanese. In reality it took just 38 months. By leapfrogging past numerous Japanese-held bases and islands, the Allies minimized the number of confrontations they had with

Close-up view of Japanese barge. World War II PT Boats Museum and Archives, Germantown, Tennessee.

Top: Japanese daihatsu or barge. United States Navy. *Bottom:* Japanese daihatsu or barge and dead Japanese warriors. Library of Congress.

the enemy, dramatically reduced the number of casualties, and likely shortened the duration of the war by several years.[26]

MacArthur's plan called on the Allies to only invade certain strategically important islands. Other, sometimes very powerful Japanese-held islands and bases would be bypassed and allowed to "die on the vine." In some cases the Allies would only capture the part of an island that was necessary to establish a base from which the next invasion could be launched and leave the Japanese who occupied the rest of the island alone. Although this strategy proved to be militarily sound and humane, there were potential problems with it. The advantage to this strategy was that it would minimize the amount of direct confrontation that Allied troops would have with the Japanese and thus save lives on both sides. However, it would also place Allied military personnel in vulnerable positions, supply lines could be threatened, and unconquered Japanese military personnel could continue to attack American forces by air, land, and sea.[27]

Trapped and isolated Japanese forces needed supplies delivered by barges to survive, and this is why the conflict in New Guinea and the Philippines was often referred to s a "barge busting war." The Allies needed a force capable of combating these hard-to-find shallow-water vessels, and the perfect boat for this purpose was the small, shallow-drafting, and lethal Motor Torpedo Boat. As a result, PT boats were in New Guinea from the beginning of the campaign to liberate the island. They were the first Allied naval vessels to see action in New Guinea, and in New Guinea the Motor Torpedo Boat became less of a torpedo boat and more of a barge-busting gunboat.[28]

By day, most of the barge busting was carried out by Army and Navy aviators. However, the barges generally stayed hidden during daylight hours, so airmen found only limited success in the war against these vessels. At night, which was when most of the barges were on the move, it was the PT boats that were called on to stop them.[29]

When a barge was located, a flare would often be fired in the air to illuminate the target, all of the boats in the group would motor as close to shore as possible, and the full firepower of the PT boats would be unleashed to destroy the craft. With the additional guns that had been added to the boats patrolling the waters in New Guinea and the Philippines, the hail of small shells and bullets at close range would prove to be deadly even to the better armed and armored barges. In addition, sailors who were not manning deck guns and cannons on the PT boats would often fire tommy guns and automatic rifles at the barges and even heave hand grenades on to the decks of the enemy vessels. While attacking, the PT boats would often keep moving, and when they had motored out of range from their targets, they would circle back and unleash another barrage on the target. There were even a few occasions when PT boat crews, desperate to destroy a barge they confronted at close range, would drive their boat over a barge in an attempt to kill its crew and crush the enemy vessel.[30]

Frequently, the initial barrage of fire from the PT boats was so devastating that all of the Japanese barge crew was quickly killed. However, the Japanese were often able to return fire; and when defeat seemed inevitable, Japanese sailors would run into the jungle or jump overboard and swim out to sea. Most of these men would eventually drown. PT boats would try to round up swimming Japanese soldiers and sailors and capture them, but this was always dangerous and difficult. If capture was imminent, Japanese sailors and soldiers would try to stab or drown themselves and each other and would often beg the Americans to shoot them. The Japanese almost always violently resisted capture, and often if they were fished out of the water they continued to fight the Americans with

PT boat gunners "barge busting." United States Navy.

knives and even hand grenades. When this resistance proved to be futile, they would again try to commit suicide.

Often, PT boat sailors would motor up to Japanese warriors in the water, club them unconscious with boat hooks or some other object, and then entangle them in a cargo net and lift them on to the boat. They would then be brought back to the PT boat base to be interrogated. Sometimes after an enemy soldier had been located, a net would be lowered off the bow of the PT boat; and a sailor would enter the water tethered to the boat, rap the Japanese soldier or sailor off the head with a blackjack, and then tie a line around him so he could be lifted on to the boat. Unfortunately, as the war wore on, and the hatred on both sides grew, American sailors, who were unable or unwilling to coax or force the Japanese out of the water and on to the decks of the PT boats, would train their guns on the defenseless swimming enemy and kill them where they swam.[31]

If Japanese sailors were captured, they would be brought back and turned over to officers who would interrogate them. Interestingly, Japanese sailors, some of the fiercest and bravest warriors in the history of warfare, proved to be docile and cooperative prisoners. For their entire lives they had been taught that surrender was never an option, so beyond killing themselves when capture was imminent, they had never been told what to do when captured. Thus, when Japanese warriors were captured, they found themselves in a position that was never thought to be a possibility. So they did what had always been expected of them in their authoritarian society: They respected authority, and this meant cooperating with their American captors. As a result, some of the captured Japanese barge sailors did provide their American captors with important intelligence.[32]

When the barge grew quiet, and the PT boat crews believed the Japanese were dead or gone, PT boat sailors were sent to board the vessels and search for intelligence. During the occasions when my father went on barge patrol, he was sent to inspect several barges. Although I do not believe he ever found valuable intelligence, he was struck by how much the quarters of the men who had recently been killed resembled the crew's quarters

Japanese prisoners captured by Filipino guerrillas. United States Navy.

on his own PT boat. Photos of family members and beautiful young women adorned the walls, bunks were in various states of disarray, and assorted plates and dishes lay near or in crude sinks waiting to be cleaned. On one occasion they did find a lone soldier on a barge, and my father assisted in capturing the man who fortunately allowed himself to be taken prisoner without resisting.[33]

The success of the PT boat barge-busting patrols in New Guinea had a significant impact on the war in the Pacific. From November 1943 to January 1944, 147 barges were sunk; and in total, hundreds of barges were sunk by the sailors of the Mosquito Fleet in New Guinea and later the Philippines. By February 1944, the success of the PT boat patrols had resulted in a dramatic decline in barge traffic; and by late 1944 the PT boat barge patrols that originated from Mios Woendi came to an end.[34]

The success of the PT boat barge-busting operations impacted the Japanese in several ways. As a result of the American air and PT boat gauntlet, the Japanese found it much more difficult to supply their troops. This often made it necessary to try and move supplies overland in jungle-infested New Guinea. This was dangerous and impractical to the point where provisions were often left behind, and even the bare minimum of supplies could not be transported to waiting soldiers. It also forced the Japanese to use submarines to resupply troops, which meant these vessels were not available to fight Allied ships. As a result of their inability to supply troops, untold thousands of Japanese soldiers would await supplies that never came and starve.[35]

The Japanese did develop strategies to deal with the PT boat threat. They would place an unmanned daihatsu near shore in close proximity to shore batteries. They would then wait for a PT boat to arrive and attack the boat with the large, shore-mounted guns when it moved in to destroy the barge. Even without a decoy barge, PT boats had to be wary of shore-mounted guns. This was especially true in waters that had reefs near shore that could ground boats, creating inviting stationary targets for shore gunners.[36]

PT boats performed many important functions in addition to barge patrol in New Guinea. They destroyed Japanese supply depots, attacked Japanese shore batteries, fought Japanese planes, rescued PT boats and other allied craft that were stuck on reefs, prevented the Japanese from evacuating troops, strafed beaches, rescued natives who had been driven from their homes, patrolled rivers, transported American, Australian, Dutch, and native scouts to various locations on the island, and even transported the Sultan of Ternate—the man who had been governor of the "entire region" prior to the war, along with his harem—away from the Japanese and to safety.[37]

Perhaps it was the Japanese themselves who best articulated the important impact the PT boats had in New Guinea. Tokyo Rose, certainly reflecting the attitude of Japan's military leaders, called the men of the Mosquito Fleet, "War Criminals." An intercepted radio message that was translated by American code breakers explained, "At all costs American PT boats must be smashed before we can reinforce garrisons now defending New Britain and New Guinea;" and in a diary found on a Japanese sailor after his barge was captured, the PT boats were referred to as, "the monster that roars, flaps its wings, and shoots torpedoes in all directions."[38]

For the Japanese, New Guinea was a terrible place to be, especially after the Americans and their "Devil Boats" arrived. A popular saying among Japanese soldiers was, "heaven is Java, hell is Burma: but no one returns alive from New Guinea." Even American soldiers, who certainly had less difficulty on the island than the Japanese, referred to New Guinea as, "green hell on earth."[39] There were at least 157,645 Japanese garrisoned on New Guinea and perhaps as many as 200,000. Only 10,072 of these men survived the war, and of the more than 147,000 who died, only a small percentage were killed as a result of combat with the Allies. The rest starved or perished as a result of disease or some jungle related ailment. As one Japanese general explained after the war, Japan "bled itself white" on New Guinea.

The success of the American war on the barges created a desperate need for food. Starving Japanese soldiers often ate grass, snakes, raw crabs, and roots. Pack animals were slaughtered and eaten, and cannibalism became common. After the war, Japanese doctors admitted to surgically removing parts of dead bodies so they could be consumed. Japanese soldiers would enter the thick jungle in search of food. Often they would never return, killed by one of the numerous dangerous jungle creatures or a member of one of the often-violent tribes who occupied the island's interior. Both Allied soldiers and indigenous natives were killed and devoured by the Japanese. Allies were referred to as "white pigs," and locals as "black pigs."

Conditions became so dire that even Japanese corpses were consumed. In perhaps the most barbaric undertaking to preserve food, captured native men and women and allied men condemned to be cannibalized were often kept alive while they were being consumed. Skin would be stripped from thighs, arms, the chest, and ears; and noses and lips would be cut off all while the victim was alive. This was done because the flesh on a living victim would not quickly rot in the brutal, humid heat; and food could be preserved for another day.[40]

Just as the Japanese terrorized the natives, the natives terrorized them. New Guinea had numerous native tribes and many proud, healthy, and brave warriors. They all shared a hatred of the Japanese and killed and captured hundreds of their enemy. In general

6. The Battle for New Guinea and Return to the Philippines 107

New Guinea natives were tolerant of the Americans, but Americans had to also be wary of the indigenous people of New Guinea. Generally the native people and the PT boat sailors avoided each other.[41]

The PT boats of Squadron 16 began night patrols almost immediately after their arrival at Mios Woendi. The boats often motored as close as 50 yards from shore, and they engaged barges and attacked the enemy hidden in huts and the jungle along the shoreline. In addition to barge patrol, PT boats dropped off army rangers or Royal Dutch Raiders on remote parts of the island and then picked them up days or weeks later. On several occasions when these soldiers were picked up, they had Japanese prisoners; and these would be brought back to the base for interrogation.[42]

Boats would also be sent out to rendezvous with native scouts. These men would be brought to the boats to share information with officers, and on occasion they were brought back to the base so they could be questioned. These scouts lived in tiny dwellings built near the coastline surrounded by the jungle canopy and were often in close proximity to the Japanese.[43] PT boats also located and evacuated Dutch, Javanese, Formosan, and Indian army personnel who had been captured, forced to work as slave laborers, and then escaped. In October and November, 782 were evacuated by PT boats. One Dutchman, who had escaped the Japanese and then been rescued by PT *223*, claimed to have slit the throats of 12 of his Japanese captors while they slept before his escape. Of course there was no way to verify this claim.[44]

During one night patrol, PTs *298* or *299* and *301* sunk a barge and then found five Japanese military personnel in the water. The boats cautiously approached the men and proceeded to remove them from the water. One had a hidden hand grenade that was fortunately grabbed by one of the boat's sailors and hurled into the water before it exploded. Another had a knife, which he used to cut one of the officers on the boat. As another prisoner was placed on the deck, a member of the crew spied stars on the shoulder of the man's uniform indicating that he was an officer. Realizing how rare it was to capture a Japanese officer, one of the more aggressive trophy collectors on the boat proceeded to cut the stars off the man's uniform. Seeing this, other crew members jumped in grabbing the man and cutting his uniform in a frenzied attempt to acquire souvenirs from their prisoner. In minutes, the bewildered officer was standing on the deck of the boat in rags and almost naked.[45]

While on barge patrol, my father and the sailors on PT *221* found a lone Japanese warrior in the water. The man resisted being brought on board the PT boat, but the PT boat sailors were able to hook him with a boat hook and hoist him up. Just as the man was being deposited on the deck, he pulled out a hidden hand grenade and pulled the pin. Instantly, an armed sailor—perhaps my father—who had been observing the proceedings, fired a bullet into the prisoner while another sailor kicked the grenade and then the sailor overboard. As a result, in the future when the sailors of *The Omen of the Seas* found Japanese soldiers or sailors in the water, they rarely made an attempt to capture them. My father believed that most of these men drowned.[46]

On occasion, boats would see terrified natives mingling on the shore. These men and women had been driven from their homes by the Japanese and were looking to the Americans for help. PT boat crews would load as many as 80 natives on to the deck of a boat and then bring them back to their base where they would be safe.[47]

One of the most common problems faced by PT boats in New Guinea was running aground on reefs. This happened with such regularity that Lieutenant Herbert H. "Pete"

Japanese warrior being pulled onto a PT boat. PT boat sailors had to guard against Japanese prisoners trying to kill them or kill themselves. World War II PT Boats Museum and Archives, Germantown, Tennessee.

Wells, an artistic officer on PT *221* who would have a successful career as an illustrator of children's books after the war, created a "Reefer Club" membership card that was handed out to all sailors who were on boats that hit reefs.[48] In addition to being wary of reefs beneath them, PT boat crews had to keep a lookout for enemy and American planes above. For the duration of the war in the Pacific there were communication problems between PT boats and American planes and even other ships, which led to many serious and even deadly encounters. Allied aircraft patrolling the New Guinea shoreline by day would sometimes mistake a PT boat for a Japanese barge and strafe the boat; and on occasion, PT boats would mistake Allied planes for Japanese aircraft and fire on them. In total, two PT boats were sunk by friendly fire in New Guinea, and tragically 14 PT boat crew members were killed and 21 wounded. Two pilots were killed by PT boat gunners.[49]

Tragedy struck Squadron 16 soon after the boats arrived at Mios Woendi. One morning while most of the crew of PT *221* was relaxing under a canopy on the bow of the boat, Quartermaster Second Class Oliver Young jumped off nearby PT *301* and started walking toward the base to get a new pair of shoes. Below the deck of PT *301* the bilge was being cleaned with high-octane gasoline, and as a result the Baker Flag was flying which warned of the potentially dangerous activity that was taking place on the boat. Without warning, the auxiliary generator caused a spark, and this resulted in a huge explosion in the engine room. Oliver Young was still less than 200 yards from the boat, and he turned as the boat's deck was ripped open and sent flying "sky high." Motor Machinist's Mate First Class George M. Chilles was blown out of the engine room and over the side of PT *301* landing on the open lazaret hatch of PT *300*, which was tied to the *301* boat. His skull was crushed, and he died instantly.

Motor Machinist's Mate Second Class Ted Russo was also launched out of the engine room of PT *301* and on to the deck of PT *300*. He landed on one of the .50 caliber gun mounts. Although he suffered numerous broken bones and a fractured skull, it was believed he would survive. However, he died four days later from internal injuries. Motor Machinist's Mate Second Class Nolan Noack, the third man in the engine room, was hurled high into the air by the explosion. Fortunately for him he landed in the water, but he was unconscious, and he surely would have drowned had it not been for the actions of Edmund I. "Ed" Kalinowski, a motor machinist's mate second class on nearby PT *223*. Fearing that PT *301* would soon catch fire, the sailors in PT *300* took an ax to the lines that tethered their boat to PT *301* and began to back the boat away from PT *301*. In the chaos of the moment, the crew of PT *300* did not realize that Noack was unconscious and in the water to the stern of PT *300*, which was now about to back over him. Seeing that the unconscious Noack was about to be carved up by the propellers of PT *300*, Kalinowski dove into the water to rescue his squadron mate.

Men were yelling at the sailors operating PT *300* to stop, but the boat operators could not hear them above the roar of the engines. Kalinowski grabbed Noack as PT *300* was backing down and held the unconscious man in one arm, and desperately fended off the boat by pushing off its stern with his other. Obviously, Kalinowski was no match for three PT boat motors, and it was only a matter of seconds before both men would find themselves under the boat and dismembered by its screws. Sailors continued to desperately yell. Kalinowski's legs were forced under the boat, and his feet got so close to the propellers that his shoes were sucked off. Finally, the operators of PT *300* realized what was happening, and their boat was put into forward gear and driven away from the two men and into the beach. Noack lost his leg but lived. Kalinowski received a deck court martial for going overboard without orders and was fined one dollar. He also received the Navy Marine Medal, the highest non-combat decoration awarded for heroism by the United States Department of the Navy.

Others suffered from the explosion as well. Ship's Cook Second Class Russel T. Enyeart, the cook on PT *301*, was in the officer's quarters when the explosion occurred and was blown through the door to the ammunition locker, but fortunately he was not severely injured. Torpedoman's Mate First Class Jarred Rankin was on the boat and was working on a torpedo at the time of the explosion. He was blown over the deck of the boat and landed on a torpedo on PT *223*. He was seriously injured, but he did eventually recover fully. Motor Machinist's Mate Everett A. Dunbar was also blown overboard, and he suffered extreme shock.

Chilles and Russo had been with Squadron 16A from the time it had left New Orleans and had only recently been transferred to 16B. They were well known and liked by the sailors in the squadron. Chilles was given a military funeral and buried on the nearby island of Biak on the same day he was killed. The damage to PT *301* was so extensive that the boat had to be scrapped. Ironically, a number of the crew of the *301* boat had also manned the ill-fated PT *219* in the Aleutians.[50]

On July 30, 1944, General MacArthur's troops landed at Sansapor on the western end of New Guinea. As many as 200,000 Japanese troops were still on the island; but with the success of the PT boat barge busting campaign and other naval and air efforts to prevent their resupply, these remaining Japanese were in the words of Lieutenant General Robert Eichelberger "condemned prisoners."[51] The Allies did not control all of New Guinea, but that was never their goal.

In addition, Rabaul, the major Japanese base in the region, was still controlled by Japan, but its 100,000 troops had been rendered impotent. The United States controlled the waters between New Guinea and New Britain, so Rabaul had little military value. Certainly the 100,000 troops could have been better employed by the Japanese in areas that still had military value. However, the United States Navy was now so much more powerful than Japan's that if the Japanese wanted to evacuate their men to fight elsewhere it probably would have been impossible.[52]

In late November 1944, the last PT boat patrol in the waters off New Guinea was made, almost 1,500 miles to the east of where the first patrols were made more than 20 months earlier. Evidence of the success of these patrols could be seen along the shore where the remains of scores of Japanese daihatsus and supply dumps rotted. Untold numbers of field artillery pieces had also been mounted along the shore to try and combat the PT boat menace. These guns were thus unavailable to be used against Allied troops, and many of them quickly rusted in the humid New Guinea air as the Japanese were bypassed and the guns became useless. Inland thousands of Japanese skeletons were quickly being hidden by the jungle, invisible testament to the success of the PT boat barge busting campaign in New Guinea.[53]

Having lost control of New Guinea, the Japanese also lost the outer perimeter of their "absolute national defense sphere," and shortly America would return to the Philippines. This decision was not without controversy. Some civilian and military leaders argued that the Philippines should be bypassed and that the Allies should instead focus on the Central Pacific portion of the Japanese Empire. This was unfathomable to General MacArthur. He had dreamed of his return to the Philippines since he had been ferried to safety on PT *41*. The general's last words to Major General Jonathan "Skinny" Wainwright, the man in charge of the Allied forces after his departure had been, "If I can get to Australia, you know I'll come back as soon as I can with as much as I can." The general explained to President Roosevelt that the American people expected the Japanese to be driven from the Philippines and that doing so would be a great boon to the president's popularity. This assertion was certainly crass, but President Roosevelt was one of the consummate political animals of the twentieth century; and surely this argument resonated with him, especially in an election year. MacArthur also argued that America owed it to the millions of Filipinos suffering under Japanese rule and to the thousands of Allied prisoners being brutalized and dying in Japanese prison and work camps in the Philippines to come to their aid as soon as possible. Ultimately, the great general's arguments won the day. The time had come for America to return to the Philippines, and the sailors in Squadron 16 would play a small but important role in this mammoth undertaking.[54]

In early September 1944, Admiral William Frederick "Bull" Halsey, Jr.'s Third Fleet launched the preliminary attack that would be the beginning of America's Philippine campaign. Carrier-launched planes attacked shore installations in Mindanao, the Visayas, and other nearby islands, and approximately 200 Japanese planes were destroyed. The admiral concluded that Japanese air power in the Philippines was much weaker than previously believed and that the Japanese were pouring soldiers from all over their empire into the Philippines in an attempt to prevent the United States from taking this vital component of their domain. As a result, Admiral Halsey recommended to Admiral Nimitz that the United States bypass the islands of Mindanao, Talaud, and Yap and make their return to the Philippines on the island of Leyte—which was between the larger islands of Luzon to the north and Mindanao to the south—as soon as possible to limit the Japanese troop buildup. General MacArthur agreed with this conclusion, and in a few short weeks Operation King II, the invasion of Leyte, was launched.[55]

MacArthur's leapfrog from New Guinea to Leyte in the Philippines would be 1,200 miles and the longest of the war up to that point. The general who had fled the Philippines in early 1942 on four rickety PT boats now returned with one of the most formidable naval fleets ever assembled. General MacArthur sailed on USS *Nashville* surrounded by 157 combat ships of Admiral Thomas C. Kincaid's Seventh Fleet and 581 other vessels. Crowded on board some of the ships were more than 160,000 nervous, highly motivated, well-fed, trained, and equipped soldiers of MacArthur's Sixth Army; and they were all there to drive the Japanese out of the Philippines.[56]

If General MacArthur's success in New Guinea and bold decision to initiate his Philippine Campaign at Leyte enraged Japanese military planners, it also gave them an opportunity to stop the American advance in the Pacific, regain the prestige the military had when it was winning great victories with shocking regularity, rekindle the supreme confidence that all of the Japanese had had in their military in the early phase of the war, and ultimately retake the offensive in the Pacific. General Tomoyuki Yamashita, the man

USS *Nashville*. United States Navy.

responsible for Japan's defense of the Philippines said, "The Japanese will fight the decisive battle in the Philippines in Leyte." In October 1944 alone, 20,000 additional troops were brought to the island to supplement the already staggering 60,000 to 70,000 warriors who were already there. In addition, the bulk of the Japanese fleet would also motor to the waters that surrounded Leyte to support the warriors who defended the island and confront the American Navy in what the Japanese hoped would be a decisive battle that would enable their navy to again dominate the Pacific.[57]

October 20, 1944, was one of the more important days in America's long, slow, and unstoppable advance in the Pacific. On that day after MacArthur again set foot on Philippine soil, he famously remarked, "People of the Philippines, I have returned by the grace of Almighty God, our forces stand again on Philippine soil." MacArthur's words no doubt are illustrative of the enormous ego of America's most famous general in the Pacific during World War II. However, what is also beyond question is that Japan's greatest fear had become reality. The nation that had been humiliated in early 1942 was now back. In the years since its departure from the Philippines, the United States had improved its tactics; gained valuable combat experience; and developed an extraordinary officer corps to lead naval, air, and ground warriors who were up to the difficult tasks that lay ahead. In addition, the full might of the American production machine had been harnessed by the United States military. Regardless of the desperate measures they would employ in the future, Japan was destined to lose the war.[58]

Leyte was 115 miles long and between 15 and 45 miles wide. It was mostly mountainous, and thus provided ample protection for Japanese troops. In addition, September and October were rainy months, and this was also the time of year when typhoons were common. Thus, the conditions would be miserable, and American forces would have a difficult time moving men and equipment and building airstrips after they had landed.

It did not take long for MacArthur's forces to realize that not only was Leyte defended by more than 75,000 battle-hardened troops, and thousands of support personnel, most of whom would never leave the island alive, but that the enemy also had a number of small, well-hidden airfields in the island's interior, which were used by Japan's planes to launch sorties against American ships and ground forces. Unfortunately for the Japanese, American carrier-launched aircraft had destroyed more than 400 Japanese planes on Leyte prior to the invasion, and America's superior air capabilities continued to destroy large numbers of Japanese aircraft after the battle commenced. Because of these losses the Japanese had a critical shortage of aircraft, and this certainly handicapped them in their fight to maintain control of Leyte and the rest of the Philippines.[59]

The ground battle for Leyte was brutal. As tens of thousands of American troops poured on to the island, Japanese resistance stiffened. Not only did the American forces have to combat the Japanese on the ground and in the air, they also faced numerous jungle ailments such as dengue fever; filariasis, a lymphatic infection; malaria; and "jungle rot." In addition, typhoons roared, 75-mile-per-hour winds were common, and 35 inches of rain fell during the first 40 days the Americans were on Leyte. Poor drainage and huge amounts of silt made many roads and airfields unusable. When it was not raining, thick humid air made it impossible for soldiers to dry off, and constantly being soaked only added to the suffering in both armies. Sharp rocks cut boots; the smell of decaying vegetation was so vile that it caused many men to vomit; and swampy, soft ground made walking difficult and made it almost impossible to keep feet dry. The Japanese, well dug-in in trenches, spider holes, and pillboxes, made the battle for the island deadly and even more miserable.⁶⁰

On October 13, 45 PT boats under the command of Lieutenant Commander Robert Leeson left Mios Woendi bound for Leyte, almost 1,200 miles away. The PT boats and their support craft completed their arduous journey on October 21 and almost immediately began night patrols. Over the next several days they located and sunk seven Japanese barges and several other small vessels, and then found themselves engaged in perhaps the greatest naval confrontation in history.⁶¹

One of the hallmarks of Japanese war planning in World War II was their belief in the decisive battle. This had been the goal at Midway, and it was also the objective of the Japanese Navy in the Battle of Leyte Gulf. However, like at Midway where Japan divided their naval force and thus allowed the United States to win a decisive victory instead of suffering a disastrous loss, the Japanese employed a similar strategy in the Philippines. They divided their forces on land and sea, and they ultimately suffered a devastating defeat.

As the American noose tightened on the Japanese Army on the island of Leyte, the Japanese Naval Command still believed the decisive victory they had dreamed of since the war's inception could finally be obtained in the waters near the island.⁶²

Three Japanese Naval forces steamed toward Leyte: Center Force from the West, Northern Force from the North, and Southern Force from the South. The Japanese would get the decisive naval battle they wanted but not the result. Over four days and thousands of square miles the 282 ships and 200,000 sailors and airmen that made up the huge armadas of the United States and Japan would slug it out in what by most measures was the largest naval battle in history. When it was over, the Japanese Navy, the finest in the world at the war's inception, would be in ruins, and Imperial Japan would find itself in possession of an empire that spread across thousands of miles of ocean without a navy capable of protecting it.⁶³

Although the Battle of Leyte Gulf was largely a slugfest between traditional naval ships, PT boats did play an important role in the engagement. Prior to the battle's commencement, 39 PT boats were divided into three groups of 13 boats and ordered to position themselves along the coasts of Mindanao, Leyte, and Bohol west of the Surigao Strait, the narrow passage that separated Leyte from Mindanao. Obviously the boats of the Mosquito Fleet would be no match for the behemoths that Japan was sending to confront the American armada, but the boats could be the "eyes and ears of the American fleet." The United States did not have any radar-equipped aircraft available for the battle, but they did have the vessels of the PT boat fleet, and Admiral Kinkaid instructed these boats to locate the position of Japanese ships and report it to the larger American vessels. In addition, the PT boats were to harass and

PT boats at Leyte Gulf. United States Navy.

attempt to damage or even sink Japanese ships with their torpedoes when they encountered them.[64]

There is no question that PT boats made an important contribution to the United States Navy's success in the Battle of Leyte Gulf and that their performance on the night of October 24/25, 1944, was one of the most gallant in the history of the Mosquito Fleet. It was the PT boats that first located the incoming Japanese fleet, and the larger ships were thrown off balance as they maneuvered to avoid torpedoes fired from the Motor Torpedo Boats. In combating the PT boats, Japanese surface ships fired star shells and deck guns and aimed searchlights, all of which exposed the ships to American surface vessels. In total, the boats of the Mosquito Fleet fired 30 torpedoes. At least one found its mark on light cruiser *Abukuma*, and one hit destroyer *Asagumo* and played a role in its sinking.

The PT boat crews paid the price for engaging the Japanese. Of the 39 boats that took part in the battle, 30 came under heavy Japanese fire, 10 were hit, 3 men were killed, and 3 officers and 17 crew members were wounded. One PT boat ran aground during the confrontation. Looking back at what occurred on the night of October 24/25, it is surprising that more damage was not done to the small boats.

Admiral Chester W. Nimitz, not a man prone to offer unwarranted praise, acknowledged the role played by the PT boats' sailors in the battle when he wrote: "The skill, determination and courage displayed by the personnel of these small boats is worthy of the highest praise…. The PT's action very probably threw the Japanese command off balance and contributed to the completeness of their subsequent defeat."[65]

There were 4 major battles in the Battle of Leyte Gulf, and America won all of them. In total, the Japanese lost 1 large aircraft carrier, 3 medium aircraft carriers, 3 battleships, 6 heavy cruisers, 4 light cruisers, 11 destroyers, 4 submarines, 116 aircraft and most of the pilots who flew them, 300,000 tons of combat shipping, and 10,000 men. Thousands of these men chose to drown rather than be rescued. In addition, during the course of the battle for the island of Leyte, the Japanese lost 19 of their 25 transport ships and the supplies these vessels carried. This made it almost impossible for the Japanese to transport men and supplies off of Leyte when the battle for the Philippines shifted to Luzon. The United States lost 1 light carrier, 2 escort carriers, 3 destroyers, 3 submarines, and approximately 40 planes and 1,500 men.[66]

The Imperial Japanese Navy Air Service, once the finest in the world, was now a shell of what it once was. Most of its best pilots were dead, and the advantage Japanese airmen had flying the Zero had largely been erased by the improvements in American aircraft technology. It was impossible to adequately train enough pilots to replace those who had been lost; and even if they could have, Japan now lacked an adequate carrier force from which the planes could be launched. In addition, with the impending loss of the Philippines, essential oil from the East Indies was about to be cut off, which meant that Japan would have an even greater critical fuel shortage for the remainder of the war. The Japanese Army was still manned by formidable soldiers, but it was being chewed up whenever it confronted the Allied forces.

Japan's leaders should have realized that victory was now impossible. There would be no decisive battle against the United States that would result in victory. Continuing the war would serve no purpose other than to prolong the suffering of combatants and civilians on both sides. Japan should have sought peace. However, by now the United States had proclaimed that only unconditional surrender would bring the war in the

Pacific to an end, and this was unfathomable to Japan's leaders. In addition, in the Philippines, Japan would unleash a new weapon—one they believed could change the course of the war. Japan would try to win the war with history's first guided missiles by sending thousands of young men crashing into American ships in bomb-loaded planes. The kamikaze, they believed, would bring them victory in the Pacific.

On the cloudy morning of November 19, PT Boat Squadrons 13, 16, 25 and boats from Squadrons 36 and 17 left Mios Woendi bound for Leyte. Accompanying the PT boats were eight crash boats, three PT tenders, and LST *210*. To preserve fuel, the boats only traveled 12 knots per hour; and like the PT boats that preceded them, they carried 20 extra drums of fuel on each boat. Not long after the small fleet departed, the winds picked up considerably. Soon the small boats found themselves in some of the roughest water they had yet encountered. The ride on a PT boat was always "stiff," and as the wave heights grew, sailors suffered "strains, sprains, cuts, bruises, broken bones, and lost teeth." Fortunately after approximately 24 hours the seas started to calm down.

On the fourth day of the voyage, the boats anchored in shallow water at the northern tip of the Palau group of islands. In total, as many as 100 American ships were anchored here. Although there were still several thousand Japanese scattered in these islands, they generally posed no threat to the Americans and were ignored. Occasionally a small number would row out on small boats and attempt to hurl hand grenades on to the American ships, but these actions proved to be futile. Japanese planes did attack the boats on

PT boats based at Mios Woendi prepare for the invasion of Leyte. World War II PT Boats Museum and Archives, Germantown, Tennessee.

occasion, but the PT boats were generally left alone. On the sixth day of their voyage, the PT boats left Palau. For the remainder of the voyage to Leyte, PT boat crews were required to stand "condition two watches" until they arrived at Leyte. On the third day after leaving Palau, Japanese planes attacked some of the American ships that were sailing with the PT boat fleet. One cruiser was hit and badly damaged, and approximately 15 Japanese planes were shot down. At noon on the fourth day after leaving Palau, the men of Squadron 16 arrived at San Pedro Bay at the island of Leyte. The sailors had motored 1,200 miles, many of them in difficult sea conditions, in their small boats. Many had endured seasickness, and all were exhausted and grateful to be away from the constantly roaring Packard motors.[67]

The officer who was in charge of these Motor Torpedo Boats and would eventually be in command of all PT boats during the upcoming Mindoro campaign was Lieutenant Commander Nathaniel Burt Davis, Jr. If one man symbolized the swashbuckling can-do attitude of the PT boat men in New Guinea and the Philippines, it was Lieutenant Commander Davis. Born on September 6, 1911, the lean and handsome Lieutenant Commander Davis graduated from the United States Naval Academy in 1933 and would spend World War II commanding a PT boat, a squadron, and eventually a task unit. While in New Guinea, his boat attacked a Japanese barge and killed or captured all of its crew. As the barge was sinking, Lieutenant Commander Davis ignored intense enemy fire from shore and nearby barges and attempted to board the vessel in an effort to obtain intelligence. There was a huge explosion that caused the barge to sink before he could search the vessel. The Silver Star that he was awarded for his gallantry read, "His courage, leadership, and absolute disregard for the enemy fire were an inspiration to officers and men alike. His actions were in keeping with the highest traditions of the Navy of the United States."

Lieutenant Commander Davis was also awarded two Legion of Merit Medals during the war, and these tell much about the man and sailor that would lead the men of Squadron 16 during their last and most difficult chapter of the war. One read:

> The President of the United States of America takes great pleasure in presenting the Legion of Merit with Combat "V" to Commander (then Lieutenant Commander) Nathaniel Burt Davis, Jr., United States Navy, for exceptional meritorious conduct in the performance of outstanding services to the government of the United States as Commanding Officer of Motor Torpedo Boat Squadron Twenty-Four during operations against enemy Japanese forces in New Guinea, from January to November 1944. Skillfully participating in the Campaign, Commander Davis directed fifty-three combat patrols, led his squadron on twenty-five special missions and successfully effected an aircraft rescue. Developing brilliant landing party tactics behind enemy lines, on three occasions, he conducted small parties ashore to wipe out enemy installations, destroying food stores and capturing vital documents without casualty to our own forces and with a score of fourteen Japanese killed and nine taken prisoner. Commander Davis also developed the expert technique of landing large army scouting parties from PT boats and served as commander of PT Advanced Bases at Saidor and New Amsterdam Island. His outstanding initiative, courageous leadership and devotion to duty were in keeping with the highest traditions of the United States Naval Service.

Lieutenant Commander Davis's second Legion of Merit Medal was for "exceptionally meritorious conduct in the performance of outstanding services to the government of the United States during World War II." He would also be awarded a Navy and Marine Corps Medal for the heroism he displayed on Mindoro.[68]

During one raid in the Philippines in the second week of 1945, Lieutenant Commander Davis led his 14 Davis's Raiders and a group of Filipino guerrillas. They paddled

6. The Battle for New Guinea and Return to the Philippines   117

Far left, captured Japanese pilot; next to him in sling, Lieutenant Commander Davis; far right, Filipino guerrilla. Francis Gelzheiser collection.

to shore on small rubber rafts, snuck up on a group of Japanese and opened fire. In less than a minute, the massive fire of the Americans and their allies killed almost all of the Japanese.[69]

During the course of the war, Lieutenant Commander Davis was wounded, captained boats, lead Davis's Raiders on numerous missions, lead 20 special missions landing and retrieving Army and native scouts, took prisoners on 11 different occasions, destroyed tons of Japanese stores and equipment, killed scores of Japanese warriors, commanded Squadron 24, and then commanded all of the PT boats during the campaign for Mindoro. Like so many other officers and men who fought in World War II, the contributions of Lieutenant Commander Davis have largely been forgotten. However, there can be no doubt, that officers such as Lieutenant Commander Davis, who directly commanded men in combat and who continually led by example and worked to develop combat techniques that enabled American forces to win confrontations with the enemy with a minimal loss of American lives and equipment, played an enormous role in winning the war and set an example for military commanders that is still relevant today.[70]

Anchored and docked with the PT boats at Leyte was an enormous fleet of ships. The skies were cloudy and soon after the PT boats arrived, Oliver Young, now the quartermaster on PT *300*, reported that the boats were surrounded by explosions. Boat officers and crew believed that Japanese planes were attacking; and even though fuel tanks were low, the boats pushed their throttles to full speed to make them more difficult targets.

Soon the men on the small craft discovered the source of the explosions. In the distance, American ships were "furiously firing everything they had" at a swarm of Japanese planes that were attacking the ships. Some of the ships were firing their guns without setting the fuses on the shells. The shells would travel high into the air, disappear behind the clouds, and then loop back down to earth and explode when they hit the water.[71]

At night, Japanese planes would soar across the sky and drop bombs intended for the larger ships below. On many nights air raid alarms would be sounded two to three times. Initially, PT boat gunners fired at the Japanese planes, but soon an order was issued that banned all anti-aircraft fire at night by American boats and ships. It was determined that the fire burst that emanated from the American guns would provide targets for the Japanese planes; and it was feared that excited American gunners might inadvertently follow Japanese planes, fire their guns at too low of an angle, and mistakenly hit American ships.[72]

When Squadron 16 arrived at Leyte, there were still important tasks to be performed by the PT boat fleet. The battle for the island still raged, and my father and his shipmates on PT *221* and other boats from the squadron were ordered to pick up Japanese prisoners, deliver flame throwers and other equipment for the Army, and drop off soldiers on different parts of the island. They also picked up wounded soldiers and Army scouts and assisted in defending a nearby airstrip on Leyte.[73] The Japanese had a base in Ormoc Bay, on the west side of Leyte, and as in New Guinea, the Japanese used barges and other non-traditional craft to resupply their troops there. From October to December PT boats were assigned the task of stopping these vessels, and as in New Guinea, they proved to be adept at this task. In some instances, this meant that PT boats had to confront ships that were as large and powerful as destroyers. In total, PT boats destroyed more than 140 barges in the waters near Ormoc and 60 other Japanese vessels.

Lieutenant General Eichelberger acknowledged the contribution the PT boats made during the campaign for Leyte when he wrote:

> The cooperation of Motor Torpedo Boats throughout all operations on the Western half of Leyte provided invaluable support to elements of XXXIV Corps. PT squadrons located at Ormoc conducted continuous nightly sorties, sinking over 200 Japanese barges and over 200 other miscellaneous craft loaded with reinforcements, equipment, and supplies. The eagerness of the crews to close with the enemy and furnish aid to our ground forces was outstanding throughout.[74]

On one occasion, PT *221*, with my father on board, was assigned the task of taking Squadron Commander Davis to the city of Tacloban. By this point in the war, most of the city's 20,000 residents had fled. The streets were mud, few stores were open, and there was little on the shelves of the ones that were conducting business. American soldiers and sailors were everywhere, and they were often joined on the streets by abandoned gamecocks. As they wandered through the city's streets, my father and a shipmate encountered a nine-year-old girl. She played the piano, and despite having lost her family and experiencing the horrors of the war at such a young age, she had a happy, outgoing demeanor. Her father was an engineer who had been captured by the Japanese, and she asked my father that if he was ever in Manila, could he try to locate her uncle who might know where her father was. It had not been many years since my father had also faced life as a child without parents, and I am sure he was moved by the girl's plight. He agreed that if he were ever in the capital city, he would do his best to locate her uncle.[75]

While based in Leyte, PT boats were attacked by Japanese planes and kamikazes. In early November, while anchored in Leyte Gulf, a bomb landed on PT *320*. Two officers and 12 members of the crew were killed, and only one man survived. PT *134* was hit by bomb fragments that killed one sailor and wounded four others. Two crew members were killed and the boat's skipper and executive officer and eight crew members were wounded when a bomb landed less than 10 yards from PT *132*; and while on night patrol, PTs *523* and *525* were attacked by four Japanese Zeros. The planes strafed the boats and killed three officers and six enlisted men. PT *323* was almost cut in half when an early kamikaze hit the vessel amidship. Two officers were killed and nine sailors and two soldiers, who were passengers on the boat, were wounded.[76]

Recreation, commerce, and war were mixed in a surreal way while the PT boats were based at Leyte. Men would often strip and swim in the delightful waters, sometimes while Japanese planes flew overhead. Often the planes would try and mimic American planes coming in to land, and then they would release their bombs. When the Americans realized the enemy was above, ship and shore batteries would unleash relentless fire on the enemy planes. Guns were sometimes fired at low angles, and occasionally shells and bullets would dangerously skip over the water. The crew of PT *221* saw two such ricocheting shells hit American ships. Japanese planes would occasionally be shot down, and PT boat crews would be called on to try and pluck the pilots from the water. Air raid alerts were sounded two to three times per day, and when this occurred at night and 40 mm and larger projectiles were fired at enemy aircraft, the sight was "beautiful."[77]

The occasional Japanese attacks did not stop trade with the people who lived on the island. Almost daily, natives would paddle out to the PT boats and larger ships in canoes laden with woven mats, crude knives, Japanese-occupation currency, and coconuts. In return, these men wanted food, canned meat, cigarettes and clothing.[78]

The battle for Leyte was significant for a number of reasons. Allied success on the ground, sea, and in the air were proof that America's military leaders had learned to fully harness the United States' enormous production advantage. The Japanese saw the Philippines as essential to their empire, and thus invested enormous amounts of equipment and numbers of men to repel their enemy at Leyte. In total, more than 50,000 of Japan's best troops were killed on the island, and as many as 40,000 died on ships bound for it. However, this massive commitment did not alter the tide of the war.[79]

While the fighting still raged on the island of Leyte, General MacArthur planned one of his boldest moves yet in the war. He would invade the Philippine island of Mindoro. This was a risky decision. The island was in close proximity to Luzon and its scores of Japanese-controlled air fields, and it was more than 260 miles from American air bases on Leyte, which put it beyond the range of most American land-based fighter planes. However, MacArthur argued that taking Mindoro was a logical extension of his island hopping, "hit em where they ain't" strategy. By gaining control of the island, the American forces would only be separated from the Japanese stronghold on the island of Luzon by the 7½ mile Verde Island Passage; and America's main objective in the Philippines, the nation's capital of Manila and Manila Bay, would only be a 90-mile voyage across Cape Calavite. In addition, Bataan and Corregidor were on Luzon, and for millions of Americans this was "sacred ground" that had to be retaken. On Mindoro the Americans could build the vital air bases and staging grounds essential for the success of the Luzon campaign, and it was also on Mindoro where the men of Squadron 16 and their small boats would face their greatest test.[80]

7

American Production Versus the Japanese Spirit Warrior in World War II

I think the kamikaze planes were the worst fear of the PT men. You would shoot like hell, but they would still keep coming.—Quartermaster First Class William A. Bahn, PT 299

By the time the Japanese signed the surrender documents on USS *Missouri* on September 2, 1945, the United States was the most formidable military power in the history of the world, and this was largely the result of her genius for production. What makes the military capability of the United States at the war's end even more impressive is that during the period leading up to World War II the United States neglected her armed forces, and by many measurements it was not even a second rate military power.

There were a number of reasons for America's neglect of its armed forces. In the 1930s, the nation was mired in the Great Depression, and millions of citizens fought to survive each day. As a result, President Roosevelt's New Deal planners were far more concerned with improving the badly damaged American economy than they were the growing weakness of the American military relative to her potential enemies abroad.

For many Americans, World War I was still a recent and unpleasant memory. For the first time in our nation's history, President Woodrow Wilson had committed the United States to a war in Europe, hoping the war would result in "peace without victory" and an end to war in Europe. However, at the Versailles Peace Conference President Wilson was largely ignored. Allied leaders wanted their pound of German flesh, and they scoffed at Wilson's idealism and reminded him that the Americans had been latecomers to the war and that the majority of the Allied bleeding had been done by British and French boys, not American. The Treaty was harsh, and many Americans believed that American warriors had been sacrificed for an unworthy cause.[1]

Because of the passion for war displayed by the American people after the bombing of Pearl Harbor, it is often forgotten just how opposed to war and entering into a confrontation with Germany or Japan Americans were prior to the attack. Most Americans were supportive of the government's efforts to reduce the size of the world's great navies in the 1920s, and the majority of Americans supported the national government when it reduced the size of the regular Army to 140,000 soldiers following World War I. In 1937, in a poll believed to be scientific for the period, 95 percent of the American people said they did not want the United States to become involved in any future war.² A year earlier, 500,000 students participated in anti-war protests on scores of college campuses, and many argued that ROTC programs should be terminated just as zealous anti-war students asserted in the 1960s. A year prior to this, President Roosevelt signed the first of several Neutrality Acts that essentially outlawed selling arms to belligerents during war in the hope that this would prevent the United States from being pulled into a future conflict as it had been during World War I. Always the masterful politician, President Roosevelt, a champion of President Wilson's internationalism in the 1920s, famously proclaimed during the campaign for his third term in 1940, "Your boys are not going to be sent into any foreign wars."³

When the bombs were dropped on Pearl Harbor, the United States had the sixteenth largest military in the world, somewhere behind Portugal and Romania. Japan, on the other hand, had spent the decade prior to the attack building up its armed forces. In the years leading up to Pearl Harbor, 60 percent of its national budget was devoted to its military, and half of this had been used to construct a massive navy that by 1939, despite the attempt to limit the size of their Navy by the Washington Naval Conference of 1921–22, was the strongest in the Pacific.⁴

Even with the Depression and the long-standing neglect of the military, a closer examination of America's industrial capacity in the pre-war years shows that it was highly unlikely that the Japanese could ever win a war against the United States, if America properly organized its industrial capabilities to wage war, and even Admiral Yamamoto admitted as early as September 1940 that it would be difficult for Japan to win a protracted war against the United States. From 1929 to 1932 the Depression had shrunk America's gross domestic product by more than 30 percent, manufacturing by almost 50 percent, construction by 78 percent and investment by an astonishing 98 percent. Unemployment reached 25 percent and 5,000 banks went out of business. Hunger and homelessness grew while national self-confidence declined. However, even during the crisis years of the Depression, the United States produced 12 times the steel, five times the ships, five and one-half times the electricity and 105 times the cars that Japan did. In addition, it had the most skilled and productive workforce in the world and industrial geniuses who had not only invented the modern mass production system but were also capable of harnessing America's vast, untapped production capacity and creating a military machine that could quickly eclipse Japan's.⁵

At the Teheran Conference in late November 1943, Josef Stalin proclaimed, "The most important things in war are machines.... The United States is a country of machines."⁶ Stalin may have been a brutal, murderous dictator, but he understood the vital role the United States and its machines could play in winning World War II, because he realized that no country understood the machine as well as the United States and that America would make World War II a war of machines.

The attack on Pearl Harbor not only brought the United States into World War II, but it changed the hearts and minds of tens of millions of Americans. Gone were the beliefs in pacifism and isolationism that were so prevalent in the United States in the pre-war years. These were replaced with a desire to not only win the war but to do so in such a way that our enemies would never again pose a threat to the world.

Shortly after the United States entered the war, President Roosevelt went to Congress and explained that it was essential for the United States and its allies to have an overwhelming material advantage over the Axis powers. This would not only enable the Allies to win the war, but it would also reduce the loss of American lives. He proclaimed that the United States must produce 60,000 aircraft in 1942, 125,000 the following year and 120,000 tanks and 55,000 antiaircraft guns over the same time period. Achieving these goals seemed impossible when they were proclaimed, and they would have been for any other nation. However, not only did the United States generally meet these production goals, but it then surpassed them in the last two years of the war.[7]

Two-thirds of America's rapidly growing naval forces would be sent to fight the Rising Sun, which meant that it was inevitable that the United States would eventually control the seas. The Japanese Empire was spread out over hundreds of thousands of square miles. Thus most of their holdings needed to be supplied via the water. This made the war in the Pacific a war of supply, and once America's productive capacity was harnessed, she would not only be able to out supply her enemy but prevent the Japanese from provisioning much of her far-flung Empire.[8]

By the time the Japanese signed the surrender treaty, the United States had produced 299,293 aircraft at a total cost of $45,000,000,000. (All of the following dollar amounts are in 1940's dollars.) This was more than the combined wartime aircraft production of Germany, Japan, and Great Britain, and included 18,000 B-24s, 12,692 B-17s and 3,763 B-29 bombers. Grumman produced 500 F6F Hellcat fighters per month; and often when at sea, carrier-based crews would throw the planes that showed wear overboard and bring a new one on to the deck to insure that missions were not delayed. Especially important to the PT boat sailors in the Pacific was the P-38 Lightning. The United States produced 10,037 of these planes that proved to be adept at shooting down Japanese kamikazes. One PT boat veteran admired the planes and their pilots so much that he explained, "The fellows in the PTs said if they ever met a P-38 pilot in a bar, they would surely buy him a drink."[9]

At its highest level of production, Japan produced 1,000 planes per month. Despite producing only small numbers of combat aircraft at the war's inception, the United States was able to average almost 6,500 aircraft per month during the war years; and in 1944, as the United States ramped up production for the final phase of the war, more than 8,000 aircraft rolled out of American factories each month. Each American aircraft worker was able to produce four times more per day than his Japanese counterpart. In addition, not only was the United States able to produce far more planes than its enemies, but almost all of the American aircraft produced in the last phase of the war were faster, larger, and technologically more sophisticated than the aircraft piloted by the Japanese.

Fifteen hundred fifty-six warships, 82,028 landing craft and 5,777 merchant ships floated out of American shipyards. Early in the war it was clear that the aircraft carrier was the most important warship in the Pacific. During the course of the conflict, the Japanese were able to manufacture seven carriers, the United States 100 fleet, light, and escort carriers. For every 16 warships the United States produced during the war years, the Japanese produced one; and in total the United States spent a staggering $105,000,000,000 on its Navy during World War II. Just as astonishing was America's ability to produce supply ships. In 1943 alone, President Roosevelt ordered the Maritime Commission to produce 24,000,000 tons of cargo shipping, and to the surprise of many, this goal was achieved.

In addition American factories manufactured 634,569 Jeeps, 11,000 chainsaws, 2,383,311 trucks, 6,500,000 rifles, 40 billion bullets, and 88,410 tanks during the course of the war. This tank production was approximately double what the Germans were able

7. American Production Versus Japanese Spirit Warrior in World War II   123

Above: B-29 Superfortress in flight. The marriage of the technological prowess to design and build the B-29 and the ordnance it carried, and the American willingness to unleash total war on Imperial Japan, meant that Japan would either surrender or be destroyed. United States Air Force. *Right:* B-29 bombers dropping bombs on Japan, most likely containing napalm, circa July—August 1945. Library of Congress.

to produce, even though they were fighting a war for their national survival against Russia; and the tank was an essential weapon in this conflict. While all of this conventional war material was being manufactured, America still had the resources to spend 2 billion dollars on the Manhattan Project, and by the last months of the war it had

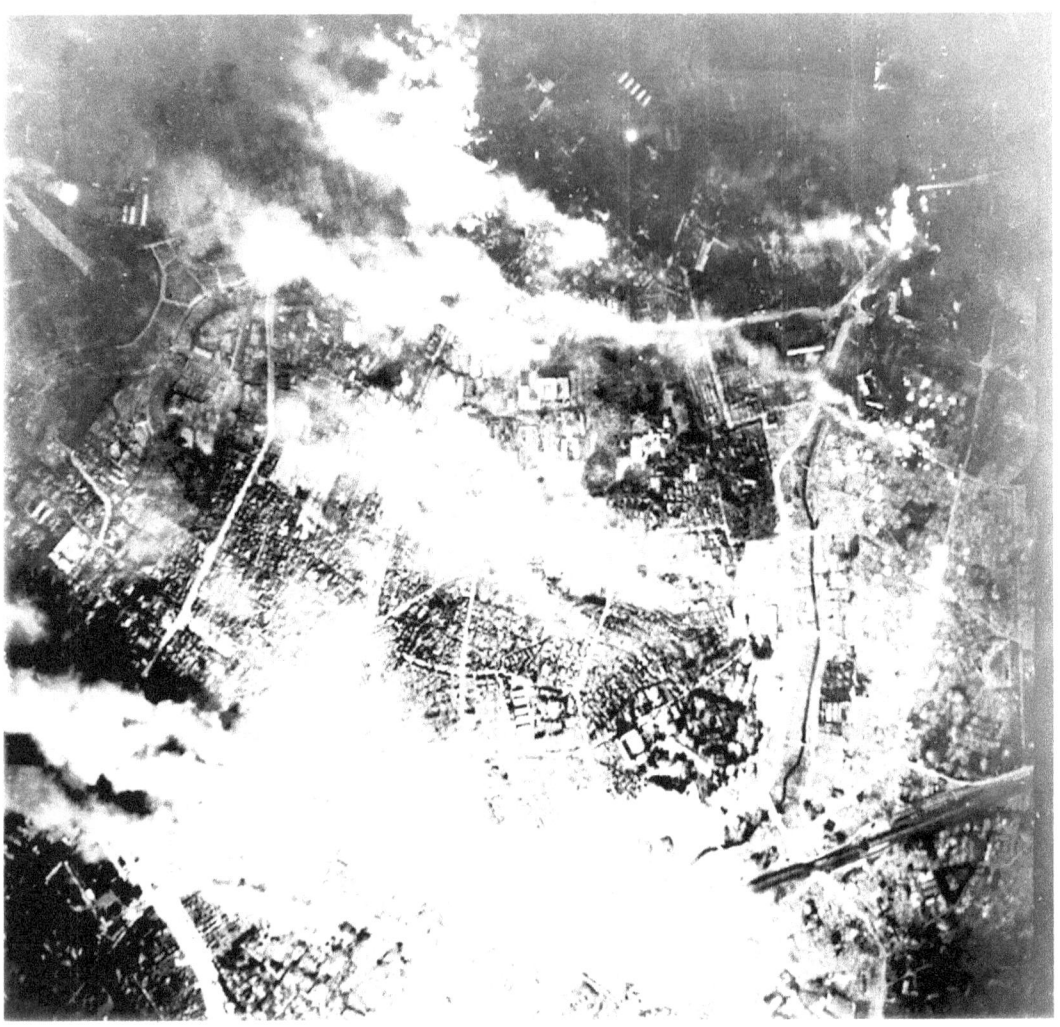

Aerial view of Tokyo after the city was firebombed by B-29 bombers on May 26, 1945. Library of Congress.

developed three atomic bombs—the most complicated weapon ever produced—two of which would play a key role in forcing the Japanese to finally surrender. By 1944, the United States manufactured six times the armaments of Great Britain, 60 percent of all Allied munitions, and 40 percent of the world's. By the war's end, America had a three-to-one advantage in stockpiled weapons over its enemies. Finally, during the last 18 months of the war, as brutal and ruthless combat was being waged throughout the Pacific, each American warrior could count on 8,000 pounds of supplies for each two pounds that his Japanese counterpart received. This fact alone should have convinced the Japanese leadership of the futility of the war they continued to wage.[10]

The most effective machine that could be used to wage war on the enemy with minimal American casualties was the airplane. Although serving on an American bomber was perhaps the most hazardous duty in the American military in World War II, it was also the best way to bring enormous destruction to the enemy with a relatively small loss of American life. However, in order to wage a successful air campaign, the American people and the United Sates military had to agree that it was acceptable to wound and kill hundreds of thousands of German and Japanese non-combatants in the process of bringing this air campaign to our enemies. Pearl Harbor hardened the American heart, and there would be little condemnation when the American air campaign indiscriminately killed and maimed hundreds of thousands.

Airpower alone could not win the war. Even the most optimistic believers in the role of the airplane in modern war had to concede that men on the ground doing the dirty and dangerous work that infantries had done for millennium would still be necessary to defeat our enemies, but airpower could dramatically reduce the number of deaths these infantrymen would have to endure to achieve this victory. The combination of American production prowess, the suspension of the longstanding reticence to kill and wound civilians from the air, and the desire to reduce the number of American casualties, all made America's air war possible and forever changed the rules for how the United States waged war.[11]

Perhaps the weapon most responsible for winning the war in the Pacific was the B-29 Superfortress Bomber. A technological marvel for its day, the plane initially had so many problems that General Curtis Emerson LeMay, the man in charge of America's bombing program against Japan, was supposed to have said that "it had more bugs than the Smithsonian," and this was certainly true. At the factories where the planes were manufactured, inexperienced workers often made mistakes that could prove to be deadly for the men who operated the aircraft; but these problems did not stop the manufacturing of the planes, and often the various problems with aircraft were repaired after the planes were built. Slowly the geniuses that designed and built the first of these planes were able to improve their soundness; and over time, the aircraft did become more reliable.[12]

This enormous plane was the perfect marriage of American wealth and technological prowess. It had four propellers that were each 16 feet long, could carry 10 tons of bombs, fly at 357 miles per hour, and stay in the air for 16 hours.[13] Even more frightening than the plane was the cargo it often carried: M69 napalm bombs.

Initial bombing attacks against Japan were conducted during daylight from approximately 30,000 feet. However, the jet stream above Japan often caused bombs to drift far from their targets, and many bombing raids ended unsuccessfully with none of the targets being destroyed. General LeMay developed an audacious plan to better utilize his new super bomber and in the process bring Japan to its knees. Rather than drop bombs during the day from high altitudes, he would send his bombers over Japan at night flying at altitudes from five to six thousand feet. By flying at lower elevations, planes could carry heavier payloads, and ordnance dropped from lower altitudes would be impacted less by winds and more likely to hit its target.

A significant percentage of the buildings in Japan were constructed of bamboo, and there were few zoning regulations even in major cities. As a result both large and small factories were often constructed in the vicinity of schools, houses, apartments, and hospitals, and fuel for fire was everywhere. This combination would have horrifying consequences for the Japanese. Rather than bomb Japan into submission, General LeMay decided to burn it, and the combination of the B-29 Superfortress and M69 napalm made this possible. Napalm was put in a cheesecloth bag, and this was placed inside small pipes that measured twenty inches long and three inches in diameter. When these pipes hit the ground, they sat for a few seconds, and then exploded sending the ignited napalm-filled cheesecloth bags flying up to 100 yards in varying directions. The substance stuck to anything, burned at 1,000 degrees for six to ten minutes, was almost impossible to put out, and was spread by water.[14] Hundreds of small 6.2-pound cylinders containing napalm could be put into one bomb, and the cylinders would be sent hurling in all directions when the bomb landed and would do even more damage when deployed in bombs that detonated hundreds of feet above the target zone scattering the cylinders even further. Each B-29 Superfortress could carry 1,000 pounds of M69 napalm in addition to the pipes and cheesecloth that housed this terrifying substance.

Before most attacks, skilled pilots would fly in at an altitude of only 500 feet 45 minutes before the majority of the B-29s arrived. They would drop napalm canisters in a giant X pattern over the city, thus dividing it into four quadrants outlined by fire. Three hundred to eight hundred bombers would shortly arrive, and each was assigned one of the four quadrants in an effort to assure that the maximum area was incinerated.

On March 10, 1945, alone, 496,000 of the napalm-filled cylinders were dropped on Tokyo. The resulting inferno consumed much of the oxygen in the air, caused rivers and canals to boil, and destroyed 16 square miles of central Tokyo, 63 percent of the city's commercial district and 18 percent of its industrial capacity. Twenty-five percent of the city's buildings were gone, 1,000,000 people were homeless, and at least 80,000 were dead. It is best left to the imagination to determine what it was like for the tens of thousands of residents who tried to flee the fire in a city with a population of six million that only had enough concrete shelters to house 5,000 people and was filled with buildings constructed of bamboo.

By the war's end, after five months of B-29-delivered M69 napalm, at least 35 percent of most of Japan's cities had been rendered into ash; and some, like Kofu, had only 25 percent of their buildings intact. All of this fire left more than 9 million urban residents homeless, and most of these people were starving.[15]

Napalm was not the only ordnance that fell on the Japanese from American bombers. America's production prowess also enabled it to produce staggering numbers of traditional bombs; and throughout the Pacific, tens of thousands of Japanese warriors were blown to bits or forced to hunker underground as American bombers dropped thousands of tons of traditional bombs on islands prior to American invasions.

There were a number of reasons for America's productive supremacy in World War II. Unlike the Axis and other Allied powers, American production facilities were not under attack during the war. German cities were leveled and much production was moved underground. Thousands of Axis factories were destroyed, raw materials became scarce and difficult to transport, and as the war dragged on, both the Japanese and Germans became more and more dependent on slave labor. These workers were always mistreated and underfed, often brutalized, and forced to work in dangerous conditions. It is not surprising that the American workforce—made up of well-fed, motivated, and paid free citizens—out-produced the workforces in Germany and Japan composed of starving slaves or workers who were often hungry and under constant fear of being blown up.

The dynamic nature of the American social and economic system also benefited American production. The need for labor in America's factories inspired thousands of black Americans in the rural south to travel north to better their lives by attaining employment in factories producing war materials. Women abandoned their traditional roles in the home or office to work in American factories, and because the United States could mechanize agricultural production more than any other nation, farmers by the thousands left the plow and learned the skills necessary to produce the tools of war. Despite the fact that these new industrial workers had virtually no experience working in factories, America's output per worker-hour during the war was two times that of Germany's and five times that of Japan's. Unlike Germany and Japan, the United States had an abundant supply of domestic energy, and American factory managers did not have to worry about production being hindered by shortages of energy or an unreliable electrical grid.[16]

American industrialists quickly reorganized existing factories that had manufactured consumer goods to build the machines of war, and almost overnight massive new factories were constructed to manufacture weapons that had barely been on the drawing board only months earlier. Early in 1941 the Willow Run factory did not exist. In March 68 acres of Washtenaw County, Michigan, farmland were leveled, and 8 months later Henry Ford's massive Willow Run plant was producing the first of the plant's 8,500 B-24 bombers. Production at first was slow, the quality of the early planes was not good, and an elderly Henry Ford and his engineers found it difficult to utilize the mass-production techniques that helped them to produce millions of cars in the construction of warplanes. However, at Willow Run as in thousands of other factories throughout the United States during the war, America's engineers used their unique manufacturing genius to overcome these problems; and by 1944 the 40,000 men and women who worked at the plant were producing one B-24 Bomber, a plane that had over 100,000 parts, every 63 minutes.[17]

Willow Run is perhaps the best example of an immense American industrial concern adapting and evolving to meet the needs of the American war effort. Prior to the war, Ford Motor Company was already one of the largest corporations in the world; and for several decades it had been at the forefront of developing and implementing a factory system that employed tens of thousands of workers and produced millions of automobiles.

Higgins Industries, the company that built the boats on which the sailors of Motor Torpedo Boat Squadron 16 spent the war, played an equally important role in America's war effort, but its pre-war history was more humble, and consequently, its contribution is even more astonishing than Ford's and more indicative of the unique productive genius of America in the mid–20th century.

Andrew Jackson Higgins, the man behind Higgins Industries, was born in Columbus, Nebraska, on August 28, 1886. Like many self-made industrialists of the last century, he came from a humble background, was an indifferent student, and failed to graduate from high school. As a young man, he worked as a logger, truck driver, miner, bank officer, and saw mill operator. He eventually moved to New Orleans, and in 1916 he started A.J. Higgins Lumber and Export Company. Higgins enrolled in a correspondence course in naval architecture, completed the course, and was awarded a Bachelor's Degree. More importantly, a foundation was created that would eventually enable Higgins to become one of the foremost boat designers and manufacturers in the world.[18]

Coastal storms that damaged company facilities, putting trust in the wrong people, debt, and the inability of companies to pay back money they owed A.J. Higgins Lumber and Export Company forced Higgins's company to go out of business in October 1923. Higgins stayed involved in the lumber and boat-building business, and in September 1930, Higgins Industries was incorporated. This enterprise focused on boat construction, and in 1937 Higgins began to design and construct landing craft that he hoped the Navy would purchase. This marked the beginning of a series of battles he would fight with established civilian and naval procurement forces. The Bureau of Construction and Repair (BCR) was the organization within the Navy that oversaw the design and acquisition of many of the vessels built for the Navy. The decision makers in this organization were generally partial to the ship designs and modifications that were produced by the BCR or companies that had long done business with the BCR.[19]

However, as war approached, and it became more and more evident that the designs of the BCR were inferior to those developed by Higgins Industries, Higgins won the day, and Higgins Industries began to produce vessels for the Navy, Marines, and Army. Not only were the Higgins craft superior to their competition, but because Higgins Industries was able to produce the vessels in a production line for the first time, the cost to construct each vessel declined. The midwestern boy who came from humble beginnings would ultimately do as much for the Allied war effort as any individual.[20]

In 1937 Higgins Industries employed 50 people, and the firm produced primarily wooden boats. By June of 1941, with the United States still not at war, 1,600 were employed, and by the summer of 1944, as American production reached its peak, 20,000 people worked for Andrew Jackson Higgins, and a significant percentage of the vessels that came off its production lines were constructed of steel.[21]

The output of these workers was astonishing. They worked in seven different plants that encompassed 5,000,000 square feet under roof. Sixty-nine train cars carrying 2,427 tons of materials arrived every day.[22] At the peak of production, the Higgins factories produced 700 boats of various design and size per month, and by the war's end a total of 20,094 vessels had reached the end of Higgins Industries production lines and were used to transport men and supplies for the Army, Navy, and Marines.[23]

On Thanksgiving Day, 1944, just months after the successful invasion of Normandy, General Dwight David Eisenhower said of Higgins: "Let us thank God for Higgins Industries, management, and labor which has given us the landing boats with which to conduct our campaign." In an interview conducted after the war, the General referred to Higgins as, "the man who won the war for us."

As the war progressed, hundreds of companies like Higgins Industries constantly improved the efficiency with which they manufactured their products, and thus America's production advantage grew geometrically throughout the war. The United States constructed a total of 3,425 of its famous liberty ships during the war. The first one was completed on December 30, 1941, and took 355 days to build. By the middle of 1942, America could turn out one every 105 days, and by the end of the war one was floated out of a shipyard every 17 days. Our enemies could only dream of such improvements in industrial productivity.[24]

Between 1939 and 1945, America's gross national product almost tripled, and its productive capacity doubled. On the day Japan surrendered, America had 12,500,000 people in uniform, and a naval fleet larger than the combined fleets of all of the other navies in the world. As Japan struggled to meet the most basic fuel requirements for its shrinking fleet in the last 18 months of the war, America's Fifth Fleet consumed 3,800,000,000 gallons of fuel in one year.[25]

This production miracle was the result of a marriage between civilian and military leaders that was sometimes rancorous but that was ultimately successful. Not only did it make America's armed forces overwhelmingly more powerful than its enemies', but it also enabled the United States to provide 50 billion dollars of military and civilian supplies and services to 50 nations during the war years.[26]

The Japanese also made a gross miscalculation about what it meant to go to war with a great western nation. Japan's leaders saw the citizens of the United States as pampered, soft, and weak, and this national weakness would make them unwilling to pay the price necessary to defeat Imperial Japan. What the Japanese failed to understand was that when fully engaged western democracies were the most lethal military powers, and the United States was just the most recent in a long line of western societies who were not only willing to fight a long and deadly war, but who were also determined to fight a war of annihilation.

When the bombs landed on Pearl Harbor, the United States was not a nation of subjects who were ordered to respond by an emperor or dictator, but a country populated by millions of free citizens who demanded that their leaders not only wage war but wage it in such a way that the enemy was decimated and forced to surrender unconditionally. In many cases what emanated from America after Pearl Harbor was not hatred but an almost genocidal desire to completely destroy the nation that had attacked the United States. This national obsession with victory and vengeance combined with the exponential improvements in the quantity and quality of our weapons meant that the United States had the will and the ability to annihilate Japan. Perhaps the greatest irony of World War II was that despite what many on both sides believed, democracies were superior to dictatorships at mobilizing for war.[27]

This fundamental miscalculation on the part of the Japanese would prove to be fatal. Even after the disaster at Midway and the obvious and stark evidence that the arithmetic of the war was heavily stacked against them, the Japanese still believed that the innate weakness of their democratic enemies would force them to the bargaining table and that a peace favorable to Japan could be negotiated. The Japanese Empire was huge, and the Japanese wanted to make World War II a war of space. Their warriors could "dig and endure" and their ability and willingness to do this—even when starving, sick, and being relentlessly bombed—would make retaking the enormous space they occupied too costly for the Great Producer.

As the war progressed and Japanese fanaticism grew, America became more determined to fight a total war, the goal of which was annihilation and unconditional surrender; and it had the resources, manpower, industrial facilities, and expertise to accomplish this. The great tragedy of the war in the Pacific was that by miscalculating the ability and willingness of the United States to wage a total war on the Japanese, the Japanese not only guaranteed the destruction of their army, navy, and air forces, but the almost total obliteration of their nation.[28]

The two nations that went to war in December 1941 were separated not only by a huge expanse of ocean but also by a cultural divide that would play a major role in how the war was fought and ultimately how it was won. Anyone who has read America's founding documents or spent any time in the United States realizes that at the center of American society is the individual. Each citizen is born with inalienable rights, and it is the job of the government to protect these. The individual is largely free to navigate his way in life and place in society. Although class, race, religion, and numerous other aspects of an individual's makeup impact a citizen's place in America's social and economic hierarchy, individual liberty and autonomy were both at the core of what it meant to be an American citizen.

All of this would have been foreign to the people and governing class of Japan. Japan was a small island about the size of Montana with a population of 72 million people on the Japanese mainland. The country had few natural resources and little exposure to Christianity and the European Enlightenment that had done much to create modern western political, social, and economic systems. Isolated and with such a large population on such a small landmass, it is not surprising that the Japanese valued stability over liberty.

At the top of Japanese society was the emperor or Tenno, which means "heavenly sovereign." He was believed to be a descendant of the sun-goddess Amaterasu and was the source of national unity and enlightened rule. The military, which was growing stronger by the decade, was directly connected to him.[29] Other than the emperor, the military was the most important institution in Japan, and military thinking and procedures were dominated by a modified Bushido Code that was based on the traditions of Japan's ancient samurai or military class that had played a central role in Japanese society since the eighth century. By the late nineteenth century, with the threat from the west growing, Japan had to dramatically expand the size and power of its military, but while doing so it still tried to maintain many of the values of the samurai. The *Imperial Precepts for the Military* was published by the government in 1882, and it explained that the samurai values of loyalty and self-discipline were now to be the guiding values of even the lowest conscript in the Japanese military. In addition, Japanese military men were expected to be frugal, stoic, obedient, courageous, and possess a war-like spirit, much as the samurai did. In short, the samurai/Bushido traditions were to guide all of Japan's warriors.[30]

Japan prior to and during World War II was the consummate hierarchical society. Individuals were required to subordinate personal aspirations to the greater society; and to insure that this occurred, each person had to do what the individual above him said. Individuals almost never argued with those in authority, and in many ways closed-mindedness was a virtue. When the war broke out, all of Japan's people were cogs in a machine that had one purpose: winning the war. Defeat was never openly discussed or seen as a possibility. Since the individual mattered little, it was expected that each warrior would not only be completely obedient to those in charge, but would also fight fanatically and without restraint. If a warrior's life mattered little, then he should always be prepared to die, and those that opposed him in battle and non–Japanese civilians were even more expendable. Thus raping the women of defeated enemies and pillaging their belongings was accepted and even expected.[31]

Japanese military training was savagely violent. Men were brutalized by those of higher rank, intellectual training was minimized, and there was no room for discussion or imagination, especially in the enlisted ranks. Often this inflexible command structure resulted in warriors who were willing to die by the thousands in frontal charges that had no chance of success, but rarely showed imagination or took individual initiative in combat.

The goal of this brutality was to create a warrior who would follow orders without question, never retreat, and above all never surrender. Victory over any enemy, even one as potentially powerful as the United States, could be achieved if the warrior was fanatical enough. If all of the men of Japan would simply forget the self, "the mind could triumph over matter," and Japan would become the most powerful nation on earth. The Japanese warrior was often expected to live on almost nothing, and to fight so vigorously that a few thousand men could engage many times their number, and in the process sap the will to fight from their enemy. All was fair in war, and winning—even against America, the Great Producer—was simply a matter of each warrior possessing enough will.[32]

The Japanese had a name for this selfless warrior filled with fighting spirit that they would unleash on the world: Yamato-damashi, or Japanese spirit or "Spirit Warrior."[33] The training to create a Spirit Warrior began at a young age, and in many ways the primary goal of Japanese education was to create Spirit Warriors. Students were taught to subordinate themselves to the emperor. Military indoctrination was an integral component of traditional school subjects such as math, science, foreign language, and physical education. Each school had its own military officer assigned to it, and his job was to make sure that the Bushido Code was woven into the daily functions of the school and that each student learned that above all his job was to subordinate his own aspirations and sacrifice everything for the good of the state. Students learned to do what they were told and follow the rules that dictated behavior in all aspects of society. They were taught to always respect those above them, to stand at attention and salute when in the presence of a superior, and to accept the vicious corporal punishment they received for most infractions—no matter how minor—quietly and without complaint or resistance. The brutality that was regularly inflicted on students by their superiors was often inflicted by these same students on those below them as their status in the Japanese hierarchy increased.[34]

Fear of death would hurt the soldier's ability to win. Consequently, students and warriors were taught that their lives meant nothing beyond what they could do for the emperor and that only by embracing dying for the emperor could victory be ensured and honor brought to the family.[35]

There were three main components to the Japanese Spirit Warrior. The first was that the Spirit Warrior was expected to fight to the death and surrender was never an option. In 1908 the army's criminal code stated, "A commander who allows his unit to surrender to the enemy without fighting to the last man or who concedes a strategic area to the enemy shall be punishable by death.... Do not be taken prisoner alive."[36] Later the Japanese military field code explained, "Rather than live and bear the shame of imprisonment by the enemy, he should die and avoid leaving a dishonorable name." It also explained, "Never give up a position but rather die." There was no instruction in any of these manuals about how to surrender.[37]

Brutality was deemed to be essential to creating a Spirit Warrior. Military recruits were slapped, kicked, and beaten with fists and bamboo poles. Beatings were at the heart of military training, and enlisted men were expected to beat those of lower rank often and without mercy. Finally, unquestioned obedience was expected of all enlisted men in the Japanese military. Officers represented the emperor, which meant that any order came from the infallible, divine leader; consequently, all orders were legal.[38]

Because the men in Japan's armed forces were deemed to be expendable, treated cruelly, and expected to be cruel to the enemy, it is not surprising that the war in the Pacific was brutal and especially deadly for the Japanese. Officers often lacked imagination, and when a battle was obviously lost, instead of surrendering or retreating, they would often order their men to make suicidal frontal assaults. Desperate Japanese soldiers would scream "banzai," a traditional greeting for the emperor, which meant 10,000 years or eternal life, as they charged into American guns and bayonets. Such acts almost never resulted in victory and instead only brought "honorable" death.[39]

The combination of single-minded soldiers, often desperate to die for the emperor and willing to engage in fanatical, suicidal frontal attacks, and leaders who often cared little for the men under their command, resulted in a staggering death rate for Japanese warriors. At Tarawa and Makin more than 99 percent of Japanese soldiers died. At Kwajulein, even though the Americans had nine warriors to every two Japanese that opposed them, the Japanese refused to surrender; and their fanatical charges resulted in the Japanese losing 21 men to every 1 American who was killed. Only 2 percent of the Japanese soldiers survived the battle. Tragically, as deadly as battle was for Japanese soldiers, only one-third of all Japanese deaths in the Pacific were the result of combat against the Allies. The rest of the fatalities were the result of Japanese leaders abandoning troops on islands thousands of miles from home. Most of these men needlessly starved or perished after suffering from a jungle or other disease.[40]

To comprehend the events that were about to unfold for the Allied forces in the Pacific in the last year of the war, it is important to understand the Japanese strategy for victory in the Pacific. After the attack on Pearl Harbor, the Japanese forces were able to "run wild" in the Pacific. Europe's Pacific powers were either controlled by Japan's ally Germany or devoting the bulk of their military resources to resisting the Nazi regime. The American fleet was decimated, and in early 1942 her ability to strike back at Imperial Japan was minimal. This meant that after the attack on Pearl Harbor, Japan was the dominant power in the Pacific. However, the Japanese High Command also realized that by attacking the United States they had awakened a sleeping giant, and most understood what this would mean.

A militarized America could create the most formidable war machine the world had ever known. American farms and industries could produce more food, ships, planes, tanks, munitions, and all of the other products necessary to wage war than all of her adversaries combined. The United States had a much larger population than Japan; and over time America could create ground, air, and naval forces far greater than the Rising Sun's. In short, America's leaders were determined to make World War II a war of production, and in that contest, no nation could equal the United States.

Japan's response to this reality was simple, lethal, and terrifying. They would force the United States to sue for a peace that was favorable to Japan not because she could equal America's production and thus win a protracted military campaign, but because Japan was spiritually superior to the United States and produced Spirit Warriors that America did not. They would make the war a confrontation between "fanaticism and firepower," and they believed that in this confrontation, fanaticism could prevail. America's overwhelming production advantage might enable its military forces to eventually win most of the battles, but these victories could only be won by killing nearly all of the Spirit Warriors they engaged; and in the process, the Americans would have to sustain enormous casualties of their own, which the Japanese High Command believed was the Achilles heel of the Great Producer. American democracy did not produce Spirit Warriors, and American citizens did not see their sons dying in battle as their highest calling. Eventually, the Spirit Warriors' willingness to kill and be killed would cause their softer, democratic opponents to grow weak, weary of war, and sue for peace. Even after the disasters of Midway and Leyte, most in Japan believed that the Spirit Warrior could still win the war and that much of the hard-won Japanese Empire could remain under Japanese control. But to achieve this victory, a new manifestation of the terrifying Spirit Warrior had to be unleashed on the American naval forces in numbers not yet seen…. The Special Attack Corps or the kamikaze.[41]

By early 1944, Japanese naval and army pilots had numerous disadvantages when they faced American flyers. At this point in the war, most of the brilliant carrier pilots who had played such an important role in Japan's stunning success in the first months of the conflict were gone.[42] At the same time that the United States was producing the best trained pilots in the world flying progressively superior planes, Japanese pilots saw their training limited, and the quality of the planes they flew remained almost stagnant. In the last years of the war, American pilots would receive an average of 600 hours of flight training and be sent into combat with state-of-the art planes. Largely as the result of the critical shortage of fuel and a desire to save fuel for a final battle on the Japanese homeland, their Japanese counterparts received fewer than 100 hours of flight training, and many kamikaze pilots were not even trained to land their aircraft for obvious reasons.[43]

Poorly trained pilots were sent into combat in planes such as the once vaunted Val dive-bomber that had not had significant design upgrades since before the war.[44] In addition, as the war progressed, the quality of Japanese fuel declined, and this reduced the performance capabilities of Japanese planes. The results were predictable. During the last two years of the war, American pilots almost always bested their Japanese counterparts when they met in aerial combat.[45]

The Bushido/Spirit Warrior mindset coupled with the desperate position Japan now found itself in the war made the formation of the Kamikaze Force inevitable. Believing that if land and sea forces were making such extraordinary sacrifices, the commanders of Japan's Imperial Navy Air Service and Army Air Force argued that Japanese pilots should also make additional sacrifices; and in desperation, the Japanese created and then unleashed their Kamikaze Force. In the months that followed, Japan would become more dependent on these suicidal warriors in their fight against the Allies; and although these human-powered guided missiles proved to be deadly, terrifying and a huge problem for the American forces in the Philippines, they never threatened to change the course of the war as the Japanese hoped.

The suicide planes were named after the divine wind or large typhoon that came out of the East China Sea and swept across the Sea of Japan in 1274 and again in 1281 and destroyed the invasion forces the Kublai Khan had sent to Japan. One hundred and fifty thousand invaders were drowned, and the myth grew that the Japanese people had been chosen by the gods and their land was unconquerable. The name kamikaze comes from "god" kami and "wind" kaze. Interestingly, this name was used by the Americans during the war as the name for all suicide attacks, but it did not come into favor in Japan until the years after the conflict ended and the United States was occupying Japan. Warriors in the Imperial Japanese Navy called the Kamikaze Force Shimpu Tokubetsu-Kogekitai. Shimbu means "gathering of courageous forces." Members of the Japanese military used the abbreviated names To, Tokko-tai or Tokubetsu-Kogekitai when referring to the Kamikaze Corps.[46]

Officially, all pilots in the Kamikaze Corps were volunteers, and most were told by Vice Admiral Takijiro Onishi or some other high-ranking officer after they volunteered, "Having stepped up to the task, you have all become young gods with no earthly desires."[47] At least officially, first sons, only children, and children from single parents were not eligible for the suicide services; but it is impossible to know how rigidly the Japanese adhered to this rule, especially in the last desperate months of the war. Most of the kamikaze pilots were between eighteen and twenty years of age.[48]

The first official suicide units were formed in the fall of 1944 when the battle for the Philippines was about to commence. On October 19, Vice Admiral Onishi went to Clark

Field near Manila and asked Zero pilots to volunteer to be special pilots. Pilots were told they would be flying planes loaded with 550-pound bombs into enemy ships. Future kamikaze missions would be loaded with bombs of different weights depending on variables such as the length of the flight and the availability of bombs. The largest bomb used was 1,763 pounds, but the 550-pound bombs employed in the earliest attacks were used on the majority of missions. Despite the price these young men were being asked to pay, all volunteered, and in the future when groups of young pilots were asked to join the Special Attack Corps, a large majority almost always enlisted.[49]

Why did so many young Japanese men agree to fly these missions? Certainly the indoctrination process aimed at creating Spirit Warriors that had begun when the pilots first started school played an important role. Most also believed that their lives were not their own and instead they belonged to a higher authority and ultimately the emperor. It was deemed to be an honor to die for the nation, and their Shinto beliefs taught them that when they died their spirits would join the spirits of other deceased warriors at the Imperial Palace in Tokyo's Yasukuni Shrine.[50] In addition, many of the pilots were still teenagers or in their early twenties, and at a point in their lives when they were susceptible to peer pressure. The nation had to be spiritually mobilized if it was to win the war. Each citizen had to do his part in this mobilization, and crashing a plane into an enemy ship would not only bring honor to the young pilot, but would lead to an eternity of honor for his family.[51]

Before taking off on what was almost always their last mission, there were a variety of rituals performed by each pilot. Some would recite the *Song of the Warrior*:

> In serving on the seas, be a corpse saturated with water.
> In serving on land, be a corpse covered with weeds.
> In serving the sky, be a corpse that challenges the clouds.
> Let us all die close by the side of our sovereign.

There was usually a ceremony where food was served and the pilot drank sake. Prior to this, a final letter had usually been sent to the pilot's family, and in the envelope or package the young man almost always included nail clippings, hair, or even a finger that would be cremated and then placed in the family shrine.[52]

Certain articles often accompanied the young pilot when he entered the plane's cockpit. Most wore some combination of the hachimaki or headband and sen-nin-bari or thousand stitches belt, and many also took a mascot doll or masukotto ningyo and/or a sword. Often one or more of these items was made by a family member or female admirer, and generally it was the pilot's choice as to which, if any, of these items went with him on his final flight.[53]

Surprisingly, kamikaze pilots often took off with no real plan; and as the war waged on, attacks seemed to become even more random. Pilots were often told to attack a ship of their choosing, and rarely did a group of suicide pilots coordinate plans before they began their mission. What they all knew was they were expected to die trying to sink an American ship or boat, or destroy a shore installation; and even if they changed their minds during the mission, most had little training landing planes, so they would most likely crash-land and die even if they did not intentionally ram into a target.[54] The first kamikaze pilots had much success. Not only were the Allies unprepared for this new weapon, but early kamikaze pilots tended to have more experience than the young men who would pilot the planes in the last phase of the war.[55]

Most Japanese did not see the special attack mission as an act of suicide. Instead, it was viewed as a military tactic that enabled one pilot or a small number of pilots to destroy an enemy ship; and on rare occasions, one suicide plane could set off an explosion that would damage more than one ship. The pilot's death was a byproduct of this tactic, not the goal of the mission.[56]

Initially, aircraft carriers were the preferred targets of the suicide planes. The elevators that lifted the planes up to the carrier decks created a pathway for explosions and fire to penetrate into the large hanger lockers in the ship's interior, and it was difficult to contain these fires.[57] As the use of the suicide planes increased, all ships and boats were deemed to be worthy targets, and the Japanese did not appear to discriminate between different kinds of vessels when launching their attacks. Although both the Japanese Army and Navy had Special Attack Units, they rarely coordinated attacks. If they had, it is likely the units could have damaged Allied naval forces even more than they did.[58]

There were two basic attack routes used by the kamikaze pilots. The first required them to fly to an altitude of 16,000 to 20,000 feet and use the clouds for cover. They would then dive at their target at a 45 to 55 degree angle. This steep attack angle made it more difficult for Allied gunners to hit them, but it also made it more difficult for pilots to adjust their flight-path if necessary; and many of the planes that attacked this way crashed harmlessly in the water. The advantage of this attack route was the plane achieved great speed by the time it hit its target and would penetrate deeply into the ship's deck and potentially do more damage when the ordnance carried by the plane exploded. The second attack route used was to fly in from a low angle and attempt to crash into the less well-defended stern of the ship or boat. This low attack trajectory made it more difficult for radar operators to detect the attacking planes, and it also made it more difficult for ship and boat gunners to fire at them since the lower trajectory of their fire was more likely to hit nearby vessels. Planes flying at this lower angle that hit their targets often did less damage than planes that dove from high above because they would be unable to achieve as fast a speed as their diving counterparts. Once the attack route was determined, pilots would seek out a suitable target, steer their planes toward it, and then prior to the crash arm the one or two bombs they carried.[59]

The kamikaze was a ferocious weapon, and it took a psychological toll on the men who had to face them. Not only did sailors have to fear that their boats or ships would be blown up by the suicide planes, but they also had to ask themselves what kind of warrior would fly a bomb-laden plane into a ship? American leadership worked hard to prevent the American public from learning about the new weapon. Allied officers and enlisted men were told not to mention the kamikazes when they went home on leave. Mail was checked to make sure that letters did not mention kamikazes, and the majority of Americans did not learn of the suicide attacks until April 1945, when they were used by the hundreds in the Battle of Okinawa.[60]

The arithmetic of defending against the kamikaze was frightening, and even Admiral Halsey, not a man who scared easily, admitted that the kamikaze was "The only weapon I feared in war." As Admiral John Sidney "Slew" "Popeye" McCain, perhaps the American officer who was most instrumental in developing the American strategy to combat the suicide planes, explained, "Before the innovation of the suicide attacks…, destruction of eighty or ninety percent of his attackers was considered an eminent success. Now one hundred percent destruction of the attackers is necessary to preserve the safety of the task force."[61]

When the Special Attack Force was first unleashed, American ships were caught off guard, and no tactics had been developed to avoid or destroy this new weapon. However, in short order new protocols were developed and these became more effective as a greater number of suicide planes were encountered. Initially, American boats and ships responded to kamikaze attacks by concentrating massive firepower on the man-guided bombs. This was easier said than done. Often planes arrived out of nowhere and surprised the crews and more than one would attack a given ship. When one plane or group of planes was destroyed others might soon arrive hell-bent on blowing up the same vessel.[62]

In time naval leaders developed more complex tactics to prevent the suicide planes from achieving their goals. When a fleet of naval craft sailed together, the destroyers—referred to as "Tom Cat" picket destroyers—with the most up-to-date radar and aircraft homing devices to assist American pilots in locating Japanese planes, would sail up to 60 miles from the rest of the ships. Planes returning to aircraft carriers were instructed to fly over these destroyers and turn in a predetermined direction. The main fleet would then be instructed that these planes were not kamikazes. This was done to prevent kamikazes, referred to as "Tail-End Charlies" when they hid among American planes, from flying in close proximity to American planes as the American airmen were on their way back to their carriers and then breaking away at the last minute and crashing into American ships. In addition, carrier-launched planes would form combat air patrols or CAPs. If necessary, CAPs would fly into the returning American planes, seek out any Japanese planes among their ranks, and "delouse them."[63]

Finally, the composition of the Naval Air Force was changed. Prior to the kamikaze, a typical American aircraft carrier sailed with 38 fighters, 36 dive-bombers, and 18 torpedo-bombers. Once the United States Navy realized the full potential of the Japanese kamikaze, carriers sailed with as many as 73 fighters and only 15 dive-bombers and 15 torpedo-bombers. The logic of this was simple, the further from American vessels a kamikaze could be destroyed, the less likely it could damage or sink an American ship. Fortunately, by the time the Japanese were employing suicide planes against the Allies, the pilots that took off from American carriers and airfields were almost always superior to the ones behind the controls of the kamikaze, and the once-vaunted Zero or other aircraft flown by the Japanese pilots were almost always inferior to the planes flown by American pilots.[64]

It is difficult to determine when the first kamikaze attack occurred in World War II. In mid–1944, as the force was being formally organized, some Japanese pilots, acting on their own, occasionally attempted to fly their planes into enemy ships after they had been hit, and some intentionally crashed into American planes destroying both planes in the act.[65] On the morning of October 21, 1944, during the invasion of Leyte and just days before the fateful Battle of Leyte Gulf, HMAS *Australia* was hit by a Japanese plane that had been hit by defensive fire. The captain of the vessel and 19 others were killed, and 54 were wounded. Some sources classify this as the first official aerial suicide attack against Allied forces; but others dispute this conclusion because although the Japanese pilot rammed into the ship intentionally, it was not a pre-planned suicide mission.[66]

On October 24 and 25, 1944, the first official kamikaze attacks occurred during the Battle of Leyte Gulf. Ten Allied ships were hit and the 512-foot escort carrier USS *Saint Lo* was sunk killing 114 men.[67] As the battle raged for the Philippines, the Japanese became more and more dependent on the Kamikaze Force, but even fanatical Japanese military leaders realized that suicide planes could not defeat the United States. However, they hoped these terrifying manned bombs would improve morale at home, set an example for all military and non-military personnel, delay further advances by the United States into Japanese held territory, and force the Allies to reconsider their insistence on unconditional surrender and instead negotiate a peace that was favorable to Japan.[68]

The suicide plane was a terrifying weapon. They attacked both small boats and large ships. They often came out of nowhere, and a quiet, peaceful morning could be interrupted by a lone plane or two crashing in to a boat or ship, killing dozens, if not hundreds, and even sending the vessel to the ocean's bottom. Even kamikaze hits that failed to do great damage to the ship could be terrifying. Exploding suicide planes would send a barrage of metal, gasoline, and often the blood, arms, legs and other body parts of the dead pilot hurling all over the vessel's deck. There is no doubt that hundreds of gunners throughout the Pacific Fleet lost sleep knowing their skill or lack of it might be the difference between life and death for the men on their ship.[69]

How successful were these suicide attacks? Initially, the Japanese had hoped one plane could destroy one ship. Had these results been achieved, there is no telling how this would have impacted the outcome of the war. Fortunately, the suicide planes never approached this level of success.[70] In the Philippines there were 650 kamikaze attacks. Approximately 27 percent of these planes hit their target, and three percent of the vessels hit were sunk. This percentage was almost doubled at Okinawa, the last major battle of the war.[71]

Although the Japanese often exaggerated the impact of the suicide attacks, they did cause serious damage to the American naval force in the Pacific. In total there were 2,550 kamikaze attacks in World War II, and 407 Allied vessels were damaged or destroyed by these suicide planes. The exact number of fatalities caused by suicide planes during the war is debated by military historians. As many as 12,000 men were killed by kamikazes and more than 10,000 were injured.[72]

The success of the kamikaze led to the creation of many more suicide weapons, although none of these were as widely used or as successful as the suicide plane. Had the war not ended when it did, and the United States invaded Japan, it is likely that an enormous variety and number of suicide weapons would have been employed by the Japanese as their cause became more desperate.

Suicide soldiers were equipped with a pole that had an explosive charge at the end. The warriors would run at a tank and drive the explosive-tipped pole into it causing an explosion that would disable the tank and kill the soldier. Suicide swimmers would swim to docked or anchored boats, attach bombs to the vessel's hulls below the water line, and then explode the bombs.[73] Fukuryu or "Crouching Dragons" were men equipped with underwater breathing suits and explosive-tipped poles who would swim through the water or walk on the sea floor underneath an enemy naval vessel and then drive the explosive tipped pole into the boat's hull blowing a hole in the hull and killing the man who had made it.

"Sherman Carpets" were a particularly sinister suicide weapon. Children equipped with backpacks filled with explosives were trained to throw themselves under tank treads and set off the explosives. The explosion would kill the child and disable the tank. This suicide weapon was to be employed if the United States invaded Japan, although there is some evidence that they were used during the Battle of Okinawa.[74]

The famous Type 93 or Long Lance torpedo that had served the Japanese so well in the war was modified into a suicide weapon. The torpedo was cut in half and widened to make room for a pilot. The fuel tank was enlarged, and a small air tank and a 3,418-pound bomb, almost three times the size of what the torpedoes normally carried, were installed. These Kaitens or "Turn toward Heaven" were generally launched underwater from the deck of a submarine.[75]

Midget submarines were tiny submarines that were employed by the Japanese for most of the war. The pilot was expected to approach the stern on an enemy ship, drop a depth charge set to explode at a shallow depth, and then attempt to flee. It was unlikely that the man operating the vessel would live through the blast that followed.[76]

In the Philippines, the Japanese deployed suicide boats called Shinyo or "Ocean Shakers." These were plywood craft 16.5 to 21 feet in length powered by a car engine. They had a light machine gun mounted on the bow and were generally loaded with depth charges, 260 pounds of dynamite, or they had bombs mounted on the bow. They would be hidden near shore under the jungle canopy or in caves, and would be sent out at night. They could travel up to 100 miles, and once they found their target, they would drop their depth charges next to it or ram the craft and detonate the bomb in the suicide boat's bow. They almost never returned once they were sent out after an enemy vessel. During the battle for the Philippines, PT boats regularly patrolled off the coast of Luzon and other islands in search of these weapons so they could be destroyed before they were unleashed on American vessels.[77]

In August 1944 a call was sent out all over Japan for volunteers to operate a new secret weapon that some believed could change the course of the war. Hundreds of men responded, and it is likely that all were shocked and perhaps awed when they saw the aircraft they would pilot to their deaths.

The craft was between 18 and 20 feet long with stubby wings attached halfway down its metal fuselage. At the base of the suicide weapon were two tail rudders made of cloth-covered plywood, and on the bottom were three rocket nozzles that stuck out from the three rocket engines mounted in the craft's lower section. Several things made this weapon unique. First, it was one of the few rocket-powered machines that would be piloted by a man used in World War II. In addition, unlike the conventional planes flown by kamikaze pilots, this new weapon was designed to be a suicide weapon. Once it was launched, it would be impossible for the pilot to survive.

The new weapon was called the Maru Dai Special Attack Craft, but the more common name was Oka or "Exploding Cherry Blossom." American sailors disdainfully referred to them as Bakas, which was Japanese for fool or idiot. Okas, with the pilots inside, would be harnessed to a Japanese Mitsubishi G4M "Betty" bomber. The range of each Oka would be determined by the altitude of the bomber when the Maru Dai was released. Generally, it was calculated that Okas could travel up to 10 times the altitude the bomber had reached when the weapon was let go, which meant that under most circumstances a Maru Dai could travel approximately 20 miles to its target once released. The aircraft carried a 2,600-pound armor-piercing warhead that the Japanese believed was powerful enough to sink even the largest Allied ship. In September 1944 the first Okas were built, and in total 800 were constructed. It was hoped that they would change the course of the war.[78]

As the battle waged for the Philippines, and it became clear to the Japanese that American forces would soon take the island of Leyte, 100 Okas and a number of support personnel were loaded on to the Japanese aircraft carrier *Shinano* bound for Formosa and the Philippines. Unknown to the officers and crew on the ship, they were being followed by the American submarine USS *Archer-Fish* (SS-311). On November 29, the submarine hit *Shinano* with four torpedoes; and soon the ship sank taking her crew, the 100 Okas, the Okas' technical support personnel, and their pilots to the ocean's bottom.

On December 1, 88 newly manufactured Okas were transported over land to Kure. From here they were to be sent to the Philippines and Formosa. With the successful American landing on the island of Mindoro in December 1944, the Japanese became desperate to stop their advance and to prevent the Americans from taking the vital Philippine island of Luzon and continuing their advance toward Japan. Okas and their pilots and support personnel were loaded on to aircraft carriers *Unryu* and *Ryuho* bound for Luzon. On December 19, while the Japanese ship was still hundreds of miles from its destination, submarine USS *Redfish* (SS-395) thwarted the Japanese plans when it sank *Unryu*. This raised the total of Okas destroyed by the Americans to approximately 138, and the deadly aircraft had yet to attack an American ship. *Ryuho* and the Okas onboard were rerouted to Formosa, and the suicide weapons would play no role in the battle for the Philippines. For the remainder of the war they would be launched only from planes that took off from mainland airfields. This eliminated any chance that the new weapon would dramatically impact the outcome of the war unless the United States was forced to invade the Japanese mainland. Had the new weapon arrived at the Philippines in time to be used at Mindoro, it is possible that the reduced American air presence would have resulted in the frightening weapon sinking many American ships.[79]

As the war progressed, all Japanese citizens, including women, children, and the elderly, were expected to be Spirit Warriors if the war came to them. In June 1944, thousands of civilians on Saipan were forced to participate in the "dying game." Civilians were used as shields, and mass hangings of civilians were common to insure that no Japanese man, woman or child was alive when defeat came. Thousands fled to Marpi Point on Saipan's northern tip to avoid the advancing American soldiers and Marines, and hundreds leaped off the cliffs to the rocks and surf 200 feet below and met their death. Whole families jumped together, parents stabbed, shot, and strangled children and one woman jumped while in the act of giving birth. Those who were reluctant or unwilling to join in the mass suicide were encircled by the Japanese soldiers. Some were shot, and this terrified the rest into making the fateful leap. In total, 22,000, or two-thirds of the civilian population, died, and thousands of these because they too adhered to the Spirit Warrior belief that it was better to kill oneself than to be defeated and live to tell of it. This "militaristic collectivism" that insisted that civilians and warriors were linked in Japan's efforts to win the war also led to horrifying actions by civilians as the battle was waged on Okinawa and numerous other islands in the Japanese Empire. The conclusion reached by American warriors doing the killing on the ground and those charged with planning the final chapter to the war in the Pacific was that to defeat Japan the United States would have to be willing to fight a war of "extermination"; America would have to, "kill them all."[80]

After the war ended, Japan's naval minister Admiral Mitsumasa Yonai explained, "When you took the Philippines, that was the end of our resources."[81] Clearly with no hope of ever gaining control of the sea or air, and without even the minimal raw materials necessary to wage war available, Japan could not win the war. With an impending Allied invasion of Japan on the horizon, many in the highest ranks of the Japanese military and government believed that if Japan was invaded the entire nation needed to die fighting their enemies or commit suicide rather than surrender.[82]

On June 8, 1945, Emperor Hirohito and Prime Minister Kantaro Suzuki endorsed Ketsu-Go or "Decisive Operation" as the "fundamental policy to be followed henceforth in the conduct of the War." Military leaders planned to have tens of thousands takayari butai, old men and women and children, armed with long wooden spears tipped with whatever was available, confront the Americans on the beaches. Fuel had been carefully stored in reserve for the 10,000 planes, at least half of which would be manned by suicide pilots charged with sinking loaded American troop carriers, and 3.5 to 5 million soldiers and a staggering 32 million men and women who made up the national militia were all readied for the final battle.

The propaganda that had worked so successfully to persuade the Japanese to sacrifice themselves rather than accept American victory on Japanese held islands in the Pacific was also employed on the mainland. Civilians were told that the Americans would rape women and girls, eat children, and send dogs to kill young boys and girls. American Marines were barbarians who had murdered their own mothers before they went to war.

This was what millions of Japanese civilians believed awaited them. Few questioned those in authority or the need to sacrifice everything in defense of the motherland. Earlier in the war Prime Minister Hideki Tojo had pledged "death of the entire nation if the war was lost," and Tojo's sentiments still prevailed in both civilian and military populations.[83]

Each citizen would be expected to choose death over surrender, and if defeat came, it would only come after the Japanese people had fought, died, or killed themselves and were no more. Even children were not spared from this thinking. The young were taught to defend kokutai or "national polity," and if necessary they were told that the entire Japanese race would perish to defend this.

The date set by the United States for Operation Olympic, the invasion of Japan, was November 1, 1945, and we can only imagine what the final clash between America, the Great Producer, and the Japanese Spirit Warrior would have meant for both the invaders and the people of Japan.[84]

More than 70 years after the war's conclusion, many still question America's decision to drop atomic bombs on Hiroshima and Nagasaki. The reality in 1945 was that Japan would only have surrendered without the bombs after it fought and lost a horrific battle on the home islands that would have killed or maimed millions or after an Allied blockade, probably lasting years, caused Japan to "die on the vine." Experience throughout the Pacific with this latter policy proved that before Japan would have succumbed, millions would have starved or died of disease. Even Emperor Hirohito acknowledged after the war that the bomb allowed the Japanese to "save face." The target of the atomic bombs was not just the cities that were incinerated by them but the mind of the Japanese people. In the end, something needed to break the Spirit Warrior mindset that had played such a significant role in Japan's decision to go to war and in the way millions of Japanese warriors fought and died so desperately and courageously throughout her far-flung Empire. The will of the Spirit Warrior had to be changed, and tragically, it took two atomic weapons and tens of thousands of lives to do this.

Certainly, none of the men in Squadron 16 knew anything about Spirit Warriors, the Okas or most of the other Japanese suicide weapons. They had heard of and even seen kamikaze planes in use, but it is unlikely the men of Squadron 16 realized how many suicide planes awaited the American naval forces that were soon to depart for Mindoro. Up until this point in the war, my father and the men in Squadron 16 had been relatively lucky. They had motored thousands of miles, navigated through violent seas, and endured cold, loneliness, homesickness, anxiety, and fear. They had been in close proximity to battle and engaged the Japanese in a limited way while on barge patrol, but for the most part, they had avoided the full ferocity of the war. Soon their luck would end, and they would be left on Mindoro to defend the island against the Japanese and their suicide planes piloted by Spirit Warriors.[85]

8

Mindoro

We hated to see the dawn come, because sooner or later one of our PT boats was going to get hit. —Unidentified PT boat sailor on Mindoro

Invasion: December 12–15, 1944

On December 12, 1944, the Visayan Attack Force, under the command of 50-year-old Rear Admiral Arthur Dewey Struble, left Leyte bound for the island of Mindoro. The men leading this first convoy to Mindoro had several goals. First, they hoped to land troops on the island's beaches and quickly drive inland and capture the Japanese airfields and the city of San Jose. These airfields were thought to be in poor repair, but American military leaders were confident they could quickly be made functional. They next wanted to land naval personnel on the island, establish a base for PT boats, and then construct additional airstrips as needed.

Sailing as part of this large and formidable fleet was my father in Task Unit 70.1.4, which was under the command of Lieutenant Commander Davis and composed of PT boat Squadrons 13 and 16, and boats *227* and *230*. Fearing Japanese attack from the air as they motored to Mindoro, all of the PT boat sailors were ordered to stand condition two watches; and obviously, all crew members would be required to be on duty if the boats came under attack. It is doubtful if my father or any of the men in Squadron 16 thought much about American production or Spirit Warriors while on this voyage. Their world was a tiny boat, their fellow sailors in Squadron 16, a huge ocean, and the distant—and I imagine mysterious—island of Mindoro.[1]

The island they were about to invade was the seventh largest in the Philippines. It measured 58 miles wide and 110 long at its largest points. Its name came from the Spanish *Mina de oro* or gold mine, although none of the precious metal was ever found on the island. Its interior was wild, thickly vegetated, and mountainous, with Mount Halcon, the highest peak on the island, reaching an elevation of 8,481 feet. The perimeter of Mindoro was flat, and beaches and mosquito-infested marshland stretched along the shoreline. Most of the island's 117,000 inhabitants lived along the coast and supported themselves by farming citrus, bananas, coconuts, rice, maze, and sugarcane. Eight indigenous tribes with an unknown population lived in the island's interior. For the most part, these people kept to themselves, but during their time on Mindoro, my father and his squadron mates did occasionally encounter them when they hiked into the island's interior.

In the southern part of Mindoro was Mangarin Bay. This was a deep and well-protected cove close to San Jose, the island's most important city; and it was in Mangarin Bay that the PT boat crews would build their base. Although quiet, sparsely inhabited, and little influenced by the outside world in the years leading up to World War II, the island did have a long and interesting history. The people of Mindoro had traded with the Chinese as early as 972, and Charles Mann concluded in *1493: Uncovering the New World Columbus Created* that it was on Mindoro that Spanish, Chinese, and Filipino traders first exchanged goods, thus beginning the global trading system that dominates the economies of the world today. It is doubtful if my father and his shipmates knew any of this as they motored their boats and readied their psyches for the ordeal they were about to face.[2]

Although the United States would eventually control almost all of Mindoro, General MacArthur initially intended to occupy only the southwest coast of the island around San Jose. This area was an alluvial plain that extended five miles inland and about 33 miles along the island's coast. The town of San Jose was a short five miles from the beaches. Fortunately, there was no real road system on the island, and the few trails that existed were easy to seal off or control, thus preventing the Japanese troops on the island free movement.

Many in the Pentagon opposed the Mindoro invasion because they thought it was too risky. They believed the island was surrounded by too many other Japanese controlled islands, feared the destructive power of the newly formed Kamikaze Force, and worried that the invasion fleet could not be provided with adequate air cover during the 550-mile voyage. Admirals Nimitz and Kinkaid both argued with General MacArthur against the invasion. They feared that American ships would be too vulnerable to kamikaze attacks, especially when they passed through the narrow Surigao Strait, and they also worried that the rainy weather over Leyte would prevent supporting aircraft from flying. Ultimately General MacArthur won the argument.

To increase the chances that the invasion would be a success and to hopefully reduce the losses that the invasion fleet would suffer, the Americans did several things prior to the invasion to confuse the Japanese. First, they did not bombard Mindoro, and instead ignored it in the weeks and days before the invasion; and they instructed the Filipino guerrillas on the island to lie low and not engage the Japanese. They also sent out a series of dummy radio messages from a variety of different ships in different locations that they knew the Japanese would intercept. These were designed to confuse the Japanese and make it more difficult for them to ascertain America's next move. They hoped that this lack of action by American bombers and the guerrillas would trick the Japanese into believing that Mindoro was not the next island in the Philippines that the Americans planned to attack.

Naval planners had initially set December 5 as the date for the Mindoro invasion. However, despite the difficulties caused by postponing such an enormous undertaking, Admirals Kinkaid, Halsey, and Nimitz all agreed the invasion should be put off 10 days, and they were able to convince General MacArthur that this delay was warranted. There were several reasons for the postponement. First, the airstrips on Leyte that would be vital for the planes that would provide air cover for the Mindoro invasion force during the first part of its journey were not complete. In addition, the pilots, sailors and ships in Task Force 38, which would also provide air cover for the invasion fleet, needed additional rest and repair after the recently won Battle of Leyte Gulf.[3]

During the Battle of Leyte Gulf, Admiral Halsey got a taste of the destructive potential of the kamikaze. Although the Japanese disaster at Leyte Gulf made the Philippine Sea an "American Lake," he was fearful of what the "kami boys" would do to American ships and boats as they fanatically fought to maintain control of Mindoro and then Luzon. Admiral McCain had pondered this problem extensively and proposed sending Task Force 38 and its seven heavy carriers, six light carriers, nine battleships, 16 cruisers, 60 destroyers, 540 planes, 150 dive bombers, and 140 torpedo bombers to within striking distance of Luzon to guard all of the airfields on the island and destroy Japanese planes on the ground and in the air should they successfully take off. Named the Big Blue Blanket after the Naval Academy's Football Team, Admiral McCain's plan was both brilliant and audacious.[4]

There were more than 100 airfields in Luzon, and the plan called for all of them to be covered by the Blanket. For the first time in the war, Marine Corps fighters and naval aircraft would be integrated. Huge numbers of planes would have to fly round the clock. Fighter planes would attack Japanese aircraft if they successfully took off, and dive-bombers and torpedo-bombers would work to destroy Japanese airfields. The Task Force 38 operation over Luzon proved to be one of the most successful operations of the war, and although it would not protect the warriors on Mindoro past the initial phase of the operation, it did do much to insure the safety of American ships and sailors while the task force operated over the skies of Luzon.[5]

As the invasion fleet motored away from Leyte, none of the men in Squadron 16 knew of the Big Blue Blanket and the degree to which American airmen were endeavoring to protect them. Tom Hart remembered that the seas were calm and the sky relatively clear; and fortunately for the Americans, when darkness came each night of their voyage at approximately 7:15, there would be little moonlight to light the skies above the boats and ships motoring toward Mindoro. Although many of the men on PT *221* were nervous, no crew members got seasick.

The Attack Force, composed of almost 160 boats and ships, was a formidable fleet. Leading the way were the ships of the Mindoro Attack Group, followed by the Close Coverage Group, and then the PT boats, which motored in the rear of the armada surrounded by destroyers. Thousands of soldiers were also packed on ships and in landing craft. Initially, many of these men were to parachute on to Mindoro during the invasion. However, the available airstrips on Leyte were filled with fighters and bombers with little room left for troop transports. Thus, the airborne phase of the Mindoro Campaign was cancelled.

Prior to the main armada's departure, Slow Tow Convoy had sailed. This was made up of six slow-moving tugboats, three destroyers, two destroyer escorts, an Army aviation gasoline tanker, two LCTs (landing craft tank) and several other vessels that joined at the last minute. Despite its head start, the main invasion force would eventually pass the Slow Tow Convoy, and the ships in this group would be the last to arrive in Mindoro.[6]

Although the Japanese realized that the Americans would ultimately move on Luzon, they did not believe that Mindoro would be the next Philippine island the Americans would invade. Not only was Mindoro 262 miles from the nearest airfield on Leyte, and thus beyond the range of most island-based fighters, but it was also surrounded by enemy airfields; and to get to Mindoro, the invasion force would have to pass several enemy-held islands. In addition, Japanese military leaders believed that the island was too rugged for additional air bases, and thus would be of little value to the Americans. Their doubts were reinforced when the Americans did not bomb the island and Filipino guerrillas did not initiate any actions prior to the invasion. Instead, the Japanese surmised that Palawan, Paney, or Negros, which were all closer to Leyte, would be the next target. This miscalculation by the Japanese triggered the implementation of one of the great acts of barbarism that occurred during the Philippine Campaign, and I believe my father went to his grave unaware of the relationship between the invasion of Mindoro and this war crime.[7]

My parents lived in the house that I grew up in Fairfield, Connecticut, for almost 40 years. A short distance from the house is an entrance to Interstate 95, and my father traveled on this highway thousands of times during the decades he lived in Connecticut. If you travel several miles east on the highway toward the city of Bridgeport, you pass under a section of Route 25 that runs from Bridgeport to Newtown named for Colonel Henry Andrews Mucci; and as you approach the Route 25 overpass on Interstate 95, Colonel Mucci's name is easy to see on the commemorative sign. I am sure my father saw the Colonel's name on the overpass thousands of times. He also traveled on the section of Route 25 named for him on numerous occasions. Although my father had seen Colonel Mucci's name often, I do not believe he had any idea who he was until 2002 when Hampton Sides's *Ghost Soldiers: The Epic Account of World War II's Greatest Rescue Mission* was published. This book chronicles the heroic mission of the 121 Army Rangers and 600 Alamo Scouts, under the command of Colonel Mucci, to rescue 513 survivors of the Bataan Death March, who were imprisoned at Cabanatuan Prison Camp on the Philippine island of Luzon. I read the book, and then recommended that my father read it, which he did. Several years later, the movie, *The Great Raid*, with Benjamin Bratt playing Colonel Mucci, came out; and my father and I agreed that the film did an excellent job portraying the events in the book. What neither of us realized was that the brutal opening scene of the film was linked to the invasion of Mindoro, and despite reading the book and seeing the film, I do not believe that my father ever learned how the two events were related.

During the first day of its voyage to Mindoro, the Visayan Task Force encountered no Japanese resistance. The movement of the armada did not surprise the Japanese, but because they expected the Americans to be bound for Palawan, Paney, or Negros they focused their air power over these skies. The Japanese sent 186 planes, including as many as 50 kamikazes, from Leyte, Luzon, Negros, and Panay to attack the convoy; but because they did not realize where it was heading, they did not find it. Instead, many of the planes were sighted by American Task Force 38, and the fighter aircraft from its carriers destroyed approximately two-thirds of the Japanese planes and forced the rest to flee. In addition, other planes from Task Force 38 prevented Japanese aircraft waiting on the Luzon airfields from taking off for the remainder of the day.

On Palawan, in the town of Puerto Princesa, were 150 American prisoners of war. These men had survived the Bataan Death March, starvation, beatings with clubs wrapped with barbed wire, lack of medical care, overwork, daily humiliation, and other cruelties inflicted on almost all Japanese war prisoners, but most of these men would not survive another day. The prisoners had constructed three crude air-raid shelters to protect themselves from American bombs. The Japanese had allowed the construction of the shelters, but they had insisted that the entrances only be large enough for one man to get in or out at a time.

On December 14, anticipating an American invasion of Palawan that would not occur until February 28, 1945, the 150 prisoners were called back from their work details at noon. Soon two American Lockheed P-38 Lightening fighter aircraft arrived overhead, and the prisoners were sent into the air-raid shelters. Once the men were inside, some of the men and the shelters were doused with gasoline and set on fire. Quickly the soldiers inside the shelters burned, suffocated, and desperately attempted to run out of the narrow exits, many of them on fire, where they were shot by the Japanese. Some did escape and leaped off cliffs to the island's beaches, but most of these men were hunted down and shot. In total, 139 soldiers were murdered.

Eleven men did escape the slaughter and informed the American military what had happened. Fearing that the men imprisoned at the Cabanatuan Camp on Luzon would face the same fate, the Americans hastily planned Colonel Mucci's raid, and the courageous Rangers were able to rescue all of the men who were still alive at the Cabanatuan Camp. I believe the film and the footage of the rescued men at the film's end meant a great deal to my father. As an old man it reminded him that long ago in a far-off place called Mindoro, he and his squadron mates had done their part in liberating the Philippines and helping to save the lives of those men in the old newsreels.[8]

For the most part, the escort carriers and the Big Blue Blanket proved to be extremely effective, and only a small number of Japanese strikes on the Mindoro-bound boats and ships took off from Luzon. From December 14 to 16, American pilots from Naval Task Force 38 located and destroyed more than 200 Japanese planes still on the ground in Luzon, and 68 more in the sky before they could do any damage to American ships.[9]

In addition to the planes from the six escort carriers and Task Force 38, the invasion force would also be protected by land-based Army Air Force planes when weather permitted after they reached Mindoro. The American success at striking the Japanese aircraft at Luzon did not prevent Japanese planes from taking off from airfields on Mindoro, Formosa, and the Central Philippines and preying on the ships in the convoy. However, there is no question that the airmen in the Big Blue Blanket saved untold numbers of American men and ships as the armada sailed for Mindoro and during the first day of the invasion. Unfortunately, forces beyond the control of even the United States Army and Navy would bring an end to the safety screen of Task Force 38; and after Mindoro was taken, the Japanese would again successfully launch large numbers of planes from Luzon in an attempt to destroy ships in future convoys bound for Mindoro and vessels that had made it to the island.[10]

On the second day of the voyage, Japanese kamikazes located the Mindoro-bound fleet, and suicide planes would attack and terrify the American forces for the remainder of the Mindoro campaign. As the suicide planes dove toward the ships below, gunners from the fleet's ships would greet the human-powered bombs with ferocious barrages of anti-aircraft rounds. Most planes were hit and disintegrated before the pilots hit their mark, but at 3:00 in the afternoon, as the convoy was about to round the southern Cape of Negros in the Sulu Sea, the PT boat sailors got a taste of what was coming. A lone Val with a bomb hung on each wing flew over land, making her hard to detect on radar, and set her sights on light cruiser *Nashville*, which had been MacArthur's flagship during the invasion of Leyte and was now serving as the flagship for the Mindoro invasion force. The 10,000-ton, 608-foot ship was manned by 900 sailors and 42 Marines and was filled with reporters, high-ranking Navy officers, various other VIPs, and Brigadier General William C. Dunckel, the Commander of the 503rd Parachute Regimental Combat Team and 19th Infantry Regimental Combat Team of the 24th Division, that made up the invasion force. Due to the number of high-ranking personnel on the ship, some sailors called the vessel "Brassville."

A number of the gunners on nearby ships thought the suicide plane was a Marine Corsair and held their fire; and because gunners were confused and surprised, only a few rounds were fired at the plane before it found its mark. It hit on the ship's port side just aft of Rear Admiral Struble's cabin. The plane's two bombs instantly exploded destroying the ship's fire communication system and igniting some of the ship's ammunition and shells. Tracer rounds went off by the hundreds, bodies and body parts filled the air and scattered over the ship's deck, and men were blown and jumped overboard.

For 20 minutes the ship's crew fought the fires that had been ignited by the attack, and during this time, *Nashville* never left formation. Almost immediately after the plane hit, the flag bridge was destroyed and 133 men were dead and 190 wounded. Among the dead were Captain Everett Woolman Abdill, Rear Admiral's chief of staff; Colonel Bruce C. Hill, the general's chief of staff; and most of General Dunckel's staff. The General was burned over much of his body, but he did not go back to Leyte for medical attention. Almost all of the 41 Marines who were killed by the blast or who died due to injuries caused by the explosion were teenagers.

Exceptional damage control was initiated after the attack. Minutes after the suicide plane hit, destroyer USS *Stanley* and YMS *315* motored to the wounded ship and helped to fight the fire and rescue many who were wounded or who had been forced to leap overboard by the fire and explosions. Rear Admiral Struble, General Dunckel, and their surviving staff officers were then transferred to destroyer USS *Dashiell* and continued to Mindoro. *Nashville,* escorted by destroyer *Stanley,* slowly made its way back to Leyte Gulf.[11]

Two hours after the tragic hit on *Nashville*, 12 more Japanese planes arrived. PT boat gunners helped to drive them away, and three of the planes were shot down. One aircraft exploded mid-air as it was about to hit battleship USS *West Virginia*. Later, seven kamikazes and three fighter escorts descended on the 376-foot destroyer USS *Haraden*. Again, massive fire was brought to bear on the incoming planes, and nine were taken out of the sky. However, when fighting the kamikaze, a 90 percent success rate was not enough. The last plane slammed into the bridge on the starboard side of *Haraden*, and its momentum then sent the plane crashing over the ship's deck, wreaking havoc as it went. The forward stack and fire and engine rooms were disabled, the ship's radios and radars were no longer operational, and 14 men were killed and 24 wounded. No longer operational for combat, *Haraden* limped back to Leyte.

Shortly after the attack on *Haraden*, the Japanese pilots turned their attention to the Slow Tow Convoy, which was now behind the main invasion force. The destroyers escorting the slow-moving craft did their jobs well, and none of the Japanese planes found their mark. Two badly damaged enemy planes crashed so close to an Army gasoline tanker after they had been hit that two men on the craft were blown overboard, but this was the extent of the damage done to the convoy.[12]

That night, Rear Admiral Theodore D. Ruddock, the man in command of the escort carriers, ordered the ships under his command to motor toward the island of Palawan. He hoped that this would fool the Japanese into believing that the fleet's destination was Palawan, not Mindoro. This course change, in addition to the aerial bombing that had taken place earlier, did fool the Japanese. Certainly none of the Americans who carried out the ruse ever imagined that it would result in the slaughter of helpless American prisoners of war.

The Japanese hoped that on December 14 they could bring great destruction to the convoy, but these plans failed for two reasons. First, most of the Japanese planes that took off that day determined to sink Mindoro-bound American ships were destroyed by the aircraft of Task Force 38 before they got far from their airfields on Luzon. One 40-plane raid took off, but these were quickly intercepted by 106 American fighter planes from the Big Blue Blanket, and most were quickly destroyed. Eight planes did eventually find the convoy, but all of these were either shot down by concentrated anti-aircraft fire or crashed harmlessly into the water. It is possible that more planes would have located the Mindoro-bound vessels, but the enemy believed the Americans were bound for Palawan and thus Japanese pilots did not have an accurate location for the Mindoro-bound invasion force.[13]

Early in the morning of December 15, a day dubbed "N" Day, the Visayan Attack Force began to arrive at Mindoro. Tom Hart and his shipmates on PT *221* spied the island in the distance through the clouds and sun-filled sky. Their "long and wet trip" was over.[14] The seas were calm, and the conditions were perfect for an amphibious landing. A small Japanese vessel was sighted near shore and destroyed, and then a deafening roar thundered through the fleet as destroyers began to bombard the coast. The only people present on the shore were Filipinos. Some herded carabao, others carried babies and household belongings, and a few were waving American flags. Most quickly fled the beaches. Realizing that further bombardment was unnecessary, it was halted, and General Dunckel boarded a PT boat and was taken ashore.[15]

As landing craft motored up to Blue and White beaches, which were on the southwest corner of the island between the Bugsanga River and Caminawit Port, and began unloading soldiers from MacArthur's Sixth Army, the spirits of the invaders were buoyed when they set foot on the gradually sloping beaches and found the sand solid and well suited to driving trucks and other motorized vehicles over. More importantly, there was little Japanese resistance, and some of the Americans were greeted by grateful Filipinos bearing gifts of eggs, bananas, and even fried chicken.[16] In short order, 11,878 combat troops, including members of the 503rd Parachute Regiment, 9,578 members of the Army Air Force, and 5,901 service troops, whose primary job was to build and repair airfields, were on the island. Had the aviators of the Big Blue Blanket not done their job so well, it is likely that Japanese fighters would have greeted these men with vicious strafing. Instead the invaders found relative peace.

Twelve hundred men had been brought to offload the 27 LSTs, and a "conveyor belt" was formed to unload the ammunition and other supplies as quickly as possible. Soldiers and sailors grabbed a box of ammunition, carried it to the beach where it was stacked, and then got back in line and soon grabbed another box. This procedure continued, without break, even as Japanese planes attacked from above, until the vessels were unloaded. Hard work and hard sand made the unloading go more quickly than anticipated, and the job that was expected to take two days was largely completed just before dark. In total 27,600 tons of supplies were offloaded, another testament to the American supply juggernaut.

In one of the more unusual chapters in the history of PT Boat Squadron 16, Lieutenant Joe Loftus, a Supply Officer in the squadron who spoke Japanese, took control of an abandoned Japanese radio on Mindoro. By the time the Japanese realized they were communicating with an American, Lieutenant Loftus had received information that he shared with his superiors.[17]

Landing barges on Mindoro, December 1944. World War II PT Boats Museum and Archives, Germantown, Tennessee.

Days before, all but five hundred to one thousand Japanese troops had been removed from the island, and the anticipated bloodbath that had greeted American troops at so many islands in the Pacific was temporarily avoided. It is doubtful if anyone was more relieved at the lack of Japanese resistance than Rear Admiral Struble, who had been at Normandy the previous June for the invasion. This lack of Japanese resistance is one of the clearest examples of the genius of America's island-hopping strategy. After the American success in taking Leyte, the obvious next target would be one of the previously mentioned islands. Believing that one of these islands is where the Americans would land next, the Japanese had removed most of their troops from Mindoro to fortify these islands only to be surprised and infuriated when General MacArthur boldly sent his forces to the more distant island of Mindoro.[18]

As the Mindoro invasion fleet was arriving at the island, a lone Japanese reconnaissance plane flew over the invasion force and reported his findings to his superiors. Not even the Big Blue Blanket could completely protect the American forces. Almost immediately, 15 to 20 kamikazes and as many escort planes, some of which had participated in the Battle of Leyte Gulf, took off from Davao and Clark airfields on Luzon and from airfields on other Japanese-held islands bound for Mindoro, determined to disrupt the American landing. Carrier-launched American Combat Air Patrol planes warned United States' ships that Japanese planes were coming, and within half an hour after their arrival, the wonderful peace that greeted the American forces was terminated by the distant hum of incoming planes.

At 8:00 a.m. American land-based Army planes arrived at Mindoro, and the aircraft carriers, their planes, and supporting ships began to head back to Leyte. Slow Tow Convoy had still not reached Mindoro. Shortly after they departed, the Japanese planes made the returning ships their target. A kamikaze set his sights on destroyer USS *Ralph Talbot*.

Japanese "Betty" bomber flying over Mindoro. World War II PT Boats Museum and Archives, Germantown, Tennessee.

The plane was ripped apart by anti-aircraft fire, but its pilot had navigated close enough to the destroyer that wreckage from his plane fell to the deck of the American ship. Minutes later, another plane took a different route to the destroyer and attacked from high above. It too was destroyed before it could hit its mark. Two attacked escort carrier USS *Marcus Island*. The first struck the ship's lookout tower with its wing and beheaded the lookout before it crashed 20 feet from the ship. A second plane arrived seconds later, was hit by fire from the ship, and then crashed doing minor damage to the ship. Over the next 40 minutes, 6 more planes attacked. Four were shot down and two driven off. No serious damage was done to the American vessels.[19]

Soon after the invasion force arrived at Mindoro, Lieutenant Commander Davis led PT *221* and four other PT boats into Mangarin Bay to search for a site to construct a PT boat base. The remaining 18 PT boats in the task force were ordered to stay with a group of LSTs that were motoring toward the bay. Within minutes the five boats in the bay were confronted by 11 Japanese planes. Three of these set their sights on the American destroyer USS *Howorth*, which had participated in the earlier bombardment of the island and was now in Mangarin Bay and in close proximity to PT *221* and several other boats from Squadron 16. The first plane flew over *Howorth*, took heavy fire from the destroyer and the nearby PT boats, dove in an attempt to crash into the ship's deck, and crashed in the water 50 feet from the vessel. The second plane appeared, and the gunners on the *Omen of the Seas* opened fire on her. The plane banked, providing an excellent target for the PT boat's 40 mm gun, only to have the gun jam. The suicide plane then proceeded to fly over the destroyer hitting the ship's radar antenna and forecastle and depositing plane wreckage and Japanese body parts on to the ship's deck before falling into the sea. The destroyer was only slightly damaged.[20]

The combined fire of the destroyer and nearby PT boats successfully shot down the third kamikaze, and then the fourth plane set her sights on the *Omen of the Seas*. Tom Hart, manning the twin .50 caliber machine guns, and his shipmates poured fire at the manned bomb while the boat operators frantically maneuvered the fast-moving vessel to avoid being hit. Just as the plane was about to hit the *221* boat, the wall of bullets aimed at the aircraft did their job, and the plane "cartwheeled across the water's surface" and then disappeared under the water just short of its target. The crew of PT *221* had performed well in its first direct confrontation with a Japanese suicide plane.[21]

The kamikazes next turned their attention to the LSTs outside of the bay. Lieutenant Commander Alvin W. Fargo, Jr., Commander of Squadron 13, ordered the 18 PT boats that had not yet entered the bay to get between the LSTs and the planes and do all they could to shield the larger vessels from the kamikazes. Ten planes converged on the LSTs and the PT boats. Seven attempted to strafe the PT boats, but all missed their mark, and three were shot down. Two more were brought down by the gunners from the PT boats and LSTs, but two of the suicide pilots were able to reach their targets.

One plane was hit but still broke through the massive anti-aircraft fire from the boats and hit the 328-foot LST *738* amidship. The plane penetrated the main deck, broke through into the tank deck where 218 drums of high-octane gasoline, 12 tons of 75 mm ammunition, small arms ammunition, anti-aircraft weapons, and 200 to 300 flasks of oxygen were stored. The high-octane aviation gas was ignited first, and this set off the other explosives, which ripped the ship's fuel tanks open and caused a series of enormous explosions. The order was given to abandon ship, and dozens of men jumped into the fiery, oil laden waters, many swimming through the flames to get to safety. While life rafts were being lowered, there was a second large explosion. The 376-foot destroyer USS *Moale* moved in to help extinguish the flames, but it was repelled by two more explosions that emanated from the LST. Wheels, vehicle parts, and anything else that was on the deck when the suicide plane hit were sent flying through the air. *Moale*'s bow was badly damaged, one of her crew was killed and 10 wounded, and all attempts to fight the fire on LST *738* were terminated. As the ship was being destroyed by fire and explosions, frantic PT boats darted in to pull desperate sailors to safety. PT *224* alone rescued 76 men that morning. The LST was damaged beyond repair and later sunk by naval gunfire, and *Moale* had multiple holes in her bow from the explosions from the LST.

While LST *738* was burning, five planes attacked LST *472*. Nearby PT boats unleashed massive anti-aircraft fire but failed to stop the planes. The first crashed into the water on the port side of the ship. The second made it through the ship's defenses and crashed on its deck, setting off a series of explosions and destroying its water mains and chemical fire-fighting equipment. A third plane came in with its guns blazing, was hit by a nearby ship, flew just over the LST, and crashed off her port beam. A fourth Japanese plane now strafed the LST, missed its target, and then crashed off the bow of the ship; and a fifth and final plane then attacked and was destroyed as it attempted to crash on the ship's bow.

Destroyers USS *O'Brien* and USS *Hopewell* motored toward the burning LST in an attempt to render aid, but they were forced to turn back by the large explosions that emanated from the LST. As the LSTs burned, PT boat crews simultaneously fired at Japanese planes that bolted across the sky looking for additional targets to menace and worked to rescue the desperate crews from the two LSTs. PT *221* spotted the burning LSTs and immediately motored toward the damaged ships. *The Omen of the Seas* nosed up to one of the LSTs that was in the "worst condition" to help save the men in the water only to be violently jolted by one of the explosions. All of the sailors on the PT boat were sent flying, and Robert Carlson was hit with shrapnel in the shoulder. The men on PT *221* quickly recovered and proceeded to pull approximately 25 men from the water, including most of the members of the Army Medical Unit who had been sent to tend to the sick and wounded on Mindoro. Some men were burned or injured in other ways, but all remained calm. A doctor who was pulled to safety immediately started to give first aid to the wounded.[22]

While the crew of PT *221* was hauling men from the water, more enemy planes arrived. One aimed at LST *605*, which was scheduled to be the PT boat base ship, and missed. Moments later the men on PT *221's* 40 mm bow guns brought tremendous fire to bear on a plane determined to crash into a nearby ship. It got dangerously close to its target, started to smoke and then cartwheeled along the surface of the bay, spraying water and flames and then sank from sight.

When the wounded were brought aboard the PT boats, first aid was administered, fractures were splintered, the burned were covered with sheets and blankets, and morphine shots were given to reduce the pain. The most difficult part of the rescue operation was getting the victims up the six feet of cargo net that hung from the side of the boats. Not only were many of the wounded unable to help themselves, but the boats were also often forced to move quickly as they engaged the Japanese in a desperate sea-to-air battle.

My father manning the twin .50 caliber machine guns. Francis Gelzheiser collection.

As men were being pulled from the water, Ensign Raymond W. Rosenthal, an officer on PT *224*, observed a helpless man in the water that he feared would soon drown. The young officer, who had been a competitive swimmer in college, asked the boat's captain, Lieutenant Robert J. Wehrli, if he could enter the water to save the man. A short, heated discussion ensued, with Lieutenant Wehrli arguing against Ensign Rosenthal entering the water. Ensign Rosenthal finally convinced the boat captain that he could save the sailor and was granted permission to attempt the rescue. PT *224* located the near-dead sailor, and Ensign Rosenthal jumped into the water and was left alone with the wounded man as PT *224*, in the heat of battle, motored away. Shortly after Ensign Rosenthal reached the wounded man, PT *223* motored by. Lieutenant (jg.) Harry E. Griffin, the captain of the boat, was shocked to see Ensign Rosenthal in the water, but soon the young officer and the wounded sailor were pulled to safety.

Unfortunately for the PT boat crews, most of the equipment to build the PT boat base in Mangarin Bay was on LST *472* and was lost as a result of the destruction done by the kamikazes. Like LST *738*, LST *472* was damaged beyond repair and sunk by American naval gunners. In total 200 thankful men were rescued by the PT boats on this first day on Mindoro, and most of these were plucked from the water while Japanese planes were attacking from above. Six of LST *472*'s sailors were dead, and several more were badly wounded. LST *738* lost one of her crew and 10 more were injured.[23]

During the first days on Mindoro, my father was on PT *221* on two separate occasions when kamikazes attacked. Although this was a terrifying experience it was not the most haunting memory he had of the early hours on Mindoro. While the battle with the suicide planes raged, the PT boat crews raced to rescue as many sailors who had leaped or been blown overboard as possible, and the skill and courage of the sailors in Squadron 16 saved many men. Some of these warriors were wounded and required assistance from the sailors on board the PT boats. On several occasions, just as the *Omen of the Seas* arrived and my father and his shipmates were trying to pull a man from the water, an enemy plane appeared, and the wounded American had to be left behind as PT *221* darted away to avoid being hit. My father always wondered if some of those men failed to stay afloat until they could be rescued later and drowned, and what must have gone through the wounded men's minds as their squadron mates motored off just as they were about to be pulled to safety?

After battling the kamikazes, some of the PT boats tied up to an old Japanese floatplane dock. Two Japanese were quickly killed by the PT boat men, and the remainder of the enemy, who were nearby when the PT boats docked, fled into the jungle. Lieutenant Commander Davis, always an aggressive warrior, armed with grandees, a Bowie knife, and at least two firearms, and Chief Commissary Steward Al Piotter headed into the jungle looking for nearby Japanese. They quickly found five in a foxhole, and when they refused to come out and surrender, Lieutenant Commander Davis hurled a grenade into it killing three and forcing the remaining two to surrender. As many as 12 additional Japanese warriors were located by the PT boat sailors, and as many as 10 were killed and the rest were captured.[24] Within 90 minutes American infantrymen had walked more than a mile through sugarcane fields encountering little resistance, and to the relief of all, it was determined that the island of Mindoro was going to be occupied with a minimum loss of American life.[25]

By 4:00 in the afternoon, Lieutenant Commander Davis had supervised the construction of a crude advanced PT boat base in a tiny cove in Mangarin Bay. A nearby

PT boats most likely in Mangarin Bay, Mindoro. World War II PT Boats Museum and Archives, Germantown, Tennessee.

thatched-roof house was designated the officer's quarters, and sailors and soldiers located areas inland and on and near the beach to sleep. All but one of the huge landing craft that were not destroyed by the Japanese had been unloaded. The American and Australian troops were already frantically repairing and building airfields, and the remaining Army planes that were providing close air support on Mindoro were ordered back to Leyte to beat the bad weather that was predicted in the near future.[26]

The skies grew quiet as the sun began to set over Mindoro. PT *297*, with PT *224* approximately 250 yards off its stern, began to motor out of Mangarin Bay on a night patrol. They had not completed the passage between Ilin Island and Mindoro when three Japanese planes appeared. Two Vals approached the starboard bow of the boats at an altitude of approximately 150 feet with their guns blazing. The two vessels immediately opened fire, but failed to bring the planes down. The lead aircraft flew past the boats, turned right, and came back and passed over PT *224* from starboard to port bow at an altitude of roughly 40 feet. The plane released a bomb, which hit the water approximately 60 feet off the boat's port bow. Water splashed all over the boat's deck, but the bomb caused no damaged to the boat or injuries to its crew. The PT boats were firing at the aircraft, and after the bomb was dropped, the sailors could see that the plane had been hit and was on fire. It continued to fly low in the sky and disappeared over the trees near the Mindoro shoreline and then crashed out of the sight of the sailors on the boat.

The second Val returned and flew over PT *224* at approximately 300 feet and dropped two bombs that hit 50 yards off the boat's starboard and 30 yards to its port. The boats continued to unsuccessfully fire on the plane, and it soon circled around and approached the craft from the stern. The plane was only 50 yards in the air when it began to dive at the boat. Massive fire from the boat's 40 mm guns was directed at the aircraft. In addition, turret gunners unleashed constant fire, and much of it ripped into the aircraft. Suddenly, the plane broke its dive abruptly, and crashed just 60 feet off the boat's port quarter, so close to the PT boat that her crew could feel the flames that came from the plane as it crashed. The men on PT *224* were convinced that their gunners had destroyed the plane and saved their vessel and the men on it from almost certain destruction. The third aircraft was destroyed when it attempted to crash into PT *224*, just missed the boat's fantail, and then rammed into the water just feet from the boat. Miraculously, despite the plane crashing so close to the boat, the vessel was not damaged, and none of the men on it were injured. The boats continued on into the night to carry out their assigned tasks.

Later, Motor Machinist's Mate First Class Al Holmes commented, "Those planes were so close to the boat, you could see the color of the pilot's eyes. We wouldn't have needed to use the guns. We could have thrown potatoes at them." Torpedoman's Mate John Novak, who directed the 40 mm gun crew, and the men under his leadership were commended for courageously staying on their guns and continuing to fire even when the plane was frighteningly close to the boat; and turret gunners Gunner's Mate Second Class Albert C. Clark and Radar Man First Class John W. Fuller did, "outstanding shooting during all of the attacks made by the Vals."

During the patrol, the boats continued to have difficulties. PT *224* struck an object and her rudders were damaged, forcing the boat to cancel the patrol. While seeking out an anchorage for the night, PT *297* went hard aground on the north side of Ilin Island. Torpedoes and other heavy objects on the boat were thrown overboard, but this still did not lighten the boat enough to float it off the reef. The boat remained there for the night, and all attempts to free the vessel the next day failed. The boat remained grounded until it was eventually pulled off by several PT boats, but while being dragged off the reef the vessel's bottom was damaged so badly that it had to be beached until it could be placed in dry dock and repaired.

Fearing a night attack as darkness fell on the American soldiers and sailors on Mindoro, the boats were pulled as near to shore as possible and covered with branches. Between fear of Japanese attack and the hungry mosquitoes, few of the sailors slept well. PT Boat Squadron 16 Commander Colvin, eager to improve the efficiency at which the boats under his command could be supplied and loaded with fuel, worked with several sailors welding a damaged section of a small railway that ran from San Jose to the water's edge at Mangarin Bay. As a blue light from the welding torch flickered in the darkness, my father and his shipmates on PT *221* looked up and spied a lone Japanese plane overhead heading for the light from the welder's torch. The surprised welders ran for cover, and as the plane released its fragment bomb, nearby sailors ran frantically in the darkness, falling over rocks and sometimes into the water in order to escape the bomb blast.

It exploded near the welding project. Chief Motor Machinist's Mate Alfred "Al" Abeckerle was a crew member of PT *200* and had been trying to move drums of 100-octane gasoline to nearby PT boats whose fuel tanks were almost empty. When the enemy plane arrived, he had run terrified into the black night as the plane was about to drop its bomb and leaped into the water just in time to have shrapnel from the fragment bomb wiz past him and splash into the water just missing him. When it grew quiet, he went to Lieutenant Commander Colvin and said, "Captain, I think we'd better get the hell out of here." Lieutenant Commander Colvin replied, "I think you are right," and the welding project and efforts to refuel the boats were ended for the night. Fortunately, the well-placed bomb missed the fuel drums, and no man was wounded by the shrapnel sent flying near the men who were working. Several other planes flew low over the base that night dropping bombs, but these also missed their targets.[27]

Despite the vicious attacks that my father and his shipmates endured during their voyage and after their arrival on Mindoro, as evening arrived on December 15, my father felt relatively safe. Yes, the voyage from Leyte had been difficult, and the aerial attacks during and after their arrival had been terrifying; however, even though a number of the ships had departed Mindoro for Leyte, there were still many ships anchored nearby, and this huge naval force would be a match for whatever the Japanese could throw at the Americans. However, a new reality arose when the remainder of the invasion fleet and a large number of the invasion force troops also set sail back to Leyte as soon as the ships were unloaded. These ships made it back to Leyte undetected by the Japanese. Less than 24 hours after the huge armada's arrival, the only naval force left to defend the island of Mindoro were the 23 PT boats under the command of Lieutenant Commander Davis.[28]

The Japanese were both surprised and enraged by the successful American landing at Mindoro. The American forces on the island were a direct threat to the supply lines necessary to maintain Japanese forces on Luzon, and Japan's control of Manila and the Philippines was now in jeopardy. The Americans had to be driven from Mindoro, and the way the Japanese went about trying to remove the Americans from Mindoro and prevent the success of the inevitable invasion of Luzon was indicative of the new thinking that now dominated the Japanese high command.

The Japanese were reluctant to confront the American Navy in a traditional battle fearing that another Leyte Gulf–like defeat would essentially bring an end to their naval presence in much of the Pacific. Instead, General Yamashita, who was now in charge of the Japanese defense of the Philippines, would rely on the more than 100 airfields that the Japanese still controlled in the Philippines and the traditional and suicide planes that could be sent from these to confront the Americans. For the remainder of the war, it would primarily be the fanatical, and often suicidal, Spirit Warrior in the air and his equally fanatical counterpart on land who would confront the American forces and try to preserve the Japanese Empire that was steadily shrinking and growing weaker as it combatted the America production juggernaut.[29]

December 16–17, 1944

Although Army Air Force planes were supposed to take over for the Navy's carrier-based aircraft early in the morning on December 16, weather prevented them from arriving on time. Fortunately, the naval aircraft were able to stay for one more day until the weather improved, and the Army planes arrived at Mindoro from Leyte late that afternoon.

Early in the morning of December 16th, 1944, Tom Hart observed a lone plane he believed was a Mitsubishi Ki-46 Reconnaissance Aircraft, also known as a "Dinah" by the American forces, fly into Mangarin Bay. The plane flew in very low and set her sights on PTs *230* and *300*, which were returning from night patrol. The aircraft strafed PT *230* and missed. The PT boats anchored and docked nearby quickly opened fire on the aircraft but failed to destroy it. It then banked, circled back, and flew in low just above the shrubbery at the island's edge and toward LST *605*, the last remaining ship on Mindoro, which was unloading supplies on the beach. The plane, that some PT boat sailors surmised was trying to crash into the LST's open door, was finally hit by gunners, and a part of its tail was blown off. The aircraft burst into flames, flew under the bow of the LST, and crashed near the vessel igniting 21 drums of gas and causing a huge explosion.

Al Abeckerle was removing gas drums forward on the lower tank deck of LST 605 and was there when the plane hit. When he heard the ship's gunners open fire, he yelled for the men to take cover, and soon a Japanese plane crashed into a "large pile of fuel drums." The explosion that followed lifted the front end of LST 605; and flames, sand, and debris were sent flying everywhere. In addition, 100-octane gasoline from leaking fuel drums had flooded the tank deck, and frantic sailors immediately manned hoses attached to salt-water pumps in an attempt at extinguishing the flames before the LST exploded. As more Japanese planes arrived, men ran for cover. Some found safety behind large crates that contained the Packard engines used to power the PT boats. Thomas S. Allison, a chief machinist's mate on PT 219, lacked a safe place to hide, ran into the brush, and then raised his hand at the enemy planes overhead and yelled, "You buck-toothed bastards, come down here and fight like men."[30]

The hand of fate or just random luck often determined if a man lived or died on Mindoro. When the plane arrived, my father was near LST 605 working on the electrical system of one of Squadron 16's boats. My father saw the plane coming and believed that the boat he was working on was about to be hit. He quickly started to run, only to realize too late that the pilot was not after the boat he had fled but LST 605, which he was now running toward. When the explosion occurred, my father was near the LST and was temporarily "paralyzed," knocked unconscious, and sent flying through the air. As secondary blasts were going off all around my father, a fellow serviceman ignored his own welfare, ran toward the explosions, grabbed my father like a "sack of potatoes" and ran with him to safety. My father always believed that the man's selfless act saved his life. However, he never learned his identity; and on several occasions when I asked him what happened to his rescuer, he explained that as far as he knew he was killed shortly after the rescue in a subsequent attack. I do not know the man's fate, but I am sure that my father always regretted not thanking him for his courageous act.

Others who found themselves near where the suicide plane hit were not so lucky. Five men were killed, including one Squadron 13 PT boat sailor who was "completely eviscerated by the explosion," and 11 more were wounded. In addition, a three-week supply of fuel was destroyed.[31]

Soon after the arrival of the "Dinah" that attacked LST 605, the PT boats were ordered to untether from the docks, pull up their anchors and motor out into Mangarin Bay. Soon dozens of Japanese planes arrived including high bombers, fighters, seaplanes, and kamikazes. The pilots of these aircraft expected to find the large naval fleet that had arrived at Mindoro the previous day; and they were incensed that the Americans were not only occupying Mindoro, but also that the large, target rich fleet had escaped. They proceeded to unleash a massive aerial assault on the remaining PT boats. This was the beginning of five straight days of general quarters. Over the next 20 days, Japanese planes would raid the Mindoro boats and bases as many as 29 times per day in an effort to destroy the American forces. Bombers, fighters, seaplanes and float planes would all participate in these attacks, but it was the kamikazes—most of which were Japanese Zeros due to their speed and evasiveness—that would prove to be the most feared and deadly aerial adversaries.

With Task Force 38 no longer plying the waters around Luzon, and her planes no longer patrolling the skies over the island, Japanese planes would take off from Luzon and other Japanese-held islands and bomb and strafe the Americans on Mindoro or attempt to crash into PT boats. With few planes of their own, and limited anti-aircraft weapons, the American's defense was dependent largely on the gunners of the PT boat fleet.[32]

Four suicide planes soon attacked. Three set their sights on PT *230*, captained by Lieutenant (jg.) Bryan F. Kent, which had still not returned to the dock from its night patrol and had just avoided being hit by the gunners on the plane that crashed into LST *605*. The boat roared to full speed, and employed "broken-field running football tactics to the problem," and maneuvered erratically to make it difficult for the suicide planes to hit their target. While it was fleeing the three aircraft, her gunners concentrated fire on the lead plane that dove in a "gradual sweep increasing to an angle of about 70 degrees." The boat captain "maneuvered at high speed to present a starboard broadside to the incoming plane." Lieutenant (jg.) Kent feinted in several directions and then turned hard right rudder just as the plane was about to hit PT *230*. The aircraft crashed into the water 30 feet off the boat's starboard bow. Shortly, another suicide plane set its sights on a nearby PT boat, skipped just under the boat's bow, and bounced up and onto a nearby beach. This was the only suicide plane that did not crash in flames during the Mindoro campaign.

Almost immediately another plane set her sights on PT *230*. Plane and boat maneuvered radically in a deadly cat-and-mouse game, and a desperate last-second turn to port caused the plane to miss and crash 45 feet from the boat. Only seconds passed when the third plane to attack PT *230* came in for the kill. This time it attacked from high above and came down at a 70-degree angle. Again the skilled crew maneuvered their craft frantically to the left and the right. As the plane made its final course adjustment, Boat Captain Kent "swung suddenly at right angles," and the desperate crew watched as the suicide plane crashed just a few yards off the boat's stern. The explosion that followed lifted the stern of the boat out of the water and engulfed the crew in flames, smoke, and debris. Miraculously, the boat was undamaged and no one in the crew was hurt. Fate was with Lieutenant (jg.) Kent that day. He and his crew had guessed three times, and each time they had guessed correctly. Fate would not be so kind to all of the PT boats on Mindoro.[33]

The Japanese suicide planes next set their sights on PT *77*. One came roaring in for the kill. In a quick and brilliant maneuver, Boat Captain Frank A. Tredinnick reduced the boat's speed at the last minute, and the plane, unable to adjust to this surprising maneuver, crashed harmlessly in the water 10 yards in front of the PT boat. Another kamikaze pilot decided to give his life in order to destroy PT *223*, which was motoring next to PT *221*. The skilled crew of this craft turned hard to the right at the last minute. The pilot was unable to change his course and died crashing into the water between PTs *223* and *221*, just 10 feet from the targeted boat. Next, Lieutenant (jg.) John R. Erickson's PT *298* came under attack by two suicide planes. The boat desperately maneuvered to avoid being hit. One plane came in from high above the second aircraft, and the boat's gunners "fired a steady stream of shells at one plane," causing it to crash 15 feet off the boat's port bow. The second plane came in from a lower altitude and set her sights on the boat's stern, strafing as it dove. Intense fire was returned by the men of PT *298*, and the suicide plane came so close to accomplishing its mission that it scraped the paint off of the boat before it crashed three feet off the boat's starboard. The shock from the plane's crash sent one man flying over the side of the boat.

Miraculously, none of the sailors on PT *298* suffered serious injuries, although one was averted when the sailor manning the 20 mm gun on PT *298*, not realizing his shipmate had been blown off the boat by the kamikaze crash, opened fire on the sailor in the water believing it was the Japanese suicide plane's pilot. Fortunately the gunner's shipmates realized the mistake he was making and got him to stop firing before he hit his shipmate. Soon after this close call, Al Piotter looked up and saw PT *223* "disappear in the cloud of flame and smoke." He thought the boat had been hit, but when he looked again, "he saw she was going wide open with her bow out of the water still shooting."[34]

Before the PT boat crews could catch their breath, another kamikaze flew in for the kill, but the combined fire from numerous PT boats knocked it out of the sky before it could get close to a boat. Throughout the morning's battle, all of the PT boats based in Mindoro engaged the Japanese. Frantic gunners fired continuously, and in the words of Tom Hart, "All kept their heads." As the boats' gunners fired at the Japanese planes streaking across the sky, one seemed to set her sights on PT *221*.[35] As the plane raced in toward the stern of the boat, the stern 40 mm failed to eject its shells properly and jammed. Tom Hart and his shipmate James Donald frantically worked to clear the jam. For reasons that will never be known, the plane flew over the boat and set her sights on another target. In addition to the planes that were destroyed trying to crash into PT boats, eight more planes were shot down by the Motor Torpedo Boats. The battle against the Japanese Kamikaze Force in defense of Mindoro was just beginning.[36]

During the first days in the battle for Mindoro, either in the afternoon after he survived the explosion of LST *605* or the following day, a young soldier approached my father and asked him to help repair the ignition system on a landing craft that he and his fellow soldiers were using to ferry them around Mangarin Bay and the adjacent shoreline. My father agreed and quickly made the needed repair. He then asked his commanding officer if he could go with the soldiers on the landing craft across the bay. His goal was to drop the troops off and then use their craft to ferry an abandoned Japanese freighter that was docked near where the PT boats were stationed to an anchorage in Mangarin Bay, thus making more room on the dock for the squadron's boats. The officer replied, "Go ahead, it's your funeral," and my father boarded the vessel and headed across the bay with the soldiers. He left the soldiers off, and then proceeded to the freighter.

As he was tying up the vessel, a lone American soldier came out of the jungle clutching his arm, which had been shot by one of the Japanese troops that were still scattered throughout the Mindoro jungle. My father applied a tourniquet, bandaged the wound, and then asked the young man to go to sickbay. He refused and instead barked, "I'm going to find the son of a bitch that did this to me, and I'm going to gas the Japs one." He then asked my father to go with him into the jungle. My father agreed; but before they left, the soldier grabbed a jerry can filled with gasoline and handed his rifle to my father. They then set out to find the pillbox where the Japanese were hidden when the soldier was shot. As they neared it, the soldier proceeded to circle around the pillbox and up a hill so that he could station himself over the enemy's dug-out position. He intended to pour the fuel into it and then ignite the gasoline and force its inhabitants to exit and expose themselves. As he made his way up the hill, my father proceeded forward and found himself almost directly in front of the pillbox. With no warning, an armed Japanese soldier ran out of the pillbox right at my father. "Shooting from the hip," my father fired a single shot and downed his adversary. My father's wounded comrade was now positioned above the pillbox. He quickly poured the contents of his can into it and ignited the fuel. The flames forced a second armed man to run from his hiding place, and this time with the rifle properly positioned, my father shot and downed him. Finally a third man, screaming and engulfed in flames but still clutching his rifle, came running out from his hiding place, and my father fired a final, well-placed shot, and he too was quickly killed.

Quiet ensued, and my father closely examined the men he had killed and then returned to the PT boat base. Francis Gelzheiser, a man so gentle, decent, and respectful of all life that he often rescued errant insects in his house and carefully deposited them outside, had just fired three shots, each of which had killed a man at close range. He had "joined the Navy in 1942 because I liked the water and couldn't see fighting in hand to hand, close fighting, where the enemy is seen face to face before killing." Not surprisingly, he confessed to me late in his life that he was "haunted by the three dead Japanese."

Sometime after my father shot the three Japanese soldiers, he went back to his electrical shop. He took out his knife and a file, and on the knife's bolster he etched a groove for each of the men he had killed. I believe at the moment he was proud of what he had done, and that these marks served as a kind of trophy to forever remind him of his accomplishment. I also believe that at some level he hoped to add grooves to the knife in the future. My father never said this to me, but it is the only conclusion I can make.[37]

December 17 began peacefully for the PT boat sailors on Mindoro. Late the night before, Slow Tow Convoy had arrived. Although it had been attacked several times while meandering toward Mindoro, the destroyers and destroyer escorts assigned to protect the ships in the convoy did their job well. They shot down at least five Japanese planes and prevented the aircraft from doing any damage to the American ships. The convoy unloaded its cargo during the night and then departed back to Leyte early in the morning. By the time it got back to Leyte, the convoy was motoring at just one knot per hour so as not to leave any vessel behind. No ships were hit by the Japanese on the return voyage, despite Tokyo Rose's claim that the convoy had been annihilated.

To the south off the coast of Panay, ships in the Slow Carrier Task Force, whose planes had patrolled the skies over the Mindoro-bound ships, came under attack. Suicide planes set their sights on carriers USS *New Mexico*, *West Virginia*, and *Marcus Island*. All failed to hit their mark; and in total five planes were shot down by the ships' gunners, four were destroyed by their planes, and four crashed into the water.

Up to this point, the PT boats had been anchored or tied to trees near shore in an attempt to keep the boats hidden from the Japanese. This made it difficult to resupply boats, so in the late morning PT *221* and several of the other boats motored to the small rickety dock near their primitive base and attempted to load supplies. PT *221* was the first to arrive, and the boat's crew tethered their boat directly to the dock. Three more boats soon joined the *221* boat; but since the dock was only large enough to tie one boat directly to it, the additional boats were tied to one another outward from PT *221*.[38]

The crews immediately began loading fresh water and other supplies. Tom Hart took his position as lookout on the aft 40 mm gun and was putting on his helmet and talking with a shipmate when the late morning quiet was broken by the unmistakable crack of the 40 mm gun from the boat tied next to PT *221*. Hart looked up, and was shocked to see three planes frighteningly close to the four boats flying at an altitude of approximately 1,000 feet. His fellow PT boat sailors were equally surprised, and in the chaotic seconds that followed, they responded to the planes in very different ways. Some men were so shocked to see the aircraft that close that they froze and did nothing to protect themselves or their shipmates. Others heard Lieutenant Wells, the third officer on PT *221* and the only officer present, yell, "Get off the (expletive deleted) boat." This resulted in at least six sailors jumping off the boats into the water and many others running for shore. Lieutenant Wells gave the order because he feared the boats were "going to go up like a string of firecrackers." Radioman Second Class Ralph Records obeyed the orders and proceeded to flee so quickly that his shoes fell off. All of the men on the boats expected at least one of the aircraft to crash into the four boats and perhaps destroy all of them.[39]

Several of the boats' gunners did man their positions and opened fire on the incoming aircraft. However, the scattering of the crews made this more difficult. Tom Hart had immediately manned his 40 mm gun; but to properly operate this weapon a pointer was necessary, and these men had left the boats in the chaos. The job of the pointer was to elevate and lower the gun barrels to match the target's position. Thus without a pointer, it was almost impossible for the gunners to fire accurately at the incoming planes. One of the planes strafed PT *224*. Two of the bullets ripped into the arm and shrapnel penetrated the right cheek of Ship's Cook Second Class George Walsh, who was manning the forward 20 mm gun. The bullets caused him to fall through the open hatch into the crew's quarters, but the wounded Walsh quickly scrambled back to his gun and immediately commenced firing.

Realizing the boats were sitting ducks as long as they were tethered together, frantic sailors tried to untie the boats and motor them into Mangarin Bay where they could better maneuver to avoid the planes. Unfortunately in the chaos of the moment, even this did not go well. Crew members started to motor away before the lines connecting the boats were untied. This stretched the lines so tight that they were impossible to loosen, and sailors had to scramble to find knives to cut the boats loose. Soon the boats were backing down only to hear anguished cries. Boat operators then realized that they were about to back over and kill some of the men who had abandoned ship and were in the water off the stern of the boats. Boat operators quickly changed course and started to motor forward only to hear similar cries from men swimming off the boats' bows. Soon, all of the sailors in the water had been cleared away from the boats, and the proper pointers and gunners had taken their position on most of the boats' guns. As the craft started to motor from the dock, a deafening roar was heard as most of the guns from the four boats opened fire.

In one of the stranger and more difficult to understand events in the history of Squadron 16, none of the three planes attempted to crash into the four boats even though one well-directed crash most likely would have destroyed all four boats. Instead, after firing on the boats, they continued on. One aircraft that had been hit by the PT boat gunners flew over the shore and strafed the house designated as the Officers' Quarters, where the officers were meeting. Hearing the planes coming, the officers ran out of the house into the nearby brush and dove into foxholes that had been left by the Japanese. The plane then set its sights on an insignificant supply dump, crashed into it, and inflicted only limited damage.

Almost as soon as the four boats had cleared the dock, two Japanese planes returned. The boats opened fire on the aircraft. One plane set its sights on a small tanker in the bay. The pilot dove and at the last minute realized he was going to miss his target. He was able to pull out of his dive, and then he set his sights on another nearby vessel. The chaos that had impacted their ability to properly respond to the earlier attack now gave way to the professionalism that was generally the hallmark of the PT boat crews in World War II. Accurate and intense fire was directed at the plane, and it began to smoke from a hit from one of the boats. In a last, desperate attempt to damage an American vessel, it set its sights on a PT boat. The second Japanese plane joined in this hunt and the two planes crashed into the water trying to destroy PTs 75 and 84. One plane landed so close to PT 75 that five men were blown overboard, and four sailors on the boat suffered shrapnel wounds from flying debris.[40]

That night, two PT boats went on an important mission. The boats motored to a guerrilla hideout at Abra de Ilog on the north coast of Mindoro. Here they met Lieutenant Commander George F. Rowe, the United States Naval officer attached to the Mindoro underground, and delivered sealed orders from General MacArthur. They then picked up 11 American pilots who had been shot down and rescued by the guerrillas. As they motored back towards Mangarin Bay, they stopped to pick up two men who had been assigned to watch the island's coast. The Filipino guerrilla forces played an important role in the battle for the Philippines, and the ability to navigate close to shore, pick up and deliver men and orders made the PT boat a very important link between the Allied and guerrilla forces[41]

On December 17, 300 miles east of Luzon, the sailors and pilots of Task Force 38 who had done so much to protect the Mindoro invasion armada two days earlier and continued to attack the Japanese planes on Luzon, suffered a terrible tragedy that my father, and I am sure most of the men in Squadron 16, did not learn about until decades after the war. A number of the ships in the task force were low on fuel, and attempts were being made to fill fuel tanks at sea so the attacks on the Japanese on Luzon could continue.

Refueling while at sea was a skill that the United States Navy worked hard to perfect during World War II, and it was a difficult, time consuming and potentially dangerous task even in the best conditions. The ships of Admiral Halsey's Task Force 38 had been ordered to motor 450 miles to the east so they could refuel and then continue to maintain the Big Blue Blanket over Luzon. Halsey was reluctant to rescind this order, which would have exposed the Mindoro invasion force to more Japanese air strikes.[42]

Weather forecasting in World War II was primitive by today's standards, and this was especially true in the waters surrounding the 7,000 islands that made up the Philippines.[43] On the morning of December 17, the barometer began to drop, wind speeds picked up, and wave heights began to dramatically increase. The ships in Task Force 38 were ordered to continue to take on fuel and stay in formation. Admiral Halsey received inaccurate weather information and unwittingly ordered the fleet to motor directly into a typhoon that was eventually named Typhoon Cobra but is today generally referred to as Halsey's Typhoon. The results of this order would be catastrophic. At 1:00 a.m. the barometer dropped to 29.88. An hour later the barometer had fallen .13 inches. "Singer's Law" was a weather-prediction rule followed by mariners of this period that stated that if the barometer dropped .10 of an inch or more in three hours or less, the mariner was in the path of a typhoon, and the seamen better "haul ass." At one point in the storm, the barometer dropped .74 inches in an hour, and eventually fell below what the instruments could read to an estimated 26.30, which would have been the lowest reading ever recorded by the United States Navy up to that point. At 1:00 a.m., winds had picked up to 26 miles per hour. They continued to increase until they roared at more than 125 miles per hour, and gusts of 164 miles per hour were recorded.[44]

To compound the problem, many of the destroyers had spent their days at sea circling the larger vessels in search of enemy submarines and thus burned more fuel than the larger ships in the fleet. They had fuel tanks that were more than one-half empty, and several of these ships had tanks that were less than 20 percent full. This lack of fuel meant that these vessels had too little ballast. Enormous waves caused the ships to roll dangerously, and the fuel would move with the ship altering its center of gravity and causing some of the ships to pitch to more than 70 degrees and come dangerously close to capsizing. In addition, several of the older destroyers had been refitted with new combat information centers, modern radar antennae, and additional guns and ammunition. This added up to 510 tons to the small ships and made them more top heavy, less stable in the water, and more likely to make extreme rolls in the violent seas.[45]

Task Force 38 continued to battle the winds and seas for almost 48 hours with disastrous results. Ships were difficult to control and often sailed blindly, and there was the constant fear of a collision. Venturing on to a ship's deck was often suicidal. Sailors were washed overboard and drowned, crushed by pounding ships, or cut to pieces by enormous propellers. Fuse caps were ripped off of shells making them live, and some exploded as they crashed into bulkheads. Heavy equipment like freezers crashed from bulkhead to bulkhead. Sailors who were forced to venture on to their ship's deck had to crawl on their bellies backwards against the wind, but this created a vacuum which made breathing difficult, and rugged sailors were reduced to tears when they confessed to their shipmates that they could not swim.

The waves, some of which reached the terrifying height of 100 feet, forced several ships to roll to 78 degrees.[46] As destroyers USS *Hull*, *Monaghan*, and *Spence* made their extreme rolls, water poured into their smokestacks and disabled their engines. Unable to keep their bows into the wind, all three ships were overcome with water and sank. Fortunately, some of the smaller destroyers with near empty fuel tanks were able to add seawater to empty tanks. This added ballast made the ships more stable, and likely reduced the number of ships that were sent to the sea's bottom.[47]

For the sailors who were thrown overboard or who did not go down with their ships, their ordeal only got worse. First they had to survive the storm and the enormous waves with little water and food. The oil-filled water was blown into men's faces, rafts were often in poor condition, and the survival supplies that had been stowed on them were often lost in the chaos. When the storm subsided, their problems did not. During the day, the temperature rose to 100 degrees, men died of thirst, and some desperate sailors made the fatal mistake of drinking seawater. Clothes were ripped off by the wind and violent waves, and near naked sailors, floating only 15 degrees from the equator, had their skin badly burned by the tropical sun. The salt caused temporary blindness and body sores, and often these bled causing sharks to surround, terrify, and sometimes maim and kill the sailors. Brave men fought to not only save themselves but their fellow sailors, and as was the case so often in World War II, extraordinary acts of courage were common.[48]

As the typhoon raged, aircraft carriers rolled violently, screws came out of the water, and enormous waves crashed over flight decks that were almost 60 feet above the water. Planes were ripped from their fittings and crashed into each other and structures on carrier decks. They careened into guns damaging the weapons beyond repair and started fires as aircraft fuel was ignited forcing men to venture out on to the roller coaster–like decks and fight these blazes.

In total 146 aircraft were lost in the storm. Many of these were thrown over the side to prevent them from crashing and catching fire. Two pilots returning to their carriers found decks that were rolling violently and full of crashed planes and other debris. Unable to land, they rolled their planes upside down and bailed out into the violent waters below.[49]

Decades after this epic struggle for survival, the courage displayed by many of the men of Task Force 38 should not be forgotten. Nameless sailors jumped into the turbulent seas, lines in hands, to rescue fellow sailors who had been swept off ships' decks.[50] On USS *Taussig* with all of the ship's power out, Dr. John Blankenship tied himself to an operating table and performed an emergency appendectomy by the light of an oil lamp.[51] A young lieutenant (jg.) named Gerald "Jerry" Ford was the officer of the deck on light carrier USS *Monterey*. Lieutenant (jg.) Ford had seen much action prior to the great typhoon, including battling the Japanese for two days during the Battle of Leyte Gulf, but the storm would be the greatest challenge he would face during the war. Shortly after the storm began, he smelled smoke, climbed up to the ship's deck, and was quickly sent flying across the vessel's surface. Only the two-inch metal lip on the border of the deck prevented him from being sent into the ocean. In time, fires were ignited below deck, and three of the ship's four boilers stopped working. If the fourth went out, not only would fire be raging throughout the ship, but the ship would also be uncontrollable and at the mercy of the violent seas.

Learning of the catastrophe on *Monterey*, Admiral Halsey instructed her captain, Stuart "Slim" Ingersoll, to abandon ship. Captain Ingersoll replied that he believed the ship could be saved, and he charged Lieutenant (jg.) Ford with going below and extinguishing the fires. Beneath the deck of the burning ship were approximately 18 aircraft. The storm had caused them to break loose, and not only had the fuel in the planes ignited, but pieces of the planes were crashing violently into each other and bulkheads. Thick black smoke filled the compartments below deck and wafted through the vessel's ventilation systems, and enormous stockpiles of ordnance were on the verge of being ignited and detonated which certainly would have sent the ship to the ocean's bottom seven miles below. Lieutenant (jg.) Ford put on a gas mask and led a group of sailors below. They rescued the wounded and then started fighting the flames. As one man was burned or became overwhelmed by smoke and heat, he would drop to the back of the line, and another sailor would step up. Relentlessly, the team led by the future president extinguished the flames and drove forward. The fire was brought under control, the three damaged boilers were repaired and made operational, and the ship was saved.

Although Lieutenant (jg.) Ford would go on to become speaker of the House of Representatives, vice president and president of the United States, he almost never talked of his actions during the harrowing hours when he battled smoke, flames, flying metal, and terror below the deck of *Monterey* during the worst hours of Typhoon Cobra.[52]

When the winds died down and the waters grew calm, the officers and crew of Task Force 38 counted their losses, and it soon became clear that they had survived one of the great maritime disasters in naval history. In addition to the three destroyers and 146 planes that had been lost, eight other ships were seriously damaged. Admiral Halsey ordered the surviving ships to motor to a base at Ulithi, hundreds of miles from their position. Fortunately the man in command of destroyer USS *Tabberer*, or *Tabby*, disobeyed this order. Lieutenant Commander Henry Lee Plage was a 29-year-old naval reservist. He was tall, athletic, loved by his men, and handsome enough to be called Cary Grant. Most of the sailors on his ship had been to sea for less than three months, and 90 percent of his enlisted men were still teenagers.[53] Despite losing her radar and radio antennas, having her mast and pilot house ripped off in the storm and receiving an order to leave the area and get needed repairs, Lieutenant Commander Plage elected to stay in the region where the storm had occurred and search for survivors.[54]

All available crew were ordered to the deck to participate in the search. The ship maneuvered in a calculated box pattern to make sure that the search was as thorough as possible. Twice Lieutenant Commander Plage was ordered to terminate his search, and twice he refused this order. In order to see better, all deck lights were extinguished. Not only was the badly damaged ship now vulnerable to attack by Japanese submarines, but because the damage to the deck made the vessel resemble a submarine, she was almost attacked by an American ship.

For 51 hours the ship's crew searched. Sometimes men would be found too weak to swim, and sailors from *Tabby* would tie a line around themselves, jump overboard, and swim, sometimes through sharks, to the weakened sailor and pull him to safety. Often when life rafts with men in them were located, the small craft would be surrounded by sharks. From the deck of *Tabby* men would shoot the dangerous creatures to prevent them from killing their fellow sailors.[55] In total the men of *Tabby* rescued 55 of the 93 sailors who were pulled from the water after the storm. After they were convinced that there was no chance of more rescues, *Tabby* steamed to Ulithi. Her crew had gone 60 hours without sleep, but it is doubtful if any of the sailors on board complained about this. Despite blatantly disobeying orders, Ship's Captain Henry Lee Plage, who feared a court martial awaited him as a result of his insubordination, was awarded the Legion of Merit, and his crew received the first Unit Commendation Ribbon ever awarded by the United States Navy.[56]

When Admiral Halsey learned that the officer who had disobeyed his orders and risked losing his ship in order to save lives was a naval reservist, he responded, "How can an enemy ever defeat a country that can pull boys like that out of a hat." Lieutenant Commander Henry Lee Plage was not a man bred for the military, and had war not come, he most likely would have lived out his life in quiet obscurity, certainly unmentioned in any military history book. When war did come, Lieutenant Commander Plage responded. Resourcefulness and a healthy skepticism of blind obedience were the byproducts of being raised in a nation that prized liberty over conformity, and it is likely that this upbringing resulted in the young Lieutenant Commander Plage disobeying orders. It may also be the reason that the men in charge of the young officer awarded him a medal instead of sending him to the brig. It is fitting that after *Tabby* was repaired just one month after the great storm, she steamed north to take part in the Battle of Iwo Jima. Anchored close to the island when Lieutenant Commander Plage was called to a meeting on shore, the ship's crew fittingly watched as the American flag was raised on Mt. Suribachi.[57]

Almost 800 sailors died as a result of the massive typhoon, and 80 more were injured. These men had been instrumental in attacking the Japanese on Luzon and preventing their planes from reaching Mindoro during the early hours of the Mindoro Campaign, and it was Admiral Halsey's dedication to this task that made him so determined to refuel his destroyers. His mission was to prevent Japanese planes from flying and attacking the men and ships that had landed on Mindoro. The men charged with this task displayed great skill and bravery in carrying out this mission, and it is unfortunate that most of the sailors in PT Boat Task Unit 70.1.4 never knew of these sacrifices which undoubtedly saved the lives of some of the Mosquito Fleet sailors on Mindoro.[58]

On one of his first nights on Mindoro, perhaps as the men in Task Force 38 were battling for their lives, my father, exhausted from the Japanese attacks and working non-stop to set up the PT boat base and keep the boats' electrical systems running, decided to sleep on the beach in an attempt to stay cooler. As nightfall came he found a spot on an empty beach, and enjoying the cool evening breeze, he started to go to sleep. However, even after sunset, the Japanese planes continued randomly to bomb and strafe, and to reduce his exposure and make sure that they did not see him from above, he moved to the edge of the beach, dug a crude fox hole, covered himself in his mosquito netting, and fell asleep hidden under a bush. After an unknown amount of time he awoke to find his body covered with fire ants. If he laid still, the creatures did not bother him, but with each slight movement numerous ants would sting him, and in a short period of time he had painful welts on much of his body, and he started to feel "paralyzed" by the ants' poison. Still fearful of the Japanese, he removed his mosquito net, left the safety of his hiding place, and ran for the water in an attempt to remove the insects. The cool water was comforting, and soon he encountered a fellow sailor floating nearby. He called out, got no answer, and then swam to the man and pushed him. His silent comrade quietly fell to his side, and in the moonlight it was revealed that the man's lower half had been severed in an earlier bomb attack. Quietly, my father swam back to shore with the half-man in tow. He spent the night in the sand with the ants and their painful bites, the continued bombings, and the nightmare of his floating, half-comrade, whose corpse now rested nearby.[59]

December 18–24, 1944

In the days following their arrival at Mindoro, the PT boats began to patrol the coast of the island. There were different goals for these missions. Because of their relatively shallow drafts, PT Boats were well suited to ferry raiders behind enemy lines to engage the Japanese troops on the island; and on more than one occasion Lt. Commander Davis himself led a group of PT sailors on these raids. These men were called Davis's Raiders, and they wore this moniker proudly. PT Boat crews would try to determine where shore-to-shore troop movements were occurring. They would also make contact with Filipino scouts behind enemy lines, take part in reconnaissance missions to search out mines and shore defenses, and search for hideouts from which the Japanese could launch suicide boats, which were a deadly addition to the Japanese arsenal late in the war.[60]

Although these patrols were often conducted at night, circumstances required daylight patrols, and too often these resulted in encounters with kamikazes. PT Boats had certain advantages over larger vessels when dealing with these adversaries. They were fast and could turn quickly. They had enormous firepower for their size and could often destroy a suicide plane before it hit its mark. While firing at their adversary, PT boat crews would try to evade the plane by running in a zig-zag course. If they failed to destroy their enemy, they would wait until the pilot had committed to his final flight path, and then at the last possible moment quickly turn to port or starboard hoping the plane would be unable to follow their route and crash harmlessly in the water.[61]

Although I am not sure if my father would have agreed, Tom Hart called December 18 "the roughest day on Mindoro," and on this day luck ran out for one of the boats in Squadron 16. During the morning hours the skies over Mindoro were surprisingly quiet. In the early afternoon a medium Japanese bomber or "Nell" appeared, and immediately the PT boat crews opened fire on the aircraft. Hundreds of rounds were aimed at the plane, but none brought the aircraft down, and it was able to unleash three or four bombs and then escape. Fortunately, none of the bombs hit their target. Soon several Japanese fighters or Oscars appeared. One set its sights on a PT boat, but it crashed harmlessly in the water unable to hit the frantically moving craft. American P-38s arrived and shot down two Japanese planes but not before two of the P-38s were hit and the pilots forced to bail out. Both of them parachuted to safety and were unharmed. Soon another plane arrived from the same direction as the suicide plane, and most of the PT boats immediately opened fire on it. Tom Hart and his fellow gunners on PT *221* were shocked when none of the ordnance they were firing brought the plane down, but all were glad that their fire had missed when the plane veered to one side and the gunners could identify the plane as an American PBY (Catalina Patrol Bomber). Unfortunately, one of the boats did not recognize the plane as American, and its gunners continued to fire for another 30 seconds.

The skies grew quiet until late afternoon. The all-clear signal was flashed and the sailors in Squadron 16 began to relax when three more enemy planes appeared. This time they were "Vals." One dropped a couple of bombs, but these missed. Another dove and strafed the boats, but the combined fire from the PT boats forced it to turn away. The pilot appeared to have made the decision to leave when he suddenly banked his plane and set his sights on PT *300*, ironically named *Kamikaze Val* by her crew. Squadron Commander Lieutenant Commander Colvin was the captain of PT *300*. He spotted the kamikaze, and immediately initiated evasive procedures. However, despite the vessel's quick turns and the hail of bullets discharged at the plane, the manned weapon kept coming. As the kamikaze bore in, PT *221* and other PT boats in the area frantically fired at the plane until it got so close to the *300* boat that they had to stop for fear of hitting their own squadron mates. At the last minute, Lieutenant Commander Colvin ordered a sharp swing to the starboard. The pilot had anticipated this maneuver and turned his plane in the same direction at the same time. The plane slammed into the boat amidship of the engine room. Almost immediately fire engulfed the boat, there was a huge explosion that sent all but three of the men on the boat flying into the water, and the vessel was split in half. Watching this from the water nearby, the men on PT *221* feared that the entire crew was dead. The stern portion of the boat, weighted down by the engines, sank immediately, and the burning bow floated on the surface. Eight of the sailors on PT Boat *300* were dead or mortally wounded, and seven, including Lieutenant Commander Colvin, were seriously wounded. As Japanese planes strafed them from above, sister PT boats arrived; and while gunners fought off the planes above, PT boat sailors worked to retrieve the survivors. Lieutenant Commander Colvin, despite his wounds, ordered the boats to rescue his crew members first.

PT *300*'s Torpedoman Second Class Everett Nussman displayed particular bravery that afternoon. Operating the starboard twin .50 caliber guns, he kept firing his guns until the suicide plane was only feet from his boat. Then he dropped to the bottom of his gun turret just as the plane hit its target. The explosion caved the turret in on him, but he was able to wiggle free and jump into the water. Ironically, he was the only man in the crew who was not killed or seriously injured. Machinist's Mate First Class Joseph Brunner was a shipfitter who was acting third officer on the boat. When his body was retrieved from the water, the only mark on it was a bullet hole through the chest. It was possible that he had been hit by one of the strafing Japanese planes, but many of the sailors on *Omen of the Seas* quietly believed that one of the gunners on the nearby PT boats who was trying to fight off the Japanese planes, continued to fire when the suicide plane was too close to the *300* boat and hit Brunner. Of course, none of the men who quietly pondered this would ever know the truth.[62]

PT *300* had been ordered to go on night patrol that evening, and Oliver Young, who was scheduled to crew the *300* boat, was walking towards the intelligence shack for a briefing when the air-raid alarm sounded warning of the arrival of Japanese planes. PT *300* immediately cast off and headed for the outer bay where it could maneuver to avoid enemy planes, and it departed before Young could get back to the boat. On board PT *300* was Motor Machinist's Mate Second Class William Dudas, who also served as the trainer on the 40 mm cannon. Dudas was also Young's best friend. When the kamikaze came, Dudas continued to fire fearlessly at the plane until the kamikaze crashed into the boat, seriously wounding Dudas. When the wounded from PT *300* were brought back to shore, Young was waiting, terrified about what he was about to learn. Bill Dudas was still alive, but mortally wounded. As Young held and comforted his friend, Dudas continued to murmur, "Momma, Momma." Young asked the Navy corpsman the prognosis. The reply could not have been worse, "Every bone I checked was broken, and I cannot shoot enough pain killer in him to stop the pain." Bill Dudas was dead 45 minutes later. Fifty-five years after his friend was killed, Oliver Young still teared up when he told of the event, and explained that, while on Mindoro, he would see much death, and there were days when the "bodies were stacked up like cordwood on the shore until they could be checked and buried. But it was different with my buddy Bill."

This was not the end of Oliver Young's story. When the inevitable telegraph arrived at the Dudas' residence telling of Bill's death, his sister was alone. She was beside herself with anguish, and called Oliver Young's family for help. Young's mother answered the phone and thought that Bill's sister had gotten a telegraph saying that Oliver Young had died. Believing that her boy was now dead, Mrs. Young fainted and remained passed out on the floor until she was revived some time later. When Young was home on leave he visited Bill's family. Again, decades after the event, Oliver teared up when he recalled that the family asked if Bill had been brave in the face of death. Young assured them that he had been, that he courageously continued to fire until the suicide plane hit, and that he deserved a posthumous medal for the courage he displayed that day. "Of course that wouldn't bring him back to life, but it would have shown what a wonderful guy he was."[63]

The bow section of PT *300* tormented the PT boat sailors on Mindoro by burning all night. William A. Bahn explained years after the war, "Every time we looked we thought of the fellows who were killed and about the wives and mothers when they got the telegrams. That was the 18th of December and they would probably get the news for Christmas."

Part of the horror of war is its randomness. Lieutenant Commander Colvin, a fine officer, had waited until the last instant, guessed which direction to turn to avoid the kamikaze and guessed wrong. As a result, the plane and boat had turned in the same direction at almost the same time resulting in disaster for PT *300*. He would have to live with the terrible outcome of this split second decision for the rest of his life.

The eight sailors killed on PT *300 Kamikaze Val* were: Radioman Third Class Joseph G. Amos, Quartermaster Second Class John W. Ball, Seaman First Class Albert J. Basso,

Fire Controlman First Class Valmore Beauregard, Gunner's Mate Third Class Albert E. Boone, Motor Machinist's Mate Second Class John R. Bowers, Machinist's Mate First Class Joseph M. Brunner, and Motor Machinist's Mate Second Class William L. Dudas. Most of the sailors on PT *300* had been together for more than a year. They were shipmates and friends, and those who gave their lives that day would always be remembered by the shipmates who survived and the squadron mates who served with them.

Shortly after the destruction of PT *300* more Japanese planes appeared. All of the PT boats in Mangarin Bay opened fire on the aircraft, but none of them hit their targets. Unfortunately, PT boat gunners did hit an American F-40 Corsair, and at almost the same time Japanese planes shot up a P-38. Both American pilots managed to bail out of their burning planes and were rescued unharmed after their planes exploded in the water. Not surprisingly, the pilot shot down by friendly fire was incensed that it had been the PT boat gunners that destroyed his plane. Two Japanese planes were shot down by American P-38s.[64]

Despite the loss of PT *300*, the sailors on Mindoro had to continue to carry out their duties. As night began to fall, Lieutenant Commander Davis motored away from the base with sealed orders for the guerrillas hiding out on the other side of the island. The package was delivered to Lieutenant Commander Rowe, and after the package was dropped off, 11 American pilots who had been rescued and sheltered by the guerrillas were brought aboard the boat to be brought back to the PT boat base.[65]

That evening, PT *221* was scheduled to go out on night patrol, but the events of the day had prevented the boat's crew from refueling until early evening. As night descended on the base, they were just beginning to add fuel to their craft when an alert sounded, and the *Omen of the Seas* immediately motored away from the fuel barge and into the bay. PT *223* was also anchored near the fuel barge, and her crew was unable to move as far away from the fuel barge by the time the Japanese planes arrived. Boats were ordered not to fire to avoid giving up their positions to the Japanese pilots. Seven bombs were dropped in a row. The first hit the PT boat base that was under construction and the last landed near the fuel barge, which was just off the shore. PT *221* was far enough away from the explosions to be out of the range of the flying shrapnel, but PT *223* was not so lucky. It was so close to the bombs that its crew could hear them "swish" as three landed off the boat's starboard bow and three off its stern. The force of the bomb blasts was so powerful that six sailors from PT *223* were blown off their boat and into the water. All of the men began to swim to shore, but Gunner's Mate Second Class Ladislav Micgl needed help. Several sailors, including Lieutenant Commander Davis, quickly swam out to assist him, and all of the sailors safely reached shore.

Quartermaster Second Class Robert E. Hopkins was hit in the chest and the arm with shrapnel; Ed Kalinowski was hit by shrapnel in his right leg; Torpedoman's Mate First Class Charles Mahoney, who had been operating the smoke screen, was struck by shrapnel in his right leg; and Gunner's Mate Third Class Angelo Cortese was wounded when a fragment from one of the bombs struck the base of the aft 40 mm gun, glanced upward, and penetrated his abdomen. One of the bombs that exploded near PT *223* sent shrapnel through the bow and stern of the craft, and 40 mm ammunition on the boat's stern caught fire. Gunner's Mate Third Class Ed Reitz may have saved PT *223* and the men on her when he quickly threw the ammunition that had been hit overboard thus preventing it from setting off a string of explosions that likely would have destroyed the boat.[66]

After the December 17 Japanese attack on PT *224*, Torpedoman's Mate Second Class

Bob Spofford removed the shrapnel from George Walsh's cheek, and Walsh was then sent to "a little shack" on Mindoro. Almost as soon as he arrived, there was a Japanese air raid and as men ran for cover, the terrified Walsh was inadvertently left on the porch as bombs exploded nearby. After this attack ended, more wounded were brought to the shack. All of the injured were then transferred to the small train that had recently been repaired and transported about three miles inland to a small Army hospital. During the night, there was another air raid, and this time Walsh could hear the shrapnel "hitting the side of the building."

Joining Walsh in the hospital the next day was PT *223*'s Angelo Cortese. Walsh talked with Cortese, and Cortese told him that he "had just written a letter to his mother." Although the injury did not appear to be serious, the young man died four days later. It is likely the letter arrived a week or two after his passing. Another sailor Walsh encountered in the hospital was Ensign Harry Hilliard. Ensign Hilliard had been on PT *300* when the boat was hit, was burned over much of his body, and was "covered from head to foot" with bandages and resting. Shortly after the death of Angelo Cortese, Squadron Commander Colvin, still recovering from his wounds, wished Walsh and Hilliard "good luck" and then informed them that they were being "shipped home." Their time on Mindoro was over.[67]

Before sunrise on December 19, thirteen Japanese planes flew over Mangarin Bay and dropped flares that illuminated the bay and the surrounding shoreline. One landed close to the *Omen of the Seas* lighting up the small vessel and making her an easy target. PT boat sailors feared the worst, but the sun rose and the flares burned out, and still no planes attacked to destroy the targets lit up by the flares.

While the PT boat crews built a base for their boats, fought Japanese aircraft, and patrolled the shoreline of Mindoro and nearby islands, hundreds of men worked dawn to dusk in the island's hot, bug-infested interior constructing and repairing landing fields from which planes could take off and land to defend Mindoro and aid in the future attack on Luzon. In addition, the PT boat base force kept the boats running, and constructed a sickbay and chow hall. The Japanese understood the purpose and importance of the landing fields, and planes periodically flew over in an attempt to bomb them and disrupt their construction. As the days went by some sailors moved in to abandoned native huts to better escape the rain and bugs while sleeping, and although these were often an improvement, getting a good night's sleep still proved to be difficult.[68]

During the evening of December 19, a floatplane or "Jake" flew over Mangarin Bay. PT boat gunners opened fire on the aircraft, and as the plane flew away and crashed on the horizon, Tom Hart and the other gunners on PT *221* believed that it was their fire that brought the plane down. Shortly after the destruction of the lone plane, a second arrived and flew over the docked PT boats and dropped four to five bombs aimed at the boats. Several of the bombs landed near two of the boats, but none were close enough to do damage.[69]

As it grew dark, more planes arrived, and the sailors on the PT boats manned their guns in an attempt to fight them off. Prior to the attack, Tom Hart had completed cleaning the aft 40 mm gun, and grease had soaked through the canvas that he had placed the parts on when cleaning the weapon and left a stain on the boat's deck. Hart now manned the newly cleaned weapon as Ship's Cook Third Class Elred Joyner, the boat's cook and ammunition passer, raced up the ladder to assist in the defense of the boat. Joyner was lanky and over six feet tall, and as he bounded down the deck to assist Hart, his heel hit

A warehouse on Mindoro. World War II PT Boats Museum and Archives, Germantown, Tennessee.

the grease spot left by Hart when he had cleaned the gun. Years later, Tom Hart described what followed:

> His feet shot forward and upward ... and his six foot frame appeared momentarily suspended horizontally in space before he crashed to the deck. He was on his knees in an instant, threw back the lid of the ammunition box, extracted a clip of shells, and leaped to his feet, only to crash to the deck again with the added weight of the clip of ammunition across his chest. Again he rose quickly but held to the framework of the gun with one hand as he passed Hart the ammunition. Rapidly, efficiently, he bent down, seized another clip of shells and thrust them at Hart but again the treacherous deck betrayed him. He was on his feet quicker than ever this time, holding the gun, his face livid with rage. He roared, "You son-of-a-bitch, if you ever spill another drop of oil on this deck, I'll pound your head to pulp."

While Joyner was screaming with rage, bombs were exploding, guns firing, men shouting, and the organized chaos of battle was everywhere. Joyner did not care. Instead he was completely focused on Hart, the slippery spot on the deck, and his falls. For years the PT boat men would laugh at this episode, and I think remembering events like this helped them to buffer the memories of the war they wanted to forget.[70]

On December 20, the morning brought quiet and several wonderful hours of peace. At noon, two enemy planes arrived and flew over the just completed Hill Field named after Colonel Bruce Craighill Hill who had been killed during the attack on *Nashville*. PT boat gunners fired at the planes but were unable to bring them down. Shortly after these planes flew off, two more arrived and fire from American P-38s and P-47 Thunderbolts that took off from the just-completed airstrip destroyed both aircraft. Surprisingly, one Japanese pilot elected to parachute to safety and he was eventually captured by PT *220*. Pilots electing to parachute over enemy-held territory were rare in the Pacific. Most chose the fate of the second plane that was hit. He guided his plane toward a PT boat and attempted to crash the vessel but missed his target dying in the explosive crash. Additional planes arrived throughout the course of the day, and in total 29 enemy planes attacked on December 20. Army pilots taking off from Hill Field were able to shoot down 11 of these aircraft. Three American P-47s were lost during these aerial battles.

That night the *Omen of the Seas* was sent out on patrol. It only had to motor a few miles to a section of beach near Dongon Point. Once there it was assigned the task of preventing enemy barges from landing. No barges were encountered, but an enemy plane did fly over within 100 yards of their boat. Anxious crew members waited for the command to commence firing, but orders had been given to not fire on Japanese planes while on night patrol unless they attacked first. Additional planes flew nearby, although none of these got as close to the boat as the first. Shore-based searchlights spotted these aircraft, and radar-controlled 90 mm shore batteries opened fire on them.[71]

While returning from their first all-night patrol on Mindoro on the morning of December 21, the *Omen of the Seas* encountered PTs *220* and *222* also on their way back to the base. The two boats had shot down a floatplane as the sun was rising. On board the boats were Filipino guerrillas who the boats were taking back to the PT boat base and a Japanese pilot that the natives had captured and turned over to the Americans. That same day PT *223* was patrolling along the Mindoro shoreline when it struck a reef and damaged all three of its screws.

Later that day as the afternoon sun was high in the sky and the tired crew of PT *221* worked on routine maintenance, one of the more unusual events in the history of PT *221* occurred. An alert was sounded which brought the sailors to their battle stations. Soon a Japanese Mitsubishi A6M3 or "Hap" appeared out of the clouds, and it made a dive for one of the PT boats, missed its target, skimmed over the water, banked sharply, and set its sights on the *Omen of the Seas*. Tom Hart and the gunners on PT *221* had been firing at the plane since its arrival, but as the plane banked and created an easy target for them, the 40 mm gun that Hart was operating stopped firing. Just prior to this, all of the boat's motors had mysteriously shut down, and the small craft sat near motionless in the water with the gun best positioned to hit the fast-moving plane not working. PT *221* now found itself a perfect target for this kamikaze, and all members of its crew awaited the plane's impact and the explosion that would follow. Tom Hart explained years later, "I thought, this is the end." He was not afraid, and only felt "a dull sense that his life was about to end." Ensign Joseph F. Rafferty, who was at the boat's wheel unable to turn the craft when the plane was coming, felt sure the end was near, and "felt nothing.... I just thought this was the end," and he believed that this was the thought that went through the minds of all the men on the boat as the plane approached.

Hart kept trying to fire the 40 mm, and when it continued not to fire, he dropped another clip of shells into the weapon, again felt nothing as he pulled the trigger, and even attempted to add a third clip in a desperate attempt to get the gun working. Still the gun was silent. Looking down as he frantically added the new clip, Hart awaited the inevitable explosion that would end his life and the lives of his shipmates and destroy his beloved PT *221*. It never came. Instead, when Hart looked up the plane had wheeled and was flying low over the water. It had passed up a stationary target with its main gun not firing and set off for a different boat. Continuing on its low flight path, the pilot found his new prey and was destroyed before it could do any damage. To add additional mystery to this event, when the skies quieted, all three engines started; and when Tom Hart inspected his weapon, it was not jammed, and there was nothing wrong with it. The experienced gunner would go to his grave pondering why the kamikaze pilot had spared the men of PT *221* and why at that moment the motors had stopped running and the boat's 40 mm gun had failed to fire?[72]

During these first days on Mindoro, life for the PT boat sailors and soldiers on the island was not only dangerous but exhausting. Although military construction crews had made operational the first airfield on December 20, its presence did not prevent the Japanese from continuing their attacks on the men and boats stationed on Mindoro or on the supply ships that would arrive in the future. Hot meals were almost never served; and for two weeks, when hot food was provided, it consisted of dehydrated potatoes and spam. Many sailors were so busy patrolling, maintaining the boats, and engaging the Japanese planes that days would go by and they would eat almost nothing.

My father's skills were in great demand during this period, and at one point he went 68 hours without sleep. Not only was he going out on patrol in PT *221*, but he was also working almost nonstop to keep the electrical systems in the squadron's boats functioning properly. Electrical systems in World War II PT boats were temperamental to begin with; and problems with radios, radar, batteries, lights, and anything else connected to wires were increased by the heat, humidity, and salt air of the Philippines. While helping to load .50 caliber ammunition on to PT *221* toward the end of his 68-hour sleepless marathon, my father was approached by an officer. When the officer addressed my dad, he did not respond, and although my father was standing, the officer soon realized that my father was asleep. Sleeping while on duty was a serious offense in the United States Navy, especially in a war zone, and there was discussion of a Court Martial. However, when the circumstances were examined, cooler heads prevailed, and my father was verbally reprimanded, told to complete the tasks at hand, and then given a few hours to get some sleep. It is likely that the squadron's officers realized that seriously punishing my dad would have served little purpose and removed one of the squadron's best electrician's mates from duty when his skills were most needed.[73]

When men were given time to sleep, slumber was often fitful and hard to achieve. To keep hidden, boats continued to anchor near shore or tie directly to branches on the shoreline. Nights were hot and humid, and mosquitoes and other bugs were inescapable. One sailor explained that many sailors looked like they had "the measles" each morning after a night of being stung by mosquitoes and other bugs. Sailors also feared numerous other insects on the tropical island, especially a venomous "black widow like spider" that was common and seemed adept to locating and crawling on sleeping sailors. In addition, a sailor had to wonder as he drifted off to a fitful sleep if that night would bring a Japanese plane and his death.

The old saying proclaims that "all is fair in love and war," and if romance was not to be found on Mindoro, the sailors took the latter half of this maxim to heart. During the first days on the island, supplies were hard to obtain, especially after the LSTs that held many of them were destroyed by kamikazes. Often at night sailors in the squadron would be sent on "mid-night small stores," which essentially meant that men would comb the island and locate and abscond with materials necessary to keep their boats running.

PT Boat Squadron 16 Electrical Group, on the island of Mindoro. My father is in the rear row, fourth person from the left. The look on his face reminds me that the person in this photograph is a man I never knew. World War II PT Boats Museum and Archives, Germantown, Tennessee.

Some sailors became masters at acquiring what was needed on these late night patrols, and although the officers realized what was going on, they always looked the other way. What mattered was that the boats were kept operational.[74]

The success of the Mindoro invasion could only be continued if the island could be resupplied; and during the evening of December 19 the first resupply convoy, composed of 11 destroyers escorting 25 ships, 14 LSTs and 6 chartered freighters, sailed out of Leyte bound for Mindoro. Unfortunately, these vessels would not be protected by escort carriers or the pilots of Admiral McCain's Big Blue Blanket. Early in the morning of December 21, two Japanese planes attacked the convoy, dropped several small bombs that missed their targets and then flew off. Three more Japanese planes then arrived. One of these was shot down, and the remaining two were forced to flee by American Combat Air Patrol planes.

At approximately 6:30 that evening, 20 more Japanese planes attacked, and these were intercepted by 12 Army P-38s. Although outnumbered, the superior skill of the Army pilots and quality of their aircraft prevailed, and within short order, eight of the enemy planes were shot down. However, at approximately 7:15 p.m. five fought their way through the defending American aircraft and set their sights on the Mindoro-bound ships below. Despite the enormous ordnance aimed at these planes, four made it through the defensive fire and set their sights on three ships and began their suicide dives. One crashed into LST *460*, another LST *749*, the third exploded on liberty ship SS *Juan de Fuca*, and the fourth missed his mark and exploded in the water next to destroyer USS *Foot*, only slightly damaging the vessel.[75]

The three successful suicide planes had done their work well. All three vessels were forced to leave the convoy, and four of the destroyers were ordered to stay behind to protect them and rescue their crews. What happened on LST *460* was particularly terrifying and spectacular. The suicide plane approached the ship at a 45-degree angle, and Lieutenant (jg.) J.B. McClendon had to dive on to the deck to avoid being hit by the suicide plane just before it smashed into the ship's mast and then crashed into the conning tower. The plane's engine broke through the conning tower, wheelhouse, and wardroom and then into the tank deck and landed on top of a stockpile of ammunition. Burning plane parts were scattered throughout the ship, and the pilot's body landed on one of the ship's 20 mm gunners. The ship was carrying gasoline and ammunition, and as fire spread throughout the vessel, the sky was lit up by the flames from the burning fuel and the massive explosions from the ignited ordnance. The enormous blasts could be heard miles away, and desperate men leaped overboard to escape the flames and eruptions that came from the ship. Men lost limbs and were burned beyond recognition; and as crews fought the fires, ammunition and shells continued to explode, maim, and kill. The inferno on the vessel made it necessary to abandon the ship. Half-burned, burning, and hysterical soldiers and sailors leaped into the water, while others, driven temporarily mad by their wounds or the trauma of what they had witnessed, refused to leave the ship and had to be forced overboard. Some men, unable to locate lifejackets, grabbed on to men who were wearing them, but no longer in need of the devices because they were dead.

LST *749* was hit amidship by one plane carrying two bombs. One exploded on the deck, and one penetrated into the provision room and exploded, killing all of the crew who were there. The ship's steering was destroyed, and as a fire roared through the doomed vessel, LST *749* plowed forward, the crew unable to control the speed and direction of the ship. The 376-foot destroyer USS *Converse* moved in to assist, and immediately four Japanese planes attacked. She continued to render assistance to the sailors in the burning LSTs while under attack. Three of the Japanese planes were shot down by the destroyers and the fourth fled. Hundreds of men from the two LSTs were rescued by *Converse* and other ships. Ultimately, LSTs *749* and *460* found their way to the bottom of the Sulu Sea. There were dozens of casualties among the ships' crews, and 107 of the 774 soldiers on the two ships were killed, a striking example of the destructive potential of the Japanese Kamikaze Force.

Juan De Fuca was hit in the number two hatch. Fortunately, there was no flammable material near where the suicide plane crashed, and the fire was quickly put out. Two men were killed and 17 injured as a result of the suicide attack. In total, as many as 45 Japanese planes attacked that day, and 15 were shot down. It is a testament to the skill of the American pilots who defended the convoy and the gunners on the ships that more ships were not lost.[76]

Later that same day, destroyer USS *Bryant* was sailing off the southern tip of Mindoro as part of Task Group 78.3.13 when a single Zero flew toward her starboard bow. In an attempt to avoid the plane, the ship turned hard while increasing its speed to full. Gunners set their sights on the plane and both 20 mm and 40 mm rounds hit the aircraft. The ship continued to turn sharply, and the plane's pilot, despite the damaged condition of his aircraft, attempted to adjust his course to match the course alterations of the ship.

The plane hit 50 yards off the ship's port beam, and flying debris from the aircraft wounded one sailor.[77]

The surviving ships in the convoy motored on, and on December 22 they arrived at Mindoro without further incident. The LSTs were quickly unloaded, and as dusk approached, the vessels were on their way back to Leyte. The Japanese were still determined to destroy these ships, but this task was made more difficult because American planes could now fly from airstrips on Mindoro.

Shortly after leaving Mindoro, the returning ships were attacked by four kamikazes. Three of the suicide aircraft were shot down by American P-38s in the sky over their targets. But the fourth, diving almost vertically, survived the fire from the planes and vessels below, and set her sights on destroyer USS *Newcomb*. The skipper of the ship, Commander I.E. Macmillan, ordered full speed ahead and a sharp turn to the right. The suicide pilot got frighteningly close to its target and crashed just yards from the ship's bridge. No damage was done to the ship, but it is likely that at least a few of the sailors on *Newcomb* thought they were breathing their last breaths, and perhaps even a heart beat or two was skipped as the suicide plane was in the last few hundred yards of its dive. Later that day, a fifth Japanese plane was shot down attacking the convoy, and 10 more were destroyed by P-38 pilots in the skies over Mindoro.[78] Late at night on December 21, a lone plane flew over Mindoro, dropped several bombs, and scored no hits but disturbed the sleep and rattled the nerves of the men trying to rest.

The next day Lieutenant (jg.) Pete Rock, the beloved captain of PT *221*, boarded a plane and was sent back to the United States. For my father and the other sailors on PT *221*, this was a sad occasion; and Tom Hart, years later, explained that he felt a sense of "desolation" when he learned that Lieutenant (jg.) Rock would no longer be in command of PT *221*. It had been 20 months since the small boat had motored out of New Orleans, and during that period the men on *Omen of the Seas* had experienced much. There had been few constants in their lives as they journeyed thousands of miles over unfamiliar waters, but the one steadying force had always been Boat Captain Rock. He had the sense to realize that a PT boat was not like other naval vessels, and that the men who crewed these boats were a unique kind of sailor. They resisted formality and were often unwilling to embrace many long-standing naval traditions. However, they had also proven themselves to be adept seamen and able warriors. Lieutenant (jg.) Rock gave the men under his command the space they needed, and allowed them to ignore many of the formalities that other boat captains insisted their crews respect. He could be firm but kind, and he had the ability to lead men and command a motor torpedo boat in combat. Under him, the green sailors that left New Orleans had grown into superb sailors, become close friends, and displayed their metal during the difficult early days of the Mindoro campaign.

Lieutenant (jg.) Rock had developed a deep respect for the men under his command. Days before departing for New Guinea, he had been interviewed by the *San Francisco Chronicle* and said, "My crew is one of the best in the Squadron," and I am sure that he meant this. The young boat captain would go on to have a successful career in the United States Navy, and retire long after the war had ended having earned the rank of Lieutenant Commander. After the war, he would share beers with the sailors who had been under his command at PT boat reunions, and like so many of the men who came to these events, it is unlikely he ever again experienced anything like the early days on Mindoro. Not surprisingly, the sailors who served on PT boat *221* would always respect the man who had led them, and after he left Mindoro, he was fondly remembered and missed.[79]

Some of Squadron 16's officers. PT *221* Boat Captain Pete Rock, front row, far left; Squadron 16 Commander Almer P. Colvin, front row, center. Francis Gelzheiser collection.

At 6:30 in the evening, three enemy planes flew over Mangarin Bay and were soon pursued and shot down by American P-38s. In the pursuit of the enemy planes, one of the P-38s was hit by enemy fire, and the pilot was forced to bail out of his plane. He safely parachuted to the water and was quickly picked up by a nearby PT boat. After dark, more Japanese planes arrived. They dropped bombs that failed to hit any boats, but did land near a group of soldiers on the beach making coffee, killing three and injuring two.[80]

As night fell on December 22, PTs *220* and *222* motored to Log Anchorage off the Mindoro coast and picked up Lieutenant Commander Rowe, an American prisoner of war who had escaped his Japanese captors, and two Japanese prisoners of war. At first light in the morning, the two boats raced through the Mindoro Straits and motored within sight of the Japanese garrison on Luzon. Five American aviators who had been shot down over the island more than a month before and had thus far avoided being taken captive by the Japanese paddled out to the PT boats in native bancas, which resembled canoes. When the pilots were taken aboard, the two PT boats motored back towards Mindoro and got to within an hour of their destination before a Japanese floatplane overtook them at approximately 11:00 a.m. The plane circled twice trying to determine if the two boats were Japanese or American. The tense PT boat crews held their fire, hoping the plane would leave without attacking. The aircraft suddenly flew over the boats, first dropping bombs that barely missed them and then it returned for a strafing run at the small vessels. The plane's guns had barely fired when the combined fire from both of the boats found their target in their crossfire. The plane was hit, crashed just astern of the rear boat, and quickly sunk into the water.[81]

December 23 was the quietest day thus far for the PT boat sailors on Mindoro. PT *221* spent much of the day patrolling along the shoreline of Mindoro but encountered no Japanese in its search. When night came, the *Omen of the Seas* motored into a channel that separated Mindoro and a small island at the eastern edge of Mangarin Bay and anchored. To make sure the boat was not exposed to enemy planes, a stern anchor was dropped near shore, and swimmers brought a line tied to the bow to shore, pulled the bow in and tied the line to a tree. Branches were then cut with machetes and placed on the boat to further camouflage it. Hidden on the shoreline, hungry mosquitoes feasted on the sailors all night, and sleep was almost impossible. Planes flew over during the night and dropped bombs, but none came close to the boat except a phosphorous bomb which exploded 100 feet above the water, and soon thin streams of light were trickling down toward the boat. Another plane flew in that was barely 100 feet over the water, and the gunners on the boat could have easily shot it down. However, as on most nights, the order had been given not to fire on enemy aircraft at night unless the plane fired first. The plane passed, and then turned around and again flew low over PT *221*. The men on the boat continued to hold their fire, and they still could not determine if the aircraft was American or Japanese. After the second pass, the plane flew harmlessly into the horizon. At this point the sailors concluded that it was an enemy aircraft, and I am sure that all were relieved that both the men on the *Omen of the Seas* and the pilot in the plane had decided to allow December 23 to come to an end peacefully.[82]

At some point during the last week of 1944, the Army base on Mindoro received a radio message explaining that a group of American soldiers on Mindoro had been ambushed, and that they were pinned down on a beach, and one of their men had been wounded and needed to be rescued and given medical attention. A location was given, and PT *222* was sent to find the soldiers and bring the wounded man back for medical care. The soldiers were located, but the PT boat could not get close enough to shore to bring the wounded man aboard. Lieutenant (jg.) Robert Roth asked for volunteers, and George A. Dwyer, the quartermaster on PT *222*, immediately answered the request. Dwyer, an excellent swimmer, then entered the water with a knife in his mouth and a flashlight in one hand and proceeded to push a yellow raft through shark-infested waters until he reached shore one-half mile from the boat. Once near land, he proceeded to signal the boat and listen to audible signals from land, which eventually directed him to the location of the wounded man and his comrades. When Dwyer found the soldiers, he saw the newly dug graves where two Americans had recently been buried, and then carefully loaded the wounded man in his raft. Dwyer pulled the man back to the boat, and the soldier was immediately taken to the base at Caminawit Point where he received medical attention. For his efforts, George Dwyer received the Navy and Marine Medals for valor beyond the call of duty.[83]

December 24 was also uneventful. Boat crews were able to clean guns and complete various other chores on the boats. The day before, Robert Carlson had decided that the best way to clean his mattress cover was to tie it to a line, and let it drift behind the boat. Unfortunately, he forgot about it the next day, and when the boat backed down in the morning, a propeller caught it, and the cover became wrapped around one of the screws that had been damaged earlier. Now the men had to both repair the damaged screw and free the mattress cover while the vessel was still in the water.

A Japanese plane did fly over the island and dropped a bomb that landed on a 1,000-barrel supply of gasoline adjacent to Hill Airfield. The explosion that resulted was spectacular, and the supply of aircraft fuel was now limited. Thus many flights had to be cancelled, but other than being startled by the huge explosion and fireball that followed, no one was harmed.

Patrols were an essential function of the PT boat force in the Philippines, and much of the time and energy of the sailors of the Motor Torpedo Boat fleet were devoted to preparing for and going on these patrols. On occasion, boats would be sent on patrol during the day. One of the goals of these missions was to draw Japanese fire from shore guns. PT boat gunners would return fire, and if they did not destroy the enemy ordnance, they at least hoped to set fire to the area near the weapons. Two to five planes, usually B-25s and P-38s, working in conjunction with the PT boats, could then locate the fire and destroy the guns from the air.

Although the goal of the majority of the patrols was to survey the shorelines of Mindoro and nearby islands in search of the Japanese, numerous other tasks were performed. American and Filipino warriors and guerrillas were dropped off and picked up, American pilots who had been shot down and prisoners who had escaped the Japanese and were under the protection of Filipinos were picked up, demolition teams were dropped off and picked up, and on occasion, Filipinos and their canoes were brought to a prescribed location, and the men and their boats would depart and sometimes be picked up days later. There were even a few occasions when PT boats took Marine and Army Air Corps pilots on missions with them so they could become more familiar with the boats and thus more able to identify them from the air. This was done to reduce the chance of friendly fire attacks on the small boats.

Each PT boat patrol was different, but there were certain procedures and routines that were followed before, during, and after most missions. The majority of the patrols took place at night. Crews would meet at between 3:00 and 4:00 in the afternoon to be briefed on where they were going and the goal of the patrol. There was also often a discussion about what procedures would be implemented if there was an emergency and the crew had to abandon ship.

Prior to leaving, the PT's captain and officers would check to make sure that all of the systems in the boat were functioning properly and that there was adequate fuel and ammunition for the night's patrol. If more than one boat was going on the mission, a "section leader" boat would be assigned. The engines would then be started and they would send out a cloud of smoke when first turned over. They would then be allowed to adequately warm up. For the remainder of the patrol the roar of the engines would be the dominant sound heard by the sailors. Generally, the boat would be joined by one to three other PTs, and occasionally a destroyer accompanied the small boats to provide additional firepower, but solo PTs did go on patrol. As the PT boat roared forward, the famous rooster tail wake would follow the boat. If there was a chop on the water, the boat would bounce violently, and salt spray would cut into the eyes of the sailors. Often, it rained on at least part of the patrol, and this added to the discomfort of the men on the boat's deck. Shortly after the boat left the dock, the cook would invite a portion of the crew to come below and eat a light meal, which often consisted of sandwiches and coffee. When these sailors were done, the next group would eat. Usually, this was the only food they would consume until a light breakfast was served on the voyage back to the base.

Boats would often head out to an assigned section of the Mindoro coastline or to a nearby island, and sometimes their destination was as much as 100 to 150 miles from their base. Once they arrived at their destination, their speed would be reduced. If there were multiple boats on the patrol, one PT would motor as close as 100 yards from shore. Some boat captains were more cautious, and they would avoid going too close to shore or entering small inlets or rivers. Others were more aggressive, and they would go dangerously close to shore. Often boats would motor past the same piece of coastline several times, and all of the sailors were expected to keenly focus on the shoreline in search of anything that indicated an enemy presence. One sailor was usually assigned to listen carefully to the radio, and another would intently watch the radar screen. Sailors not assigned to other tasks would peer through binoculars keenly focusing on the shoreline. The guns were manned at all times, and if the enemy was located, the outer boats would move closer to shore, and multiple guns from each PT would be directed at the target. Gunners would carefully watch the trajectory of tracer rounds to determine if they were firing accurately. Once a boat started firing, the light from the firing ordnance exposed the PT's position, and usually this meant that shore or barge guns would soon find the boat in their sights. Consequently, the boat would often move as it fired, and then circle back and commence firing to avoid being hit by the shore guns.

Below deck few lights were left on, and these were only in sections of the boat without windows or where the windows had been carefully covered. No lights were allowed on the deck, and on some nights it was so dark men had trouble seeing their hands in front of them. On other nights, when the moon was full and the sky cloudless, it was easy to see through the night. These well-illuminated nights were dreaded by many of the PT boat sailors, because the good visibility also made it easier for Japanese warriors on land, sea, and in the air to see them.

As the dawn was coming, the boat crew would set a course back to base, push the throttles forward and head home. At this point, the men could relax a bit, although they still had to worry about a confrontation with enemy planes and running aground. My father talked often of the beauty of the sunrises over the Philippines. He loved to gaze at the horizon from the deck of the *Omen of the Seas* as the sun rose. The sky would turn a mixture of orange, yellow, blue, and red, and I believe that the beauty and peacefulness of these moments helped him to momentarily forget that he was at war. Over the course of our lives together, we enjoyed hundreds of early morning fishing expeditions, and he always grew quiet and looked to the east as the sun was coming up. Although he almost never talked of the war, he did periodically remark about how he loved watching the sun come up over Long Island Sound and how it reminded him of the beautiful sunrises he saw in the Philippines while on patrol.

As the boats neared the base, the young sailors on the PTs did what young men with powerful boats and cars always do, they pushed the throttles to their limits and raced to get back to the base first. Part of the reason for this contest was simply young men enjoying the speed and the competition of the act, but there was also a more practical rationale for the race. The boat that arrived first was also the first to get to the fuel dock. Refueling could take significant time, and only one boat could refuel at a time, so being the first in line meant the crew could get its tanks filled first, and thus move on to the post-patrol chores and be the first to get some much needed rest.

PT boat crews were supposed to completely fill the 3,000-gallon tanks on their boats, but many crews secretly disobeyed this order. Although having adequate fuel was essential to the success of any mission, many PT boat sailors believed that the added speed that could be attained as a result of having fewer gallons of fuel in the tanks resulted in some PT boat crews secretly taking on only the fuel they deemed to be necessary for a mission. Once the refueling was completed, the boat would motor to the dock, mooring, or anchorage where it was berthed, and the crews would get to work. The boat's captain and perhaps one or two other officers would immediately go to the commanding officer's office and report on all of the actions of the mission and then sometimes participate in an intelligence meeting. The gunner's mates would take the boat's guns apart, repair any part of the weapon that was not functioning properly, and then oil and grease the weapons as necessary. Ammunition that had been exposed to salt water was discarded. Machinist's mates would check the engines and perform maintenance as was needed. Other members of the crew would clean the vessel, scrub the bilge, make necessary repairs to the hull, take on water, check and repair the smoke generator, torpedoes, and in some cases depth charges, and make sure the vessel was fully supplied for the next patrol. Members of the base force would repair electrical systems, motors, and other components on the boat as necessary.

The post-patrol maintenance and cleaning took many hours. The blazing Philippine sun would make any metal on the boats hot to the touch and create stifling conditions in which men had to work. On some boats, men only had to complete the tasks associated with their job on the boat. For example, a boat's cook only had to make sure that the galley was clean and stocked and then he could rest. On other boats, men who had completed their tasks were expected to assist other sailors with their chores until all of the post-mission tasks were completed. When the boat was fully cleaned and needed repairs completed, the crew would wash up and then get some rest. Often boat crews would get a day or two off between patrols, but it was not uncommon for boats to go on missions two and three nights in a row; and on occasion, crews would be exhausted after spending as many as 10 consecutive nights on patrol.[84]

As evening came to Mindoro on Christmas Eve, 1944, in an effort to avoid the mosquitoes that had been ravaging the sailors while they tried to sleep, the crew of PT *221* motored the boat to the east shore of the bay and anchored there. Ensign Rafferty took out a pint of whiskey that he had been keeping since they had left the United States, mixed it with powdered lemons, and the crew of PT *221* shared a peaceful Christmas drink together. Somewhere on the island of Mindoro, homesick sailors and soldiers tuned in to Tokyo Rose, and she sent Bing Crosby's *I Love You* or *I'll Be Seeing You* over the airways, which of course made the men who heard it even more homesick. Random planes flew over the island that night and dropped bombs, but fortunately none did any damage.[85]

December 25–26, 1944

In the 10 days since they had landed on Mindoro, the sailors and soldiers stationed there had done an admirable job of building a military infrastructure on the primitive island. Tents had been constructed to house a sick bay, radio shack, and chow hall, and the construction of new and improvement of old airfields continued. Base force sailors

First Mass celebrated on Mindoro after the American invasion. World War II PT Boats Museum and Archives, Germantown, Tennessee.

continually worked to keep boats running, a task made extremely difficult by the number of hours the boats were operating and the regularity at which boats collided with reefs, logs, and other submerged and floating obstacles.

Shortly after the sun rose on Christmas morning, each boat was allowed to leave only six sailors to man the craft so that the remaining crew members could attend a simple Christmas religious service. While most of the PT boat sailors were worshipping, a Japanese fighter came roaring over Mangarin Bay at an altitude of only 100 yards, but before it could do any damage, it was shot down by PT boat gunners who remained on the boats.

There was some levity later in the morning when newly arrived Ensign John Zulick stepped out of a small railroad car, which ran on the tracks repaired by the crew supervised by Lieutenant Commander Colvin and was thus named "Colvin's Railroad," and announced for all to hear, that since he had arrived "the War was over and all hands could relax." He continued to banter on but none of his words could be heard because the air was filled with explosions caused by the Japanese dropping stick bombs aimed at the white house that was being used as the operational headquarters. The bombs all missed, but they did prove just how wrong Ensign Zulick was.[86]

PTs *221* and *227* were sent out on what was called the "southern patrol." The water was rough, and for most of the day the sailors had their teeth rattled by the pounding of the boats in the turbulent seas, and they were soaked by the salt spray that blasted over their boat's bow each time it landed. Their mission was to transport six men to an LST that six days earlier had been hit by a bomb in the stern and made inoperable by the explosion and the extensive fire that had engulfed much of the ship. Fearing the LST would blow up, the captain of the vessel had ordered his crew to abandon ship and board another vessel. After being abandoned, the ship had drifted for several days; and when the PT boats found her, the fires that had damaged her were out, and she was drifting near a small island. The job of the men on the PT boat was to try and repair the large craft and bring it back to the base in Mangarin Bay. For the rest of Christmas, the PT boat crews and their passengers worked to pump the water out of the abandoned vessel, and as night fell, the ship's bilges were relatively dry. They were able to get the LST's motors started, but its steering was in poor repair. After failing in their attempt to get the ship underway, the PT boats headed the 50 miles back to their base, and the six men who had been brought to repair the LST were left behind to continue working on the ship. The seas continued to pound, and the soaked, beaten up, and exhausted PT boat sailors made it back to their base as Christmas day was about to come to an end.[87]

After returning from this difficult patrol, the crew of PT *221* hoped that December 26 would be quiet and peaceful, and during the day their wish was granted. There were no alerts, and no patrols had been scheduled for the crew of the *Omen of the Seas* that night. By 5:30 in the evening most of the cleaning and maintenance tasks had been completed when PT *230* pulled along side of PT *221* and announced that for that night the boats would be exchanging crews. The reason for this unusual trade was that the crew of PT *221* was still worn out from the difficult night patrols they had been on over the last few days. PT *230* was in poor repair and had patrolled little over the previous 48 hours, so her crew was in much better shape. Thus the crews were exchanged so that the fresher crew could be sent out on the better functioning boat. PT *221* with the crew from PT *230* and PT *223* were now sent on a mission. Some PT boat historians report that the boats were to carry an army radar team to Abra de Ilog on northern Mindoro so they could observe the Japanese in the strait between Mindoro and Luzon. Tom Hart, who was there when the crew exchange was made, reported that the boats were to take 10 Filipino guerrillas and supplies to a guerrilla camp on northern Mindoro. It is possible that both accounts are correct, and that the boats had two missions that night.[88]

The crew of PT *221* was not happy with the exchange. They had spent the day cleaning and doing maintenance on their boat, but now another crew would enjoy the fruits of their labor. In addition they were now manning a boat that was in poor repair and in which they were not familiar. Once the exchange was made, the crew of PT *221* motored PT *230* to a quiet spot in Mangarin Bay and all on board hoped to soon be getting a good night's rest. However, as they were about to drop the anchor for the night, orders were barked over the radio that PT *230* and several other boats were to proceed immediately to the main PT boat dock.

As they motored up to the dock, the sailors were surprised by what greeted them. Men and officers were frantically boarding the boats and leaving with any weapon they could find. Carbines, pistols, Thompson submachine guns, and numerous other firearms were being handed out, and those who had yet to receive a weapon were determined to get one. Tom Hart and the crew of PT *221* soon found out why their fellow sailors were so desperate for weapons. An enemy task force was on its way, and it was feared that soon the Japanese would invade Mindoro.[89]

At 4:00 in the evening, the pilot of an American Liberator based on Leyte was returning from a patrol of Cam Rahn Bay when he spotted a Japanese fleet traveling at approximately 20 knots toward Mindoro. He immediately reported his discovery, and soon 92 fighters, thirteen B-25 Bombers, and a "number" of night-fighting P-61 Black Widows took off from the newly completed airbases on Mindoro to confront the Japanese fleet. In addition, approximately eight American planes took off from Leyte to join in the fight.[90]

The fleet they were confronting was small when compared to the armadas that the Japanese had sent into harm's way earlier in the war, but it was still formidable; and it would be the next-to-last offensive naval operation the Japanese would conduct in World War II. Second Striking Force, under the command of Rear Admiral Masanori Kimura, was composed of cruisers *Oyodo* and *Ashigara*, and six destroyers. They had departed Cam Rahn Bay, Indochina, on Christmas Eve, and they were going to rendezvous with aircraft carrier *Unryu*. However, on December 19 the American submarine *Redfish* had sunk *Unryu* and its cargo of Okas in the East China Sea as it was on its way to join the Mindoro invasion fleet. The Americans were unsure of the goal of the Japanese fleet, but when a group of cargo and transport ships were discovered motoring from Luzon toward Mindoro it was feared that Mindoro would be bombarded and then paratroopers and soldiers from troop transports would be landed in an attempt to retake the island. The only American naval force left on Mindoro to confront the Japanese fleet was the Motor Torpedo Boat fleet under the command of Lieutenant Commander Davis.[91]

Lieutenant Commander Davis determined that initially his small boats should avoid direct confrontation with the much larger Japanese ships. He was fearful of an impending invasion and believed that the PT boats could best be used to repel troop transports near shore. Thus the initial job of the PT boats was to scout the Japanese fleet and report back their actions to the officers on Mindoro. PTs *80*, *77*, *84*, and *192*, under the command of Lieutenant Commander Fargo, were to patrol 10 miles to the north and in line with the approach course of the Japanese ships. The *78*, *76*, and *81* boats, under new Squadron 16 Commander Lieutenant John Stillman, were to patrol north of Ilin Island one mile outside the entrance to Mangarin Bay and try to protect the four liberty ships anchored near the southern shore of Mindoro. And PTs *230* and *227*, led by Lieutenant (jg.) Robert Keeling, were told to patrol the outer portion of Mangarin Bay and support the other PT boats as needed, and if necessary to relay messages from Lieutenant Commander Fargo and Lieutenant Stillman to the base.

The crew of PT *221* was not happy with the situation in which they now found themselves. They were not familiar with the idiosyncrasies of the boat they were manning, only two of the boat's three engines worked, some of the deck guns operated differently than the ones on the *221* boat, and they also found it difficult to locate needed materials because each PT boat crew stowed things in different locations on the boat. Attempts were made to call back PTs *221* and *223*, but initially these boats could not be reached by radio. The 11 remaining PT boats had bent screws, were out of the water on a cradle, were missing generators, had motor defects, radio trouble, and various other problems that made them unsuitable for combat unless absolutely necessary; so they were ordered to stay in the bay near shore and defend against Japanese landings if they occurred. All boats were ordered to scout but not attack the Japanese fleet until ordered. They were then expected to engage the enemy with "torpedoes, deck guns, and depth charges" in what would be a desperate attempt to repel the vastly superior enemy naval force.[92]

If Mindoro was invaded, General Dunckel would be in charge of its defense. The general had troops of the 24th Infantry Division and the 503 Parachute Infantry Regiment as well as the PT boat sailors who were not manning boats under his command. PT boat sailors who had not yet secured weapons were now assigned rifles, and along with many of their counterparts in the Army, told to dig in on the beach and the tree-lined Mindoro shoreline. Their job was to repel the feared invasion force if the invaders were able to fight their way through the determined men in the PT boat fleet.[93]

At approximately 8:30 that night, American airmen located the Japanese fleet roughly 40 miles northwest of Mindoro, and 30 minutes later one of the more intense nighttime air-to-air, air-to-sea, and sea-to-sea battles to take place during the war in the Pacific began. A short time later PTs *80*, *77*, *84*, and *192* located the enemy, and for 80 minutes the boats came under heavy fire from Japanese ships and aircraft. The sailors on PT boats *227* and *230* observed the battle from their assigned position and reported that the "sky lit up like Times Square" from enemy ship anti-aircraft fire, and "there did not appear to be a square foot of air space that did not have tracers cutting through it. The American tracers burned with a red light; the Japanese with a white light, and both the American and Japanese pilots were flying their planes with lights on to confound the anti-aircraft gunners." In addition, "flares from enemy ships and planes were everywhere, and enemy planes were dropping bombs on shore and attempting to bomb several ships (LSTs) which lay in the harbor." One pilot later said, "It looked like hell upside down."

Tom Hart from behind the guns of the unfamiliar PT *230* viewed a surreal scene off in the distance. "The enemy task force was lobbing hundreds of shells, about half of which were illuminating shells. The illuminating shells burst about one hundred to two hundred feet above the surface of the water and descended very slowly by parachute. The entire bay and parts of the shore were lighted up fairly clearly. The surface of the water was pock-marked by falling shell fragments and occasional bombs." A plane dove and targeted an American LCM. The small craft, now operating at full speed, "twisted and turned" to avoid the strafing from the plane and the three bombs dropped by the aircraft. All of the enemy ordnance missed the fleeing vessel.[94]

Outgunned PT boats continued to come under Japanese attack, and for more than an hour they hid behind boat-generated smokescreens and ran zigzag courses at full speed to avoid bombs from Japanese planes and shells from enemy ships. At one point, two or three Japanese destroyers were chasing after four PT boats, and their shells exploded all around the boats sending shockwaves, water, and fear toward the boats' sailors. To make their situation worse, American planes flying from Mindoro to attack the Japanese ships and planes mistook the PT boats for Japanese naval vessels and landing craft and relentlessly strafed and bombed them. PT boat crews desperately tried to communicate to the American pilots that they too fought for the Stars and Stripes, and PT boat sailors reluctantly did not fire on planes fearing they could be American. PT boat gunners grew more and more anxious, and to insure that they would not fire at the American planes, Squadron 13 Commander Fargo kept repeating, "Hold your fire! Hold your fire! They're friendly!" One PT boat gunner responded, "Some god damned friends."

At approximately 10:00, PT *230* had just completed relaying the message that PTs *221* and *223* were returning to base when an "unintelligible voice came over the radio from PT *77* saying, We have been hit and have casualties and damage to the boat." One bomb, that most likely had been dropped by an American plane, had landed just off the stern of PT *77* and damaged the vessel and wounded her captain, Lieutenant (jg.) Frank Tredinnick and 11 men. Another bomb landed dangerously close to PT *84* and blew a man overboard. After retrieving the sailor, PT *84* was ordered to escort the damaged *77* boat back to the base.[95]

Lieutenant Commander Fargo requested permission to attack the Japanese ships, but his appeal was denied, and he was instead instructed by Lieutenant Commander Davis to proceed southward with PTs *80* and *82* and prepare to defend Mindoro if the Japanese attempted to land on the southern beaches. While they were passing through the strait that separated Ilin Island and Mindoro, they were attacked by an enemy floatplane and were only able to avoid being hit by running at high speeds and turning the boats erratically.[96]

The Japanese ships, under the command of Rear Admiral Kimura, continued to motor closer to the Mindoro coast. They approached Lieutenant Stillman's three boats off Ilin Island at 10:15 and certainly had vastly superior firepower and could have destroyed the small vessels, but at this point in the war Japanese naval commanders were reluctant to risk losing their ships, and the admiral did not blast his way past the PT boats. Finally, at almost 10:40, the Japanese fleet motored toward and then along the Mindoro coastline to shell the town of San Jose, the airfield, and Beach Red. These ships were joined by Japanese planes that had taken off from Luzon, and they also strafed and bombed the town and airstrip. American planes continued to relentlessly strafe and bomb the Japanese ships, and this distracted the ships' gunners and damaged the ships' guns and control stations, making accurate fire difficult.[97]

My father had vivid memories of this portion of the battle. He was a sailor in the United States Navy, but now he found himself on a Philippine island, that I doubt he had ever heard of just a few weeks earlier, in a hole on a beach being shelled by the Japanese Navy readying himself for an invasion that he was sure was about to occur. Although he did not realize this at the time, there was a comic element to the sailors' attempts at being infantrymen. Several Navy men, eager to do all they could to protect themselves from enemy shells, dug holes so deep they could not see out of them. My father and other members of Squadron 16 who were not manning the boats, helped to prepare for the impending invasion by digging a large foxhole that they reinforced with layers of 100-pound bags of hardened flour and 12-inch by 12-inch mahogany timbers. In this reinforced hole they mounted two 40 mm guns, four 20 mm guns, six to eight twin .50 calibers plus a number of small arms. My father dug a shallow hole nearby and waited, rifle in hand. The following day, soldiers, with more experience in coastal defense, explained that their endeavor was "foolhardy," and that "had their flour reinforced bunker been hit by a tracer bullet, it would have sent the entire group into God's Little Acre." Flour, it turned out, would do little to repel Japanese ordnance.

The sailors waited as bombs exploded along the beach. Slowly the explosions crept closer to my father, and he believed they were about to land on the section of beach he occupied. However, after approximately 40 minutes, the shelling suddenly moved inland toward the newly constructed airstrips, and then stopped, and the Japanese left without doing significant damage to San Jose, the airfield, or the men dug in on the beach.[98]

The Japanese gunners next fired a number of shells at Lieutenant Stillman's PT boats. All of the shells flew over the boats, and some landed within 100 yards of the vessels. American planes continued to attack relentlessly, and enemy ships now began their retreat fearful of the planes that were menacing them from above. Lieutenant Stillman again asked permission to attack, but he was again told to hold fire as long as American planes were engaging the enemy from above.

As the Japanese ships departed, they encountered the liberty ships anchored near the southern shore. One of the Japanese ships started to fire low over the water, and these shells ricocheted over the surface barely missing some of the nearby LSTs, and finally at approximately 11:00 p.m., after being lit up by star shells, one of the shells hit liberty ship *James H. Breasted* on its port side and set it on fire. Other ordnance aimed at the American ships ricocheted over the water and landed dangerously close to nearby PT boats. Earlier, *James H. Breasted* had mistakenly been attacked by American planes; and in the chaos of the night, the ship was hit by both aircraft bullets and bombs, but it was never determined what damage was done by the Japanese ships and what by friendly American aircraft fire. After the battle ended, some even claimed the ship had been hit by a torpedo launched by a Japanese midget submarine.

Soon after the LST was hit, a desperate voice, "choking with fear," called on the radio for help. PT *230*, with the crew of the *221* boat on board, saw the S.O.S. signal flash on the water and moved in to help. They found several men in the water, and it was assumed they were from the burning ship. Later it was learned that these men had been on another LST and abandoned it when they believed it was going to be destroyed by the Japanese air and naval fire. After these men were pulled from the water, a larger number of men were removed from the water who had in fact been on the now burning *James H. Breasted*. As the Japanese ships were departing, two of Lieutenant Fargo's PT boats were ordered to attack the Japanese ships that were menacing *James H. Breasted*, and as they quickly motored their craft across Ilin Strait to confront the enemy ships, both PTs went aground preventing them from engaging the Japanese. They could not be removed from the reef until the next morning.[99]

As the Japanese fleet rapidly retired to the north at just past midnight on December 27, it shelled the Mindoro coast as it went. Although some of the Japanese vessels were damaged, they had not lost any ships. This was about to change. Throughout the night of December 26/27, Lieutenant Commander Davis had continued to attempt to communicate with the crews manning PTs *221* and *223* to try to get them to return so they could support the other boats in the defense of the island. Finally the two boats were raised on the radio, and they proceeded back to their base at full speed. At approximately 1:00 a.m., eight miles north of Dongon Point, the two boats ran into the retreating Japanese fleet. The PT boat officers radioed to their superiors asking permission to attack the enemy ships, and Lieutenant Commander Davis replied, "Give them hell and then haul ass."

Aboard the PT boats some of the crew members were elated that they would get a chance to confront the hated Japanese, and others thought the men who had requested and granted this permission for this attack had "flipped their lids." Now the order had been given, and all hands nervously manned their battle stations. The two boats then set a "collision" course for the Japanese ships, and soon the Japanese spotted PT *221*. The *Omen of the Seas* immediately found itself in the glare of enemy searchlights; and enemy gunners, seeing their target, began to fire dangerously accurate rounds at the craft, and "five inch shells began bursting all around her." At this point, survival was the primary goal of the men in the small boat, and they implemented the second part of Lieutenant Commander Davis' order. They pushed the throttles to full speed, opened the smoke screen generator, which immediately became stuck and released smoke so quickly that it soon ran out, and ran a zigzag course in an effort to avoid the frighteningly close fire emanating from the Japanese guns. In their efforts to avoid the Japanese shells, they barely missed grounding on a reef. Unfortunately for the Japanese, their sailors were now fully focused on the fleeing PT *221* and unaware that PT *223* was motoring nearby and within torpedo range.

As the Japanese directed intense fire at PT *221*, Lieutenant (jg.) Griffin, the captain of PT *223*, ordered both starboard torpedoes to be fired one after the other at a range of approximately 4,000 yards. At this point in the war, the torpedoes on the Motor Torpedo Boats were superior to the ones used earlier in the conflict, and both ran "hot, straight, and normal." The improved reliability and accuracy of the weapons paid off. Several minutes later, there was a flash and then an explosion on the third ship in the Japanese line. Of course PT *223* did not wait around to determine how much damage it had done, and instead it opened up the three Packard engines and fled at full speed. However, later that day when PT boats were sent out to look for Japanese and American survivors of the battle, a boat located one lucky sailor from PT *84* who had been blown overboard and lost during the battle and five Japanese sailors from destroyer *Kiyoshimo*. This was the newest and most modern and powerful ship in its class in the Japanese Navy. During the night before, it had been hit and damaged by American planes, but it had been the torpedo from the tiny PT *223* that had sunk the pride of the Japanese fleet.

After being pulled from the water, one of the rescued Japanese acted in a particularly arrogant manner toward the PT boat sailors, and several lobbied to shoot the prisoner. Fortunately he was spared, and when interrogated by officers after he was brought back to base, it was learned that the prisoner was a quartermaster, who had valuable intelligence that he shared with his American captors. The men of the Mosquito Fleet must have smiled when a rescued American pilot who had been shot down during the battle remarked when he surveyed the deck and armaments of the small boat, "Never in the world would I ever attack anything like this."[100]

On December 27 at 2:00 a.m., Rear Admiral Kimura's fleet motored back to Cam Rahn Bay, and the aerial and PT boat forces that had confronted the Japanese force could now lick their wounds and evaluate the damage done to the enemy and the price paid by the American forces. Not only had one of Japan's newest and most powerful destroyers been sunk, but all of the other ships in the Japanese fleet had been damaged. At this point in the war, with her once vaunted Navy facing failure after failure, and protecting supply routes becoming almost impossible, losing any ship or the use of a vessel while it was being repaired was a serious blow to the Japanese naval forces.

Inexperienced American pilots who had flown only minimal hours at night, flying mostly from only recently completed and primitive Mindoro airfields, performed heroically and generally with commendable skill. Many flew into battle, attacked the Japanese, and then flew back to Mindoro, rearmed, and then took off to confront the enemy again. Twenty-six American planes were destroyed in the battle, including B-25s, P-38s, P-47s, P-40s, and a PMB patrol bomber, but fortunately most of the men who piloted these aircraft were rescued. The Japanese fleet would never again confront the Americans in the Philippines.

The battle did reveal problems that the PT boat sailors had confronted before. American planes still all too often mistook the small craft for Japanese vessels, and friendly fire attacks would continue to plague the sailors of the Mosquito Fleet for the duration of the Philippine Campaign. Lack of accurate charts continued to hinder navigation, and the PT boats that went aground during the battle were lucky that they were not destroyed by the enemy. One of the PT boat's greatest assets was that it could navigate near shore, but as long as boat crews could not measure water depth electronically or lacked access to accurate and complete charts of the waters in which they were navigating, grounding would be a problem. The night of December 26/27 had been terrifying for both the PT boat sailors in the boats and those waiting in holes on the beaches along the Mindoro shoreline. There is no doubt that all enjoyed the peace that came after the Japanese fleet fled. This peace would not last for long.[101]

December 27, 1944–January 4, 1945

Late in the afternoon of December 27, the crew of PT *221*, now reunited with their boat, and PT *223* were sent to pick up a pilot who had been forced to parachute from his plane. After much searching, the pilot was located. He was wearing a lifejacket, which briefly gave the PT boat sailors hope that they were on a rescue mission and not a body recovery. But when they got closer they saw that the man's face was in the water, and their hope faded. A macabre debate ensued about how to get the man into the boat. Some sailors argued that a slip noose should be lowered onto the pilot with boathooks, tightened, and then the man should be lifted onto the boat. One sailor protested this explaining that the man might be alive, and even if he was dead, he did not think it right to "lasso" the pilot to get him on to the boat. Ultimately, the sailor with reservations lost the argument, and the pilot was lifted into the boat with the rope. He was dead, and the body was transferred to another PT boat, and PTs *221* and *223* continued on with their mission.

Each of the two PT boats was loaded with about 1,000 pounds of supplies and a number of guerrillas. The boats were to take the supplies and men to the guerrilla forces on northern Mindoro. Because the seas were rough and water was continually crashing over the boats' decks, many of the sailors were concerned that the guns were getting so wet that should they be needed in a confrontation with the Japanese, they would not function properly. When the boats reached their destination, they motored into a small bay where they were scheduled to meet the guerrilla forces. The PT boats flashed a light, and this was quickly answered by a light from shore. Soon a strange sailing craft approached the PT boats. It was about 60 feet long and 10 feet wide and was powered by two sails that were each about 20 feet high by 10 feet long and woven from coconut leaves. The boat also had a small cabin and storage room.

The sailboat soon rendezvoused with the PT boats, and the men in all three boats worked frantically to unload the supplies from the PT boats to the sailing vessel. The PT boats would not be returning to base empty-handed. As soon as the sailing boat approached the PT boats, five American airmen emerged from the guerrillas' craft and happily jumped into one of the PT boats.

Three of the men, a lieutenant and two sergeants, had been on the same bomber, and their story was fascinating to the PT boat sailors. Flying a mission over Manila, they faced "flack that was terrific," and their aircraft was one of several bombers that was hit by enemy fire and crashed into Manila Bay. They managed to get into a rubber raft but were unsure of how to best avoid being captured by the Japanese, who they were sure would soon be after them. Shortly they saw a small boat approaching, and fearing it was the Japanese, the lieutenant drew and aimed the one pistol they had at the approaching boat. They agreed that if it was the enemy, they would not be taken alive, and the three airmen waited for the worst. As the boat got closer, the men on the raft realized that the men on the approaching boat were all wearing straw hats, and all of the airmen were relieved when they heard one of the men on the cautiously approaching vessel say, "We save you." One hour later the three very lucky airmen were in the guerrilla camp eating ice cream.

The lieutenant had learned a great deal about the Filipino guerrilla operation. The guerrillas were very numerous in that part of Mindoro and on Luzon. Sometimes they outnumbered the Japanese in a region, and they would periodically hunt them down and kill them. Occasionally the Japanese would try and locate and destroy these forces, but these actions were surprisingly rare. Whenever there was a bombing raid and Allied planes were shot down, men from the guerrilla forces would quickly paddle out to try and locate and rescue the airmen before the Japanese could find them. Since the vessels used by the Filipinos were almost all hand or wind powered, the rescuers always risked being seen by Japanese planes and/or ships and killed.[102]

On December 27, as rain pelted the ships, a second, larger, resupply convoy steamed out of Leyte bound for Mindoro under the command of Captain John B. McLean. Sailing with this enormous fleet that took up more than three square miles was Captain George F. Mentz, the commander of a diversionary attack group, comprised of the LCIs and PT boats, that was scheduled to launch attacks against southern Luzon prior to the main assault on the island. The 99-ship Task Force 77:11 was composed of LSTs, LCIs, PT Boat Squadrons 8, 24, and 25, liberty ships, an aviation gas tanker, aircraft tenders, Army supply boats, Army and Navy crash boats, nine destroyers, and PT boat tender USS *Orestes*, which served as the flagship for Captain Mentz. No aircraft carriers sailed with this enormous fleet. The convoy ferried a contingent of troops to reinforce the soldiers who were on Mindoro and provide additional material to continue the construction of the Mindoro airfields that would be vital in the impending invasion of Luzon.

The soldiers and sailors manning the convoy and the PT boat sailors who awaited them in Mangarin Bay would now experience the full wrath of the Japanese Spirit Warrior. For most of the three days that the convoy motored toward Mindoro, it would either be under attack by Japanese fighters, fighter bombers, torpedo bombers, and kamikazes, or enemy planes would be on the radar of the convoy's ships.

Captain McLean's flagship, the 2,050-ton, 376-foot destroyer USS *Bush*, would sound general quarters 49 times in 72 hours. Defense against the aerial onslaught was made more difficult by the lack of American air support provided for the convoy. Weather conditions on Leyte prevented American pilots from flying for most of the three days, while their Japanese counterparts, taking off from Luzon, had clear skies which enabled them to fly undeterred by weather and easily locate their American prey below.

Early in the morning of December 28, six Japanese planes approached the convoy. With no American air cover to protect the ships in the convoy, ships' gunners were the sole protectors of the vessels under attack. One suicide plane set its sights on an LCI, but LCI *1076* shot this plane down. Another plane was quickly shot down and another attempted to crash into aviation gas tanker USS *Porcupine* but missed its target and slammed into the water.

There are certain events in war that remain with the witnesses forever. One such event followed the attack on *Porcupine*. The 422-foot liberty ship SS *John Burke* was carrying needed ammunition to Mindoro and was so loaded with this cargo that she sat much lower in the water than normal. Kamikaze pilots flew above the ship free to carefully choose their targets due to the lack of American air cover. Through the clouds, one spotted *John Burke* and began its screeching descent. Despite a hail of fire from *John Burke* and nearby ships, the plane was able to score a direct hit between the ship's second and third cargo holds. An explosion occurred that was followed by a brief silence and then a massive explosion that sent out shock waves that shook virtually all of the 98 remaining ships in the convoy. Many vessels were rocked so violently that they reported being hit by enemy torpedoes; men on far away ships were sent flying so hard that ribs were broken; PT boat *332,* which was 500 yards away, had the seams on her side opened up by the force of the after-shock; and liberty ship SS *William Ahearn* was damaged so badly from the explosion's concussion that she could no longer maintain speed, and she was forced to limp back to Leyte. All of this pales to what happened to *John Burke.*

The second explosion, which was heard more than 20 miles away, sent a mushroom cloud into the sky that hid the ship from the rest of the convoy. Anxious sailors on nearby vessels strained to see through the cloud as they sped to help their fellow mariners. Slowly, as the cloud lifted, their worst fears became reality. What they saw was nothing: no ship, no detritus, no floating desperate sailors, no bodies ... nothing. *John Burke* had ceased to exist. The first explosion had ignited the ammunition. The second one, fueled by the exploding ammunition, was so severe that the ship was destroyed and sent to the ocean's bottom before any man could escape. All 68 mariners were lost, and no bodies were ever recovered. In addition, a small Army freighter that was near *John Burke* when the suicide plane hit was damaged so badly by the concussion that it also sunk. Two of the men on this ship survived the explosion, but one died shortly after he was pulled from the water.

Liberty ship SS *William Sharon* was hit at about the same time as *John Burke.* Its superstructure in flames, the 340-foot destroyer USS *Wilson* moved in. Firefighters from

John Burke **shortly after it was hit by a Japanese kamikaze. World War II PT Boats Museum and Archives, Germantown, Tennessee.**

the ship boarded *William Sharon,* which was loaded with thousands of gallons of gasoline and tons of TNT, and began to fight the fire. They were forced to leave the vessel when a "Flash Red" was sounded, and then re-boarded her just in time to be on the burning vessel when her ammunition boxes started to explode forcing the ship to be abandoned again. *Wilson* returned a third time, and again firefighters boarded *William Sharon,* and this time after a two-hour battle, the fires were put out, and *William Sharon* was saved. It was then towed back to Leyte without moving her cargo to a Mindoro-bound ship. In the hold of the returning *William Sharon* was a supply of beer for the tired PT boat sailors on Mindoro, and had they known this, I am sure the PT boat sailors would have greatly lamented this course reversal.[103]

During the afternoon and early evening, the Japanese attacked five more times. A Japanese torpedo ran the length of LCI *624,* and although it scraped the ship's flat bottom from bow to stern, it did not explode.[104] Four PT boats were hit by Japanese strafing attacks, but no PT sailors were killed or wounded. At approximately noon, American Combat Air patrol planes arrived, and they provided the ships with some protection from the menacing Japanese aircraft. However, bad weather forced these planes to return to Leyte three hours later, again leaving the convoy with no air support. At approximately three o'clock, the convoy was motoring off the southern point of Negros when 20 to 30 Japanese planes arrived, and they proceeded to attack the American vessels for almost the next two hours. Three of these planes were shot down.

At seven o'clock that night additional enemy planes arrived. Pittsburgh-built LST *750* was hit by an aerial torpedo in the engine room. The vessel was badly damaged and started to list to the port. This caused its cargo to shift, and eventually it rolled so badly that one of its propellers was out of the water. Men fought the fires, and others remained at their guns and continued to fire on the Japanese planes above. After an hour, it was determined that the ship could not be saved, and it had to be abandoned. American ships fired 150 five-inch rounds into the vessel, and the LST went to the bottom of the Mindanao Sea. While under attack, sailors from LCIs *1006, 1005, 1001,* and *1000* rescued 183 men who had been on LST *750.*[105]

By 8:15 that night the aerial attacks had ended, but PT boats in the convoy reported that the waters were dotted with black floating objects, and it was soon determined that the Japanese had dropped a large number of mines in the water. Fortunately, only one was detonated, and the explosion caused only minor damage to one American vessel.

Japanese planes were on American radar screens all night, and Captain McLean, knowing that more attacks were coming, pleaded with the commanders at Leyte to provide him with air cover the next day. Leyte would not be able to provide these planes, but the newly constructed airfields on Mindoro were put to good use, and aircraft from the island greeted the convoy before the sun rose on December 29. In the morning, the convoy was under attack for about 90 minutes. Three enemy planes were shot down by gunners on American vessels including the sailors on PT *352* who hit a Japanese plane as it was diving toward an LST. Throughout the day five different groups of Japanese planes attempted to reach the convoy, but fortunately American planes drove them off before they could attack the vessels in the convoy. During the night, Japanese planes attacked the convoy for eight hours. Six more planes were shot down, and PT *355* again proved the value of the small boats when its crew shot down a kamikaze determined to crash into a destroyer.

As morning came on December 30, three more Japanese aircraft were shot down

In late 1944 a resupply convoy was sent from Leyte to Mindoro. It was attacked by traditional and suicide Japanese aircraft. The smoke in the lower center of this photo is from a kamikaze that was shot down. Francis Gelzheiser collection.

not long before the beleaguered convoy arrived at Mangarin Bay. One of these planes was a kamikaze that had set its sights on an escort destroyer and was destroyed by a PT boat as it dove toward its target. Most of the men on the convoy's vessels had slept little if at all during their voyage, and there were casualties on many of the boats and ships.

Shortly after the convoy's arrival, the PT boats were placed under the command of Lieutenant Commander Davis. These boats were a much-needed addition to the PT boat fleet on Mindoro. Many of the boats that had arrived with the invasion force needed repairs, and generally the boats that arrived on December 30 were still in good condition and capable of immediately carrying out the numerous tasks required of the PT boats on Mindoro. Captain McLean wanted to unload the convoy as quickly as possible, and for most of the morning and early afternoon the skies were quiet, and the crews unloading the ships were able to do their work unimpeded by Japanese aerial assaults. There can be no doubt that all of the sailors who had manned the convoy and those who were stationed on Mindoro hoped that this peace would continue. Sick bays were full, and men were exhausted. Unfortunately, the worst was yet to come.[106]

When the Kamikaze Corps was created, the Japanese believed that this was a weapon that could fundamentally alter the course of the war. Although the suicide planes never proved to be as effective as initially envisioned, for one horrifying minute on the afternoon of December 30, 1944, the new weapon showed just how destructive it could be. At 3:40 in the afternoon, under clear skies, five Type 99 assault planes—most likely piloted by Takashi Amachi, Hobuhide Kugimoto, Tadoa Mukohse, Yutaka Ooishi, and Genji Sawada—appeared scattered in the sky above, and began their suicidal dives. Soon, all five broke through the American air cover that protected the boats that were still being unloaded in Mangarin Bay. General quarters sounded, and tired sailors, many of whom had been up all night, manned their battle stations. In about 60 seconds, despite the best efforts of these men, four American ships were in flames.

A single Val kamikaze was sighted about four miles away approaching at an altitude of approximately 2,000 feet and heading for the 328-foot Chicago-built PT boat tender *Orestes* captained by Lieutenant Kenneth Mueller. PT *355* was only 50 feet from *Orestes* when the suicide plane arrived, and its crew joined other PT boats and the gunners on *Orestes* and nearby vessels to fill the sky with bullets and anti-aircraft ordnance, frantically trying to stop the plane before it hit its target. This was the second attempt by a suicide plane to destroy the ship and her crew of 351 men. While motoring to Mindoro, she had successfully fought off a suicide plane; however, on this day she would not be so lucky. Gunners desperately continued to try and stop the plane even when they realized that their firing angle was so low that American ships and men were at risk of being hit. LCI *1072* fired so low that she shot away her mainmast, and an American P-38 that was chasing one of the kamikazes was most likely hit by fire from LCI *1000* as its gunners were desperately trying to stop the suicide plane before it found its mark. As the plane approached *Orestes*'s bullets met their mark, and just before the plane hit the ship, it banked, and hit the water just yards from the vessel.

Decades later, my father remembered this moment well. He was watching with fellow sailors as the plane hit the water and had joined in a brief but gleeful roar when he believed that a ship and her crew had been saved from disaster. Instantly, the roar was silenced. The plane was so low to the water when it hit that it bounced upward into the starboard side of *Orestes* sending its bombs into the ship in an upward direction. The explosives penetrated into the ship setting off a series of explosions and fires that would prove to be disastrous.

On the deck, 40 mm and 20 mm shells were ignited, setting off more explosions. Broken, burning, and terrified men leaped overboard, and many others, including Boat Captain Mueller, were soon forced to abandon the ship. Aviation gas was ignited spreading an even more intense fire. Desperate crew members on *Orestes* attempted to fight the fires only to find out that the fire mains were broken and power was lost.

Top: USS *Orestes*, shakedown cruise, Chesapeake Bay, May 1944. *Bottom:* Side view of *Orestes* prior to ship being hit by a kamikaze. Both photographs, World War II PT Boats Museum and Archives, Germantown, Tennessee.

Orestes shortly after it was hit by a kamikaze. World War II PT Boats Museum and Archives, Germantown, Tennessee.

Captain Mentz had been seriously wounded and was covered in blood, and his chief staff officer, Commander John Kremer, Jr., had been fatally wounded. Commander A. Vernon Jannotta, the commander of the LCI flotilla, ordered LCIs *624* and *636* to ignore the flames, fumes, intense heat, explosions, and mangled bodies and motor toward the burning *Orestes* to help fight the fire.

Despite the fact that the burning ship contained 37,000 gallons of high-octane gasoline, huge stores of ammunition, and large numbers of torpedo warheads, Lieutenant Commander Davis ordered his PT boats to the side of *Orestes* in an attempt to save the ship and its crew. My father on an unidentified PT boat joined in the rescue, and for more than 90 minutes he and his shipmates worked to save the men from the "human barbecue" that was *Orestes*. The wounded, some horribly burned, were fished from the oil and inflamed water by PT boat crews. Lieutenant Commander Davis asked for volunteers to enter the burning ship to fight the fires. Sailors from the Mosquito Fleet immediately volunteered, and soon PT boat men equipped with handheld fire extinguishers and hoses were finding their way on to the burning ship. As these men courageously battled the flames, huge explosions were being set off on the ship, and blood, flames, bodies, and body parts were strewed everywhere. As water sprayed from the hoses hit the flames, it immediately made a strange hissing sound as it turned into steam and smoke.[107]

Proving that you should never judge a man's heart, courage, or character by his physical stature, Tom Hart immediately volunteered to board the ship, fight the fire and rescue the survivors. He left a detailed account of what happened that day, but he makes

Orestes shortly after it was hit by a kamikaze. World War II PT Boats Museum and Archives, Germantown, Tennessee.

no mention of the great risk that he and his fellow firefighters were taking or of the courage they displayed:

> The PT boats had just rounded the corner of the sandy point and emerged into the bay when enemy planes appeared overhead. They were very high, but one immediately nosed into a steep dive. There was a P-38 in hot pursuit. The enemy plane, diving at terrific speed, was headed for an LST. The PT boats and other boats and ships opened fire. The enemy plane was not hit but, unfortunately, the P-38

was. It pulled out of its dive and flew slowly away flames streaming from it. The enemy plane continued its dive and the boats and ships continued firing at it as long as they dared without hitting their own craft. It soon appeared evident that the plane would miss its target. It disappeared behind some ships and everyone thought for a moment that it had crashed into the water. Seconds later the plane appeared, skimming a few inches above the water among half a dozen ships. The pilot had done a magnificent unbelievable feat in pulling his plane out of the dive at such speed and low altitude.

Some of the boats opened fire again, disregarding the danger to the other craft in the bay. After skimming among the ships the plane ... banked sharply and crashed into the Orestes.... A column of flame and smoke shot upward, and the ship began to burn.

The water around the boats was soon full of swimming men. The PT boats edged in among them and began hauling them aboard.... A whaleboat, which was picking up survivors, came alongside the *221* and asked Mr. Rauh to rush the burned man to the base. The man had not been wearing any clothing except for a pair of dungarees at the time his ship was hit. He had received a flash burn over his entire body above his belt, except for parts of his face. His outer skin had been scorched loose and hung on to him in tatters like ragged clothing. The underlying skin did not appear to be burned except on the back of his neck and showed clean and white as paper. Anderson applied a gelatin compound to his body and gave him a shot of morphine. He gave little indication of the pain he must have felt. He was a cook on one of the Elco squadrons that had arrived with the convoy from Leyte. He and several other cooks from the Elco boats had gone aboard the *Orestes* to stock up on food for their boats. Several of them lost their lives....

Lieutenant Commander Davis had a hose in hand and was already fighting the fire when Tom Hart joined him. They would hold the hose on the flames until they were overwhelmed by the smoke and flames, and then pass it off to another sailor. As they fought the fire, random and ferocious explosions emanated from the burning ship as ammunition was ignited by the fires that raged throughout the vessel. Ignoring the obvious danger, Lieutenant Commander Davis then led Tom Hart and a small number of volunteers on to *Orestes* to try and extinguish the flames and save as many of the wounded as possible. Tom Hart recorded the horror of what they encountered:

The plane had crashed just back of amidships and the entire upper deck in this area was a mass of twisted jumbled metal and loose smashed cargo. Among this wreckage the flames roared. There was one explosion aboard, but none of the firefighters was injured. On the port side of the ship, a long row of men who had apparently been in chow line lay in every form of dismemberment and mutilation. Some were eviscerated, their intestines strung over the deck, others had arms and legs torn off or twisted grotesquely or hanging by shreds of flesh. Some were blackened by fire. One man lay by himself, untouched by fire and almost unmarked. He lay on his back with dull eyes wide open and staring at the sky; on his face there was a look of surprise frozen there by death. More than an inch of blood washed back and forth among the bodies with the rocking of the ship. Over this mass of blasted humanity men tramped and stumbled dragging fire hoses. Further inside of what had once been part of the superstructure a large refrigerator packed with meat had been blasted open and its contents hurled about. In that area huge chunks of meat and parts of men were so mangled and intermingled with twisted metal and burning wood that it was difficult to tell which was human and which was not.

The firefighters kept advancing on the fire beating it back. The blood and water washing over the deck soon became so hot that it was painful to stand in it. Water was also being poured through the holes in the deck through which smoke was pouring from below. Hart and George Dwyer, Quartermaster on the *222*, took turns on one of the fire hoses. Hank Pierotti, Fran Claugherty, and Don Carter, all from the *222*, were also aboard fighting the fire. An officer ordered them to take canvas and cover the dead men. The fire appeared finally to be under control, and everyone thought it would soon be out.

A sudden alert and report of more enemy planes approaching brought an order for everyone to abandon the ship. The LCI was still alongside, and the men and fire hoses were quickly got aboard.

As the LCI pulled out, it was discovered that Dwyer was still aboard the *Orestes*. He ran to the stern and slid down a dangling line from which he was seized and dragged aboard at the last possible second.[108]

In addition to fighting the fire, Lieutenant Commander Davis located and carried two seriously wounded men out of the burning ship to safety. Motor Machinist's Mate Second Class Charles R. Jones was on nearby PT *298* when the suicide plane came at *Orestes*. PT *298* and other nearby boats "set up a tremendous barrage from both sides of the *Orestes*, in an attempt to blow the kamikaze out of the sky," and he believed that these rounds had killed the pilot just before he slammed into the doomed ship. One of his best friends, Ensign Freddrick A. Zeithan, was in charge of *Orestes*'s carpentry shop. Jones knew that this was located near where the suicide plane hit and his heart sank when he realized that in the instant the plane crashed into *Orestes* his friend had been killed.

As the PT boats motored toward the burning ship, the heat was overwhelming, and the water around the boats was in flames. Some of the men manning the stern guns of *Orestes* had leaped overboard and now desperately swam for the PT boats. PT boat men leaped into the fiery water in an attempt to save some of the struggling survivors of *Orestes* who had abandoned ship or been blown overboard and were now barely alive and on the verge of drowning. Some of these survivors died before they could be brought back to the PT boats, and this "devastated" the boat crews. PT *298* saw two men on the other side of a large wall of flame near *Orestes*. They tried to push a rubber raft through the flames to the desperate sailors. Only one of the men was able to reach the raft, and he was saved. The other man could not reach the raft and did not survive.

Additional PT boats arrived, and more sailors jumped into the oil- and fire-covered water to try and rescue the wounded. Those on board the boats threw lines to those still strong enough to grab them. Men on the top deck of *Orestes*, terrified that more explosions on the ship were to come, leaped into the water, and desperately swam to the PT boats. When the sailors were brought on board the PT boats, crew members worked hard to help the men expel the sea water that many had swallowed, and then rendered first aid. Finally, sailors tried to identify the bodies of the dead. Many were burned so badly that the only way to identify a sailor was by his dog tag, and while all of this difficult work was being done, the air was filled with the smell of burning men, an odor that many of the men who were there would never forget.[109]

After about 90 minutes, most of the fire was under control, but before all of the flames were extinguished, an LCI was lashed to each side of *Orestes* and the ship was pushed up on the beach about a mile north of Caminawit Point.[110] PT boat sailors continued to render first aid to the men who had been aboard *Orestes*, and members of the PT boat fleet were saddened to learn that at least four of the seriously wounded and five of the dead had been PT boat men who had boarded *Orestes* to get supplies. Provisions earmarked for the Mosquito Boat Fleet had been destroyed, and as a result, in the days that followed the attack, PT boat crews would be challenged by critical supply shortages.

The most seriously wounded were evacuated to the Army's Second Field Hospital near San Jose. Salvage of *Orestes* would begin almost immediately, and the ship would eventually be towed to San Pietro, California. In August 1945, after 202,500 man-hours of labor, the ship would again be operational.[111]

On December 31, officers wrote out a formal, classified Deck Log Remark Sheet that

Men who were burned after *Orestes* was hit by a kamikaze being cared for by PT *189* sailors. The decisive and courageous actions by PT boat sailors after *Orestes* was hit saved many lives. World War II PT Boats Museum and Archives, Germantown, Tennessee.

described the damage done to *Orestes*. It illustrates the military potential of the fully committed Japanese Spirit Warrior.

> **Hull**: One bomb hole 24" × 30" between frame 31 and 32 on the second deck. Second seam above the water line torn four (4) feet. Strake seam torn one (1) foot. One hole eight (8) feet long at frames 28 and 29, full width of sheer strake. Boiler room completely destroyed. Carpenter Shop completely destroyed. After end of A.C. Auxiliary generator room destroyed. Navigation bridge partially destroyed. Wheel House partially destroyed. Framework supporting "A" frame badly damaged. Main Deck damaged heavy at Frames 31 and 34. Main Deck damaged at frame 36, light. Main deck damaged by holes at frames 28 through 31. Main Deck warped at Frames 34 through 36. All officers quarters on Main Deck and Galley destroyed by fire. The compartments Second Deck damaged by fire are as follows: Dispensary, Ship's Supply Office, P.T. Officers Quarters, Messing Compartment. All piping between Frames 28 through 34 Second Deck and above destroyed. Forward Torpedo racks damaged. Ventilating systems throughout ship destroyed or damaged. Electrical damage as follows: Estimated 40 percent of all wiring burned out or water damaged. All main power feed lines for D.C. generator room burned out or otherwise damaged or destroyed. Power panel, A.C. Auxiliary generator damaged by fire and shrapnel. Degaussing cable between Frames 28 and 34 damaged. Gyro and repeaters unserviceable. Machinery damaged as follows: Steam Boilers, Evaporators destroyed with all excessory [sic] pumps. All carpentry machines, and tools destroyed. Both 4400 A.C. generators damaged by fire. Ship's service air compressor destroyed. 50 h.p. Winches for "A" Frame burned out.[112]

In addition to the damage done to the ship and its contents, 57 officers and men were killed, and many of their bodies were so badly damaged by the explosions that followed

Damaged deck of *Orestes*. World War II PT Boats, Museum and Archives, Germantown, Tennessee.

the attack that they were never recovered. Seven officers and 86 men were seriously wounded.[113]

At almost the same time *Orestes* was hit, suicide planes also found their way through tremendous fire from nearby ships and hit destroyers USS *Pringle* and USS *Gansevoort* and the aviation gas tender *Porcupine*. The 376-foot *Pringle* was hit in the after deckhouse, but was not seriously damaged, and it was able to motor to the beach and continue to provide defensive fire.[114] *Porcupine* was attacked while anchored off Beach White by a Val suicide plane. The pilot was able to land a bomb on the ship's main deck before he crashed, and the explosion that resulted ripped open the fuel tanks and flooded the engine room with oil. In addition, the plane's engine penetrated the hull under the water line causing water to flood in to the ship. The fire that resulted from the attack eventually destroyed the vessel. Seven men died and eight were wounded as a result of the sacrifice made by the suicide pilot.

The 348-foot *Gansevoort* raced at full speed just outside of Mangarin Bay and fired frantically in an attempt to destroy the kamikaze that had set its sights on her. Despite these efforts, the plane found its mark, and struck the ship on its main deck killing or wounding 34 of its crew. The explosion from the crash had cut the ship's steering and

Two views of *Porcupine* after it was hit by a kamikaze. Both photographs, World War II PT Boats Museum and Archives, Germantown, Tennessee.

electric power and blew apart her main deck. Destroyers USS *Philip* and *Wilson* motored to *Gansevoort*. Their crews fought the fires and prevented the destruction of the ship. Rescue crews and boats were able to tow the vessel to the PT boat base for needed repairs, and by early February, the PT boat base force had the ship back in service.[115]

Two hours after the successful attacks on the four American ships, Japanese bombs

Gansevoort after it was hit by kamikaze. World War II PT Boats Museum and Archives, Germantown, Tennessee.

found their mark on liberty ship SS *Hobart Baker* and sunk the vessel off the Mindoro beach. One merchant sailor was killed in the attack.

As the sun was going down on December 30, exhausted PT boat sailors boarded PTs *75*, *78*, *220*, and *224* and the boats motored out of Mangarin Bay for a night patrol. Soon a lone Japanese plane appeared, but before it could do any damage the gunners on all four boats opened fire and the plane was quickly shot out of the sky. As they journeyed into the darkness, it is doubtful if any of the young men on these boats lamented that December 30, 1944, was coming to an end.[116]

The year 1944 would not end quietly for the men on Mindoro. On the morning of December 31, liberty ships SS *Simon G. Reed* and *Juan de Fuca*, a vessel that had been damaged while convoying to Mindoro, were bombed by Japanese planes, and the damage to the ships caused them to run aground on Barriage Reef just off Mindoro. As a result of the successful Japanese attacks on the last two days of 1944, there were serious supply shortages on Mindoro. Samuel Eliot Morison, the preeminent scholar on the American Navy in World War II, concluded that "not since the Anzio operation had the Navy experienced such difficulty supporting an amphibious operation after the initial landing." In addition, naval leaders were fearful that as the Japanese perfected how to best employ their kamikazes, future invasions and the critical supply operations that followed would become increasingly more difficult. This was especially troubling because the planned invasion of Luzon was only 10 days away.[117]

Quiet settled over the PT boat base at Mangarin Bay on the night of December 31, 1944. The wounded had been sent to sick bays. Earlier, my father had been assigned the task of finding shelter for 21 crew members of *Orestes* who had not been injured in the attack. He had located a large supply tent and set it up. This is where this group of sailors from *Orestes* spent the last hours of 1944.

As he often did, my father went to sleep on a nearby beach. Just before sunrise on the first day of 1945, he was awakened by the faint roar of a plane engine in the distance. As the aircraft neared its target, the Japanese pilot, eager to make his mission a success, cut off his engines and silently glided his small bomber or "Washing Machine Charlie" just above the treetops, toward the newly raised tent. The plane dipped and unleashed one terrifyingly accurate fragmentation "daisy cutter" bomb on the tent below.

The ordnance did its work well. It detonated about 20 feet above the tent as it was designed to do and unleashed a thunderous explosion and bomb fragments on the men resting inside. Immediately 11 men were killed and 10 seriously wounded. Screams pierced the warm night air, and my father joined his shipmates in an attempt to rescue his new-found comrades. The dead, wounded, and healthy were tangled in the downed, shredded tent. Fearful that any light might provide a target for other planes, the PT boat sailors conducted their rescue in the dark. Randomly, my father pulled men to safety. Returning after removing one man, my father heard a voice, and he thought it was "Johnny Mac," a PT boat sailor from *Orestes* he had met hours before and who ironically was the brother of a friend from Pittsburgh. The voice was muffled, and it came from under the tent. Seeing an arm protruding from the downed tent canvas, my father leaned down, grabbed the arm, and pulled hoping to drag the man from underneath the tent to safety. Instead, he stumbled backward clutching "a bloody stump," the severed arm of his friend's now dead brother.

At that moment, my father succumbed to the war. Screaming "loud enough to be heard in Japan," and still clutching the arm, he slowly backed away and then "ran and ran and ran and ran." Minutes later he found himself surrounded by the safety of the Mindoro jungle. Here, he and the arm waited … paralyzed and on the verge of insanity. My father did not remember how much time he spent in the jungle. Perhaps just the remaining nighttime hours and part of the next day, or all night and the next day and the next night … he did not know. When he emerged, "bloody stump" still in hand, officers and enlisted men glanced at him and in subdued voices talked about what had happened, and if something in Fran was broken. Was he able to perform his duties? Did he instead belong in a "looney bin." Was he now just another casualty of Mindoro? How long the awkward period lasted my father did not remember. Finally the silence was broken when Lieutenant (jg.) Harry Griffin, the captain of PT *223*, yelled out "Gelzheiser, you were supposed to be down at the boat this morning to fix the auxiliary generator, and we cannot go anywhere without it. Now get your butt over there and fix it."

The command caused the trap-like mind that would serve him so well after the war to focus. He walked to the supply tent, got his tools, and went to work. Thoughts of terrifying explosions, fragment bombs, kamikazes, screaming blackened men, severed body parts, floating bodies, and the war were forced inward. He regained his focus … he did his job. The auxiliary generator was repaired, and boats were readied for battle. Talk of "sending Fran home" ended. Mindoro was not done with him. The incident was never mentioned by any officers or fellow sailors, and it would be more than 50 years before he shared this chapter of his war story with me.

I do believe that the events that followed the crashing of the kamikaze into *Orestes* haunted my father for the remainder of his life. Decades later, when I was examining comments and questions on an online PT boat forum, I found an entry from a woman whose father had died on *Orestes*. She wanted information about what had happened. I explained this to my father, and he got very quiet. He then looked at me and quietly said, "You should give me her phone number so I can call her, she needs to hear the truth."[118]

The kamikaze attacks continued into the early days of 1945. On the night of January 1, 1945, a kamikaze was again able to pierce the Mandarin Bay defenses and hit the 442-foot liberty ship SS *John Clayton* killing 6 and wounding 11. To keep the vessel from sinking, the ship was beached.

Mercifully, the last kamikaze strike came three days later, but this final suicide attack on Mindoro again illustrated just how effective a weapon the suicide plane could be. It was about 5:00 in the evening and my father was taking a quiet break on a beach. Lieutenant Commander Davis walked by and stopped to talk with my dad, and my father asked, "How are we doing?" Lieutenant Commander Davis responded that things seemed to be "going better." Just as he said this, four Japanese planes flew over Mangarin Bay at high altitude and set their sights on four separate targets. As one Val dove toward sea plane tender USS *Half Moon*, PT boats and tenders unleashed massive fire on the aircraft. The plane dropped two bombs, one bounced over the ship's fan tail, both failed to explode, and the aircraft then fled south trailing smoke. The second plane was hit by fire from PTs *78* and *81*. The aircraft, with smoke and flames trailing it, set its sights on the 442-foot liberty ship SS *Lewis L. Dyche*. The ship was loaded to its gunwales with ammunition and was on its way to support the invasion of Luzon when it and several other vessels broke off from their convoy and headed for Mindoro. It was floating on the waters outside of Mangarin Bay when the burning kamikaze crashed into it causing an enormous explosion that disintegrated the ship and killed all 71 hands. The concussion from the explosion was so great that men on shore were almost knocked to the ground. PT Boats *78* and *81* were a quarter of a mile away and were still lifted out of the water and their hulls and engines were badly damaged by the concussion from the detonation and from falling debris. Two PT sailors were killed and 10 wounded. An unexploded shell sent flying from *Lewis L. Dyche* after it was hit landed on LCI *621* and killed one and wounded four. My father and Lieutenant Commander Davis were almost knocked over by the force of the shock wave.

Motor Machinist's Mate First Class Maurice Smith had just picked up his "evening chow" and returned to PT *81*. Just after his return, the boat was motoring away from base for its evening patrol when the kamikazes arrived. Smith observed the battle between the naval vessels and Japanese planes, and after watching what he believed was the last Japanese plane crash in flames, he descended below deck to take an engine reading. About halfway through the engine check there was a huge explosion and then what he believed was a second because the "implosion that brought the air back to the boat took so long." The explosion on *Lewis L. Dyche* was so violent that the largest piece to come off the ship was about the size of an "army cot." The engine hatch from PT *81* went up into the air, and when it came down it crashed halfway into the engine room and shut down the engines. Pieces of the hull, doorknobs, light sockets, ball bearings, and other debris fell on the boat putting 36 holes in the craft. One 15- by 18-inch piece of hull flew just over Maurice Smith's head and smashed the fresh water line on the starboard engine, and flying pieces of metal punctured all four torpedoes and one of the gas tanks. The implosion returned with such force that approximately 25 feet of deck were flattened behind the engine hatch and the engine room telegraph was destroyed. The wave created by the explosion was so powerful that shore gun emplacements were "washed out." Almost all of the men on board the *81* boat were cut and badly banged up and had to be sent to sick bay. Decades after the explosion, Smith also remembered that the hot dogs and sauerkraut he was about to enjoy for dinner were blown all over the crew's quarters. Most of the base force was there to welcome Smith and his shipmates when they returned to base; and needless to say, Smith was grateful when an officer greeted him with three to four ounces of "medical alcohol."

Minelayer USS *Monadnock* and oiler USS *Pecos* were also damaged by the explosion's concussion and falling debris. Despite the damage to the *Pecos*, she was still a lucky ship. Not long before the devastating attack on *Lewis L. Dyche*, she had been hit by a Japanese bomb. Fortunately for all on board the ship, the bomb failed to explode, but the energy from the falling explosive was so great that it radically bent one of the vessel's port cargo booms when it hit.

The third Japanese aircraft strafed a nearby airfield and was shot down, and the fourth was hit by anti-aircraft fire. With smoke trailing, it flew off to the south. PT *298* picked up the wounded from the damaged vessels and transported them to the Army hospital, and PT *223* towed the damaged PT *78* back to base.[119]

January 5–September 15

When the American forces arrived on Mindoro, they did not intend to remove all of the Japanese warriors from the island. As long as the Japanese did not impede the construction and operation of the airfields, the naval base, and the other military facilities on the island, they would be ignored. To counter any Japanese attempts at infantry action on Mindoro, the United States regularly ferried troops on PT boats and other vessels to various parts of the island to collect intelligence and periodically confront the enemy. Attempts were made by Japanese soldiers to thwart the construction of the airfields on the island, but these were met with stiff American resistance and the attempts all failed.

In early January, approximately 400 Japanese troops were assembled at Batangas on the island of Luzon and taken by boat to Mindoro. These troops were combined with soldiers still on Mindoro. American troops were brought in to counter the Japanese force, and a series of skirmishes were fought at various locations on the island throughout January and February. Often it was PT boats that ferried American soldiers to areas occupied by the Japanese. On January 6, approximately 400 Japanese soldiers engaged a company of American infantrymen at the town of Pinamalayan and forced them to pull back. The Americans brought in reinforcements, and drove the Japanese out five days later. Soon after this defeat, the Japanese tried to take the airfield at San Jose, but this attack also failed. Eventually the Japanese were relegated to hiding on the island and trying to survive malnutrition, disease, the heat, and confrontations with the Filipino guerrillas. Many Japanese soldiers still occupied parts of Mindoro when the war ended.[120]

During the early days of 1945, General Walter Kruger's Sixth Army was pulled out of Mindoro to prepare for the impending invasion of Luzon, and these troops were replaced by General Eichelberger's Eighth Army. In addition, Major General Roscoe B. Woodruff relieved General Dunckel as the commander of the 24th Infantry Division. This meant little to the sailors of the Mosquito Fleet, but it did give them an excuse to throw a party at the paratroopers' headquarters in honor of the command change, and I am sure that all of the sailors and soldiers attending enjoyed the punch concocted with five gallons of

PT boat torpedo alcohol. Unknown to the sailors, many of these paratroopers who were based on Mindoro would participate in the battle for Luzon and hundreds would make the dangerous and deadly jump on the tiny island of Corregidor. These men would endure some of the worst fighting of the war, and many would be injured and killed in America's efforts to retake the "Rock."[121]

By the end of the first week of January, the number of Japanese attacks was reduced, and the PT boats began to patrol even more extensively along the Mindoro coast and Luzon in anticipation of the American invasion of that island. PT boats would journey out at night and make contact with guerrillas, land scouts and raiders behind enemy lines on Mindoro, southern Luzon, and nearby islands. PT boats would strafe Japanese shore positions, set fire to Japanese bases and installations, and destroy boats and docks.

Lieutenant Commander Davis was informed by his Filipino guerrilla contacts on Mindoro and Luzon that a large number of Japanese "midget" suicide or "Q" boats were hidden in Batangas Bay, Luzon. When Lieutenant Commander Davis informed his superiors of this, they were doubtful that the boats existed. Always a man of action, Davis organized a raid with two PT boats and two planes for air cover. Davis and two or three sailors then landed at Batangas, absconded with a suicide boat, and then proceeded to tow it back to the PT boat base. However, on their return voyage, the PT boats and the cargo they towed were attacked by American planes, and the Japanese craft was sunk. After listening to his account of what happened, Lieutenant Commander Davis' superiors were convinced of the existence of the suicide boats.[122]

After Lieutenant Commander Davis proved the suicide boats existed, PT boats would often lead search and destroy missions against these menacing craft that were a growing component of the Japanese arsenal in the Philippines. The small wooden craft would often be hidden along the coast of Luzon, and PT boat crews would motor dangerously close to shore seeking out the hiding places of these boats and then destroy them. In total, PT boats motoring from Mindoro destroyed more than forty of these deadly boats.[123]

During the first week of January, PTs *80* and *82* were sent on a daytime mission to the eastern side of Mindoro to fire on the shore where Japanese craft had been sighted. In the skies above, American B-25s were also bombing and strafing the shoreline. While the planes and boats were unleashing their ordnance, two American Corsairs flew into sight. One wobbled its wing indicating to the boats below that it recognized them as American, but the second mistook them as Japanese, flew in low, and opened fire on the two PT boats with its .50 caliber machine guns. The shocked crews did not return fire, and the plane soon flew away, but not before two men on PT *82* had been killed. The pilot of the Corsair later said he believed the PTs were Japanese vessels, and that the B-25s were strafing them.

Shore-to-shore movements between Mindoro and Leyte and other nearby islands almost always involved PT boats. Sometimes the PTs would deliver men and supplies alone, but if large numbers of men or quantities of supplies were needed that were too large for the PTs to carry, then the PTs would escort larger LCIs. PTs would bring supplies and men to Mindoro from Leyte and then from Mindoro to Luzon. PT boat crews did extensive exploring of the coastlines of Mindoro, Marinduque, and southern Luzon, and learned a great deal about Japanese defenses, mines, beaches, water depth, and the best places to land troops.

During one of the patrols, PTs *188* and *149* made the first voyage during the day between Mindoro and Luzon since the Japanese took the Philippines in early 1942. On their return voyage, they motored near a large Japanese shore gun on Verde Island, and the Japanese opened fire on the two boats. This exposed the location of the guns to the Allies, and soon American bombers were able to destroy the menacing weapons.[124]

On the night of January 14/15, PT boats *73* and *75* delivered supplies to the guerrillas on Abra de Ilog on Mindoro and then continued on patrol. To the northwest of Mindoro near Lubang Island, PT *73* hit a reef and became grounded. Efforts were made to get the vessel off the reef, but these had to soon be aborted when Lieutenant Commander Rowe let it be known that more than 300 Japanese soldiers were on Lubang. The men on PT *73* were then transferred to PT *75*, the *73* boat was set on fire so it could not be used by the Japanese, and the sailors from the two boats motored back to base.[125]

PT *221* was kept busy during this period. On the afternoon of January 7, PTs *220* and *221* were given a bag containing important information that needed to be delivered to the task force that was proceeding to Luzon for the impending invasion. The two boats motored at high speeds, delivered the bag at dusk, and then immediately turned around and headed back to their base on Mindoro at full speed as night was falling. They had almost made it back when the boat suddenly stopped causing Tom Hart to violently collide with a bulkhead. Two hard shocks quickly followed, and then the *221* boat sat motionless in the water pitched solidly atop a coral reef. PT *220* was immediately warned by radio to alter its course so that she too would not become grounded.

The grounding had caused serious damage to the *Omen of the Seas*. The steering gear in the rudder room was ruined, and one of the rudders was protruding through the bilge. They immediately radioed their superiors on Mindoro, and shortly, two LCMs, one of which carried Squadron Commander Stillman, arrived. It could certainly be argued that the sailors on PT *221* had been negligent when they grounded their boat, and many of the men expected Lieutenant Stillman to yell at them or even threaten that the men responsible for the accident would be punished when they returned to base. Surprisingly, Squadron Commander Stillman "did not display any anger or bawl anyone out." Instead he surveyed the situation and then determined the course of action that would be taken.

The PT boat and LCM crews worked for hours to lash lines to the grounded vessel and pull her free. Unfortunately, the boat had hit the reef at 8:30 in the evening, and this was also when the tide reached its peak. This meant that with each passing minute, there was less water under the boat until the next high tide arrived early the next morning. Not surprisingly, after six hours of hard work, they were no closer to freeing the craft than when they started. After several early morning attempts to free the boat failed, the crew on the LCM broke out a steel cable, and after a great deal of effort they were able to attach it to the base of the aft 40 mm gun mount. By the time this had been accomplished, it was no longer high tide, so the boat crews determined that it would be best if they awaited the evening high tide. As the tide went out, waves crashed over the now exposed reef and rolled the boat and cracked more of its hull, and additional pumps had to be temporarily installed in the boat to remove the water that was flooding into it at an increasing rate.

When high tide came that evening, the LCM began to drive forward in an attempt to slowly drag the boat from the reef, but after much effort, the boat moved only a few feet, and then the cable snapped. The two LCMs returned to their base with Lieutenant Stillman; and although upset that the boat was still grounded, he was more concerned that the men had had enough rest and nourishment. He then ordered half of the men to go to shore and get some much needed sleep.

The next morning, they did not work to free the boat. This gave the crew time to swim in the clear water and examine the abundant and different kinds of coral and fish that lived on the reef. Some of the coral reminded Tom Hart of "miniature dead trees." Others were, "lace-like, reddish-brown forms nearly a yard across." Other colors observed included various shades of white, brown, gray, pink, and blue. The fish were equally as interesting and beautiful. Most hovered motionless on the reef. They were a variety of colors, and nearly all had adapted well to their environment and were almost indistinguishable from the coral. For men who loved the natural world like Tom Hart and my father, viewing such unusual and abundant beauty surely was a wonderful distraction from the horror, exhaustion, and fear that had dominated so much of their time in the Philippines.

Days later PT *221* was freed from the reef and towed back to the PT boat base. Her badly damaged bow was dragged onto the beach so that water would not flood in, and her stern, which did not have hull damage, remained afloat. Although the crew of PT *221* was assigned shore duties as their boat was being repaired, the combination of the reduction of Japanese attacks and the inability of PT *221* to join in the patrols that continued daily from the base in Mangarin Bay, meant that for the first time the men could pursue leisure activities on Mindoro. As days melted into weeks, a kind of normalcy took shape on Mindoro.[126]

One of the first things my father and Tom Hart wanted to do was explore the interior of the island. San Jose was about five miles inland, and men could get there by following the tracks of the miniature railroad that ran from the town to the coast.

After their journey, the sailors found a town with a population of about 1,500 permanent residents. Houses were built of bamboo, and they had no running water or electricity. They sat on posts that elevated the dwellings four to five feet above the ground; and they had thatched roofs, small porches, and stood 20 to 50 feet apart. Stone ovens were used for cooking, and women prepared rice by pounding it with a bamboo pole. When coconuts were needed, small boys would quickly scurry up the tall, narrow trees, find several that were ready to be consumed, and toss them to boys who waited below. There was little furniture in the homes, and most of this was built with bamboo.

Many American soldiers walked

My father climbing a coconut tree. Francis Gelzheiser collection.

Dwellings on Mindoro, December 1944. World War II PT Boats Museum and Archives, Germantown, Tennessee.

the town's streets that were filled with a few small cars, horses, cows, and the most popular animal on the island, the carabao or water buffalo, which was used for plowing, riding, and as a source of milk. There was a large sugar refinery; but as a result of the war, there had been almost no sugar grown on the island in two years, so the refinery was not in use. The war also halted much of the commerce in the town, and the Japanese had taken most of their goods from the few stores that were open. Interestingly, most of the natives spoke neither English or Spanish. Instead, the majority of the people in this part of Mindoro spoke Tagalog, which along with English was the official language of the Philippines, so it was difficult for the Americans to communicate with them.[127]

Some of the sailors explored the flora and fauna in the island's interior. Between their base and the mountains in the center of the island, the soil was muddy and walking was difficult. Strange plants and trees were everywhere, and although large mammals were scarce, there was an abundance of interesting birds and a species of giant lizard that grew to be four feet in length. Close to the mountains, the ground rose and became dryer. Here there were small farms that grew corn and tall, fruit-filled coconut trees in straight rows. Cattle, pigs, and carabao grazed freely, and many of these mingled with the numerous small children that played unattended by adults.

There were also numerous dangerous and enormous snakes on Mindoro. The Philippine cobra, one of the deadliest snakes in the world, lived on the island; and the reticulated python, which reaches a length of more than 20 feet and is one of the largest snakes in the world, could also be found there. When we were young, my father often told my brother and me about walking through the interior of Mindoro on a narrow path and being followed by a large and strange creature. My father would move and so would the creature, and when he stopped moving so did whatever was following him. Finally, he left the path to confront whatever was following him, and he saw the largest snake he had ever seen. My father then made his way back to the base as quickly as possible, and he always believed that the enormous reptile was stalking him.

There were a number of very primitive people living in the interior of Mindoro; and although soldiers and sailors were told to limit their interaction with them, my father did periodically encounter these natives during his walks in the island's backcountry. On one occasion, he met a fierce-looking man who did not seem to want to harm my father. However, he was holding a shrunken head, and he wanted to sell it to my dad. My father declined to purchase it, and periodically during my youth I playfully admonished him for not acquiring the head. Soldiers and sailors were told that under no circumstances were they to have intimate relations with the native women on Mindoro. One soldier refused to listen, and journeyed inland in pursuit of satisfying his lust. He was found dead on a trail that my father and other sailors walked on periodically, naked from the waist down with his testicles and penis cut off and shoved into his mouth.[128]

Although the Filipino people smiled often and appeared to be kind and gentle, many of them were able and sometimes ruthless warriors. One such man was a guerrilla leader named William Dotson. Dotson arrived at the PT boat base on Mindoro shortly after the island was invaded. Two weeks prior to his arrival, he had been shot through the back by a Japanese sniper, and as a result he had grown pale and weak. Fortunately for him, the bullet had passed between his backbone and vital organs and he did not need surgery, and with rest and convalescence his health returned. The son of an English father and Filipino mother, Dotson was larger than most of his countrymen, and although he had a bright smile that he regularly displayed, he was also a merciless and sometimes cruel killer.

On one occasion, a Japanese warrior had been sent from a submarine to shore to learn as much as he could about the guerrilla operations in the area. He was caught spying on their camp and "Bill," as Dotson was often called, proceeded to interrogate him. He promised to return the man to his submarine if he answered Dotson's questions, and as Japanese prisoners often did, he cooperated fully. Dotson then loaded him on to a small boat, and rowed out to where the submarine had last been seen. He then told the man, "Before I let you go I have something for you to give your captain." He then tied a line attached to a large stone around the man's neck and pushed him overboard. As the man descended to his death, Dotson yelled, "Give that stone to your captain."[129]

On another occasion, Dotson was in control of a Japanese prisoner who was going to be executed. The man asked for a cigarette and then the opportunity to write his mother before he was killed. Dotson complied, and the cigarette and letter-writing materials were provided. For some reason Dotson became incensed when he saw the prisoner writing in Japanese, and proceeded to pull out his gun and shoot the man in the back of the head. On another occasion, a Japanese prisoner irritated Dotson by continually complaining that he was hungry. Without warning, Dotson took out his knife, cut off the man's ears, and then forced the prisoner to eat them.[130]

Another well-known guerrilla that the PT boat sailors interacted with was a lieutenant known as "Willie." Willie spoke Japanese and English fluently and was "slightly" Japanese in appearance. He was small in physical stature but had enormous courage and proved this by posing as a Japanese official and wandering about Japanese-occupied

Manila and gathering important intelligence for the Allies. On one occasion, he gathered a group of Japanese soldiers in the heart of Manila and gave a speech on the glory of Japan. Willie's father and Dotson's were colleagues at the University of Manila, and like Dotson, he dressed well and had a gentlemanly demeanor, but he was also a ruthless killer, shooting at least one Japanese man at close range between the eyes. He was pleasant, fearless, and good spirited, and those who knew him best claimed that he was most happy when he was in danger.

Willie was captured by the Japanese at least once, and his escape was a testament to his courage and cunning. Willie and another Filipino were in a small boat taking soundings near the shore of Manila. When a Japanese patrol boat saw what they were doing, Willie's colleague jumped into the water and evaded capture, but Willie was detained. When brought before Japanese authorities, Willie acted as if he understood no Japanese or English, and instead communicated in Filipino. He gave evasive answers to the Japanese officer, and after a brief interrogation, two men were ordered to take Willie to the beach and shoot him. Of course Willie understood what the two men had been told, and as he was escorted through the dark jungle to the beach, he plotted his escape. As they walked, Willie was able to remove a knife from its hidden sheath and cut his hands free. When the soldier to his rear stopped to light a cigarette, Willie leaped at him just as the match's flame flared in his face and impacted his sight and pushed the soldier over a nearby small bank. He then turned to flee into the jungle just as the lead soldier was turning to shoot him, and although the man got off a round, he was not hit, and he was able to make his way to safety.

The guerrillas and the PT boat sailors enjoyed each other's company, and during one conversation, a sailor asked one of the guerrillas how they went about capturing Japanese prisoners. Without hesitation he responded that the Japanese were often easy to locate, even in the jungle, because they smelled like fish. Curious, a sailor inquired what Americans smelled like. This time the guerrilla hesitated, and then responded that Americans smelled like goats. He was relieved when the sailors laughed at this description of their smell.[131]

My father had several encounters with Japanese prisoners. On one occasion, he was on PT *221* when they picked up detainees from the guerrillas and brought them back to the PT boat base. On other occasions, my father saw boats from the squadron return to base with captives. Prisoners were always turned over to officers, and they were always interrogated out of sight of the enlisted men. He once implied that he thought the officers would get rough with the prisoners if they believed this was necessary to get them to supply information. But he never saw detainees being mistreated, and since Japanese prisoners had a reputation for providing information once captured, it is doubtful if the officers interrogating the captured men had to abuse them to get information.

My father's most unusual encounter with a Japanese prisoner occurred when he was on PT *221* during the violent early days on Mindoro. A Japanese pilot had parachuted from his plane after it had been hit by American fire, and he was found floating in the water. The *221* boat was dashing about Mangarin Bay firing at enemy planes, and they did not want to stop the boat long enough to remove the man from the water. Instead, they quickly tied his parachute to the back of the boat, and then proceeded to furiously drive around and engage the enemy. When calm returned, they carefully brought the worn-out man aboard. Unlike almost all Japanese warriors who were about to be taken prisoner, he did not resist and instead surprised the men on the *Omen of the Seas* when he said, "God bless America" in almost perfect English as they were pulling him toward the boat. They soon learned that not long before the war, he had been a student at Harvard University, and he had been there at the same time as one of the officers in the squadron. When the two men met, they talked of different professors at the university and even acquaintances they had in common. He said he knew America well, and he did not believe much of the propaganda that he had been told by his officers. He even allowed himself to be captured, a disgrace in the eyes of his countrymen, because he knew he would be treated decently by the Americans.[132]

There were a number of problems that had to be overcome by the base force on Mindoro. Rain, wind, salt air, Japanese air raids, kamikaze attacks, lack of spare parts, bugs, and heat all made it difficult to maintain and repair the boats in Task Unit 70.1.4. The successful attacks on American shipping that was bound for or had arrived at Mindoro meant that early on spare parts and much of the equipment that was to be used to build the PT boat repair facilities were lost. In addition, tasks that should have been routine—such as unloading spare parts from ships, moving them to storage facilities, and then moving them into the PT boats to be installed—were all made more difficult due to the crudeness of the facilities and lack of equipment designed to assist in these endeavors. American grit, ingenuity, and resourcefulness helped to overcome all of these difficulties, and although on most days a number of PT boats would not be operational, the base force was always able to keep enough of the boats in good repair so that the Mosquito Fleet could carry out its assigned tasks on Mindoro. The construction crews working to build a military infrastructure on the island also did admirable work. Not only had the Japanese airstrips been quickly repaired, but new ones were constructed, one of which was large enough for heavy bombers.[133]

Base life on Mindoro did improve as the weeks went by. Additional tents were set up, and these served a variety of purposes. Several were made into barracks to provide some sailors with better living arrangements. Large tents were made into workshops that were used by the base force, and one all-purpose tent was periodically fashioned into a crude movie theater so that the men could enjoy an occasional film when off duty. A tent was set up that housed an officer's club that was open on Wednesdays and Saturdays. The bar was the tail from a P-38 that had been shot down, and officers would receive several "chits" per week that could be used to purchase beers. There was much revelry inside the small club, and officers regularly could be heard loudly singing profanity-laced songs.

Often a base radio could be heard playing familiar songs such as *Rum and Cola*. Some men had become more spiritual during their time at Mindoro, and religious services were generally well attended. As is true in all wars, sailors periodically received "Dear John" letters from wives and sweethearts, and after one sailor on PT *221* received such a letter from his wife, he proceeded to leap off the boat while it was moving in an attempt to commit suicide. The troubled sailor was relieved of duty and sent home. Filipino farmers and merchants would venture to the PT boat base and sell chickens and a variety of fruits and vegetables, much to the delight of the PT boat sailors. One fruit that created division among the sailors was the durion. This was a large green fruit that grew on trees in the jungle. Inside the fruit was a tough, fibrous white tissue, and from this flowed a milky, sticky fluid, and inside this fluid were large seeds, each of which was surrounded by tender, lemon-yellow and delicious flesh that could be eaten raw or roasted. It also emitted a terrible odor. Some sailors loved the exotic fruit so much they were willing to

Top: After the fighting had quieted down on the island of Mindoro, a crude movie theater was set up. While operating the projector during a movie, my father stopped the film and announced that President Franklin Roosevelt had died. The president's death had a profound impact on my father and his squadron mates. *Bottom:* Warehouse near PT boat base on Mindoro. Both photographs, World War II PT Boats Museum and Archives, Germantown, Tennessee.

put up with the smell. Others schemed to abscond with the fruit when they were purchased and get rid of them before they could be cut up and emit their hated odor.[134]

Sailors in Squadron 16 adopted a variety of pets, the most unusual of which was a monkey called Tojo, who preferred beer to water. Often the primate would walk up a man's back as he was about to take a drink from his can of beer, and while clinging to the sailor's back attempt to grab the beer out of the sailor's hand and drink it.[135]

Ed Kalinowski and Motor Machinist's Mate First Class William Kiendzior "liberated" a truck from the Sea Bees and headed out for a nearby village. They soon became stuck in quicksand, and while they waited for a truck to come by and pull them out, they had to remain in the vehicle while it slowly sunk because every time they attempted to get out, a nearby water buffalo started to charge at them.[136]

Although there were few large mammals on Mindoro, Tom Hart and some of his fellow sailors who liked to hunt journeyed into the jungle in search of the Mindoro Tamaraw. This brown dwarf buffalo had short horns and stood approximately 40 inches in height and only lived on Mindoro. They were difficult to locate, and there were no reports of American military men killing one. In addition, there were small numbers of wild carabao, deer, monkeys, civet cats, wild hogs, porcupines, crocodiles, lizards, and over 300 species of land birds on the island. Most of these were hard to find, and other than birds, most of the other creatures were rarely seen. Generally the hunts ended unsuccessfully.

The PT boats continued to patrol and attack Japanese bases along the shoreline, and sometimes the results were devastating. With the *221* boat temporarily out of commission as a result of the grounding, Tom Hart asked to go out on a patrol in PT *223*. The *223* boat was to join PTs *222* and *298* from Squadron 16 and PT *75* from Squadron 13 on a mission to the southern coast of Luzon where they were to bombard an enemy base. Several days earlier, guerrillas had been landed near the base. At a predetermined time, two B-25s, and four P-38s would release their bombs near the beach and strafe the warehouses on the base and then the PT boats would open fire. The guerrillas, hidden in the nearby hills and woods, would kill any Japanese fleeing the attack. They were to then rush the guards who were protecting a number of suicide boats on a nearby river, kill them, and then capture one or two of the small boats and bring them out to the waiting PT boats.[137]

The B-25s arrived on time and unleashed their bombs and a frightening barrage of 75 mm rounds. The PT boats were briefly delayed when PT *223* got temporarily grounded on a reef, but when they arrived in Pagapas Bay, they did their job with terrifying efficiency. Motoring less than one-half mile from shore in groups of two, the boats "shelled, bombed, and strafed from 8:50 that night until after ten o'clock." Tom Hart alone unleashed 500 rounds from his twin .50 caliber guns, and he accomplished this rate of fire even with his weapon jamming several times. All gunners on all of the boats were firing simultaneously, and the noise was so loud that an "explosion" went off inside Tom Hart's head that forced him to drop to the ground for a minute and prevented him from hearing in one ear for a week. The surprise was so complete and the combined fire from the bombers and PT boats so devastating, that there was no enemy fire directed at either the planes or the boats. The boats then motored closer to shore, shot up a Japanese luger they found, and then waited for the guerrillas to bring out the Q boats. After 20 minutes they determined that the guerrillas would not be coming, and the boats returned to base unsure of the success of their mission.

Several days later, the guerrillas were picked up, and the men who took part in the raid learned the results of their work. Upon seeing the PT boats, hundreds of Japanese soldiers ran into the warehouses or hid behind the thickets near them for cover. The massive fire from the boats sent thousands of rounds into these structures and through the vegetation hiding the Japanese, and when the attack ended, the guerrillas counted approximately 300 Japanese dead and wounded being carried back into the hills. Evidently, the reputation of the deadliness of the small boats had preceded them, and in their attempt to hide from the boats, they ran into the PT boats' primary targets and were slaughtered. Unfortunately, the suicide boats were too well guarded to be captured, and the guerrillas were unable to abscond with any.[138]

A few days after this attack, PTs *222*, *230*, and *75* were sent out to attack another Japanese base. After unleashing the full firepower of the three boats, the PTs returned, and it was later reported that as many as 200 to 300 Japanese and Filipinos were killed. Surprisingly, the guerrillas were not upset at the death of so many of their countrymen, because those killed were thought to be "enemy sympathizers." On this attack, there was "considerable" enemy return fire from mortars, rifles, and machine guns, and Lieutenant (jg.) William B. Helme, who had recently been put in command of the now dry-docked PT *221* and had joined the raid for the experience, had an enemy rifle bullet pass through his leg. Much of the fire directed at the PT boats came from several buildings along the shore. These received the bulk of the PT boat fire, and members of the crew believed they killed a large number of the enemy who were in these buildings. In addition, four steel barges, two luggers, and two Q boats were sunk.[139]

Throughout January and into February, PT boats continued to patrol the waters surrounding Mindoro and Luzon. These patrols took place during the day and at night, and the boats targeted Japanese shipping and shore installations. A number of luggers and sailing vessels were destroyed, as well as Q boats that were often found hidden along the shore.

PT boats and their crews were periodically sent to set up small fueling stations and repair bases on distant parts of Mindoro or on nearby islands. On these small, isolated installations, the lack of formality that was the hallmark of the PT boat fleet often reached the point where sailors later admitted that it was almost like they were in "McHale's Navy." Chief Radioman Robert Street was a member of Squadron 16 when he and nine other sailors were tasked with setting up a small refueling and repair base at a place called Mog Pog on the island of Marinduque, which was east of Mindoro. Although they could never prove it, the men chosen believed that their superiors thought they were "rabble-rousers" and sent them on this mission to get rid of them. When the sailors arrived at Mog Pog, they were greeted by friendly natives who offered them refreshing coconut milk and some very strong "booze" called "Wild Tiger." The sailors were then told that there were three Japanese nearby hiding under an old brick schoolhouse. There were a small number of soldiers with the PT boat sailors, and these men quickly aimed a bazooka at the building and leveled it on top of the Japanese.

The men then proceeded to create their small base complete with a crude kitchen, mess tent, work tent, a kerosene-operated refrigerator, and most important of all an ice cream maker that they had "liberated" from a dock while in Bremerton, Washington. A radio was set up, and Tokyo Rose was heard playing American music throughout the day. Anchored just a short distance from shore were two enormous barges that were carefully covered with dirt and jungle growth to camouflage them. Fuel was stored in one barge and ammunition and torpedoes in the second, and allied ships regularly arrived to get fuel or munitions, or have repair work done.

The men on this small base baked bread, ate wild tomatoes that were brought to them by the Filipinos, and a dessert called "mura" that was made from green coconut, canned milk, and sugar. As often as possible, "mura" was consumed before the sun came up, because once it did thousands of flies would arrive that would get into the sailors eyes, ears, nose, mouth, and food.

The resourceful sailors also installed running water and a shower. On a hill above their small base was a spring. They ran a pipe from the spring to their base, and by the time the water reached the shower they installed, it had been warmed by the sun. One day two young, attractive Filipino women arrived at the base and asked the sailors if they could use the shower. Not surprisingly, the sailors immediately replied in the affirmative, but were then disappointed when the women proceeded to shower with their clothes on.

Although I am sure their superiors would not have agreed, some of the men stationed on this small base believed the most important thing on Mog Pog was the still they built. A 40 mm ammunition case was lined with copper, and an Army field kitchen that somehow found its way to the base was mounted on half of a 50-gallon steel drum. The still sat on top of this. Condenser coils were then connected to another 50-gallon drum, and spring water was run through this for cooling. This produced a "grade A number one still."

The Filipinos would deliver a concoction made from local plants called "tuba" for five cents a gallon, but this fee was eventually waived and instead they would trade the tuba for a small amount of the alcohol that was distilled from it. The still was placed on the hill near the spring that provided the water for the shower and base, and eventually they produced enough 160-proof alcohol to supply everyone on the small base and guests that might show up. In addition, when the weekly supply boats arrived from Mindoro, they would bring 20-gallon jugs that would be filled for the men at the PT boat base in Mangarin Bay. As they learned about the small outpost, sailors from Mindoro would find their way to the base for a few days of drinking and relaxation, and thus the base became known as "Paradise Island." In time, the creative sailors on Paradise Island were even able to concoct their own lemon daiquiri by mixing one pint of "terrible concentrated lemon juice," one quart of their home made "gin," a pint of sugar, and water in the ice cream machine.

The longer the sailors stayed at Mog Pog, the more traditional military discipline faded. Most wore nothing but worn-out cut-off dungaree shorts. They would fish by hurling hand grenades into the water and then collect the dead fish that rose to the surface. They had two pet monkeys, and the creatures spent many afternoons with the sailors lounging on the dock "enjoying the refreshments with all of us ... and dipping their hands into the drinks for they were too tired to get up." When Army crash boats or naval vessels showed up to get supplies, all were invited to relax and have a drink. Officers were often shocked to see the state of the American military men manning this small base, but most allowed the enlisted men to relax with a cold drink or two, and many eventually joined the festivities. Some even gave the sailors cigarettes in exchange for the drinks they had enjoyed.

At sunrise one day a Japanese submarine arrived and at one point it was only 300 yards from shore. There were no lights on at the base, and tents and other structures had been blended into the jungle so the Japanese did not realize the sailors were there. A quiet discussion ensued. The men made a quick accounting of all their weapons, and although it was determined they could probably win a firefight with the men from the submarine, they still determined that "discretion was the better point, and kept low and out of sight and quiet." The sailors on the submarine never did realize they were right next to the base, and in time, the vessel sailed off. Half seriously, Bob Street said many years after the war, "We didn't have enough food to feed all those prisoners anyway, so we let them go."

The sailors found an old, broken-down convertible car, fixed it up, and had transportation to nearby towns and villages. On one occasion they drove the vehicle to the town of Santa Cruz, installed a 110-volt alternator and lights in a number of locations, and the townspeople were so grateful that the mayor invited them over for lunch. An old "speed boat" was found in the jungle, made operable, and used by the sailors as a pleasure craft. They also had a dugout canoe with outriggers that they could use to explore the nearby waters. Over time, the sailors who established the base were sent to other locations, and the new inhabitants decided that they could make some extra money by selling the alcohol produced by the still for one dollar per gallon. This led to a crackdown on the men on "Paradise Island," and 30 years after the war, Bob Street believed that the man responsible for the sale of the alcohol had been arrested for bootlegging.[140]

When my father had free time, he would spend it exploring the island or working

My father on the helm of PT *221*. Francis Gelzheiser collection.

on some personal project in the electrician's shop. After the Japanese torpedoes had been found on the beach in late December, he managed to take one apart and remove a number of the monel nuts from the weapon.[141] He then spent hours carefully filing these into rings for men and women. Instead of a precious stone, he would comb the beaches for conch shells, and then carefully cut out a piece of shell and mount it in the ring. He primarily made rings for women, and soldiers and sailors eagerly purchased these to send back to their wives, girlfriends, sisters, and mothers. He only made one man's ring, which he gave to me on my sixteenth birthday, and I have worn it ever since.[142]

Two of the rings made by my father after the fighting on Mindoro came to an end. The rings were made from nuts he removed from a Japanese torpedo and shells he found on the beach. Bob Gelzheiser collection.

It was only late in his life that my father talked about the violence he experienced on Mindoro, but from the time I was a boy he loved to tell the story of the Japanese warriors who slipped right under his nose and received only a smile and a wave from my father and his shipmates. Shortly after the Americans had retaken Mindoro, my father approached a young native boy and asked him if he knew the whereabouts of the Japanese. The boy looked at my dad with a puzzled expression and said that my father had seen them the day before. Surprised, my father asked his question again, and this time the boy told him that not only had my dad seen the Japanese, but he and a fellow sailor had waved to them as they paddled right past *The Omen of the Seas*. Shocked, my father now realized what had happened. The day before a group of what he believed were Filipino natives had paddled right past my dad and his shipmates in a large dugout canoe. The American sailors had smiled and waved at the men as they paddled by, but now my father was learning the truth. These innocent natives were in fact Japanese soldiers or sailors in native garb who had cleverly evaded American detection. My father always smiled when he told this story, and I am sure that after the war he was grateful that he and his shipmates were so easily duped, and that the Japanese had escaped unscathed.[143]

On January 17, PTs *222*, commanded by Lieutenant Robert J. Roth, and *223*, under the command of Lieutenant (jg.) Griffin, motored to Ilog Anchorage and then to a small bay south of Fuego Point. Here they dropped off a highly trained scouting team that consisted of an American officer who the PT boat sailors referred to as "Captain Guts" and a Filipino scout they referred to as "Phil." The two men were to undertake a very dangerous scouting mission behind Japanese lines, and before departing on their two-man rubber raft in the middle of a small bay, "Captain Guts" told the PT boat sailors that if they failed to pick them up in two days, the two reconnaissance men would be "dead men." The officers on the PT boats assured them they would not abandon them and they would return to the pick up point at the prescribed time. The boats then motored back to base.[144]

The return voyage was a "nightmare." The two boats set out at 3:50 in the afternoon the following day, and they were immediately confronted with 20- to 30-foot swells. They fought their way north and then east to Ilog Anchorage, and by the time they arrived there, every sailor was seasick. They then continued to the rendezvous point and arrived at 1:00 a.m. As they motored close to shore, one of the gunners on PT *222* had his finger spasm, and he inadvertently pulled the trigger on his gun and fired off a few rounds. This not only alerted any nearby Japanese of the presence of the two boats but also "scared the hell out of everybody." The boats continued to search for the two scouts first at the designated pick up point and then at the alternate site. It was at the second location that they saw a flashlight flash, and two men from PT *222* lowered a rubber raft into the water and paddled to shore.

When they arrived, only "Captain Guts" was waiting, and he had several bullet wounds. Earlier that day, the captain and "Phil" had been captured by an eight-man Japanese patrol. They were beaten and interrogated, but then escaped with their handguns. While they were pursued, they killed two or three of their pursuers, and "Captain Guts" was shot. Phil stayed behind to fight a delaying action, and "Captain Guts" ran "like hell" to Fuego Point where he was picked up. It was later learned that "Phil" was killed.[145]

Weeks later the PT boat sailors learned that the intelligence gathered by "Captain Guts" on the position of Japanese forces had been shared with Admiral Thomas C. Kinkaid, the man in charge of the Seventh Fleet, and that this information had played an important role in the battle for Luzon. "Captain Guts" also shared with the admiral the important role the PT boats had played in the success of his mission, and the admiral agreed that the PT boat sailors were playing a vital role in the campaign to win back the Philippines.[146]

Tragically, the last American PT boat sailors to die in the Philippines were not killed by the Japanese. On February 1, Lieutenant Stillman, the commander of Squadron 16 who had replaced Lieutenant Commander Colvin after he was injured, led a patrol consisting of PT Boats *77* and *79* along the shores of western Luzon. The day before, American ships had been attacked by more than 30 Japanese suicide boats and midget submarines during the landings at Nasugbu in western Luzon, and one sunk submarine chaser USS *PC 1129*. Shortly after *PC 1129* was sunk, destroyer escort USS *Lough* attacked a group of more than 20 of the small but lethal boats. The sinking of *PC 1129* and the presence of so many suicide craft made all of the sailors in the nearby waters nervous.[147]

Lieutenant Stillman had been charged with seeking out these deadly suicide craft and destroying them. He was told to remain south of Talin Point to avoid being engaged by American warships, and his boats never did cross this line. Three miles south of the point, PT boats *77* and *79* were illuminated by the starshell of American ships. These vessels were wary of the Japanese suicide vessels that had been in the area the day before, and they had been ordered to fire on any suspicious looking craft in the area. At least one PT flashed "PT ... PT ... PT...," but these signals were either not seen, not understood, or ignored. In addition, the destroyers claimed they sent out radio messages to the PTs, but the sailors on the smaller vessels said they never received these messages. As the PTs continued toward destroyer escorts *Lough* and USS *Conyngham,* the captain of *Lough* believed that the flashing PT single was a Japanese trick and that his ship was being confronted either by Japanese suicide boats or small craft similar to American PT boats. In a last attempt to make sure he was not about to fire on an American vessel, radio operators on the destroyers were ordered to send out messages on the radio frequency used by PT boats inquiring if any "Martinis" were in the area. Tragically he got no response.

The boats continued to motor toward the destroyers, and the sailors on the destroyers concluded that the boats were hostile. Lieutenant Commander Blaney C. Turner, *Lough's* captain, ordered his men to fire 40 mm and five-inch guns at the boats that were approximately 1,200 yards away. Shortly after *Lough* commenced firing, destroyer *Conyngham* also started firing at the two American vessels. The PT boats and the destroyers continued to attempt to contact each other by radio, but none of the vessels heard the transmissions.[148]

The two PT boats fled southward at full speed. The *77* boat, which was the same vessel hit by friendly fire during the night of the Japanese bombardment of Mindoro, hit a reef; and as its crew was abandoning ship, it was hit amidship by a shell from *Lough*. The crew was sent flying and the boat was destroyed. The *79* boat would have escaped the pursuing ships, but it slowed down to avoid the reef and swung to starboard making it an easy target for the pursuing ships. A shell from *Lough* scored a direct hit on the boat's port side and the boat exploded and quickly burned. Three sailors on PT *79* were killed by the shell, including Lieutenant (jg.) Michael A. Haughian, the captain of the boat. The remaining 30 men from the two boats swam the two miles to shore where they were hid from the Japanese by Filipino guerrillas until their rescue by PT boats two days later.[149]

Tragically, Lieutenant Stillman was not among this group. After PT *77* was hit, he removed his clothing, put on a capo life jacket, and began to swim in a different direction than the rest of the sailors in search of help. Some of the men who were there believed he was attempting to swim at the attacking destroyer to tell them of their mistake and to get their assistance for his men. Others thought he was going to a more distant island in search of assistance. Lieutenant Stillman was never seen again.

Days later, the body of a decapitated officer was found on an island near where the PT boats had been hit, and many of the sailors who served on Mindoro went to their graves believing that this was Lieutenant Stillman and that he had been captured and beheaded by the Japanese. In reality, this was not his body, and we have never learned his fate. What we do know was that Lieutenant John H. Stillman was a fine officer who had battled the Japanese in the Solomons and on Mindoro. He was loved and respected by the men who served under him. He had risen through the ranks to become an officer, and as he displayed when the crew of PT *221* grounded their boat, he was patient and fair, and certainly his last act is a testament to his courage and willingness to sacrifice for the sailors under his command. Years after his passing, Lieutenant (jg.) Robert Roth said the following about Lieutenant Stillman: "I had the pleasure of his company during the long trip going to Mindoro. Even though he knew he would be our next skipper, he took his turn of the watch and always respected the fact that I was skipper of the *222* and that the decisions concerning the welfare of the boat and crew were mine. In conversations with Lieutenant Stillman during this trip, he indicated that he would like to stay in the war zone until the war was terminated."[150]

One of the last hardships faced by my father and his fellow sailors on Mindoro had nothing to do with the Japanese. I did not learn of this until my father's final years, and I was surprised by how profoundly sad he became as he told me of the event almost sixty years after it occurred. In mid–April 1945, Mindoro was still a war zone, but relatively peaceful. It was evening, and a number of sailors were enjoying a movie, the name of which my dad could not remember. My father was the projectionist, and midway through the film, he was quietly handed a note with a message that he had to deliver to the men in the room. He stopped the film and announced that President Franklin Roosevelt was dead. My father asked for three minutes of silence, but he said it was five to eight minutes before someone said they thought that was enough, and the silence ended. My dad only told me this once, and I was surprised by how choked up he got recounting the story. My father was not a particularly political person, and if I had to define his politics, I would call him a fair-minded moderate. Why then was he so upset by the death of President Roosevelt?

First, Roosevelt was his commander-in-chief. Regardless of one's views on his politics, President Roosevelt had been a steady leader during a very difficult period in America's history; and I believe to many young warriors he was the trusted face of the American government that had sent them into harm's way. In addition, it had been New Deal programs that enabled my father and his sister to leave "The Home." Roosevelt was the face that he connected with this opportunity; and perhaps in some way, the patrician president became a far-off father figure who had helped him through the Depression and watched out for him as he fought a difficult war on a far-off island in the Philippines.[151]

Many of the warriors on Mindoro and throughout the United States Navy had a similar reaction to Roosevelt's death. Some refused to believe that he was dead. Sailors and officers stopped what they were doing and "stared into space." Others remarked or thought, "He cannot be gone, we have not won the War yet." Some "cursed and some cried," and it is likely that all felt a sense of loss. Perhaps the most powerful sentiment felt by my father and millions of other American warriors scattered throughout the world was that they desperately wanted the war to end, and they wanted to go home. Most knew nothing about Harry Truman, their new commander-in-chief, so naturally many wondered if he would be able to lead the Allies to victory as quickly as the more experienced and beloved President Roosevelt.[152]

During their last weeks and months on Mindoro, the sailors in Squadron 16 had a variety of tasks to perform, and some of them were fondly remembered decades later. PT boats were sent on patrols to Cuyo Island, 90 miles south of Mindoro, and Palawan Island which was south of Cuyo. After the first boats returned from Cuyo, the other sailors in the squadron were told of the beauty of Cuyo Island and the women who lived there, and many sailors volunteered to go on these patrols. The island was primitive, and the water surrounding its main dock was not deep enough to accommodate a PT boat, so boats would have to anchor not far from the dock and wait for a small rowboat to take them to shore. When the PT boats arrived, dozens of men and women would line the docks waiting for the sailors to come to shore. The small village on the island was shaded by tropical trees, cooled by a wonderful sea breeze, and surrounded by gently rolling hills covered with beautiful vegetation.[153]

The town had neat, shrub-lined streets, and the houses were attractive and well built by the standards of the Philippines. Most of the homes had well-attended vegetable gardens in front, and these gave off a pleasant aroma as the sailors walked the streets. Banana, coconut, and papaya trees grew randomly throughout the village, and these provided additional shade and a tropical exoticness to Cuyo. A short distance out of town was an old concrete and stone fortress from the seventeenth century. The walls of the structure were more than 50 feet high, and old guns that had ceased to function long before were still mounted at the structure's entrance. Ironically, the building had been made into a

Catholic church, and when the sailors went inside they were impressed with the beautiful colored draperies that adorned the church's walls.[154]

As the sailors walked the streets of the town, friendly citizens would invite them inside for coffee or a glass of tuba. American furniture, dishes, and even books could be found in many homes. A number of the people the sailors encountered spoke excellent English, and a surprisingly large percentage of the town's inhabitants were of Chinese ancestry. Undoubtedly, what most attracted the Americans to the town was the large number of beautiful, well-dressed, and sometimes flirtatious young women. Because so many of the men from the village had gone off to fight with the guerrillas, there were at least three young women for every young man in the town; but the PT boat sailors were never allowed to stay more than a day or two in the town, so the sailors had to be content with admiring the town's young females from a distance.[155]

During the month of February, the sailors in Squadron 16 were sent on numerous patrols with a variety of goals. After the loss of PTs *77* and *79*, PT boats were sent to search for the crews of both boats, and after these sailors were rescued they continued to search for Squadron Commander Stillman. During the first week of February, PTs *222* and *223* landed scouts on Palawan Island to scout for the impending invasion of the island, which would take place on February 28 and not include boats from Squadron 16. Days later, the same boats returned to pick up the scouts.

Boats would often be sent out at night to patrol the shoreline of Luzon. On occasion they would rendezvous with American aircraft and form a sea-air strike force. Periodically small Japanese ships, barges, and Q boats would be located, and the aircraft and PT boats would coordinate attacks to destroy these crafts. Late in February, new sailors started to arrive in Mindoro, and those who had been there during the island's "terrible hours" told "sea stories" to the squadron's new members. Training exercises were conducted regularly, and these were taken very seriously since all of the sailors participating believed that the war was far from over, and their small boats would be called on to confront the Japanese at some time in the future.[156]

On March 2, 1945, PTs *235* and *242* escorted two larger vessels to Balanacan Bay on the island of Marinduque, which was 20 miles east of Mindoro. Over the next several weeks, PT boats from Squadron 16 would motor to the island to drop off troops and patrol the waters around Marinduque, small islands that were nearby, and Luzon which was only 11 miles to the north. Periodically, these boats would be involved in small skirmishes with Japanese soldiers scattered along the islands' shoreline, but none of these resulted in any casualties for the PT boat sailors. The boats did locate several Q boat nests, which were hidden along the shoreline of these islands. When discovered, the boats' gunners would open fire and destroy the small but deadly weapons.[157]

PT boats from Squadron 16 also continued to ferry scouts and numerous Army and Navy officers to various points on Mindoro, Luzon, Marinduque, and other islands in the region, and picked up Japanese prisoners and wounded guerrillas and brought them back to Mindoro. On March 11, PTs *223* and *298* motored out of Mandarin Bay and the next day took part in the shelling of Simara Island prior to the American Army's landing on the island.

On April 6, PT boats *224*, *235*, and *298* were sent on an unusual mission. Led by Squadron 16 Commander Lieutenant Roger Hallowell, the boats delivered supplies to Culion Leper Colony in Coron Bay on the island of Culion. Established in 1906 with funds from the United States, the colony was an attempt to deal with leprosy in the only way known in the early twentieth century: Isolate those afflicted with the disease. For its time, the lepers who lived in the colony were treated humanely and received good care. It was hoped that by isolating those with the disease that the affliction could be eradicated in the Philippines. My father went to the island on several occasions. Although many of the people living there were afflicted with leprosy, he never talked negatively about the experience, and instead seemed to have fond memories of the people and the island's beauty.

The sailors were treated very well on Culion, and the supplies brought by the PT boats were much needed. The people that the sailors met seemed proud of the society they had created. They had their own silver pesos that had "Culion Leper Colony" embossed on one side, and these were used for currency on the island. It appeared to the sailors that the island was "lost in time," and the people living there had no idea how the war was progressing.

One day the town's residents and the PT boat sailors decided to have a dance. That evening the townspeople came dressed in their finest traditional Filipino clothing. The town orchestra played some "oldies" like *Doing the Lambeth Walk*, and everyone seemed to enjoy the festivities. One "white man," who had been on the island since the Spanish American War, lived in the community. He had not been treated badly by the Japanese, and he believed that the island with its mild climate, warm breezes, and friendly and kind people was his "Shangri-la" and he never desired to leave.[158]

Life on the PT boat base in Mangarin Bay became more enjoyable after the Japanese threat had largely been extinguished. Sailors watched movies on crude log benches, and on one occasion a USO show came to the island and entertained the sailors and soldiers. Periodically a ship would come to Mindoro, and on one occasion an Army hospital ship with a Merchant Marine crew arrived and anchored in Mangarin Bay. Almost immediately PT boats, including PT *221*, motored out and "buzzed" the ship, and much to the delight of the PT boat sailors, women from the ship journeyed to the deck and waved at the sailors. The crew of the ship was invited to join the sailors on the PT boat base for an evening of "jollification," and soon PT boats were motoring to the ship, picking up merchant mariners, and I am sure more importantly the nurses, and bringing them to shore. Much beer and other alcohol were consumed that night and "a bit of levity" was enjoyed by the PT boat sailors on Mindoro and their guests.[159]

During April and May PT boats would motor near shore by day and night in search of Japanese submarines. Periodically planes would crash, and the boats would be sent out to rescue the downed airmen. Unfortunately, on several occasions the pilot was found, but he was no longer alive. At one point, a number of Army Air Force planes were crashing shortly after takeoff. It was believed that some kind of sabotage was responsible for these accidents. To insure the safety of the pilots in the downed planes, PT boats were always kept on patrol to pick up pilots after their planes were forced to land or crashed. Philippine guerrillas continued to be supplied, training continued daily, and exercises were often coordinated with the airplanes based on Mindoro, especially the P-38s. In addition, boat crews practiced strafing runs and various other kinds of target practice.[160]

On June 5, 1945, Motor Torpedo Squadrons 13, under the command of Lieutenant Commander Fargo, Jr., and 16, under the command of Lieutenant Hallowell, were detached from Task Unit 70.1.4 to form Task Unit 70.1.7, Seventh Fleet, and ordered to leave Mangarin Bay and take part in the invasion of Borneo.[161] Borneo had long been important to the Japanese war effort because of its oil supply, but its significance had dwindled by this point in the war because it had become almost impossible for the Japanese to successfully transport this fuel to Japan. Still, MacArthur deemed it necessary to take the island.

On June 9, the two PT boat squadrons arrived at Brunei Bay, Borneo, in British North Borneo, and soon the small boats began their coastal patrols. In short order, the boats destroyed six barges and a 60-foot schooner; but after these attacks, it became harder to find enemy vessels to engage. PT boats from Squadron 16 escorted the landing craft that first took General MacArthur to shore on Borneo, and the sailors who witnessed the general walking to the beach and then into the "forest" were "thrilled by the general's military manner and by the bold way he walked into the forest," although they were surprised that the General MacArthur was not holding his famous corn cob pipe.[162]

Later, as the boats motored into Victoria Harbor, many of the PT sailors hoped to enjoy liberty in this small outpost, which had formally been part of Great Britain. These hopes were extinguished when the larger ships bombarded the small town and "the town wasn't there after that." MacArthur called the Brunei Bay operation "flawless," and after sporadic fighting along the coast and interior of the island, Borneo fell to American and Australian troops on August 15, 1945, just weeks before the war ended.[163]

The boats continued to perform many of the same tasks in the waters around Borneo that they had performed in New Guinea and the Philippines. They patrolled daily, motored into unknown and uncharted rivers in search of the enemy, strafed the Japanese whenever they were located, fought and sometimes destroyed Japanese planes, located and destroyed Japanese barges, searched for Japanese submarines that continued to patrol the nearby waters, made contact with and transported native guerrillas, brought intelligence to guerrillas or transported intelligence obtained from guerrillas back to base, transported high ranking American and Australian military officers to meetings on shore or on ships, transported prisoners, and picked up and delivered mail. On the morning of June 21, PTs *241* and *75* of Squadron 13 were escorting an Australian Survey party on an LCVP, also known as a Higgins boat, along the Klias Peninsula to Nosong Point. The craft was about one quarter of a mile from the shore when the ramp in the ship's bow accidentally opened and the LCVP sank. The two PT boats quickly rescued the 16 officers and men and returned them to base.[164]

One evening while on patrol, PT *298* located a submarine on its radar screen. They searched for the vessel for several minutes hoping it would come to the surface so they could sink it with a torpedo. Quartermaster Second Class Robert A. Beer was peering over the port side of the boat taking a short breather when he saw a torpedo "run exactly between my feet." Beer and a shipmate watched the torpedo go under the boat and into the "twilight," and the two sailors were forever grateful for the shallow draft of their wooden vessel.[165]

It was not until July 9 that the extensive repairs needed on PTs *220, 221, 222,* and *224* were completed and the boats were able to leave Mangarin Bay. After several short stops along the way, they arrived at Puerto Princessa on Palawan Island on July 11, refueled, and then departed late that night for Sapo Point, Muara Island, Brunei Bay, Borneo, where they joined the other boats in Task Unit 70.1.7. The newly arrived boats, all of which were in reasonably good repair, immediately began to patrol the enemy-held coastline to the north and south of Brunei Bay, Borneo. Many sailors also worked to build a base on Sapo Point on Muara Island, where PT boats could be repaired and maintained.[166]

On one occasion, PTs *221* and *222*, while on patrol, motored into a cove named Gaya

Head. At approximately 7:00 in the morning, they navigated to within a couple hundred yards of shore and came under fire from a Japanese sniper. Although a number of rounds came dangerously close to the boats, none hit their mark, and the boats were never able to accurately determine where the shots came from so they were unable to return fire.

On the night of July 19, PTs *224* and *242* went on patrol. They motored north, had no contact with the enemy, and at 11:45 they arrived at Usakan Bay. Usakan Jetty was illuminated, and the nearby huts were fired on with 60 mm high explosive mortars. Thirty minutes later a 40-foot prahu—a large sailing vessel commonly used by the people in those waters—was observed half beached 300 yards south of the jetty and was strafed and destroyed. The boats then patrolled south to Gaya Bay, and they arrived there at sunrise. The boats motored along the shoreline about 900 yards off the beach, and at approximately 7:30 enemy machine gun fire was directed at the boats from native huts. The boats then motored north and observed a large explosion near the town of Jesselton. At 8:07 the boats rendezvoused with seven Australian Kittyhawk fighter aircraft north of Gaya Island and then motored into Jesselton Harbor and strafed the huts that the sailors believed housed the machine guns and warriors that had fired on them earlier. The pilots of the Kittyhawks, who had earlier been briefed on the probable location of the enemy, then flew in and bombed and strafed the area, hitting a number of targets and setting several fires. Machine gun fire from the hills behind Jesselton was directed at the planes. In response, the two boats made two strafing runs from approximately 1,100 yards from shore and accurate machine gun fire was now directed at them. There were no casualties, and although the PT boats returned fire, it could not be determined if the enemy machine gunners had been killed. The boats departed the area at 8:55 in the morning and returned to Victoria Harbor at 12:19 with no further encounters with the enemy. This was typical of the patrols that the PT boats went on throughout July and early August.[167]

On August 15, 1945, PT Boat Task Unit 70.1.7 was ordered to terminate all operations, although some boats were still required to motor from Muara Island to Lebuan Island to pick up official mail and maintain contact with the 9th Australian Division. For the remainder of the month, boats continued to practice firing and torpedo tactics. Motor Torpedo Boat Squadron 16, still under the command of Lieutenant Hallowell and comprised of PTs *220*, *221*, *222*, *223*, *224*, *235*, *241*, *242*, *297*, *298*, and *299*, and Motor Torpedo Boat Squadron 13, under the command of Lieutenant Commander Fargo, Jr., now comprised Task Unit 93.4.64 and operated out of Muara Island, Brunei Bay, Borneo.[168]

The boats of Task Unit 93.4.64 performed a number of "mop up actions" during the last weeks of the war. Each night, boats from the task unit would go out on patrol and try to locate and destroy the large number of Japanese who had been bypassed by the Americans when they had gained their stronghold on the island. There were a number of minor actions with these scattered Japanese troops, but with each night the enemy became harder to locate. In hindsight, it was best for both sides that confrontations at this point in the war were rare. When the war ended, the PT boat sailors in Task Unit 93.4.64 were shocked to learn how many Japanese troops were still hiding in the interior of the nearby islands.[169]

The Japanese surrender, which was announced on August 15, 1945, but not signed until September 2, 1945, did not end the duties for the men in Squadron 16. Shortly after the surrender, on the island of Halmahera, Lieutenant General Ishil, the commanding general of the Japanese Army forces on the island, Captain Fujita, the commander of the

Japanese Naval forces, and several additional high-ranking Japanese officers were picked up by six PT boats and taken to 93rd Division headquarters on Morotai. Here they surrendered 37,000 troops, 4,000 Japanese civilians, 19,000 rifles, 900 cannons, 600 machine guns, and a large number of other supplies that had been trapped on the island since the arrival of the PT boats.[170]

On September 10, PTs *220*, *224*, *299*, *74*, *75*, and *84* motored out of Maura Island bound for the Sarawak River. The boats refueled at Tanjong Point on the morning of September 11, picked up a contingent of Australian troops, and then motored down river to Pending, where the Japanese surrendered the Kuching garrison. The Americans and Australians were angry that the defeated Japanese kept them waiting in the 98 degree heat, and when the Japanese commanding officer and his staff finally arrived on a small loading dock to be transported to the surrender vessel, the Allied coxswain on the launch pushed his craft to full throttle, motored next to the dock, made a sharp turn and threw a large "knee high wake" over the highly polished boots of the Japanese officers. Needless to say, none of the Allied officers or enlisted men who witnessed this made any effort to hide their glee.

On a more serious note, hundreds of English and Australian prisoners of war who had been held captive in Kuching were quickly liberated. All had suffered greatly under Japanese imprisonment. One of the freed prisoners was American Agnes Newton Keith, author of *Three Came Home* and other well-known books, who along with her husband and young son had been prisoners for three and a half years.[171]

On September 12, several boats from Squadron 16 returned to Mindoro, and the remainder of the boats stayed in Kuching and continued to ferry liberated prisoners of war to Motor Torpedo Boat tender USS *Willoughby* or the Australian Hospital Ship *Namunda*, which was anchored off the coast of Tanjong Po. On September 13, 210 Allied evacuees who had been loaded on to *Willoughby* were transported to Victoria Harbor, Brunei Bay, escorted by PT boats.[172]

PT boats continued to ferry Americans, Australians, and even Japanese military personnel and civilians throughout the region in the weeks following the war's end. In mid–September, PT *220* transported Lieutenant Colonel Tatsuji Suga to *Willoughby*. The American–educated colonel had been in charge of all Japanese prisoner of war and civilian internment camps in Borneo; and despite the fact that he was not as cruel to his prisoners as most of the men under his command, he was in charge of an internment system that was one of the most brutal in the war and responsible for thousands of deaths and untold suffering. Some of the men under his command were executed for war crimes after the war, but Colonel Suga committed seppuka or ritual suicide shortly after the PT boat dropped him off and before he could stand trial. The colonel was from Hiroshima and thus incorrectly thought that he had lost his family when the atomic bomb exploded and also believed that after surrendering ritual suicide was the only honorable thing for him to do. In 1950 a film was made of Agnes Newton Keith's *Three Came Home*, and Sessue Hayakawa played the role of Colonel Suga.[173]

The PT boat sailors still on Mindoro grew restless in the weeks after the war's end. They had answered the call of duty when their nation had gone to war, but when the hostilities ended, they wanted to get back to the United States and get on with their lives as civilians. Men spent their time playing baseball, softball and fishing.[174] Sailors built crude sail boats to navigate the waters near Mindoro. They would pilot their boats to nearby islands, meet with the natives and then journey back to Mindoro. Since most were not experienced sailors, men sometimes got lost, or found themselves in open seas with no winds. Most stopped these voyages when they realized that their lack of experience could result in sailors being swept out to sea or stranded on a beach unable to return to their base on Mindoro.

Men hunted, and on several occasions they encountered "old wrinkled pygmies" clothed only in a loincloth and armed with bows and arrows. They crafted rings from coins, spoons, and shells, and not surprisingly various kinds of "jungle juice" were created. One of the most popular drinks manufactured was distilled from raisins and other unknown ingredients. It was powerful, and tasted good enough to be popular with many of the sailors.[175]

On the last day of February 1945, the first sailors from Squadron 16 had been sent home. When sailors were given their orders to leave, it was always bittersweet for the men who were left behind and sometimes for the sailors who were going home. Many PT boat squadrons in World War II had much turnover, and this often prevented shipmates and squadron mates from growing close. Squadron 16A was different. Most of the men who crewed the six boats had been together since they motored out of New Orleans bound for Panama three years earlier. Close friendships had developed, and the hardships encountered as boats traveled thousands of miles, often in difficult conditions, and then faced the Japanese in combat, had resulted in shipmates learning to trust each other. Saying goodbye not only meant that sailors would lose the company of a good friend, but also a man they knew could be counted on when times were difficult.

This journey always took weeks and sometimes months to complete. Sailors were "on their own" and instructed to find their way home "any way you can." The route of the return journey differed with each sailor, and many spent days and weeks at various ports throughout the Pacific. My father did not leave Mindoro and the Philippines until the spring of 1945, and he did not arrive in the United States until mid–August, more than 100 days later. Along the way he spent long peaceful days on slow moving ships and stopped in New Caledonia—where he was fascinated by the people, flora, fauna, and the

My father, far right, and three squadron mates, "bound for home from the Philippines." Francis Gelzheiser collection.

island's natural beauty—and Australia where he was treated like a hero. For the rest of his life he would talk fondly of the people he met in Australia and the beauty of the country. When he returned home, he was able to go home and visit his sister and invalid mother, and then he was sent to several bases in the United States until his discharge from the United States Navy on October 11, 1945.[176]

For some of the sailors, returning to America created a new set of problems. Several of the men in the squadron who had quickly married in Seattle were divorced soon after they reunited with their wives. Others had "battle fatigue," and others "ulcers and other ailments" that were most likely related to the stress endured during the first weeks on Mindoro. Men went on week-long drinking binges, and at least one sailor drank away his money and then proceeded to fill his sea bag with radio head phones and tools from his boat's engine room and was caught trying to send the stolen goods home. He was broken to Third Class.

This was a difficult and confusing time for the men of Squadron 16. Until the atomic bombs were dropped on Hiroshima and Nagasaki in August of 1945, the war in the Pacific still raged; and all of them expected to soon be sent to Borneo or some other island in the Pacific to prepare for the invasion of Japan. While they waited, some men were sent to Melville to train PT boat sailors, others were temporarily stationed on naval bases scattered throughout the United States, some were sent to Borneo, and some got married, one sailor for the second time. I am sure that all of the men from Squadron 16 were anxious for the war to end and to be discharged from the Navy.[177]

The sacrifices made by the Americans on Mindoro were significant, and the success achieved by the PT boat sailors on the island played an important role in the ultimate Allied victory in the Philippines and in the greater war against Japan. During their first 30 days on Mindoro, the men stationed on the island had to respond to 334 alerts. In total, the Japanese crashed 200 kamikazes during the fight for Mindoro, and the sailors manning the PT boats were present for a large percentage of these attacks. In addition, approximately 103 conventional Japanese bombers and fighter aircraft were destroyed in the skies above Mindoro and over the convoys motoring to the island.[178]

In a period of a few weeks, roads were built enabling huge amounts of fuel, munitions, and supplies to be transported and stored. Airstrips were repaired and constructed, and the planes that flew from these did much to insure the success of the attack on Luzon and the liberation of the Philippines that would follow. If not for the aircraft that flew from Mindoro, the destruction done to the ships in the enormous fleet that sailed for Luzon would have been far greater than it was, and hundreds and perhaps thousands more men would have been killed by kamikazes. In addition, bombers that flew from Mondoro did much to disrupt the shipping between Japan and Formosa and Southeast Asia.

All of the construction on the island was done with minimal equipment and supplies and under the duress of almost daily Japanese attacks.[179] In addition to the airfields that played such an important role in the battle for Luzon, Mindoro's proximity to the island also made it a valuable base for American Army troops. The 503rd Parachute Regimental Combat Team (RCT) was based on the island, and the soldiers who made up this team played an important role in the fight to drive the Japanese from the Philippines.[180]

The sailors in Task Unit 70.1.4 were in the center of the fight for Mindoro from the beginning, and they were a key reason for the success of the operation. PT boat gunners shot down at least 20, and perhaps as many as 30, Japanese planes, outmaneuvered suicide planes when fanatical pilots made the decision to die in an effort to sink one of the small boats, and assisted in destroying dozens of kamikazes. Every Japanese plane that attacked a PT boat or that was destroyed when a suicide pilot attempted to crash into one was a plane that the Japanese war machine could not use against another American ship, and each one of the planes that was destroyed would further strain Japan's productive capacity, reduce its critically limited supply of pilots, and limit its ability to wage war.

PT boats in Squadron 16 also sunk at least 20 barges, seven lugers, 23 sailing vessels, 20 suicide boats, and one destroyer. They participated in attacks on Japanese Naval vessels when the ships of the Rising Sun returned to Mindoro in late December of 1944 and took part in the bombardment of three towns. PT boats stopped Japanese trade between Mindoro and nearby islands, and played a key role in protecting the almost 300-mile route from Mindoro to Lingayen Gulf in Luzon for Allied vessels. They rescued pilots whose planes had been shot down, and often crews risked their own safety when they motored in to fiery waters perilously near exploding ships and pulled hundreds of men from the water after their ships had been hit by kamikazes. Because the boats were deemed to be "expendable," they were sometimes asked to motor dangerously close to shore to draw the fire of Japanese shore batteries that could then be destroyed. They also motored close to the shores of Luzon to gather intelligence, attack enemy strongholds and destroy suicide boat bases. They landed and picked up guerrillas

PT boat squadrons 13 and 16 Mindoro "score card," compiled by the sailors in squadrons 13 and 16. The fog of battle often made it difficult to impossible to determine which ships, boats, or planes were responsible for destroying Japanese aircraft, ships, etc. Different sources provide different "score cards" for the PT boats on Mindoro. The following was listed on the back of the "score card," compiled by the PT boat sailors who took part in the battle for Mindoro: Luke seaplane, Val Fixed Landing gear, Zeke Zero, Sally 2 Engine Bomber, Betty 2 Engine Bomber, 27 Aircraft, 29 Sail Transports: 110–150 ft. long, 25 landing barges, 1 FTD Fox Tare Dog Comb transport and freighter, 4 Ammo and Fuel Dumps, 1 Command convoy, 2 Truck Convoys, 23 Q boats: 18 foot suicide boats (1 man), 1 enemy dock torpedoed, 1 destroyer. Total 124. World War II PT Boats Museum and Archives, Germantown, Tennessee.

and patrolled day and night along the coast of Mindoro to insure the enemy there could not be resupplied. The price paid by the PT boat sailors was significant. More than 10 percent of the men who sailed with the invasion fleet to Mindoro were either killed or injured badly enough that they had to be evacuated from the island.

Captain Robert J. Bulkley, Jr., in his seminal work on PT boats in World War II, *At Close Quarters: PT Boats in the United States Navy*, wrote:

> Both in lives and material, the Mindoro campaign was the most costly that the PTs had in the Southwest Pacific. Yet the damage they did far overbalanced their losses. They met and overcame the most savage air attacks the enemy could mount…. Together with Army bombers, they sank one of the newest and finest destroyers in the Japanese Navy. They stopped Japanese interisland traffic, cut off evacuation from Mindoro to Luzon, and ferreted out and destroyed small craft in the harbors. They cleaned out whole nests of suicide boats. They supported the guerrillas on Mindoro and Luzon, and carried out many valuable reconnaissance missions.[181]

After the success at Mindoro, the flow of oil was almost completely cut off from Japan, and this and the military reality Japan faced after the loss of the Philippines meant there was no realistic path Japan could follow that would lead to them winning the war. However, the culture of the Spirit Warrior that had been so ingrained in the Japanese people and their leaders prevented them from surrendering and ultimately cost Japan hundreds of thousands of lives.[182]

Approximately 200 to 400 Japanese ground forces died defending Mindoro, and another 200 to 300 fled into the jungle and were more or less ignored by the American forces as long as they did not initiate an engagement. Many of these men starved, succumbed to various jungle ailments, or were killed by Filipino guerrillas or by the aboriginal people who lived in the mountains. These rugged indigenous people had little contact with the Americans and had no qualms about killing Japanese soldiers when they encountered them.[183]

The contributions made by the sailors in the Mosquito Fleet did not go unnoticed by the American military or the Japanese. In a gathering of high-ranking Naval officers, Admiral Kinkaid told of "how proud he was of the PT boat people assigned to his Seventh Fleet, how he was aware that they were highly trained and highly efficient in all areas, how courageous and dedicated to duty they all were, and how their leadership and performance was playing so vital a part in the success of his entire Seventh Fleet. To all hands; a Well Done."[184] General George Marshall, the chief of staff of the United States Army and a soldier not easily impressed or willing to dispense with unwarranted praise, expressed to General MacArthur, "What you have done on Leyte and are doing on Mindoro are masterpieces." Rear Admiral Selman S. Bowling, the commander of Task Group 70.1 and the man in charge of all American PT boats in the southwest Pacific in World War II, wrote to Commander N. Burt Davis: "Please tell all hands with you that all hands here greatly admire the spirit and guts shown by your whole outfit in getting established, holding on, and dishing it out as well as taking it, and express my approval … well done."[185]

The comments made by the Japanese also illustrated the impact the PT boats had in the battle for the Philippines. I am sure more than one PT Boat sailor grinned when told that Tokyo Rose had announced for all to hear, "Show no mercy to the captured PT men. They are barbarians." Throughout the Pacific, the Japanese referred to the Motor Torpedo Boats as "Devil Boats of the Night" as a result of the massive destruction the small craft brought to the Japanese on both land and at sea.[186]

It is doubtful if most of the men in Squadron 16 realized the role that luck or fate played in their surviving the war. Had American radar men not mistook thousands of Dusky Shearwaters for the Japanese fleet, it is unlikely the Japanese would have escaped Kiska, and the battle for the island would have been deadly for both sides and likely resulted in the destruction of some of the PT boats in the Aleutians.[187] The Japanese did not realize that Mindoro would be the next island invaded after the American success on Leyte. Consequently, the island was not well defended. Although the armada that sailed for Mindoro was attacked, had the Japanese realized earlier that this was the next island that MacArthur was determined to take, the number of planes encountered would have been greater, and undoubtedly there would have been far more destruction to American ships and possibly PT boats. Even with this Japanese miscalculation, there is no question that the casualties on Mindoro would have been far higher if Vice Admiral McCain had not devised the audacious Big Blue Blanket plan which grounded or destroyed hundreds of Japanese aircraft that would have flown over the skies of Mindoro determined to destroy American ships and boats and kill the sailors in them.

It is also frightening to ponder what the results would have been had the more than 100 Okas bound for Mindoro and the Philippines in December 1944 arrived at their destination. When the men from submarines *Archer-Fish* and *Redfish* fired their torpedoes into the Japanese aircraft carriers *Shinano* and *Unryu*, they not only sent the ships and their cargo to the ocean's bottom, but they forced the Japanese command to reevaluate how they would utilize their new suicide weapon. Fearful that they would lose another irreplaceable aircraft carrier, they ordered the carrier *Ryuho* to change course and motor to Formosa, and her 58 Okas were unloaded there. It is doubtful if the sailors on *Archer-Fish* and *Redfish* realized that their actions possibly saved hundreds of American lives and perhaps dozens of American vessels and PT boat sailors. It is also unlikely that any of the sailors in Squadron 16 ever realized the horror that those brave submariners spared them.[188]

PT boat sailors were still on Mindoro when the war ended. Years after the war, Ensign Jim Martin of PT *298* fondly recalled that on V.J. Day Boatswain's Mate Second Class William "Bill" Jackie invited him to his tent to sample some "jungle juice" that he and his tent-mates had concocted from raisins. The brew was powerful, and as a result Ensign Martin recalled that the celebration was brief. It is likely that similar celebrations were held by other sailors and soldiers on the island. I am sure that no drink was ever as sweet or as well deserved. I also imagine that beneath the laughter and revelry, the alcohol also helped to dim the nightmares that I am sure confronted many of the sailors and numbed the deep sadness that most must have felt.[189]

Few Americans were aware of the battle for Mindoro in the last weeks of 1944 and early days of 1945. While the men of Squadron 16 were battling kamikazes and Japanese planes, tens of thousands of American soldiers were desperately trying to hold off the last German offensive of the war in the Battle of the Bulge. Of course this epic confrontation captured the nation's interest, and it would be the horrific battles in places like the tiny island of Iwo Jima that would capture the nation's imagination in the Pacific and become part of the mythology of the war. I believe my father and his squadron mates understood why their contributions to the war were largely forgotten, and they accepted this.

General MacArthur understood the importance of Mindoro. After the island was secured he explained, "I was at last ready for Luzon.... Mindoro was the gate." The United States Navy also appreciated the sacrifices of the PT boat sailors on Mindoro. For the courage and tenacity that they displayed on the island, my father and his fellow members of the Mindoro PT Boat Task Unit were awarded the Navy Unit Citation. It read:

> Task Unit 70.1.4 comprising Motor Boat Squadrons 13 and 16, plus PT's *227* and *230* of Motor Torpedo Boat Squadron 17, and the task unit commander and his staff:
>
> For outstanding heroism in action against enemy Japanese forces during the operations at Mindoro, Philippine Islands, from December 15–19, 1944. As the only Naval force present following the retirement of the invasion convoys, this Task Unit served as the only major obstruction to the enemy counter-landings from near-by Luzon, Panay, and Palawan and bore the brunt of the concentrated hostile air attacks throughout a five day period. Providing the only antiaircraft protection available for the personnel ashore engaged in the establishment of a motor torpedo operating and repair base, the gallant officers and men who commanded and staffed the Task Unit and who manned the boats maintained the vigilant watch by night and stood out in open waters close to base by day to fight off repeated Japanese bombings, strafing and suicide attacks, expending in three days the ammunition which had been expected to last approximately three weeks in the destruction or damaging of a large percentage of the attacking planes. Their invaluable service in support of the expeditions completion of operations ashore vital to the furtherance of the Mindoro Campaign reflects the highest credit upon the United States Naval Service.[190]

My father rarely spoke of the Unit Citation, and it was not until he died that I found the medal and citation tucked away in a box full of things he had collected in the war. Still, I believe he was proud that he had served his nation in a cause he never questioned. Until his death, he kept a laminated Japanese invasion currency bill in his wallet. This was currency the Japanese had printed that was to be used if they invaded the United States, and it was a constant reminder that the Japanese were a real threat to all that he believed in and loved.[191]

Japanese invasion currency. My father kept this in his wallet at all times. I believe it reminded him that the cause he fought for in World War II was righteous. Francis Gelzheiser collection.

9

The Battle for Manila and a Sailor's Journey into the Darkness

There was an overpowering stench of death and decay. It pervaded the air, and there was no escape.... This was not Manila. It was simply hell. —Sergeant Paul Rogers

From the moment he fled the Philippines, General MacArthur had been planning his return. The dramatic naval victory at Leyte Gulf and the successes on the ground at Leyte and Mindoro were only precursors to the primary goal of the Philippine Campaign: driving the Japanese from Luzon and liberating the nation's capital city of Manila. Luzon had a pre-war population of 7,384,798, and it was the most developed island in the Philippines. Manila had a population of 684,000. Manila Bay was one of the world's great natural ports, was only 1,800 miles from Japan, and was deemed to be a potentially important naval base that could be used in the coming advance toward the Japanese homeland. Much of the island was mountainous and covered with forests, and was thus well suited for a protracted Japanese defense. Consequently, many American military leaders believed that the Japanese would abandon Manila and fight a bloody defense in the island's interior, much the way the Americans had abandoned the capital city when the Japanese invaded the Philippines in the early days of the war.

On January 7, 1945, General MacArthur departed Leyte Gulf aboard cruiser USS *Boise* bound for Luzon's Lingayen Gulf, 125 miles north of Manila. The general was leading the largest amphibious operation of the Pacific Campaign, and the largest solely American amphibious operation of the war. Carlos Romulo, the editor and publisher of the *Manila Herald*, who remembered the terror felt by the citizens of his nation when the Philippines fell in 1942, remarked when he heard of the enormous invasion force, "Now it is their turn to quake."

Not surprisingly, during the long voyage, the huge invasion force was attacked by hundreds of kamikazes, and hundreds of men were killed or wounded. At one point during the voyage to Luzon the attacks were so severe that Rear Admiral Jesse Oldenorf, the man in charge of the invasion fleet, warned Seventh Fleet Commander Admiral Kinkaid that the continued assaults by the suicide planes on the convoy "placed the mission in doubt." Fortunately for the Americans, the strikes were brought to an end when the Japanese temporarily ran out of planes. The Japanese did still possess a large number of suicide boats, and it would be one of the jobs of PT boats at Luzon to combat these small but deadly vessels.

Landing on January 9 in the same location that General Tojo's forces had in December 1941, MacArthur's 280,000 men were ferried on 3,000 landing craft and were supported by 1,000 ships and boats in Task Group 77 under the command of Admiral Kincaid. By the end of the first day, an astonishing 68,000 troops were ashore, a testament to the ever-improving logistical abilities of American military leaders. In addition to the American warriors determined to liberate the island, 182,000 Filipino guerrillas, many of whom had waited for this moment for years, were poised to engage their hated Japanese enemy.

Ironically, the course taken by this enormous invasion force was the reverse route taken by Lieutenant Commander Bulkeley as he and the PT Boat crews desperately endeavored to bring General MacArthur and his family to safety during the catastrophic early months of the war; and when the invasion force arrived at its destination, it was appropriate that PT boats would sneak into Manila Bay under the cover of darkness to conduct important reconnaissance operations. These would be the first American boats to enter Manila Bay since General Jonathan "Skinny" Wainwright had surrendered American forces in May 1942.

At this point in the war, the full fruition of America's productive potential was being brought to bear, and Japan had little hope of winning any kind of traditional engagement with the United States.[1] However, General Yamashita still had 270,000 veteran troops from the Fourteenth Imperial Army under his command, hundreds of suicide weapons, and the belief that the fanatical Spirit Warrior could still triumph. Unfortunately for the general, the warriors he commanded were facing an American force larger than the ones that battled the Germans in North Africa, Italy, or Southern France. He publicly bragged that the loss of Leyte and Mindoro, "did not matter," but in private he understood the military reality of his situation. His supply lines were cut off, and his job was to sacrifice tens of thousands of men on the battlefield and to starvation and disease to buy time for Japan.[2]

PT boats played an important role in the campaign for Luzon. Prior to and during the battle, boats of the Mosquito Fleet made numerous sorties to the southern and southwestern coast of the island and gathered much important intelligence. They also performed heroically in the battle for the tiny but strategically and psychologically important island of Corregidor. It was here that General Wainwright and his starving and diseased Filipino and American warriors had retreated and made their last stand prior to America's humiliating surrender of the Philippines to the Japanese. During the battle to retake the island, PT boats motored dangerously close to the shore of "the Rock" and pulled paratroopers from the water who had missed the minute drop zones on the top of the island. In addition, PT boat sailors exposed themselves to frightening Japanese fire as they paddled rubber rafts to the island's narrow stretch of shoreline to rescue American soldiers who were being fired on by Japanese warriors from the steep cliffs that rose from the water's edge. Dozens were rescued, and no paratrooper drowned after he landed in the water off the coast of "the Rock."[3]

On February 3, 1945, the first American troops arrived at Manila, the city known as "The Jewel of the Orient," because of its grace and beauty. General MacArthur was obsessed with liberating the city and had proclaimed soon after America's landing on Luzon, "Go to Manila…. Go around the Nips, bounce off the Nips, but go to Manila!" United States troops had been ordered to advance into the city from both the north and south, and the 1st Cavalry and 37th Infantry raced to the city. All of the units involved were instructed to cause as little harm to Manila as possible.[4]

American leaders had requested that Manila be made an open city to spare its citizens and buildings from the war's destruction. Although the Japanese Commander, General Yamashita, had ordered the destruction of the port facilities, he had told his subordinates to spare the rest of the city. However, after General Yamashita left for his new headquarters in Banguio, the city's new Japanese leader, Rear Admiral Sanji Iwabuchi, defied orders and prepared to defend Manila with his Manila Naval Defense Force.[5]

When the Japanese gained control of Manila in 1942, the Philippines had been under the control of the United States since the end of the Spanish American War and the Spanish for more than 350 years prior to America's arrival. Many Filipinos resented being a colony of a powerful nation thousands of miles away, and thousands of Filipinos had died fighting their American occupiers in the early twentieth century.[6] From the beginning of the Japanese advance across the Pacific, the core of her propaganda message had been that Asia should be controlled by Asians. They believed that this message would resonate with the people of the Philippines and that they would prefer Japan's occupation to America's; and shortly after they successfully drove the Americans out of the Philippines, the Japanese did make efforts to win the hearts and minds of the Filipino people. School curriculums were changed, and students were taught the negative aspects of western imperialism.[7]

There were two primary reasons why the Japanese ultimately failed to win the support of the Filipino people. The first was economic. Unlike the United States whose enormous production capacity enabled her to produce enough of a material surplus to assist in the feeding and arming of most of her allies, the Japanese could barely feed and arm their own people. They could never produce a surplus, let alone one large enough to meet the needs of the people of the Philippines and the other peoples incorporated into the Japanese Empire. As a result, as the war wore on, the people of the Philippines faced shortages of food, gas, clothing, and most other consumer goods. They were far worse off than they had been when under American rule. The Japanese had issued new paper currency after their arrival; and like wealth-starved nations often do, they printed more and more of it as the war progressed. Not surprisingly, inflation became an enormous burden for the people of the Philippines. The worse the inflation and shortages became, the more the Filipino people hated their Japanese occupiers.

Perhaps even more important was the way the Japanese treated the Filipino people. Japanese propaganda may have said their expansion into the Pacific was to make "Asia for Asians," but the Japanese never viewed allied or conquered Asians as their equal. Like their German allies, the Japanese viewed World War II as a race war, and they believed that they were the superior race in the Pacific. Manila was a truly international city, and its population, known as Manilenos, included Filipinos, Americans, Chinese, Scottish, Germans, and numerous other ethnic groups and cultures.[8] Japan wanted a "pure" Asia, which in their eyes meant one dominated by the Japanese; and they made few efforts to hide their disdain for the people of Manila.

Civilians were forced to bow to their Japanese superiors, workers were often abused and exploited, and women were regularly victimized. The Japanese soldiers and sailors who occupied Manila had been brutalized since they were children, and not surprisingly many of them took pleasure in brutalizing the Filipino people. As the war raged on, conditions in the Philippines worsened, and almost all of the Filipino people longed for a return of the Americans.[9]

General Yamashita devised a plan that had some hope of success and would have spared the people of Manila the destruction of their city and tens of thousands of casualties. The general ordered the city to be stripped of anything that could aid the Americans, and then ordered all but 3,700 troops to abandon the city and most of the central plain of Luzon. Some of his forces were sent to Corregidor to defend it and Manila Bay, and thousands of soldiers were moved into the island's wild, mountainous interior where they would be out of the range of American naval guns. In the island's interior, the Americans would be forced to fight a difficult and bloody battle that would cost them many lives, sap the will to fight from America's military and the civilians on the home front, and force the United States' government to negotiate a peace that would leave at least part of Japan's hard-won empire in tact. The troops left in Manila would blow up bridges and protect supply lines, but they were not expected to defend the city or prevent the Americans from gaining control of it.[10]

Coordination and cooperation between the Japanese Army and Navy had not been good for most of the war, and this strained relationship had not improved as the American military was retaking the Philippines. In fact, most Naval and Air Force leaders believed that the reason Luzon needed to be defended was Manila, and they strongly opposed the withdrawal that General Yamashita was ordering. Most of General Yamashita's soldiers abandoned Manila; and despite the misgivings of their commanders, most of the Air Force troops also left prior to the battle for the city. However, the commanding general had not officially declared it to be an open city to be spared the worst ravages of the war.

Four thousand sailors were added to the 8,500 that were already in the city, and the 3,700 soldiers remaining in the city were added to this force. This Naval Defense Force, under the command of Rear Admiral Iwabuchi, was under the "operational control" of General Yamashita. But the Admiral interpreted this term very loosely, and he did not believe that it meant he should give up the defense of Manila. The 12,500 poorly disciplined and organized sailors and 3,700 soldiers under his command prepared to fanatically defend Manila.[11]

A great deal of confusion ensued. The Army only authorized a delaying action in Manila, but Rear Admiral Iwabuchi, believing that Manila should be defended, ignored orders and instead developed a crude and suicidal plan to confront the American Army in the city. By the time General Yamashita, the man that all parties agreed had the ultimate authority over what the Japanese did in Manila, learned of Rear Admiral Iwabuchi's decision to confront the Americans in the city, Rear Admiral Iwabuchi's men were surrounded with no way to escape. Since surrender was not an option, the utter destruction of the Japanese forces and most of the city of Manila was the only way the Americans could liberate the city. In Europe, German commanders had been ordered to destroy Paris and instead they had left the city and spared it the destruction ordered by Hitler. Manila was to be similarly spared, but Rear Admiral Iwabuchi's unwillingness to have his sailors join the Army's soldiers in leaving the city meant that much of Manila would be destroyed, and tens of thousands of its inhabitants would be killed.[12]

In the weeks following Pearl Harbor, the United States declared Manila an open city in an attempt to save it from the destruction that occurred in many of the cities of Europe. Despite this, the Japanese had bombed Manila prior to entering it on January 2, 1942. Before the Japanese arrived, as many as 200,000 people had fled Manila; but when the Japanese gained control of the city, there were still more than 600,000 Filipino and 5,000

American and British citizens living there. Many of these people were viewed as a threat and were imprisoned as prisoners of war even though they were not members of any of the Allied armed forces.[13]

The battle for Manila was the only time in World War II that Japanese and American forces faced each other in a major city. Although Rear Admiral Iwabuchi and his subordinates failed to develop a general strategy for the defense of the city other than widespread demolition, and the soldiers and sailors that defended Manila were inexperienced and often poorly disciplined, they worked tirelessly to prepare Manila for the American invaders, and the Japanese defenders proved to be tenacious foes. Naval guns, mines, depth charges, and even aerial bombs were planted throughout the city to repel the Americans. Buildings were blown up to block streets and provide fortifications behind which the city's defenders could hide. Mines were hidden by the thousands in the streets and in buildings; and even when buildings were leveled, advancing soldiers had to worry they would set off one of these devices and be blown to bits. Pillboxes were built, trees were cut down and used to barricade streets, machine guns were mounted in rooms and hallways in scores of buildings throughout the city, stairways were barricaded, fire slips were cut into walls, and barbed wire was strung up both inside and outside of structures to impede the advance of American infantrymen. In addition rifles and grenades were distributed to almost all of the Japanese defenders, and Molotov cocktails were concocted and used with terrifying regularity against advancing American troops.[14]

By February 3, the Americans were on the outskirts of Manila. MacArthur, who had a genuine affection for the people of the city, hoped to spare them additional suffering. Early in the Philippine campaign he had said, "One of the purposes of the Philippine campaign is to liberate the Filipinos; they will not understand liberation if accomplished by indiscriminate destruction of their homes, their possessions, their civilization and their own lives ... the destruction of lives and property in the Philippines must be held to a minimum." When it was apparent that the Japanese were not going to give up the city as the Americans had years earlier, there was discussion about using America's complete dominance of the sky to bomb the Japanese into submission. This bombing would have also led to the death and maiming of thousands of Filipino civilians, and MacArthur refused to authorize it.[15]

The next dilemma faced by American commanders was the extent to which artillery would be used in the battle for the city. Most military experts believe that urban fighting is the most difficult and deadly kind of warfare because urban structures provide so many well-fortified places behind which guns can be fired and men can hide. Buildings can be made into difficult to penetrate pillboxes, and artillery can be mounted in the upper stories of buildings to bring deadly fire on the enemy below. In addition, it is almost impossible for civilians to stay out of harm's way and avoid being in close proximity of the combatants, so innocents almost always die in large numbers. This was especially true in Manila because the American commanders had only limited intelligence about where the Japanese were hidden; consequently, almost all of the buildings had to be viewed as potential hiding places for the enemy. Unfortunately, this resulted in buildings being leveled that did not house any Japanese. In addition, the American commanders leading the battle and the soldiers on the ground fighting desperately for each square yard of Manila had no experience with this kind of warfare and thus had to learn the art of urban warfare as the battle progressed.

The greatest American dilemma was that America's production prowess had provided the invading Army with virtually unlimited pieces of artillery that could bring enormous fire to bear on the defending Japanese. It could do so at a long range, thus making it safer for Americans, and it could destroy the structures that were vital for the outnumbered Japanese defenders of the city. The equation for American commanders was simple, but the moral implications were awful. Stateside, mothers, fathers, brothers, sisters, friends, sweethearts, and wives wanted the warriors in Manila to come home alive and in good health; and if this meant firing thousands of rounds of artillery shells at buildings that protected the Japanese but also housed the innocent who were huddling in them in abject fear, then so be it. The war must be won with the fewest American casualties as possible. In the beginning of the battle, restrictions were put on the size of the artillery and the number of rounds used; however, as the fighting intensified, those restrictions were lifted and 75 mm guns and 155 mm howitzers were employed with frightening regularity. One sixteenth-century citadel alone was pounded with 8,000 rounds. Artillery barrages were often followed by shelling and attacks from tanks, infantrymen armed with small arms, flamethrowers, and grenades. Even with the unleashing of this enormous firepower, brutal close quarter and hand-to-hand fighting were often necessary to subdue the Japanese.[16]

It is understandable that some might question the morality of the American decision to use artillery extensively to defeat the Japanese in Manila. Some would even question the American decision to take the city rather than bypassing it and gaining control of the rest of Luzon. However, if the United States had decided to bypass the capital city, the leader of the Filipino guerrillas, Lieutenant Colonel Emmanuel V. de Ocampo, made it clear that the guerrillas would attempt to take the city themselves. This would have undoubtedly meant that the battle would have lasted longer and resulted in even more civilian casualties.

What the Japanese did to the civilian population of Manila as the Americans fought to take the city was unconscionable. At the inception of the battle, the Japanese proclaimed that anyone who was not with them was against them. This meant that essentially anyone who was not a Japanese warrior or civilian was a guerrilla and the enemy and had to be killed. This included all Caucasian and Filipino men, women, and children. As the American army advanced, thousands of innocents were bayonetted by the Japanese. As was often the case throughout their empire, mass rape by Japanese defenders was the norm. Dying and elderly women were raped, and soldiers grabbed healthy women, slashed between their legs and then raped them. Throats and bellies were cut open, and bodies were left in the streets. Older women who were not virgins, would often try to convince Japanese warriors to rape them and spare their younger sisters and daughters who were still virgins, but their pleas were almost always ignored. Homes were set to the torch with the inhabitants inside. Babies were thrown in the air and bayonetted as they came down; and civilians were rounded up and shot, bayonetted, and killed by the sword. Because the disposal of bodies was deemed to be "troublesome," thousands were left to rot, hurled into rivers, or placed into houses that were then set on fire, often with live people still inside.[17]

By February 12, the city was surrounded. There was no way for the Japanese to escape, and victory for the forces of the Rising Sun was impossible. Perhaps the Americans should have left an escape route for the Japanese in the hope that they would withdraw. This would have allowed them to leave the city and save face by not having to surrender; but even if this escape corridor did exist, it is doubtful whether the Japanese would have used it. The Japanese who remained in Manila were ready to die for their cause, and as their plight became bleaker, their brutality only worsened.[18]

The German Club in Manila was a well-constructed building; and since it was owned by Germans, who were allied with the Japanese and still resisting the Allied forces on both their western and eastern fronts, many civilians believed that they would be safe there. On February 9, 1,500 people sought refuge in the club. The next day, the Japanese blocked the exits and set the building on fire. Mothers clutching babies went out to beg for their lives and the lives of their babies. The women were raped repeatedly and the babies bayonetted. Some women had their breasts cut off, and one boy had his genitals removed, and his severed penis was stuffed into his mouth. Grenades were pitched into the basement where hundreds huddled to avoid the flames. Anyone who tried to flee was shot or bayonetted. As the killing and raping continued, many of the Japanese perpetrators smiled and laughed, and many of the civilians who survived the battle reported this same response as the Japanese unleashed their horror on innocent people throughout Manila.[19]

Three thousand people were forced into Fort Santiago. The structure was drenched in gasoline and then set on fire. Soon afterward the fort was bombarded with cannon. Undisciplined Japanese warriors walked the streets of Manila looking for houses that were still intact. Inside they would almost always find civilians terrified at the fate they by now knew was coming. Some would be shot, others bayonetted, and still others would meet their end by being blown to bits by grenades. Often the building was then set on fire. Thousands fled to schools, air raid shelters, convents, and hospitals, but none of these buildings provided safety when the Japanese arrived. The sick in hospitals were tied to their beds and then burned alive, babies were ripped from their mother's arms and smashed against walls or had their eyes gouged out and smeared on these same structures. Men were emasculated and wired together, covered in gas, and then set on fire.

Those who were spared being ruthlessly and senselessly murdered by the Japanese often died a slow and painful death from starvation. Food had been in short supply prior to the arrival of the Americans, and once the battle began, there was no food in the markets. The little food that remained in the city was confiscated to be used to sustain the Japanese forces.[20]

For some Philippine women, capture and life was worse than death. Many who were young and attractive were sent to joro houses or brothels. These were often set up near combat areas, and Japanese soldiers and sailors could make the short journey to the joro house, rape a woman, and then head back to the front line to die. To make sexual intercourse easier, some women were cut open, and some were raped as many as fifteen times per night.

The Americans brought their own brand of horror to the people of Manila. Initially, as soldiers advanced into the city, artillery was only used on targets in which Japanese soldiers were observed. As the battle for the city escalated, and Japanese resistance stiffened, it often proved to be impossible to accurately determine which buildings were being used by the enemy and which were empty or housing civilians. To ensure the destruction of the Japanese and to protect American lives, it was determined that virtually all buildings were inhabited by the Japanese and thus had to be leveled before the American advance. Initially 4.2-inch mortars were used, but when it became apparent that these could not adequately penetrate reinforced concrete, tanks and larger pieces of artillery were brought in that could pound even the most well built structures into rubble.

Despite the decision to level houses and larger buildings before the infantry advanced, the American warrior in Manila still risked life and limb with each yard that he advanced. When the buildings fell, many of the Japanese inside were killed, but many others would survive the collapse, and the only way to defeat these men was to root them out in the rubble and kill them. The rubble provided excellent cover for the enemy. Americans would slowly walk over the huge mounds that had once been large urban structures, seek out the enemy, and then confront him, sometimes in terrifying hand-to-hand combat. The most effective way to combat the Japanese in the rubble was with fire, and we will never know how many Japanese soldiers and sailors were burned alive by American flamethrowers.

The advancing Americans were aware of the thousands of Filipino people in the path of their advance, and some efforts were made to spare them. If a building was known to house a large number of civilians, it was generally bypassed. However, when the Japanese realized this, they would often occupy these structures, and fire from them on the advancing Americans. Military necessity then required the tank and artillerymen to lay waste to the building killing hundreds of civilians inside. The Japanese Spirit Warriors were determined to fight to the death, and in the process they would force their enemy to kill thousands of the people they were trying to liberate.

There were limits to what the Americans would do to reduce American casualties and kill the enemy. On several occasions, commanders asked that bombers be flown over the city so that bombs could be dropped on targets where the Japanese resistance was particularly tenacious. MacArthur called aerial bombing of Manila "unthinkable," and it was never employed in the battle for the city. Even without aerial bombing, the amount of firepower used by the Americans was extraordinary. In addition to tanks, flamethrowers, grandees, and semiautomatic weapons, 42,153 rounds of artillery were used in the battle, and much of this was fired at buildings that often held Filipino people as well as the Japanese.

Completely surrounded by the American forces and with no hope of escape or victory, the Japanese grew more desperate. Streets were mined, and Japanese warriors disguised themselves as Filipino guerrillas, infiltrated American lines, and then killed as many Americans as possible before being killed. When they realized that many of the government buildings had been constructed with reinforced concrete so they could withstand earthquakes, they sought these out and fought tenaciously from doors and windows as the Americans pounded them with artillery and tank rounds until even the best built structures collapsed.[21]

On March 3, all but sporadic Japanese resistance ended, and Manila came under American control. The Japanese strategy known as Senko-Seisaku, translated as "kill all, burn all, destroy all," which had been employed in China and on numerous islands in the Pacific, had been unleashed in Manila with expectable results. More than 1,000 Americans were killed and another 5,565 were wounded. Almost 17,000 Japanese, and approximately 100,000 Filipino civilians, or 100 for every one American, were dead, and countless other men and women were wounded or emotionally scarred for life.

When Manila fell to the Americans on March 3, the city was in ruins, and only Warsaw, Poland, suffered more damage during World War II. In addition to the immeasurable human suffering, 70 percent of the utilities, 75 percent of the factories, 80 percent of the southern residential district, and the city's entire business district were destroyed. Even General MacArthur, a man who had fought on the western front in World War I and been hardened by years of conflict in World War II, was emotionally damaged by what

Manila after the battle for the city. National Archives.

happened in Manila. It was fortunate for both the Americans and the Japanese that Manila was the only time they faced each other in an urban setting during the war.

Fortunately, the Japanese were not able to carry out their plans to execute the Allied prisoners held in Manila. Four thousand Allies were held prisoner in Santo Thomas University, and after fierce fighting, almost all of these men were liberated. In addition, more than a thousand prisoners in Bilibid prison were freed.

It is impossible to know how many of the 100,000 civilian deaths in Manila were caused by American ordnance and how many at the hands of the Japanese. Some who have studied the battle believe that the Americans were responsible for as many as 40 percent of the civilian deaths. There is no question that most of the structural damage to the city was caused by American firepower. However, despite this, the vast majority of the people of the Philippines viewed the Americans as liberators, and they treated them as such after the fighting had ended. The people of Manila showed their affection toward the American soldiers by shouting, "God bless America" and "Victory Joe" when they passed them in the streets, and Lieutenant Colonel Emmanuel de Ocampo, even went so far as to say, "If the Americans had bypassed the city an even higher proportion of the civilians would have been massacred." The people of Manila also believed that despite the horrific destruction that had been done to their city life would eventually get better now that the Japanese were no longer in control.

The Japanese defeat in Manila did not end the campaign to drive the Japanese from the Philippines. The battle for Luzon did not end until June 30, and sporadic fighting continued on the island and in other parts of the Philippines until the Japanese surrendered on August 15, 1945. The Allies suffered almost 40,000 casualties on Luzon, 2,000 of which were Navy personnel, most of whom died as a result of kamikaze attacks. The cost of the 10-month campaign to retake the Philippines was staggering for both sides. The United States suffered more than 79,000 casualties, and fewer than 100,000 of the 450,000 Japanese warriors charged with defending the Philippines survived the war. The vast majority of the Japanese dead and wounded were the result of starvation and disease. The material losses for both sides were also staggering. We will never know the number of Filipinos who died as a result of the war.

In many ways the battle for the Philippines was the decisive battle in the Pacific during World War II, and the loss of the Philippines made it all but impossible for the Japanese to maintain their Empire. Their air and naval forces, the finest in the Pacific when the war began, were in ruin. They were cut off from essential raw materials in other parts of their Empire, and even Japan's minister of the navy, Admiral Mitsumasa Yonai stated after the war, "When you took the Philippines, that was the end of our resources." Still Japan fought on. A nation that had taught millions of young men that surrender was the ultimate disgrace could not bring itself to surrender. It would take the incineration of many of Japan's cities and hundreds of thousands of its citizens, and two atomic bombs to finally get the Japanese to capitulate. It was not until March 1974, after meeting with his former commanding officer, that Second Lieutenant Hiroo Onoda, the last Japanese warrior in the Philippines, surrendered. For almost 30 years he had been hiding out north of Mindoro on the island of Lubang. Not surprisingly, he still carried the dagger given to him by his mother prior to the war that he was expected to use on himself if captured.[22]

This was the city that awaited my father. Remembering the young orphan girl he had met when he had been in Tacloban, my father and a friend journeyed to Manila in search of the girl's uncle. As they wandered the smoldering ruins of the once beautiful city, they saw nothing but death, "total destruction, rubble, nothing habitable," and despair. Body parts mingled with destroyed buildings, the stench of decaying bodies filled the air, and "there was not a house standing."

Out of the rubble emerged a seven to eight-year old boy and his ten-to-twelve year old sister, and almost immediately the boy said, "…My sister Joe, cheap, only one American dollar." "Dumbfounded but sadly not surprised" and disgusted, my father admonished the boy and told him never to do this again. The boy then explained to my dad that during the more than three years of Japanese occupation, the girl had been raped dozens of times, and both children had witnessed people being randomly beheaded and bayonetted. Perhaps after years of such horrors the boy believed that prostituting his sister for desperately needed money was a fair exchange. They "talked with the children, and shared their rations with them, but rather than gobbling them down they pocketed them." My father asked, "Why not eat?" The boy replied, "For our sick mother." Hearing this, my father and his friend instructed the boy and girl to take them to their home. When they arrived, there was no home, only rubble, and an old "claw-handed woman" sitting on a pile of rocks. The deformed women said to my father and his friend, "don't look." In the rubble adjacent to where they found the woman was a headless decaying body with the rotting head lying nearby. What could they do? They gave the old woman the little money they had on them, made the young boy promise not to try and sell his sister ever again, and they moved on. When they arrived at what they believed was the address given to them by the young girl in Tacloban that at one time had housed her uncle, there was only rubble and no sign that anyone lived there. They never did locate the uncle of the young girl they had befriended.

Whenever my father told me of his journey into Manila I could tell the memory of the little boy trying to sell his sister and the "claw-handed woman" living in rubble surrounded by death still haunted him; and on a note that I found scribbled on scrap paper after his death, he described this as his worst experience of the war. As brutal as Mindoro had been, it was still warrior against warrior. Perhaps his abandonment to the orphanage made the encounter with the young boy and girl more painful. Children and the "claw-handed woman" had not started this war, but they would face the war's consequences for the rest of their lives. As he scribbled on the note, "In Manila I encountered something far more horrible than what we encountered on Mindoro.... I volunteered for the Navy and PT boat duty as did all of my shipmates. We were taught to defend ourselves and kill if necessary. We expected to take casualties.... We were at war. We were entrusted with the fastest crafts afloat, great firepower and maneuverability. I was going home. The greatest horror awaited me now, Manila, and this was far more horrible than any of our previous encounters. In Manila we saw the real casualties of war ... civilians, overlooked, forgotten, neglected, civilians."

If the killing of the three soldiers on Mindoro had forced him to participate in war

PT boats burning at PT Boat Base 17, Babon Point, Samar, Philippines. None of the PT boats from Squadron 16 survived the war. World War II PT Boats Museum and Archives, Germantown, Tennessee.

Top: PT boats at PT Boat Base 17, Babon Point, Samar, Philippines. *Bottom:* PT *170* being burned, November 11, 1945. Both photographs, World War II PT Boats Museum and Archives, Germantown, Tennessee.

at its most personal level, his journey into Manila in early 1945 exposed him to the macabre reality of modern war. Death and its foul stench, destruction, horror, suffering, and the complete loss of hope were all that existed. I believe that this reality became one of the clearest truths in my father's life, and I am not sure if he ever fully came to terms with what he had witnessed.[23]

In November 1945, with the war over and America trying to put the conflict behind her, the *Omen of the Seas* and the other beloved PT boats of Squadron 16 were rounded up and sent to a quiet beach on Samar Island in the Philippines. They were run up on the beach at high tide and stripped of engines, armaments and anything else that was potentially useful. When the tide went out, oil was poured into the bilges, and then a flamethrower was used to set fire to the boat that was furthest upwind. The flames then spread from boat to boat. Scores of Packard engines were lined up on the shore, and most would soon be reclaimed by the jungle. A few of the newer boats had their armaments removed and were then used as temporary housing for the native population.[24]

These boats that were so beloved by the men who crewed them had become disposable inventory to the United States Navy. Fortunately my father and his squadron mates were not there for this event, and one of the few PT boat sailors who did witness the burning explained, "It was a rather sad event to watch the boats go up in flames." All of the PT Boat squadrons were decommissioned, and in total 128 boats were destroyed. None of the boats from Squadron 16 were saved. In total, the boats and sailors in Squadron 16A, had traveled more than 28,000 miles, and for more than 17,000 of these miles the boats were under their own power. From Pearl Harbor to the war's end these tiny but lethal boats and their crews had served America proudly; and although they were deemed to be "expendable," they played a vital role in the victory against Japan in the Pacific. The craft had successfully plied the waters of the Bering Sea, been run aground, taken her crews in and out of harm's way, and had more frequent contact with the enemy and at closer range than any other American surface craft in World War II. It is not surprising that Squadron 16 was often referred to as a "hard luck outfit."

The PT boats that had played such an important role in the battle for New Guinea and the Philippines were tired and leaky. Most of the boats' engines were worn out, and many frames were fractured and hulls dry rotted. They had no place in the post-war United States Navy, and unlike their steel counterparts, they could not be mothballed to be brought back to service in future wars. The PT boat men loved their boats and they loved each other. Their friendships would last into old age, and although their boats had been rendered into ash, the crews who operated them would always proudly call themselves PT Boat Men.[25]

10

Father and Son, Confessions and a Sailor's Last Voyage

There are few great men. There are only great challenges, which ordinary men are forced by circumstances to meet.—Admiral William F. "Bull" Halsey

Father and Son

Mark Kalinowski was my best friend. He was loud and crazy, and the most passionate person I have ever known. He loved baseball and the Mets, the Beatles, his family, gambling, and me. He loved, laughed, sang, and sometimes drank to excess. For him, the challenge of each day was to consume more than was possible. There were no down days, not really any down minutes for him. Every moment had to be consumed in big bites.

Despite his crazy nature, my father loved Mark Kalinowski. He loved his passion, his insistence that each moment had to be embraced, and his love of life. He knew Mark cared deeply for me, and he understood that he had a twisted but sturdy moral code. Mark was a good man to call a friend. On Christmas day, 1981, Mark Kalinowski died at the age of 25. The cause of death was murky, but it was most likely the result of a toxic buildup of medicine that he was taking for his epilepsy. At the gravesite I eulogized him, and the next day I returned to Florida to resume my teaching job.

My father attended Mark's funeral and stood near me as I read the eulogy, but he said nothing to me after his passing. My father was not a man who counseled or offered advice. He understood that one of the most basic realities of life is that some events have no explanation. Good men die and fate cannot be explained. Best friends should not die at 25! What could he say?

In March my father called and told me that he would be attending an engineering conference in Miami, and he would like to visit me in Tampa when it was over. He took a week's vacation, and I planned a canoe trip on the aptly named Peace River. This was the way of my father. He felt deeply, but he put little stock in words and great value in time well spent with those he loved.

The Peace is the most gentle of rivers. Paddling required little effort or thought, and miles passed easily and with little said. At night we would make a fire on the river's bank, cook simple meals, talk, and allow minutes to drift by as we quietly followed the dancing flames. Years later we laughed at the numerous times we went swimming oblivious to the alligators along the river.

Halfheartedly my father paddled. Rhythmically, his paddle would hit the water, but rather than driving us forward, he was satisfied to let the slow, unstoppable current drift us downstream. My father canoed much the way he planed wood. His keen, deep blue eyes surveyed all directions. Yellow coreopsis bloomed, eagles soared, sandhill cranes dotted the shoreline, and blue herons would sit in trees, gracefully fly off at our approach, re-perch out of sight, and then take off again as we encountered them. This dance was repeated dozens of times over many miles, and we never tired of it. Songbirds provided the day's soundtrack. Palmetto, cypress, cabbage palms, and mangroves lined the river's banks, and live oak trees arched over the river and provided a tunnel-like canopy and shade. Snakes slithered, and numerous small mammals scurried up and down the river's banks playing and completing their chores. All ignored us. He took it all in and said little. My thoughts drifted, and the gentle peace of the Peace River helped me to come to terms with the loss of my best friend.

At the time I knew almost nothing about my father's experiences in Mindoro. Now I wonder, did the thick Florida canopy take him back to the winter of 1944–45? Was his brilliant mind able to lock out the thoughts of kamikazes, screaming men, inflamed ships, dismembered comrades, and a young man seeking escape in the jungle while clutching a newly detached arm? Did he encounter memories of the half-man floating off the Mindoro beach or resting beside him as he tried to sleep? Did he think of the man who risked his life to save him, and did he ponder whether the man survived the war? Did he think of the *300* boat and the carnage that engulfed it all those years ago, and did he question why it was the *300* boat and not his own that was hit by a kamikaze? Did the exhaustion and well-earned sleep keep the past at bay? Did the evening campfires flicker memories of burning men and three well-aimed rifle shots? Did hatred from the past still dance through his dreams, or was all of this gone, pushed away to a place he tried to never go. Had he left the memory of their skinny, charred, lifeless bodies on Mindoro when he left in 1945, or did the remembrances of the dead men periodically dance into his consciousness and had these terrifying images joined him on the beautiful Peace River? I do not know. The old sailor kept his secrets. He had come to help heal my pain, not to confess his. In his world, fathers did not share their suffering with their sons. His war had to be kept far away.

Confessions

Sometime around my father's 75th year, we were trolling for bluefish and striped bass about six miles south of the Norwalk Islands off the Connecticut coast. We had been fishing together on Long Island Sound since I was seven, and neither of us ever tired of our time together on the water. This was a brilliant, warm, July day. There was a sheen on the water, that can only be seen on windless flat calm days, and the fishing was slow. My father was more silent than usual, but he finally quietly announced out of nowhere that a box had arrived without warning the day before. Opening it, he found a note from the wife of a PT boat shipmate. His comrade had died suddenly, and after his passing she had found a box of photos from the war. She did not want them, but rather than throw them out, she had mailed them to my dad.

My father was the steadiest man I have ever known. I never heard him swear or raise his voice, and I never saw him cry, panic, or lose his temper. I always wondered if this control was innate, or something he had learned as a means of self-defense at the

My father in the Grand Canyon. I wonder how often his mind drifted to the war during the countless hours we spent together. Bob Gelzheiser collection.

orphanage or in the war. On this day, he would maintain his control, but as he talked, I realized I was to hear things he had never shared with me. Perhaps he believed I no longer had to be protected from the truth of his war.... Perhaps it was time for him to admit the truth to himself.... Perhaps both. Regardless, the steadiness was gone. He would say a few words or sentences and pause. Long Island Sound was empty, and except for the purring motor slowly driving us forward, it was quiet. I looked at the fishing rods and the lines taking lures to yet-to-be-found bluefish or striped bass, and I quietly hoped nothing would bite. Finally he said, "For all of these years I convinced myself that it was a bad dream, that the things that happened never happened, and the things I did I never did, and then this box arrived and there was the proof that it was not all a dream." It was then that he told me the story of Mindoro for the first time.

The following spring, I invited him to come to my school and talk to my Advanced Placement United States History students. I was surprised when he agreed to come, but I was unsure what he would say. Since I was a little boy, my father had talked of his PT boat experiences, but all of the stories were fun, and my impression had been that for him World War II was more like an episode of *McHale's Navy* than a real war.

He loved to tell these funny stories, and when he did, my mom would roll her eyes. I always believed that this was because she had heard them so many times, but I now think she was angry that he painted such a happy picture of the war. He would tell of how in New Guinea or the Philippines one of the squadron's boats approached a long dock that had numerous crude huts built on it that the sailors used as outhouses. Approaching the dock at full speed, the boat made a sharp turn, threw up a huge wake, and several of the huts, each occupied by a sailor with his pants down, were lifted off the dock and dumped on to the water. Sailors from various boats laughed as they watched their shocked, half-clad squadron mates bob in the sea. Often, when not in the combat zone, they would drain the grain alcohol that fueled the torpedoes on their boats. They would then mix the fuel with whatever fruit juice was available and have a torpedo juice party. Once, on the morning after such festivities, an officer made a surprise inspection, and he wanted to see the PT boat crews display their proficiency with torpedoes. A target was set up, and as the bleary-eyed crew powered their boat past it, they launched a torpedo only to have it harmlessly float to the water's surface. A second and third attempt had the same results, and the enraged admiral admonished Squadron Commander Colvin, and then stormed away promising court-martials for all involved. Fortunately, before the formal court-martial process could begin, Squadron 16A was ordered to ship out, and there was no more talk of punishment.

He enjoyed telling of Squadron 16A missing the Panama Canal by more than 90 miles, climbing coconut trees, adopting pet monkeys and stray dogs, "fishing" by dropping explosives into the water and then collecting the dead fish as they floated to the surface, and waving at Japanese warriors as they glided by my father in a dugout canoe disguised as Filipino natives.

I did not know which war my father would share with my students. Would it be the one I had grown up with that was safe and filled with funny stories? An essential part of his being was to do no harm and to protect and look out for those around him. He did not burden others, and he kept his thoughts inside. Would he now be willing to share the truth of his war with young strangers? He entered the classroom and taped a world map on the wall marked with the numerous places he had served. The students were quiet, unsure of what to expect, and even a bit nervous that a strange man was about to talk to them. He took a sip of water, looked out at the students, and then quietly and slowly explained, "I have been accused of only telling the fun parts of my experiences in World War II. I am not going to do that today. Today I will tell you what the war was really like for me. I must tell the real story of the horrors of war, the death, suffering, and destruction since someday, in the not too distant future, you and others of your generation could be called upon to decide to make war."

From there, the stories flowed. I could tell it was difficult for him, perhaps therapeutic, but yes, very difficult. He told of how he did not want to kill men at close range, and how he loved the water and boot camp and the violent waves of the Bering Sea. He told of the soldier who was emasculated, and of not sleeping for more than 65 hours during the early days on Mindoro. I also learned of a patrol taken by him and the crew of the *221* boat up a small river, and how they came under fire from the Japanese and how lucky he and his shipmates felt when they escaped unscathed. He told of a commendation that Squadron 16 was recommended for and smiled when he told the class that the response from those in charge of awarding the commendation was, "Even a rat will fight when it is cornered … commendation denied."

My father then told the students his darkest experiences in Mindoro. His voice was almost monotone, and he showed little emotion as he described one event after another. When he finished the story of the three men he shot, he took the Navy knife off the podium I had set up for him, unsheathed it, and pointed to the three grooves he had carved in it decades ago. He handed it to a boy in the front row, and I could tell this resonated with the young man. The knife was real, and hard, and cold. On it were real grooves that meant real death, and this gentle old man had put them there. As the knife was being passed around, my father made a long pause, and then lifted up an old white envelope he had put on the podium. I recognized it, and after a moment's thought, I realized I had seen it many times. For as long as I could remember, the envelope had been kept in the top left-hand drawer of my father's bureau. I knew this because this is also where he kept his handkerchiefs and money, and periodically when I was growing up he would ask me to please get him money from the drawer. He never had to specify because I knew where he kept his money; and each time I went into the drawer, I had seen the envelope.

Now he slowly opened it up, and removed three small photos. I had never seen these, and this was a chapter from the story he had not shared with me on our summer fishing expedition. The first one he held up was of a young Japanese warrior. He was in his dress uniform, and my guess is that it was taken shortly after he completed boot camp. It reminded me of a similar photo taken of my dad that I now display in my house. He said little of the young man, and then he held up a photo of a Japanese woman. She is young and pretty and wearing clothes that look formal, even ceremonial, perhaps the photo was taken at her wedding. As he was removing the third photo he stopped. I was sitting in the back of the room. I had never seen my dad cry, but now I feared he was on the brink of an emotional collapse. His voice stuttered, his jaw trembled, and he tried to talk, but no words came out. I could see he was fighting back tears, and I could not decide if this was a moment he had to navigate himself or if I should go to him and give him comfort. In the seconds I took deciding what I should do, he composed himself and took a slow drink of water. More seconds passed, and he held up the last picture. It was of a beautiful Japanese infant. She is wearing a loose fitting polka-dotted dress, and it is impossible not to smile when you look at her photo. He then explained that he took the photos off of one of the men whose death was etched on the knife. He had killed the man, and "made the woman in the photo a widow and the infant an orphan." He went on to say, "The Japanese were human beings, just like us. They had wives, kids, families. They were doing their duty, just like us, by standards

The charred remains of the first Japanese soldier my father killed and the photos he found on the body of one of the men he killed on Mindoro. I believe that for the rest of his life it haunted him that he had made the woman a widow and the baby an orphan. Francis Gelzheiser collection.

of a different culture which we failed to understand." Soon after this confession he completed his talk, and by the time he left the room and I said thank you and goodbye, his demeanor had returned to normal. Mindoro had been pushed back inside where he had kept it for so many years.

Since then, I have thought often of this moment. He had told me that for 50 years he had made Mindoro a bad dream, and yet for as long as I could remember, the envelope had been in his drawer. Had he ever opened it? Did he know its contents? Was it a tiny Pandora's box that often tempted him but had to be left untouched for fear of all of the demons that its content could unleash? Did he hate or pity the young man in the photo? Could he forgive him for forcing my dad to take his life ... to bring so much suffering and emptiness to the innocent?

A Sailor's Last Voyage

In my father's 87th year his heart started to fade. He had always had wonderful health, but with the weakening of his heart came the slowing of his mind; and we knew the end could not be too far off. There were several hospitalizations; but he insisted, and we all agreed, that there would be no dramatic medical procedures to keep him alive. On our numerous camping trips, he had always insisted that we leave the campsite better than we found it. In the final chapter of his life, he wanted to make sure that he had left more than he had taken. He had always found it unseemly that so many finite resources were spent to keep the old and dying alive for a few more weeks or months. He had given more than he had taken his whole life, and he had seen, done and accomplished far more than he had ever dreamed. He had once told me, "We should all be like the elephants, and when our time has come, we should go away and die." His time had now come. He would go away and die, and leave the campsite in better shape than he found it.

He and I shared some wonderful moments during those last two years. In his final summer, we took one last fishing trip together. We had fished on Long Island Sound for almost 50 years. How many hundreds of sunrises had we quietly watched together, and this would be our last. We did not have to go far, only a bit more than a mile out and just north of our beloved Penfield Lighthouse. The lighthouse marked the end of Penfield Reef. The Reef was horseshoe shaped and only exposed during low tide. Often we had walked out onto the Reef in search of bluefish and an occasional striped bass. In the fall months, when I was in high school, we would journey out before I went to school; and he to work to throw popping lures at voracious bluefish feeding up for their fall migration. I remember thinking after I went home, deposited our fishing rods, and hurried off to school that no matter what happened during the rest of the day that I had already had a great day. I am sure my father thought the same thing. Days before this last fishing trip, I had caught some striped bass at a location within sight of Penfield Reef; and on this, our final trip, nature, or God, or fate was kind to us. As we looked to the east, the sun rose gloriously in the cloudless July sky, the sea was glasslike calm, and there were no other boats in sight. It did not take long for the rods to start bending, and by the end of the morning we had caught six striped bass that weighed between 12 and 20 pounds. We each landed three, and although my dad caught the largest, he never asked for help or gave up the rod.

We talked little, and my guess is my dad's thoughts were few. At some level, we both knew this would be our last time fishing together, and it was a time to be felt rather than pondered.

When we returned to the marina, I dropped him off at the gas dock where it would be easier for him to exit the boat. I offered to come pick him up with the car, but he said no. He would walk over and meet me where the boat was docked. I docked the boat, and while cleaning it, I watched him. He ran into Larry who had done work on our motors for almost 40 years, and they had a short talk. He then proceeded. His gait was stiff and slow, and even from a distance it was evident that he was now a very frail man and that the tide was ebbing for the old sailor. Sadness interrupted my morning of peace, and I could not help but wonder ... where had the time gone?

The following May he went to the hospital for the last time. I came to visit, and he was sitting up in his bed. He asked me to look out the window to "see if there were rows of chicken coops in the courtyard." He explained, "All they served in the hospital was chicken so they must be raising them." We laughed, talked about nothing, and then for the last time, the war came up. I thought I had heard all of the stories, but this one was new. He was on Attu and a PT boat had taken on water, its generator had been flooded, and it had to be rebuilt. My dad and a fellow electrician's mate decided that it needed to be flushed with fresh water, and the best way to do this would be to take the generator inland, find a stream, and submerse it. The moving fresh water would remove the salt and prevent corrosion. The young officer in charge refused their request to journey to the stream. My dad's mind seemed to regain its old sharpness momentarily, and his voice hardened as he expressed the disdain he still retained for such stupidity. When I asked him what they did, he seemed surprised at the question. "We took it to the nearest clean stream and submersed it.... It had to be cleaned." I then asked, "What would have happened if the officer found out you did this?" He replied, "We would have been court-martialed."

I smiled and thought perhaps this is one reason we won the war. My father had had one of the most rigid and strict upbringings possible in America. A small number of nuns and priests had to educate, raise, and control hundreds of orphaned and abandoned children with very limited resources. There was little love, appreciation for the individual, or encouragement to develop creativity and original thinking. And yet somehow my father developed a healthy skepticism of authority and an uncanny ability to solve problems often in very unique ways. To use a more modern expression, he had the ability to "think outside of the box." Certainly my father's impressive intellect was part of the reason for this, but I also believe that his insistence on ignoring orders and taking the generator to the stream is also an illustration of the kind of citizen produced in America as a result of her long cherished belief in individual liberty and that citizens needed to be trusted.

There were many reasons why America and her allies won World War II. Certainly her factories and farms played an enormous role, and no war can be won without warriors willing to do the difficult and terrifying work of war; and the generation that was tasked with defeating Imperial Japan and Nazi Germany showed its metal time and time again. However, America's victory was also a byproduct of the American system that put great faith in the individual, whether the son of a blue-blood steel magnate or an orphan. When my dad journeyed to that stream to clean that generator he was doing what thousands of others did during the war. Somehow, despite his upbringing, he still had developed that uniquely American willingness to question authority, have faith in himself, and get the job done regardless of what his superiors said. I am sure that under the same circumstances, German and Japanese sailors would have followed orders, and I believe that is one reason they lost the war. In my father's world, stupid orders were more stupid than they were orders so they had to be ignored. Men do not think this way in totalitarian states. They might be fanatical warriors eager to die for the cause, but they will not disobey orders to clean generators; and often keeping a boat running was more likely to bring victory than killing oneself trying to crash a plane into a boat.

If Japan produced the Spirit Warrior, one of the most determined, fanatical, and courageous warriors that world has ever seen, the United States produced Fran Gelzheiser, Tom Hart, Henry Plage, Glenn Koach, Arthur Williams, Paul Delco, and millions of other citizen sailors, airmen, and soldiers like them. The last thing these men wanted to do was to die for President Franklin Roosevelt or anyone else. They wanted to win the war and then go home to the people and nation they loved. How many millions of times during the course of the war did the innovative instincts that had been honed during boyhood or the reluctance to be blindly led help them to fix a jeep, or a piece of artillery, or modify a PT boat, or search for missing men in a vast ocean in a damaged ship when they had been ordered to do otherwise, or clean a generator in a wilderness stream? They respected but did not worship or fear authority, and all believed that the lowliest of citizens, even those abandoned in an orphanage, mattered.

On more than one occasion, hospital aides and nurses came in to take my father for tests or to cart him off to dialysis. Each time we told them no. His time had come, he was at peace, and we were going to take him home to die. Days later I returned, this time to my parent's house. I expected to find him in a wheelchair, perhaps watching the numerous birds that congregated by his backyard feeders, and I hoped we could visit for one last time. Instead he was sleeping on his deathbed, surrounded by family and a hospice nurse. In the days that followed, he said only two things: "I am on the trail," and once when he briefly awoke and my brother asked him how he was doing he instantly responded, "Great Ed, never better." To the end, he would not burden others.

I will always be grateful that, somewhere along the way, I think Mindoro and the war left him. There would be no cries in the night, tears or confessions. He was ready to die, a man deeply satisfied with the life he had lived. I know he was saddened by what the war had forced him to do, but I do not believe he died encumbered with guilt. The strength that had served him so well when he was young stayed with him. In his final hours, he did not let the pain from the war trouble his peace. In his quiet way he had a final victory. In the end, the war did not haunt him.

At the funeral there was no honor guard or bugler playing taps. In fact, there were few things in the world that bothered my dad more than taps. The previous Christmas I had received a book on the history of taps from my sister. My father barely acknowledged the gift when I showed it to him, and while taking a walk later that day, I asked him why he hated taps so much. He became quiet and edgy, unhappy that this topic had come up. He looked off into the distance and uttered, "There was no taps on Mindoro … no taps … you just dug a hole and buried them … dug a hole and buried them." This ended the discussion.

Death forces us to crystalize a person's life, and when I thought of my dad, this process was not difficult. He was the most decent, gentle, kind, honest, honorable, and brilliant man I have ever known. However, when I distilled his life even more, I determined that at his core, he was a man who loved life and had a deep need to look out for others. Perhaps this need came as a result of being abandoned at six, left in "The Home" with his sister by a father who had turned to drink and a mother who could not care for him. To be needed meant that he would never be abandoned again. Looking out for others is what he did, and this can best be seen in a small act that took place during the early days on Mindoro.

In an unusual act in a war zone, my father was summoned to Lieutenant Commander Davis's office and asked to take out the garbage. Because the relationship between officers and enlisted men in the PT boat fleet was generally very informal, this surprised my father. When he went to comply, he noticed a piece of paper on the rim of the trashcan. He picked it up and saw that it was a letter of acceptance to Naval Officer Candidate School. If he was going to accept the offer, he had to leave immediately. I am sure that my dad must have felt much pride. The kid from the orphanage who came from nothing could now become a naval officer, one of the most respected positions a man could earn during World War II. More importantly, it was a ticket off the hell that was Mindoro. He looked up and Commander Davis said, "It's up to you, but we need you here." Without a word, my father pushed the letter into the trash. In the ensuing days his skills, dedication, and courage would help to save boats and perhaps men's lives. I love this story, but no one who knew my father would be surprised by it, because putting others ahead of himself is what he did.... His nation, squadron mates, coworkers, friends, and family. If you knew my dad, you had at some point received his generous help. In the end, he accepted death with grace, and in doing so, he made his passing much easier for all of us.

My father always had a love of life, and I believe that this was deepened by his experiences during the war. When I was a boy he used to say, "Bob, life is short." This meant little to me at the time, but I now understand that he was trying to help me to understand that each moment should be savored, and we should never take the simple beauty that surrounds us each day for granted. He marveled at all things that crawled, swam, ran, flew, and bloomed. At 85, he donned a bee suit to help my sister Lynn and her husband Wayne harvest honey. More than any man I have ever known, he loved life. Once I questioned him about what he did on V.J. Day. By this point in the war, he had been sent home from the Philippines, and at some time in the future he was to be sent to Borneo to prepare for the invasion of Japan. He was in Pittsburgh when the bombs were dropped on Hiroshima and Nagasaki, and I expected to hear stories of wild partying and perhaps kisses from appreciative, pretty young women. Instead he got quiet. "I sat on a street corner and watched all of the celebrating. I looked at all of the happiness but instead of joining it I said to myself over and over ... what a waste ... what a waste."

I do not fully understand how the Japanese fit into this equation. He spent his career designing circuit breakers for Westinghouse, and often engineers from Japan were sent to his plant to confer with him. I am sure he was always respectful, but I do not believe he was ever comfortable around them. My father spent a lifetime figuring out how things worked. Whether in the lab at Bryant Electric or observing nature on a hike or constructing or repairing something in his shop, he could almost always comprehend and explain what was happening. I do not believe he was ever able to understand the men who flew the kamikazes or the culture that created them. The idea and reality of the suicide plane were so foreign to him that I believe he wanted to avoid thinking about them and have little to do with the people who created this weapon. I do not think he hated the Japanese, but I do not believe he ever forgave them. In his eighties, while on vacation, he went to pick up a rental car. When renting a car, he always specified that he wanted an American vehicle; and when they handed him the keys to a Mitsubishi he refused to take them. A disagreement ensued, and even when offered an upgraded Japanese vehicle, he refused to take it. Ultimately he drove away in a small Ford.

I believe my father could not forgive the Japanese for attacking his nation, for killing his comrades, for sending a kamikaze into PT *300* and *Orestes,* and for exploding a cluster bomb above the sleeping survivors of the ship. They had forced him to kill and to turn wives into widows and babies into orphans, and they had compelled boys to prostitute their sisters, and a claw-handed old woman and her children to starve.

War can only be understood by its participants, and outsiders like myself can only record what we have learned from those participants. War can destroy even those who have been physically unscathed by it, and others can move on from its horrors, and at least on the surface appear unharmed by what they have seen and done. Late in his life I came to understand that my father's war experiences did not consume or destroy him because he never allowed the war to destroy his humanity. Had it done so, and only once did he admit to me that it almost did, I do not believe he would have ever recovered from it.

While looking at photos in a PT boat calendar with him late in his life, I came across a photo of a Japanese sailor or pilot being hoisted up the side of a PT boat by its crew. The man was rope thin and pathetic looking, and as I examined the photo, my father told me of the similar rescue he participated in while on PT *221*. However, just as the prisoner was being dragged on to the boat's deck with a boat hook, he pulled the pin of a grenade that he was hiding behind his head. Instantly, a sailor, perhaps my father, fired a bullet into him as another kicked him and the grenade overboard. Generally, Japanese sailors and pilots who had abandoned their ship or plane would choose drowning over rescue and thus they swam away from American ships coming to their aid. After this incident, Japanese found in the water by PT *221*, who might have been saved, would almost always be left to drown. This bothered my father, but he realized the need for such a policy. What he could not abide was cruelty. Once when sharing a drink with some former shipmates at an annual P.T. Boat Reunion, a man from another squadron joined them. At some point the conversation shifted to the treatment of the floating Japanese, and the man gleefully bragged about how he and his shipmates took great joy in running over these men and "splitting their heads like coconuts." Quietly, my father and his shipmates walked away.

What frightened my father was the realization that war can strip any of its participants of their humanity, and that World War II almost took his. Not long before he died, we were taking a walk, and he brought up the killing of the three men on Mindoro. It was rare for him to bring up this topic, and the casual way that he mentioned it made it even more unusual. However, he became very emotional as he explained the final chapter to this story that he had never told me, but that he now, perhaps because death was so near, wanted to tell. After he had shot the men, he went up to each one and pushed him to see if he was dead. Each man had been killed by the single shot, but he emotionally confessed, "I don't know what I would have done if any of them were alive." This would have been the greatest challenge to his humanity, and I believe as he neared death and pondered his life, he was terrified that he would have succumbed to hate and killed wounded, helpless men. I reminded him that they were dead and he did not have to speculate.... He had survived the war with his humanity intact.

My father wanted his ashes spread on his beloved Long Island Sound, and so in

August 2011 we prepared to do so. Days before, I went to the garage to ready an American flag to fly on our boat *Harvest Moon*. I found a six-foot pole and started to fasten the flag half way up it but then smiled and said no. On my father's last day the flag would fly high and at full staff. This is how he would want it.

Before the sun was up, my family and I boarded the *Harvest Moon*, and slowly I navigated her out of the marina, past the jetty at the east end of Jennings Beach in Fairfield, Connecticut, and out toward Penfield Lighthouse. It is a journey we had made hundreds of times together. When I was a little boy, he would pilot the boat, and when we were far removed from any obstructions, he would let me take the wheel and teach me simple rules of navigation. At some point I started to operate the boat, and when he grew old, I would look out for him, much as he had done for me when I was young. We passed the spot where we had caught the six stripers the previous summer, went around the lighthouse and then anchored just west of where Penfield Reef elbowed westward and near where we had spent so many magical, timeless mornings fishing for blues. The incoming tide and gentle westward wind were in harmony, the anchor quickly took hold, and we were alone and motionless on Long Island Sound. His final voyage was about to end.

My brother's lifelong friend Jimmy had joined us. He had lost his leg to cancer at nine and been ordained as a Jesuit Priest as a young man. Jimmy had known my father for almost his entire life, and I was grateful he was there for this final act. Jimmy's words were brief but eloquent, spoken by a man who knew and understood my father and whose own suffering and religious study had brought him closer to God. My brother then gently and with great care spread my father's ashes into the easy flowing current of Long Island Sound. They hesitated briefly by the side of the boat, and then were taken up by the current and started to float westward. Weeks before, I had taken the boat to Pirates Cove at Port Jefferson Harbor, New York, a place my father and I had visited often and loved. I had repeated the long walk around the Cove's perimeter that we had taken so often and found an appropriate smooth, rounded, cream-colored stone. On it I had engraved **Francis Gelzheiser: 10/13/21–5/11/11**, and as the ashes started to drift off, my mom held it in the water and let it go. We then dropped rose petals Jimmy had brought, and they joined the ashes that glistened on the water's surface and slowly drifted westward.

With these ashes went the story of Mindoro, for the men of Motor Torpedo Boat Squadron 16 are all almost gone: the powerful and patient Lieutenant (jg.) Pete Rock; Tom Allison, who may not have understood political correctness but was a good man to call a shipmate; Verner "Swede" Carlson, who could drive in a ten-penny nail with three blows from his hammer, and Don "Shorty" LaCasse and Al Piotter and Joe Lardiere and Joe Rafferty and John "Ducky" Mathews and Ed Kalinowski and Francis Lerz and Dan Saunders and MacIntyre "Tex" Henderson and N. Burt Davis. Even my father's favorite, the gentle and contemplative Tom Hart had his memory destroyed by Alzheimer's disease and died in 2014. Historians will only give Mindoro a passing mention in their tomes on the war against the Japanese. No famous director will put the story to film, and no young, rail-thin, wavy-haired method actor will have to try to conjure up an image or personal horror that will enable him to properly portray a terrified young man retreating into the jungle clutching a severed arm. No, with the ashes went the story, and perhaps this is how it should be. My father always looked out for others, always put others before himself. He had suffered for us all, hid the truth to protect us, and now made it easy for all of us to forget. Perhaps he believed that only those who were there could understand the complex and cruel calculus of war. I admire his selfless, quiet courage greatly. However, it still needs to be said that with their decency, humility, courage, virtue, and willingness to sacrifice the men of Motor Torpedo Boat Squadron 16 upheld the finest traditions of the United States Navy and America. We should all be grateful for their sacrifices.

After my father's death, I was examining an old photo album he had put together in his youth. It was great fun seeing him so young, and one photo was my favorite. He is standing in a small yard somewhere in Pittsburgh. He is wearing an oversized dark pinstriped suit that I am sure he must have borrowed. His arms are out at his side with his palms up. His hair is dark, thick, and wavy, and he has an enormous smile on his face. I love the smile and the look on his face because they display nothing but optimism. He had been abandoned at age six, spent his youth in a catholic orphanage in the middle of the Great Depression, was sent home and then went to work to support his mother while in high school, and often he and his mom and sister had to flee their apartment in the middle of the night because of unpaid rent, but none of this was displayed on his face. This is the photo of a young man who loves life and is wholly focused on the future. On the photo he had written "Just graduated from Avalon High School…. What's next?"

My, "what" awaited him! He would attend college on the G.I. Bill and graduate with a degree in electrical engineering in less than three years. He would get a job at Westinghouse, fall in love with my mom and spend the rest of his life happily married to her, have three children, and then move from Pittsburgh to Fairfield, Connecticut. Here he would go to work at the Bryant Electric Plant, a Division of Westinghouse, in Bridgeport, and his job was to design a line of residential circuit breakers. By the time he retired he would be engineering manager, have 49 patents, and the circuit breakers that he developed would be the most popular in the world. They are still produced today, and to date, tens of millions have been manufactured. He would attend annual PT boat reunions, and share stories and beers with his squadron mates but talk little of the events that they all wanted to forget. He talked of these men often, and like him, most lived happy, productive, and simple lives. He would give generously of his time and money to the First Congregational Church in Fairfield, Connecticut, construct beautiful things, tell countless stories, help Habitat for Humanity build numerous homes for the less fortunate, enjoy an occasional cold beer, camp and build and gaze into large campfires that he referred to as "ripsnorters," fish, build and fly kites and chase butterflies with his children, laugh, garden, raise vegetables and take long hikes with my brother who shared his love of nature and keen observation skills, help my sister with numerous projects in her home and then enjoy wonderful meals made by her and her husband Wayne, take walks and travel with my mom, arrange flowers, make chicken soup, take beautiful photos, read, canoe, hike the Grand Canyon and Canyonlands, canoe the Allagash Waterway, play catch with his son, teach him to use a knife and to saw and plane wood. I am sure he could not have imagined any of this as he stared at the camera in the spring of 1940.

However, before any of this could happen, he would have to go to war. He would have to watch his comrades die, and he would have to kill. He would have to survive Mindoro and then witness war torn Manila. He would then return home and try to "let the war go and try to forget it."

Gently the ashes and rose petals drifted away. There was the slightest ripple on the water's surface, and this helped the rose petals to dance softly and the glare off the floating ashes to slightly flicker as they drifted away. From the east came a loud scream, and instantly an Osprey appeared and soared directly above the drifting ashes and rose petals. Ospreys were not common in that part of Long Island Sound, and for minutes we watched as the bird screamed and soared and never altered his course directly above my father. Silently we watched. The bird's screeches continued and grew quieter as the ashes he was soaring above drifted away from our anchored boat; but for as far as we could see, he never shifted his course from above them. None of us spoke. I looked over at my mom. Her eyes sparkled as she gazed out with a tiny Mona Lisa smile on her face, alone and at peace, I was struck by how beautiful she looked. In time, the bird morphed from being a bird to a small dot to nothing. My father was gone.

I do not understand why the bird soared across the sky following my dad. Perhaps he was some unexplainable escort to eternity, perhaps just an Osprey who liked to follow ashes and rose petals. Some events are not meant to be understood, and we can make of them what we wish. Such is the way with death. What I am sure of is that my father would have loved to see what we witnessed. If he had, he would have gotten great joy from talking about it and sharing what he had observed with others. What I would give to be sitting on the boat with him on a warm summer morning, fishing rods baited, and listening to him tell of the Osprey that soared across the sky, screeching and following the flower petals and ashes, but I will never hear such a story. My father, America's son and the finest man I have ever known, is gone. I miss him, oh my God, how I miss him. Rest in peace, old sailor, rest in peace.

Afterword: Killing

I guess I've changed some.... Sometimes I wonder if I've changed so much my wife is even going to recognize me whenever it is I get back to her or how I'll ever be able to tell her about days like today.... I just know that every man I kill, the further away from her I feel.—The fictional Captain John H. Miller, played by Tom Hanks in the film *Saving Private Ryan*

The common denominator of all wars is killing, or as Colonel Samuel Lyman Atwood Marshall wrote in *Men Against Fire: The Problem of Battle Command*, "We are reluctant to admit that essentially war is the business of killing."[1] For more than 4,500 years, men, and now men and women, have gone to war; and although the weapons and tactics have changed, all of the participants in the countless conflicts that have occurred over the millennium have either directly or indirectly been in the business of killing. The marriage of killing and war is so obvious that it hardly needs to be stated. However, what is less well understood is that despite the fact that war and thus killing have been a constant in human history, the act of killing is not natural, and most people will avoid doing it in almost all circumstances.

Man is not by nature a killer of men, and most humans are extremely reluctant to kill. By some estimates, only two percent of men are predisposed to kill. In World War II, when in close combat with the enemy, only a minority of American soldiers, perhaps as few as 15 percent, were shooting to kill, and many were more terrified of killing than of being killed. Because killing is "not natural," the act of killing has an enormous impact on the killer, often for the rest of his life.[2]

After Pearl Harbor was bombed in December 1941, the vast majority of Americans supported the government's decision to go to war. However, despite this support, 800,000 men were classified as 4-F and unfit for military service for psychiatric reasons; and even with these efforts to "weed out" individuals deemed to be psychologically unsuited for combat, 504,000 men were removed from the battlefield for "psychiatric collapse." It is likely that killing was one of the main reasons for these psychological injuries.[3]

There are a number of factors that impact an individual's willingness to kill. The closer the enemy is to the warrior, the harder it is to kill.[4] Killing with bare hands, knife, bayonet, sword or other hand-wielded, close-range weapon is the most traumatic for the killer, and likely to leave the greatest psychological scars. Killing an enemy with a firearm at close range or with a hand grenade is almost as traumatic as close- or personal-range killing. Killing with a rifle from long range is easier than from short range, and killing with artillery, bombs dropped from the air, and with shells fired from naval guns results in less long-term trauma for the killer than when killing is done at a closer, more "personal" range. In short, the less personal contact the warrior has with the enemy, the more likely he will kill, and the less long-term psychological damage he will suffer from killing.[5]

The less isolated a warrior is when asked to kill, the more likely he will carry out his assigned task. In World War II, soldiers who had developed a "mutual acquaintanceship which established pride" were more likely to stand firm and kill in the face of battle than those who did not feel a close connection with their unit.[6] During the war, infantrymen in combat with no commanders nearby would often avoid firing or fire to miss. If an officer or other enlisted man of higher rank was nearby encouraging the soldier to kill, then he was often more likely to kill. Operators of heavy weapons such as flamethrowers or bazookas, who generally worked in teams, were more likely to kill than individual soldiers with rifles; and artillery teams, naval gunners, and bomber crews, who killed from afar and were often more closely watched and monitored by members of their group, almost always did their best to end the lives of their enemies.[7]

Although killing is not natural, and a significant percentage of warriors in World War II avoided killing at close range, there were a variety of factors that made it more likely that men would kill in the Pacific than in Europe or North Africa. "Cultural distance," dehumanizing the enemy, and racial differences between most Americans and the Japanese made it easier for most American warriors to see their Pacific enemy as not like me or us, and to kill him. "Moral distance" and the belief that the Japanese cause was wrong also increased the likelihood that Americans would kill in the Pacific. Soldiers, marines, airmen, and sailors in the Pacific constantly reminded themselves that the "Japs" were a vicious, expansionist menace who had bombed the American homeland, and cruelly conquered, subjugated, and brutalized millions of people in the Pacific. The desire for vengeance and the belief that America's side was righteous and just helped many American warriors pull the trigger in the Pacific.[8]

As anyone who has been part of an athletic team knows, feeling as if you are a part of a team with a common goal can be a powerful motivator. Warriors in the Pacific often stayed in the same unit or squadron or on the same boat or ship for the entire war. This created a powerful bond, and men often feared letting their fellow warriors down. This bond also made it more likely that men would overcome their natural desire not to kill.[9]

All men, even battle-hardened generals, have a breaking point, and this is why 2 to as many as 30 percent of all battle casualties are psychiatric, and it also helps to explain why man's genius will always find less personal ways to kill.[10] However, even with modern weapons systems that enable killing from thousands of miles away, it is still necessary to send warriors into harm's way and for them to kill at close range as men have done for millennium. The results of this can be seen in the enormous number of servicemen who suffer from post-traumatic stress disorder and the tragic level of suicide among servicemen after they come home from combat. Our weapons have changed much, our psyches little. We need to all remember this when the nation makes the decision to send men and women into battle and asks them to kill.

In the years that I have spent researching and writing this book, there is one question that I have continued to ask: Why did my father go into the jungle with the soldier and kill the three Japanese warriors? My dad was an electrician's mate in the United States Navy. His job was to maintain and repair the various electrical systems and components on the PT boats, crew the boats, and when necessary man the .50 caliber guns or other ordnance. When the wounded soldier asked my father to go into the jungle with him to locate and kill the men who had shot him, my father could have declined and insisted that the man go to the sick bay and tend to his wounds. There was no order to join the soldier, no group or unit pressure to join the man in his quest to kill, my father did not know the soldier, he was not even in the Army so he had no bond with the man as a fellow soldier, and he did not have to worry that by not going he would lose the respect of fellow soldiers. Although my father told me that he was a good shot with a rifle, he had only limited training on how to use the weapon. Much military discipline comes from "habit" that is created by repeating an act over and over, and my father certainly had not developed the "habits" of the combat infantryman.[11]

Often men rise to the challenges of battle because of the encouragement of men around them. This is one reason the modern infantry officer is often only armed with a sidearm. His job is to command and to push and encourage his men. He is often there to get his men to kill not to do the killing.[12] Man is by nature gregarious and thus gains comfort and even courage from the group. There is a reason the spoken word is referred to as "the greatest steadying force in any time of crisis."[13] And yet my father was alone when he fired the three shots; and to my knowledge, the wounded soldier said nothing to my father before he fired. There was no order to kill, and there was no "cloud of battle" that often provided soldiers with "plausible deniability that they had killed."[14]

The man who raised me was perhaps the least likely killer I have ever known. My father was calm, rational, and never overwhelmed by his emotions. He had been raised by nuns and priests, schooled extensively in Christianity, taught that all humankind had value, and that killing was wrong. It is hard to fathom my father pulling the trigger, and yet, he voluntarily went into the jungle with the intent to kill.

After much pondering, I initially concluded that my father agreed to join the soldier because even as a young man, he was always willing to help people and almost always put the needs of others over his own. This sounds simple, but I imagined the soldier asking my father for assistance, and my father not fully understanding what he had agreed to do until after the three men were dead. I no longer accept this explanation. Yes, my father was always willing to help, but he also had a very clear sense of who he was, and he never agreed to participate in tasks for which he was not well suited. He was also much too smart and analytical to walk into the jungle on a strange island with an angry and wounded soldier in the middle of World War II and not understand the potential consequences.

I now believe that my father knew exactly what he was doing when he entered the jungle, and I understand that the young man who journeyed into Mindoro's interior that day was a person I never knew. He wanted to find the Japanese soldiers who had shot the American, and he wanted to kill them. In the days and hours before he killed, *Nashville*, LSTs *738*, *472*, and *605* had been hit and scores of men had been killed or wounded. He may have encountered the half man on his moonlit swim (this event may have occurred after he killed the three men), experienced the loss of friends, and watched kamikazes slam into ships and attempt to crash into PT boats. He had seen the dead piled on the shore "like cordwood," and barely missed being killed by a kamikaze while on shore. He also continued to be outraged about the Japanese attack on Pearl Harbor and the brutality that they had unleashed throughout the Pacific.

Scholars who study war generally agree that there is no way to know prior to combat who will kill and who will not, and I believe that my father's actions that day on Mindoro are proof that it is very difficult to determine prior to combat who will kill.

I now think that when my father walked into the jungle he was full of hate and wanted vengeance. He wanted to avenge Pearl Harbor, the invasion of his nation in Alaska, the destruction caused by the Japanese as they stormed across the Pacific creating their Empire, and the horror he had witnessed on Mindoro. He loved his squadron mates and wanted to protect them, and I believe that all of these events and feelings made my father different and contributed to his decision to journey into the jungle.[15]

Modern weapons allow killing to be done from afar, and contemporary battle is often impersonal and can create a sense of "littleness" in the warrior. Warriors can find themselves in a "physical wilderness" dominated by impersonal forces. The enemy on Mindoro came from the sky. His face was rarely seen, and for many Americans the men who flew the kamikazes were so foreign they hardly seemed human. Being attacked by such "indistinguishable figures" reduced the warrior's sense of the enemies' and his own importance. For many, the enemy became a "thing" and it was a thing that needed to be killed. All of this may have contributed to my father's decision to join the nameless soldier on his quest to find, and kill, the men who shot the soldier.[16]

Killing at close range and watching a man die is one of the most traumatic events that can happen in an individual's life. Although all warriors react to killing differently over the short and long term, there are certain "emotional stages" that usually follow killing, much like there are common emotional stages that people experience after the death of a loved one. Often the immediate responses to killing are "exhilaration, satisfaction, euphoria, and elation," and a sense of accomplishment. Sometimes these feelings end when the killer inspects the bodies of those he has killed, sometimes it takes longer. In my father's case, I believe these feelings continued throughout the day and contributed to his decision to etch the three grooves on his knife's bolster. Eventually, most killers feel "guilt, remorse, and emotional pain" as a result of what they have done, and these feelings are intensified if the killer had examined the body/bodies of those he has killed closeup. Over time, most killers find some acceptance, but often killing haunts the killer for the remainder of his life.

I am sure that my father felt a deep and very painful remorse and guilt for having taken three lives, and I believe he battled these emotions for much of his life, especially during his last decade when his ability to filter out the past waned and he had to come to terms with his own mortality. By the end of his life I think my father came to accept what he had done, but I do not believe he ever fully got over the guilt. I also believe that the Navy knife that had always been kept on the left-hand side of his workbench, and was almost never taken from its sheath, was not placed there as a trophy, but instead as a reminder of a terrible event in his life and of the harsh reality of how war and killing can change any man.[17]

When men kill, they often need to talk about what they have done, especially with people who have also killed or at least been in battle and thus have some understanding of what the killer has experienced. In this regard my father was lucky. During his long and slow journey from the Philippines to America, he was often in the company of other men who had experienced war. He spent days on slow moving ships, enjoyed time in Australia surrounded by friendly, grateful people, and fellow warriors. Even when he got home and enrolled in the engineering program at the University of Pittsburgh, he was surrounded by fellow G.I.s taking advantage of generous G.I. Bill benefits. I do not think my father talked with anyone about what had happened in the jungle. In fact after his death I found a note he had written saying he had not talked about the three men he had killed until he told me what had happened more than fifty years after the war, although he did believe that my mother somehow knew what had happened. Although he did not talk about killing with fellow veterans, I do believe that it was therapeutic for him to be around men who had had similar experiences. During his journey home and in the weeks and months after he arrived, I think my father worked hard to bury the memory of the war and of killing, and it was only as an old man that he again fully confronted what had happened.

During his first semester in college, my father found himself in a freshman English class. The University of Pittsburgh had created special classes that started later in the school year to accommodate warriors returning from the just-completed war in the Pacific. All of the students in the class were men who had been to war, most wore some form of military garb, and all had been out of school for a number of years. A young female professor walked into the room, looked around, said nothing, had nothing said to her, burst into tears, and quickly walked out never to return to the class. I asked my father if any of the men said anything or made a noise or gesture that might have upset the young woman, but he assured me no. She had walked in, observed the students, burst into tears, and left. Certainly being a young teacher charged with instructing battle-hardened men could have been intimidating, and perhaps she had lost a brother, boyfriend, husband or father in the war, but I now wonder. How many of those men had killed, and how many had a different countenance because they had killed, and did she see or sense this, and did it terrify her?[18]

The three grooves on my father's knife are insignificant in the context of World War II. As many as 80 million people were killed in the war, and the grooves represent three. But they are also a universal symbol for war at its most basic level. People are killed in war, and often the killers come home to countrymen incapable of understanding what it means to kill.

Writing this book, I have been confronted by the great paradox of my father and the war: The fact that in spite of being the most gentle and decent man I have ever known, my father killed. I have come to understand that it was because of, not despite, this decency that he made the decision to leave the ease and safety of civilian life, enter the conflict, and kill. Being gentle and decent did not change the fact that an existential threat confronted his nation. He, like millions of other young men, realized that it was the responsibility of all who enjoyed the blessings of liberty to do their part to destroy this threat. Being decent and gentle did not lessen this responsibility and instead made him more aware of it.

Although many would like to believe differently, the reality of the human condition is that human nature does not change. As long as there is liberty, there will be threats to it, and to defend those who wish to be free, men and women will have to journey outside the safety of "the wire" and confront liberty's enemies. When my father enlisted in the Navy and joined the war, he understood that for liberty to survive in the nation he loved, virtuous men had to confront our enemies so that those who stayed behind could remain safe and free. This reality was etched on the bolster of his knife and in the deepest recesses of his memory. For those who left the safety of "the wire" there were consequences that only they could fully understand. We should all be grateful to those who chose to leave and those who continue to do so.

We have shared the good, we have shared the bad. We are brothers—blooded by our active participation in combat operations in an unprecedented naval war.... In the history of our great nation, we have never produced finer, more courageous, or greater fighting men.... May a grateful country never forget the sacrifices you made for the good of all mankind.—From Admiral "Bull" Halsey's victory speech that was broadcast to Third Fleet during a kamikaze attack, August 15, 1945

Appendix A.
Motor Torpedo Boat Squadron 16 Honor Roll: Awards and Citations

Navy Unit Commendation

Task Unit 70.1.4 comprising Motor Torpedo Boat Squadrons 13 and 16 and PTs *227* and *230*

Silver Star with Gold Star or Oak Leaf Cluster in Lieu of Second Silver Star

Lieutenant Roger H. Hallowell
Lieutenant Philip A. Swart

Silver Star

Lieutenant (jg.) Robert J. Roth
Lieutenant Robert J. Wehrli

Legion of Merit

Lieutenant (jg.) Lowe H. Wiggers, Jr.

Navy and Marine Corps Medal

Motor Machinist's Mate Third Class Francis E. Clougherty
Lieutenant Commander Nathaniel Burt Davis, Jr.
Quartermaster Second Class George A. Dwyer
Radioman Second Class Richard L. Hunnicutt
Motor Machinist's Mate Second Class Edmund I. Kalinowski
Motor Machinist's Mate First Class William C. Moen
Lieutenant John H. Stillman

Appendix A

Bronze Star with Gold Star in Lieu of Second Bronze Star

Lieutenant (jg.) Harry E. Griffin

Bronze Star

Lieutenant (jg.) Robert R. Beasley
Motor Machinist's Mate Third Class Francis E. Clougherty
Torpedoman's Mate First Class Billie J. Goddard
Lieutenant (jg.) Thomas C. Hall
Lieutenant (jg.) William B. Helme
Torpedoman's Mate Chief Petty Officer John A. Novak
Motor Machinist's Mate First Class Frank J. Pagacz
Lieutenant (jg.) Alva C. Trueblood
Lieutenant James H. Van Sicklen
Ship's Cook Second Class George T. Walsh

Commendation Ribbon

Gunner's Mate Second Class Albert C. Clark
Lieutenant F. Gardner Cox, Jr.
Radioman Second Class Jack Crawford
Radarman Second Class John W. Fuller
Gunner's Mate First Class Thomas B. Hart
Lieutenant (jg.) Samuel W. Mitchell
Torpedoman's Mate Third Class Robert N. Spofford
Gunner's Mate Second Class Alexander J. Szczech

Appendix B.
Memorandum and Suggested Unit Citation Sent by Lieutenant Commander Davis to Rear Admiral Bowling

12 January 1945

<u>Memorandum To Captain Bowling</u>

1. Enclosure (A) is forwarded to you for your consideration as the basis of award of a Naval Unit Citation as described in Alnav 181315/224 of December 1944. I personally feel that with the exception of one or two individuals the heroism, bravery, and guts shown by these men up here was equally divided among every officer and man, and that they fully meet the requirements set forth in the Alnav in question.
2. In support of this statement is the fact that slightly more than 10% of our personnel during the first two weeks were either killed or so seriously wounded to necessitate evacuation.

N. Burt Davis, Jr.
Lt. Comdr., U.S.N.

Suggested Citation

For outstanding performance of duty during the Allied landing on Mindoro Island, P.I. as the only Naval force present for fifteen days they conducted close inshore offensive patrols in the waters of the Philippine Island of Mindoro, Busuanga, Marinduque, Tablas, Northern Panay and Southern Luzon; carried supplies to Allied guerrillas on these islands; evacuated American airmen and escapees from Bataan; participated in the successful Allied landings at Bongabong, Bulalacow and Marinduque; acted as dispatch and air-sea rescue units; fortified and held their assigned lines in the face of combined air-sea attack on the night of 26/27 December 1944, although suffering an eleven percent loss in killed or evacuated wounded at the time, they attacked and were credited with the possible destruction of one

Japanese destroyer in addition to having provided safe coverage and protection to Allied shipping then present in the area; when the LST *738* was sunk by enemy air attack on 15 December 1944, they rescued over 150 personnel from the water. They effected partial salvage of two merchant ships in addition to housing and evacuating their crews. They were the first personnel to board the USS *Orestes* and despite exploding ammunition and fierce fires below in the vicinity of boilers and torpedo stowage spaces, fought the fires and brought them under control. They effected close scouting missions off Maestco de Campo Island and Coron Bay, Busuanga; made the first landing on Ilin Island; captured two enemy aviators, much valuable technical equipment and many important enemy documents. Despite almost continuous air attack, they constructed an efficient base for operations and repair; carried out regular patrols and were officially credited with the destruction of one coastal freighter, four barges, and twenty-five enemy aircraft.

N. Burt Davis, Jr.
Lt. Comdr., U.S.N.

Chapter Notes

Introduction

1. Glenn Koach, brother of Janet Gelzheiser and Turret Gunner on a B-24 Liberator Bomber during World War II, Interview, September 2016.

Chapter 2

1. Baseball Reference, www.baseball-reference.com; Bernard Grun, *The Timetables of History: A Horizontal Linkage of People and Events* (New York: Simon & Schuster, 1975), pp. 478–480.
2. Grun, pp. 478–480.
3. Marie Gaver, sister of Francis Gelzheiser, Interviews.
4. Francis Gelzheiser, father of Robert Gelzheiser and a member of Motor Torpedo Boat Squadron 16 during World War II, Interviews.
5. *Ibid.*
6. *1940 Avalon Annual* (Yearbook), Survey.
7. Gelzheiser.
8. Captain Robert J. Bulkley, Jr. USNR (Retired), *At Close Quarters: PT Boats in the United States Navy* (Washington, D.C.: United States Government Printing Office, 1962), pp. 59–60; Gelzheiser.
9. William Breuer, *Devil Boats: The PT War Against Japan* (Novato, CA: Presidio Press, 1995), p. 69; Bulkley, Jr., pp. 59–60.
10. Lewis N. Hindley, Jr., *Personal Account of Time Spent with PT Boat Squadron 16 During World War II* (Unpublished account of PT boat experiences by Lieutenant Lewis N. Hindley, Jr., July 1, 1999), p. 8; Bulkley, Jr., pp. 59–60, 200; Breuer, *Devil Boats*, p. 71.
11. Cele Piotter, *United States Motor Torpedo Boats Squadron 16 History* (Unpublished account of PT Boat Squadron 16 by wife of Chief Commissary Steward Alfred F. Piotter), pp. 1–3.
12. Gelzheiser.
13. Bulkley, Jr., p. 447; Piotter, p. 4.
14. Breuer, *Devil Boats*, p. 198.
15. Piotter, p. 2.
16. Gelzheiser.

Chapter 3

1. Bulkley, Jr., p. 1.
2. Breuer, *Devil Boats*, p. 13.
3. Bulkley, Jr., pp. 2–3; Breuer, *Devil Boats*, pp. 7–8; T. Garth Connelly, *U.S. Patrol Torpedo Boats in World War II, 1939–1945* (Ann Arbor, MI: Nimble Books, 2010), p. 127; T. Garth Connelly, *PT Boats in Action* (Carrollton, TX: Squadron Publications 1994), p. 12; Dan van der Vat, *The Pacific Campaign: World War II: The U.S.–Japanese Naval War: 1941–1945* (New York: Simon & Schuster, 1991), p. 20.
4. Bern Keating, *The Mosquito Fleet: PT Boats in World War II* (New York: Scholastic Book Services, 1966), p. 3; van der Vat, pp. 24, 136–137.
5. Connelly, *U.S. Patrol Torpedo Boats in World War II, 1939–1945*, p. 128; Breuer, *Devil Boats*, p. 26.
6. Connelly, *PT Boats in Action*, p. 41; Breuer, *Devil Boats*, p. 14.
7. Bulkley, Jr., p. 8.
8. Breuer, *Devil Boats*, p. 19.
9. Bulkley, Jr., pp. 3–5, 7–8; Connelly, *U.S. Patrol Torpedo Boats in World War II, 1939–1945*, p. 141; Bob Drury and Tom Clavin, *Halsey's Typhoon: The True Story of a Fighting Admiral, an Epic Storm, and an Untold Rescue* (New York: Grove Press, 2007), p. 21.
10. Breuer, *Devil Boats*, pp. 38–39; Howard West, *Iron Men, Wooden Boats: The Epic Story of American PT Boats in World War II* (Westminster, MA: Heritage Books, 2005), p. 113.
11. Bulkley, Jr., p. 16.
12. Breuer, *Devil Boats*, p. 34.
13. Bulkley, Jr., pp. 16–18; Breuer, pp. 40–46.
14. Bulkley, Jr., p. 27.
15. Breuer, *Devil Boats*, pp. 65–66; Keating, p. 4.
16. Bulkley, Jr., p. 27; Keating, pp. 4–5.
17. Connelly, *U.S. Patrol Torpedo Boats in World War II, 1939–1945*, p. 128; Breuer, *Devil Boats*, pp. 63–64; James C. Rock, *Naval War College Command and Staff Course: Short paper Number Two: A Study of World War II: The Development of the Motor Torpedo Boat* (Unpublished paper written by Lieutenant Commander James C. Rock), pp. 1, 5; Victor Chun, *American PT Boats in World War II* (Atglen, PA: Schiffer Military/Aviation History, 1997), pp. 13, 19.
18. Breuer, *Devil Boats*, p. 3.
19. Connelly, *U.S. Patrol Torpedo Boats in World War II, 1939–1945*, pp. 9–10.
20. Breuer, *Devil Boats*, pp. 3–4.

21. Chun, pp. 70–71.
22. Rock, p. 3; Connelly, *U.S. Patrol Torpedo Boats in World War II, 1939–1945*, p. 25.
23. Keating, pp. 8–9; Jerry E. Strahan, *Andrew Jackson Higgins and the Boats That Won World War II* (Baton Rouge, LA: Louisiana State University Press, 1994), pp. 83, 91.
24. Keating, pp. 8–9.
25. Rock, p. 4; Connelly, *U.S. Patrol Torpedo Boats in World War II, 1939–1945*, pp. 26–27, 38.
26. Chun, p. 73.
27. Breuer, *Devil Boats*, p. 4; Bulkley, Jr., p. 31.
28. Chun, p. 82; Breuer, *Devil Boats*, p. 4; Hindley, Jr., p. 8.
29. Bulkley, Jr., p. 32.
30. Breuer, *Devil Boats*, p. 4; Bulkley, Jr., pp. 32, 265; Connelly, *U.S. Patrol Torpedo Boats in World War II, 1939–1945*, pp. 37–38; Strahan, p. 83; PT Boats, Inc., Official Handout.
31. Connelly, *U.S. Patrol Torpedo Boats in World War II, 1939–1945*, pp. 37–38; David Doyle, *PT Boats in Action* (Carrollton, TX: Squadron/Signal Publications, 2010), pp. 8, 12.
32. Bulkley, Jr., p. 24; Gelzheiser; Russ Hamachek, *Hot, Straight and True: An Anecdotal View of PT Boats in WWII* (New York: Carlton Press, 1995), p. 113; Alyce Guthrie, President, WW II PT Boats, Inc.; Connelly, *U.S. Patrol Torpedo Boats in World War II, 1939–1945*, pp. 19, 57, 80; Connelly, *PT Boats in Action*, pp. 31, 47; Chun, p. 105; Gelzheiser; *San Francisco Chronicle*, September 9, 1944; *San Francisco News*, September 8, 1944.
33. Chun, p. 75; Rock, p. 5.
34. Chun, p. 111; Bulkley, Jr., p. 33; Battleship Cove: America's Fleet Museum, Fall River, MA, Official Handout; Don Shannon, PT Boat curator, PT Boat seum, Fall River, MA, Interview, February 2017.
35. Doyle, p. 28; Chun, p. 118.
36. Thomas Hart, Friend of Francis Gelzheiser and a member of Motor Torpedo Boat Squadron 16 during World War II. Interviews; Gelzheiser.
37. Chun, p. 91.
38. Edmond Kalinowski, *The Stingers of Some of the Mosquitoes from the Mosquito Fleet, Squadron 16* (Unpublished account of PT Boat Squadron 16 by Motor Machinist's Mate Second Class Edmond Kalinowski), p. 2; Hamachek, pp. 80–81.
39. Connelly, *PT Boats in Action*, p. 16.
40. Kalinowski, p. 1; Piotter, p. 2.
41. Rock, p. 5; Breuer, *Devil Boats*, p. 14; Hindley, p. 14; Keating, p. 249; Hamachek, p. 52.
42. Breuer, *Devil Boats*, p. 69; Connelly, *PT Boats in Action*, p. 7.
43. Chun, pp. 107, 112; Connelly, *U.S. Patrol Torpedo Boats in World War II: 1939–1945*, p. 22; Gelzheiser; Doyle, pp. 5, 59; Hamachek, p. 22.
44. Hart, Interview; Gelzheiser; Chun, p. 102; Connelly, *PT Boats in Action*, p. 17; West, p. XX.
45. Bulkley, Jr., p. 32; Hart, Interview; Gelzheiser.
46. Breuer, *Devil Boats*, p. 126.
47. Connelly, *U.S. Patrol Torpedo Boats in World War II, 1939–1945*, pp. 124–125; Rock, pp. 7–8; Gelzheiser.
48. Rock, pp. 7–8; Hindley, Jr., p. 13.
49. Keating, p. 11; Hamachek, pp. 18–19.
50. Hart, Interview; Gelzheiser; Doyle, p. 35; Bulkley, Jr., p. 29; Strahan, p. 205; Captain Walter Karig, *Battle Report: Victory in the Pacific* (New York: Rinehart and Company, 1949), p. 57.
51. Breuer, *Devil Boats*, p. 167; Doyle, p. 17; Bulkley, Jr., p. 43.
52. Bulkley, Jr., pp. 123–128; Connelly, *PT Boats in Action*, pp. 34, 36.
53. van der Vat, pp. 246–248.
54. Connelly, *U.S. Patrol Torpedo Boats in World War II, 1939–1945*, p. 85; van der Vat, pp. 246–248; Connelly, *PT Boats in Action*, p. 31.
55. Connelly, *U.S. Patrol Torpedo Boats in World War II, 1939–1945*, pp. 83–87; Shannon; Bulkley, Jr., pp. 34, 295–296; West, pp. XVI–XVII; Connelly, *PT Boats in Action*, p. 17; Chun, p. 110; PT Boats, Inc., Official Handout; Hamachek, p. 95.
56. Breuer, *Devil Boats*, p. 28.
57. Bulkley, Jr., p. 34; Connelly, *PT Boats in Action*, p. 4; West, pp. XVI–XVII.
58. Breuer, *Devil Boats*, p. 118; Bulkley, Jr., p. 38.
59. Rock, p. 9.
60. Connelly, *PT Boats in Action*, pp. 31–32, 51; PT Boats, Inc., Official Handout.
61. Piotter, p. 83; Connelly, *U.S. Patrol Torpedo Boats in World War II, 1939–1945*, pp. 40, 130–131; Bulkley, Jr., p. 93; Rock, p. 8; Kalinowski, p. 2; Chun, pp. 9, 122.
62. Gelzheiser.
63. Doyle, p. 3.
64. Chun, pp. 6–9, 127, 129; PT Boats, Inc., Official Handout; Doyle, p. 29.
65. Guthrie, PT Boats, Inc., Interview, August 2015; Gelzheiser.
66. Hart, Interview; Karig, p. 57.
67. Chun, p. 137.
68. Chun, pp. 122, 130–132; Bulkley, Jr., p. 210.
69. Chun, p. 130.
70. PT Boats, Inc., Official Handout.
71. Hart, Interview; Connelly, *U.S. Patrol Torpedo Boats in World War II, 1939–1945*, p. 128.
72. Connelly, *U.S. Patrol Torpedo Boats in World War II, 1939–1945*, p. 109; Doyle, pp. 14, 17; Chun, p. 119.
73. Guthrie; Connelly, *U.S. Patrol Torpedo Boats in World War II, 1939–1945*, pp. 19, 57, 80; Connelly, *PT Boats in Action*, pp. 31, 47; Chun, p. 105; Gelzheiser; *San Francisco Chronicle*, September 9, 1944; *San Francisco News*, September 8, 1944.

Chapter 4

1. Tom Hart, *PT Boat Squadron 16 World War II Memories*. This narrative written by PT boat *221* crew member Gunner's Mate First Class Tom Hart was found in the PT Boats, Inc., archives. Please see Bibliographic Note for additional information. pp. 1, 3; Gelzheiser; Piotter, p. 3.
2. Bulkley, Jr., p. 16; Gelzheiser; Hart, p. 1.
3. Hindley, Jr., p. 13.
4. Hart, p. 2; Hindley, Jr., p. 13.; Gelzheiser.
5. Hindley, Jr., p. 12.

6. *Ibid.*, p. 13.
7. Hart, pp. 4–5.
8. *Ibid.*, p. 2.
9. *Ibid.*, pp. 2–3.
10. Gelzheiser; Hart, pp. 4–5.
11. Hart, pp. 4–5.
12. Gelzheiser; Hart, p. 6.
13. Gelzheiser.
14. Gelzheiser; Hart, p. 3.
15. Hart, p. 9; Gelzheiser.
16. Gelzheiser; Hart, p. 10.
17. Hart, p. 11.
18. *Ibid.*, p. 11.
19. Gelzheiser; Hart, p. 12.
20. Gelzheiser; Hart, pp. 13–15.
21. Gelzheiser; Hart, p. 16.
22. Gelzheiser.
23. Gelzheiser; Hart, p. 20.
24. Piotter, pp. 6–7; Gelzheiser.
25. Hart, pp. 21–22.
26. Gelzheiser; Hart, p. 22.
27. Gelzheiser; Hart, p. 23; Maurice L. Smith (Unpublished account of PT boat experiences by Motor Machinist's Mate First Class Maurice L. Smith), p. 3.
28. Gelzheiser; Hart, pp. 24–25.
29. Hart, pp. 25–26; Gelzheiser.
30. Gelzheiser.
31. Piotter, p. 7.
32. Gelzheiser; Piotter, p. 8.
33. Gelzheiser; Piotter, pp. 8–9.
34. Hart, p. 32.
35. Gelzheiser.
36. Bulkley, Jr., pp. 64–65; Gelzheiser.
37. Hart, pp. 35–36; Gelzheiser.
38. Hindley, Jr., p. 16; Bulkley, Jr., p. 66; Hart, p. 36; Gelzheiser.
39. Gelzheiser; Hart, pp. 35–36; Smith, p. 1.
40. Piotter, p. 9; Smith, p. 1; Gelzheiser.
41. Gelzheiser; Hart, p. 39.
42. Hart, p. 38.
43. Hindley, Jr., p. 17; Kalinowski, p. 5.
44. Gelzheiser; Piotter, p. 10.
45. Piotter, p. 10; Gelzheiser; Kalinowski, p. 4; Hart, pp. 37, 43–44.

Chapter 5

1. van der Vat, pp. 121–124.
2. Brian Garfield, *The Thousand Mile War: World War II in Alaska and the Aleutians* (Fairbanks, AK: University of Alaska Press, 1995), p. 5; van der Vat, pp. 121–124, 162; David M. Kennedy, *Freedom from Fear: The American People in Depression and War, 1929–1945* (New York: Oxford University Press, 1999), pp. 533–534.
3. George C. Herring, *From Colony to Superpower: U.S. Foreign Relations since 1776* (New York: Oxford University Press, 2008), p. 539; Bulkley, Jr., p. 167; van der Vat, pp. 115, 120, 129; Garfield, p. 5; Keating, pp. 1–2.
4. van der Vat, pp. 156–158, 181; Garfield, p. 118.
5. Kennedy, p. 533; van der Vat, p. 170; Bulkley, Jr., p. 167; James D. Hornfischer, *The Fleet at Flood Tide: America at Total War in the Pacific, 1944–1945* (New York: Bantam Books, 2016), p. 144.
6. Garfield, pp. 143, 159.
7. Bulkley, Jr., p. 261.
8. *Ibid.*, p. 261.
9. Garfield, pp. 24, 72.
10. *Ibid.*, pp. 160, 250.
11. Bulkley, Jr., p. 261.
12. Garfield, pp. 19, 59, 252; David Sears, *At War with the Wind: The Epic Struggle with Japan's World War II Suicide Bombers* (New York: Kensington, 2008), p. 83; Kennedy, p. 443.
13. Kennedy, pp. 233–234; van der Vat, pp. 162–163; Herring, p. 530.
14. Garfield, pp. 5–7.
15. van der Vat, pp. 177, 180; Kennedy, p. 536; Victor Davis Hanson, *Carnage and Culture: Landmark Battles in the Rise of Western Power* (New York: Random House, 2001), pp. 370–373.
16. van der Vat, pp. 172, 180; Kennedy, p. 536; James Bradley, *Flyboys: A True Story of Courage* (New York: Little, Brown, 2003), pp. 119–120; Hanson, p. 351.
17. Garfield, p. 7.
18. Kennedy, p. 536; Hanson, pp. 338, 350–351, 375, 381.
19. Hanson, pp. 334, 376.
20. *Ibid.*, pp. 335–336.
21. Hanson, pp. 335, 338; Kennedy, pp. 541–542; van der Vat, pp. 188, 194.
22. Hanson, p. 338; West, pp. 43–44.
23. Hanson, pp. 337, 340, 352, 366; Garfield, pp. 52–53; van der Vat, p. 193.
24. Garfield, pp. 3–4.
25. Garfield, pp. 3–4; Hart, p. 29; Bulkley, Jr., p. 29; van der Vat, p. 196; Hanson, p. 355.
26. Garfield, pp. 32–33, 34; Bulkley, Jr., p. 261.
27. Garfield, pp. 41–46, 49–51.
28. Kennedy, p. 543; Garfield, pp. 4, 19, 47–49; Sears, p. 83.
29. Bulkley, Jr., p. 262; van der Vat, p. 195; Garfield, pp. 99–102.
30. Garfield, p. 223.
31. *Ibid.*, pp. 223–231.
32. *Ibid.*, pp. 104–105, 196.
33. Bulkley, Jr., p. 262.
34. Garfield, pp. 142, 147, 220, 221; Bulkley, Jr., p. 262; van der Vat, p. 273.
35. Garfield, pp. 137, 189.
36. van der Vat, p. 274.
37. Bulkley, Jr., p. 262.
38. Garfield, p. 253.
39. van der Vat, p. 274; Garfield, p. 296.
40. Garfield, pp. 279, 283, 582.
41. *Ibid.*, p. 311.
42. *Ibid.*, p. 326.
43. B.H. Liddell Hart, *History of the Second World War* (New York: G.P. Putnam's Sons, 1970), pp. 500–501 (Author's note: Unless otherwise noted, in future citations Hart will refer to Thomas Hart not B.H. Liddell Hart); Garfield, pp. 310, 326, 328–331, 333; Captured diary of American-educated Japanese doctor found on the island of Attu after the battle for the island, May 12, 1943–May 29, 1945, PT Boats, Inc.

44. Garfield, pp. 394, 414.
45. Bulkley, Jr., p. 263.
46. Bulkley, Jr., p. 263; West, pp. 44–45.
47. Garfield, pp. 184, 235.
48. Bulkley, Jr., pp. 263–265; Garfield, p. 235.
49. Bulkley, Jr., pp. 267–269; Garfield, p. 236.
50. Bulkley, Jr., p. 270; Smith, p. 3.
51. Piotter, pp. 10–11; Gelzheiser.
52. Hindley, Jr., pp. 18, 20; Gelzheiser; Garfield, pp. 18–19, 70.
53. Hart, p. 44.
54. Gelzheiser; Hart, pp. 44–45.
55. *Ibid*.
56. Hart, p. 46.
57. Hindley, Jr., p. 18–19.
58. *Ibid*., p. 19.
59. Hart, p. 47.
60. Gelzheiser.
61. Piotter, p. 11.
62. Hart, pp. 47–48.
63. Gelzheiser; Hart, pp. 49–50.
64. Hindley, Jr., p. 20.
65. Hart, p. 50; Piotter, pp. 10–11.
66. Hart, p. 51; Gelzheiser; Kalinowski, p. 6.
67. Kalinowski, p. 6.
68. Hart, p. 52; Gelzheiser.
69. *Ibid*.
70. Bulkley, Jr., p. 270; Piotter, p. 11.
71. Smith, p. 3.
72. Gelzheiser; Hindley, Jr., p. 22; Piotter, p. 17; Doyle, p. 50.
73. Smith, p. 2; Kalinowski, pp. 8–10.
74. Garfield, p. 162; Piotter, p. 15.
75. Gelzheiser; Piotter, p. 13.
76. Piotter, p. 17.
77. Piotter, pp. 13, 15, 17.
78. Hindley, Jr., p. 21.
79. Bulkley, Jr., pp. 270–271; Kalinowski, p. 6.
80. Gelzheiser; Hart, p. 61.
81. Hart, p. 65; Gelzheiser.
82. Garfield, p. 71; Gelzheiser; Hart, p. 54.
83. Piotter, pp. 15–16.
84. Gelzheiser; Hart, p. 112.
85. Gelzheiser.
86. *Ibid*.
87. Hart, p. 65.
88. Hindley, Jr., p. 22.
89. Gelzheiser; Hart, p. 57.
90. Hanson, p. 360.
91. Kennedy, pp. 812–813.
92. Sears, p. 26; Drury and Clavin, pp. 6, 18, 276.
93. John Keegan, *The Face of Battle* (New York: Penguin Books, 1976), p. 304.
94. Hart, p. 57; Smith, p. 4; Keegan, p. 304; Gelzheiser.
95. Piotter, p. 131.
96. Hart, p. 6; Hindley, Jr., p. 24; Smith, p. 3.
97. Kalinowski, p. 9; Hart, p. 66; Piotter, p. 17.
98. Piotter, pp. 14–15.
99. *Ibid*., pp. 15–16, 18.
100. Letter from General William O. Butler, commander of North Pacific Fleet, PT Boats, Inc.
101. Hindley, Jr., p. 22; Hart, p. 63.
102. Kalinowski, p. 8; Hart, p. 60; Piotter, p. 14.
103. Piotter, p. 14.
104. Hindley, Jr., p. 23.
105. Bulkley, Jr., pp. 271–272.
106. Piotter, p. 16.
107. Garfield, p. 140.
108. Bulkley, Jr., pp. 272–273; Garfield, pp. 373, 379–380; van der Vat, p. 275; Gelzheiser.
109. Garfield, p. 380.
110. *Ibid*., pp. 357, 365.
111. *Ibid*., pp. 371, 372, 417, 419.
112. *Ibid*., pp. 417–419.
113. Piotter, p. 18; Gelzheiser.
114. Hart, p. 66; Gelzheiser.
115. Bulkley, Jr., p. 273; Piotter, p. 109; Hart, pp. 66–67.
116. Gelzheiser; Piotter, p. 19; Hart, p. 60; Kalinowski, p. 9.

Chapter 6

1. Gelzheiser; Piotter, p. 20.
2. Hart, p. 80.
3. Hart, pp. 76–77, 80; Gelzheiser, Naval Records.
4. Hart, pp. 76, 78.
5. Piotter, pp. 24, 31; Hart, pp. 79, 93; Kalinowski, p. 16; Breuer, *Devil Boats*, p. 16; Doyle, pp. 54, 59; Smith, p. 1.
6. Gelzheiser; Kalinowski, p. 13; Hart, p. 79; Piotter, p. 24.
7. Gelzheiser; Piotter, p. 24; Hart, p. 80; *The San Francisco News*, September 8, 1944.
8. Piotter, p. 25.
9. Hart, p. 85.
10. van der Vat, pp. 237, 246; Hart, pp. 86–87; Keating, pp. 13, 59; Chun, p. 20; West, pp. 50–52, 54, 73, 82, 90, 352.
11. Hart, pp. 86–87; van der Vat, p. 246; Piotter, p. 26.
12. Hart, pp. 86–88; Gelzheiser.
13. Bulkley, Jr., p. 250; Breuer, *Devil Boats*, p. 117; Hart, p. 178; West, pp. 280, 283.
14. Hart, pp. 98–100; Kalinowski, p. 13; Bulkley, Jr., p. 245.
15. Bulkley, Jr., p. 167.
16. Bulkley, Jr., p. 167; Breuer, *Devil Boats*, p. 89; Keating, p. 51; James P. Duffy, *War at the End of the World: Douglas MacArthur and the Forgotten Fight for New Guinea, 1942-1945* (New York: New American Library, 2016), p. 2; West, pp. 77, 105–106, 108, 109; Stanley Falk, *Liberation of the Philippines* (New York: Ballantine Books, 1971), p. 7.
17. Sears, p. 68; Keating, p. 92.
18. Breuer, *Devil Boats*, pp. 77, 117; Duffy, p. 1; Gelzheiser; West, p. 281.
19. Bulkley, Jr., p. 178; Breuer, *Devil Boats*, p. 177; Piotter, p. 30; West, p. 113; Samuel Lyman Atwood Marshall, *Men Against Fire: The Problem of Battle Command* (New York: William Morrow, 1947), p. 200; Hamachek, p. 145.
20. Keating, p. 9; Gelzheiser.
21. Breuer, *Devil Boats*, p. 77.

22. Keating, pp. 57, 228.
23. Bulkley, Jr., p. 182.
24. Breuer, *Devil Boats*, p. 112; General Douglas MacArthur's General Staff, *Reports of General MacArthur in the Pacific: Volume 1* (Library of Congress Catalog Card Number 66-60005, 1994), p. 164; West, pp. 109, 235.
25. Breuer, *Devil Boats*, pp. 101–102; Antony Preston, *Strike Craft* (Greenwich, CT: Bison Books, 1982), pp. 35, 37.
26. van der Vat, p. 340.
27. Breuer, *Devil Boats*, p. 115.
28. Keating, p. 58; Bulkley, Jr., pp. 168, 175; Chun, pp. 35–36; Breuer, *Devil Boats*, p. 8.
29. Breuer, *Devil Boats*, p. 102; Bulkley, Jr., p. 117.
30. Breuer, *Devil Boats*, p. 102; Bulkley, Jr., p. 152; Gelzheiser; West, p. 115.
31. Breuer, *Devil Boats*, p. 155; Keating, pp. 59, 111, 113, 204.
32. Bulkley, Jr., p. 240; Garfield, p. 323; Chun, p. 60; Gelzheiser.
33. Gelzheiser.
34. Bulkley, Jr., pp. 219, 244, 368, 373; Breuer, *Devil Boats*, pp. 92, 145, 178.
35. Bulkley, Jr., pp. 219, 244, 259; Breuer, *Devil Boats*, pp. 92, 145.
36. Keating, pp. 94–95.
37. Bulkley, Jr., pp. 269–273; Piotter, p. 30.
38. Breuer, *Devil Boats*, p. 83; West, p. 227.
39. Duffy, pp. VIII, 1.
40. Bradley, pp. 230–232; West, pp. 113, 279, 281–282.
41. Hart, p. 89; van der Vat, pp. 259–260, 291; Gelzheiser; Hamachek, pp. 47, 71; Bulkley, Jr., p. 181; Keating, pp. 60, 62; West, pp. 118, 279, 280; Breuer, *Devil Boats*, pp. 100–101; Chun, p. 257.
42. William A. Bahn (Unpublished account of PT boat experiences by Quartermaster First Class William A. Bahn), p. 1; Piotter, p. 27; Oliver H. "Ollie" Young, Jr. (Unpublished account of PT boat experiences by Quartermaster First Class Oliver H. Young, Jr., June 1999); Kalinowski, p. 15.
43. Chun, p. 31.
44. Bulkley, Jr., p. 259; Hart, p. 90.
45. Hart, p. 90; Kalinowski, p. 15; Bahn, pp. 1–3.
46. Gelzheiser.
47. Kalinowski, p. 16.
48. Piotter, p. 111.
49. Breuer, *Devil Boats*, pp. 117, 157; Chun, p. 21; Keating, p. 73.
50. Bulkley, Jr., p. 259; Kalinowski, p. 16; Hart, p. 91; Young, p. 1; Piotter, p. 30; Bahn, pp. 2–4.
51. Bulkley, Jr., p. 428; Breuer, *Devil Boats*, p. 172.
52. van der Vat, p. 290.
53. Keating, p. 123; West, p. 112; Richard Connaughton, John Pimlott, Duncan Anderson, *The Battle for Manila* (London: Bloomsbury, 1995), p. 80; van der Vat, pp. 341–342; Kennedy, p. 821; Samuel Eliot Morison, *History of United States Naval Operations in World War II: Volume XIII: The Liberation of the Philippines, Luzon, Mindanao, the Visayas: 1944-1945* (Annapolis, MD: Naval Institute Press, 1987), p. 3; Duffy, p. 20; William Breuer, *Retaking the Philippines:* *America's Return to Corregidor and Bataan, October 1944–March 1945* (New York: St. Martin's Press, 1986), p. XIV; Breuer, *Devil Boats*, p. 178; Falk, p. 39.
54. van der Vat, p. 31.
55. Bulkley, Jr., p. 376; Sears, p. 121; Keating, p. 207; Drury and Clavin, pp. 43–44; MacArthur's General Staff, pp. 172–173.
56. Breuer, *Devil Boats*, pp. 144, 180; Drury and Clavin, pp. 43–44.
57. MacArthur's General Staff, pp. 177–178, 191, 196, 237.
58. van der Vat, pp. 346, 349, 363; Breuer, *Devil Boats*, pp. 92, 145, 178, 182; Sears, pp. 121–122; West, p. 343; Falk, p. 24; Bulkley, Jr., pp. 219, 244, 368, 373.
59. Morison, pp. 12–14; MacArthur's General Staff, pp. 177–178; van der Vat, p. 364; Falk, pp. 9, 24, 39; Breuer, *Retaking the Philippines*, pp. 25, 28; West, p. 368.
60. van der Vat, p. 364; Sears, p. 157; MacArthur's General Staff, pp. 224, 229; Karig, p. 61; Breuer, *Retaking the Philippines*, pp. 78–79, 82.
61. Bulkley, Jr., pp. 377–378; Breuer, *Retaking the Philippines*, p. XIV.
62. van der Vat, p. 364; Keating, pp. 208–209, 212; Falk, p. 32.
63. Sears, p. 33; Connaughton, Pimlott, Anderson, pp. 64–65; Breuer, *Devil Boats*, p. 184; Kennedy, pp. 222–224.
64. Bulkley, Jr., pp. 378, 381–390; van der Vat, p. 356; Breuer, *Devil Boats*, pp. 183–188; Rock, p. 5; Sears, p. 128; Philip Lund (Unpublished account of PT boat experiences by Carpenter's Mate First Class Philip "Bill" Lund), pp. 2–6; Connelly, *PT Boats in Action*, p. 48; West, pp. 351, 353, 356.
65. Bulkley, Jr., p. 390; Keating, p. 226.
66. Drury and Clavin, pp. 6, 45, 49, 74, 75, 144; Keating, pp. 214, 227; Kennedy, p. 828; Breuer, *Devil Boats*, p. 190; Garfield, p. 69; van der Vat, p. 361; Karig, p. 84; Falk, p. 59.
67. Hart, pp. 93–94; Bulkley, Jr., pp. 376–377, 402; Breuer, *Devil Boats*, pp. 179–183; Smith, p. 7.
68. Hall of Valor, *Military Times*.
69. Breuer, *Devil Boats*, pp. 147–149, 195–198, 201–203, 205.
70. Bulkley, Jr., pp. 215, 222, 224–225, 238, 250, 254, 256, 358, 402–403, 406–408, 410, 500, 505, 514; Gelzheiser.
71. Young, p. 1.
72. Kalinowski, p. 17; Piotter, p. 35.
73. Piotter, pp. 36, 73; Gelzheiser.
74. Bulkley, Jr., pp. 295, 402; Piotter, p. 75; West, p. 367.
75. Hart, p. 95; Gelzheiser.
76. Bulkley, Jr., pp. 390, 394, 487; Piotter, p. 37; West, p. 365–366.
77. Kalinowski, p. 18; Hart, pp. 94–95; Gelzheiser.
78. Hart, p. 95.
79. MacArthur's General Staff, p. 237; Karig, p. 16; Breuer, *Retaking the Philippines*, p. 99.
80. Piotter, p. 33; Keating, pp. 17–18; Breuer, *Retaking the Philippines*, p. 66; West, p. 375.

Chapter 7

1. John Barry, *The Great Influenza: The Epic Story of the Deadliest Pandemic in History* (New York: Penguin Books, 2005), pp. 382–388, 393; Herring, pp. 482, 485.
2. Herring, pp. 439, 504.
3. *Ibid.*, pp. 494, 504–505, 509, 520–521, 523.
4. Bradley, p. 98; van der Vat, pp. 50, 54.
5. Bradley, p. 16; van der Vat, p. 70; Herring, p. 486.
6. Kennedy, p. 614.
7. *Ibid.*, p. 618.
8. van der Vat, pp. 144–147, 209, 291; Herring, p. 551.
9. Edward J. Paris, *The Mangarin Bay Fight* (Unpublished account of PT boat experiences by Lieutenant Colonel Edward Paris), pp. 1–3; Hornfischer, *The Fleet at Flood Tide*, pp. 63, 160, 185, 353.
10. Kennedy, pp. 654–655, 668; van der Vat, p. 317; Hanson, p. 341; Hornfischer, *The Fleet at Flood Tide*, pp. 1, 53.
11. Kennedy, p. 631.
12. Victor Davis Hanson, *National Review*, July 30, 2016. (Author's note: Unless otherwise noted, in future citations Hanson will refer to *Carnage and Culture*); Hornfischer, *The Fleet at Flood Tide*, pp. XXVI, 111–112.
13. Bradley, p. 263.
14. Bradley, p. 215; Hornfischer, *The Fleet at Flood Tide*, pp. 316, 362, 386.
15. Bradley, pp. 268, 289; Hornfischer, *The Fleet at Flood Tide*, pp. XVIII, 388–389, 391, 453.
16. Keegan, pp. 216–217, 239–240; Bradley, pp. 214, 304; Hornfischer, *The Fleet at Flood Tide*, pp. 231, 464; van der Vat, pp. 242–243; Kennedy, pp. 645, 648.
17. Kennedy, pp. 653–654.
18. Strahan, pp. 5–11.
19. *Ibid.*, pp. 7, 15–21, 31, 76, 83, 84.
20. *Ibid.*, pp. 31, 42, 49.
21. *Ibid.*, pp. 51, 64, 88, 227.
22. Herring, p. 541; Strahan, pp. 188–189, 228, 278.
23. Strahan, pp. 2, 292.
24. Strahan, pp. 3, 151, 174, 190, 210, 227, 292; Hanson, pp. 341, 362.
25. Strahan, p. 220; Herring, pp. 563, 597.
26. Herring, p. 550.
27. van der Vat, p. 62; Bradley, p. 138; Hanson, pp. 99–132.
28. Hanson, pp. 363, 368; Bradley, p. 164; Breuer, *Devil Boats*, p. 68; Kennedy, p. 814; Hornfischer, *The Fleet at Flood Tide*, p. 41.
29. van der Vat, p. 44; Bradley, pp. 23–25; Hornfischer, *The Fleet at Flood Tide*, p. 455.
30. Robin Rielly, *Kamikaze Attacks of World War II: A Complete History of Japanese Suicide Strikes on American Ships, by Aircraft and Other Means* (Jefferson, NC: McFarland, 2010), pp. 7–9.
31. van der Vat, pp. 44, 63; Sears, p. 126; Richard O'Neill, *Suicide Squad: The Men and Machines of World War II Special Operations* (London: Batsford, 1999), Survey.
32. van der Vat, pp. 44, 109, 282.
33. Bradley, pp. 32–34; Sears, p. 244.
34. Bradley, pp. 17–18, 34–36; Rielly, pp. 8–19.
35. Bradley, pp. 37–38.
36. *Ibid.*, p. 38.
37. Connaughton, Pimlott, Anderson, pp. 143–144; Kennedy, p. 812; van der Vat, p. 138; Drury and Clavin, p. 97.
38. Bradley, pp. 39–40.
39. van der Vat, pp. 238, 327.
40. Bradley, pp. 32–34, 143–144; van der Vat, p. 305.
41. van der Vat, pp. 199, 224; Bradley, p. 144; Karig, p. 13; Hornfischer, *The Fleet at Flood Tide*, p. 251.
42. Rielly, p. 26.
43. *Ibid.*, pp. 11–15.
44. Sears, p. 159.
45. Rielly, pp. 49–50; van der Vat, p. 351; Sears, p. 125; Kennedy, pp. 819–821; Karig, p. 19.
46. Bradley, p. 19; Rielly, pp. 1, 7–8; Sears, p. 145; Karig, pp. 17, 84; Kennedy, p. 828; Breuer, *Devil Boats*, p. 190; Garfield, p. 69; van der Vat, p. 361; Falk, p. 59.
47. Sears, p. 139.
48. Sears, p. 175; Drury and Clavin, pp. 50–51.
49. van der Vat, p. 351; Sears, p. 125; Rielly, pp. 54–57; Karig, pp. 14–15; Breuer, *Retaking the Philippines*, p. 75.
50. Rielly, pp. 16–17, 23; Breuer, *Retaking the Philippines*, p. 73.
51. Rielly, pp. 16–17; Hanson, p. 366.
52. Rielly, pp. 21–22; Breuer, *Retaking the Philippines*, p. 111.
53. Rielly., p. 16; Breuer, *Retaking the Philippines*, p. 111.
54. Sears, p. 168; Connaughton, Pimlott, Anderson, p. 151; Karig, p. 205.
55. Rielly, p. 45.
56. *Ibid.*, p 3
57. Sears, p. 152.
58. *Ibid.*, p. 154.
59. Rielly, pp. 53–57, 143.
60. Morison, p. 53.
61. Sears, p. 220; West, p. 364.
62. Morison, p. 148.
63. Morison, p. 54; Drury and Clavin, p. 75.
64. Morison, p. 55.
65. Rielly, pp. 42, 44.
66. van der Vat, p. 359; Rielly, pp. 4–5; West, p. 363.
67. Kennedy, p. 826; Breuer, *Devil Boats*, p. 191; Sears, p. 125; van der Vat, p. 350; Rielly, pp. 4–5, 318; Hornfischer, *The Fleet at Flood Tide*, p. 357; Bradley, pp. 32–34.
68. Morison, pp. 98–99; Sears, pp. 150–155, 170; Rielly, p. 47.
69. Rielly, pp. 115, 117, 157; Falk, p. 71.
70. Sears, p. 382.
71. Morison, p. 53; Sears, p. 266; Rielly, pp. 54–57; Hornfischer, *The Fleet at Flood Tide*, p. 402.
72. Rielly, p. 324; Sears, p. 337; Drury and Clavin, p. 52.
73. Rielly, pp. 101–102, 161.
74. Bradley, pp. 293–295; Sears, p. 173; Rielly, pp. 307, 313–314.

75. Sears, pp. 174, 181; Rielly, p. 90.
76. Morison, p. 139.
77. Rielly, pp. 73, 83–84, 175; Sears, p. 173; Breuer, *Retaking the Philippines*, p. 120.
78. Sears, pp. 176–179; Karig, p. 471.
79. *Sears*, pp. 170–171, 176–179, 197–198, 244–245; Reilly, pp. 219–220; Karig, p. 394; Hornfischer, *The Fleet at Flood Tide*, pp. 249, 399–400; Norman Polmar and Thomas B. Allen, *World War II: The Encyclopedia of the War Years, 1941-1945* (New York: Random House, 1996), pp. 132–133.
80. Sears, pp. 75–76, 77; Kennedy, p. 817; Hornfischer, *The Fleet at Flood Tide*, pp. 263, 271, 272, 284, 291, 406.
81. Drury and Clavin, p. 101.
82. Sears, pp. 75–77; Bradley, p. 145; Hornfischer, *The Fleet at Flood Tide*, p. 378.
83. Bradley, pp. 292–294; Karig, pp. 461–462; Breuer, *Retaking the Philippines*, p. 261; Hornfischer, *The Fleet at Flood Tide*, pp. 75, 159, 277, 279, 308, 378, 399, 408, 420–421, 471, 479.
84. Bradley, pp. 292–293; O'Neill and Survey; Karig, p. 455.
85. Rielly, p. 144; Hornfischer, *The Fleet at Flood Tide*, pp. 420, 439, 456.

Chapter 8

1. Sears, pp. 224–225; Morison, pp. 18, 25–26; Piotter, p. 38.
2. Morison, pp. 17–18; Piotter, p. 33; Breuer, *Devil Boats*, p. 197; Charles C. Mann, *1493: Uncovering the New World Columbus Created* (New York: Alfred A. Knopf, 2011), p. 392; Sears, p. 215.
3. Sears, pp. 158, 202; Morison, pp. 6–9, 18, 93; Breuer, *Retaking the Philippines*, pp. 83–84, 100, 101; Karig, pp. 65, 87, 105; Falk, p. 75.
4. Drury and Clavin, pp. 50, 74, 79; Sears, pp. 223–225.
5. Drury and Clavin, p. 76.
6. Morison, p. 22; Sears, p. 224; Hart, p. 97; MacArthur's General Staff, p. 247; Karig, pp. 106–107.
7. Morison, pp. 12–13, 18; MacArthur's General Staff, p. 250.
8. Morison, pp. 9–11, 25, 200; Sears, p. 230; Gelzheiser; *The Great Raid* (Film, 2005); Hampton Sides, *Ghost Soldiers: The Epic Account of World War II's Greatest Rescue Mission* (New York: Anchor Books, 2002), pp. 7–12, 326; *All Hands*, The official publication of PT Boats, Inc., November 2005; Breuer, *Retaking the Philippines*, pp. 130, 132, 134.
9. Morison, pp. 21–22, 55–57; Drury and Clavin, pp. 96, 98; Karig, p. 88.
10. Morison, pp. 21–22, 55–57; Drury and Clavin, pp. 97–98.
11. Sears, pp. 51, 244–247; Morison, pp. 21–24; Sears, pp. 226–229; Piotter, p. 38; Hart, p. 97; Breuer, *Retaking the Philippines*, pp. 49, 101; Karig, pp. 107, 109, 110, 114; Falk, p. 81.
12. Bulkley, Jr., p. 403; Morison, pp. 24–25; Sears, p. 228; Karig, pp. 110–112.
13. Morison, p. 25; Karig, pp. 112–113.
14. Piotter, p. 38; Smith, p. 8; Karig, pp. 106–107.
15. Harold Moss, *Beach Mission Preparing for the Mindoro Invasion: December, 1944,* accessed from https://www.mossletters.com/beach-mission-December-1944; Hart, p. 97; Piotter, p. 40; Gelzheiser; Breuer, *Retaking the Philippines*, p. 101; Karig, p. 114.
16. Bahn, pp. 1–3.
17. Moss; Morison, pp. 21, 25–26; Sears, pp. 230–232; Hart, p. 97; Piotter, p. 43; Kalinowski, p. 19; Drury and Clavin, p. 95; Karig, p. 117.
18. Morison, p. 28.
19. Morison, p. 29; Sears, pp. 216, 231; Bulkley, Jr., p. 395.
20. Sears, pp. 231–232; Hart, p. 97; Morison, p. 29.
21. Breuer, *Devil Boats*, pp. 197–198; Hart, p. 97; Kalinowski, p. 20; West, p. 370.
22. Hart, p. 98; Karig, p. 115.
23. Morison, pp. 29–30; Bulkley, Jr., p. 403; Kalinowski, p. 20; Hart, p. 98; Breuer, *Devil Boats*, p. 197; Sears, p. 232; Piotter, pp. 38, 41, 42; Kalinowski, p. 18.
24. Piotter, p. 41; Hart, p. 98; Kalinowski, p. 20; Gelzheiser.
25. Morison, pp. 21, 24; Kalinowski, p. 19.
26. Morison, pp. 31–32; Gelzheiser.
27. Gelzheiser; Kalinowski, p. 21; Hart, pp. 98–99; Piotter, pp. 43–44, 46–47; Smith, p. 8.
28. Gelzheiser; Sears, pp. 232–233; MacArthur's General Staff, p. 251.
29. Morison, pp. 14–15; Rielly, p. 62.
30. Keating, p. 233; Bahn, p. 2; Gelzheiser; Karig, pp. 370–371.
31. Piotter, p. 45; Gelzheiser.
32. Hart, p. 99; Morison, p. 33; Bulkley, Jr., p. 403; Piotter, p. 44; Kalinowski, p. 21; Rielly, p. 62.
33. Bulkley, Jr., p. 403; Breuer, *Devil Boats*, p. 199; Hart, p. 99; Piotter, p. 46.
34. Piotter, p. 45; Bahn, p. 3; Gelzheiser; Rielly, p. 151.
35. Bulkley, Jr., p. 405; Breuer, *Devil Boats*, p. 195; Kalinowski, pp. 21–22; Piotter, pp. 46–47.
36. Piotter, pp. 46–47; After Action Reports; Bulkley, Jr., p. 405; Breuer, *Devil Boats*, p. 195; Kalinowski, pp. 21–22.
37. Gelzheiser; Lieutenant Colonel Dave Grossman, *On Killing: The Psychological Cost of Learning to Kill in War and Society* (New York: Little Brown, 2009), pp. 234–235.
38. Hart, pp. 100–101; Bahn, p. 3; Karig, p. 118–120.
39. Piotter, p. 48; Hart, pp. 100–102; Morison, p. 33; Kalinowski, p. 22.
40. Hart, pp. 100–102; Piotter, pp. 48–49; Bulkley, Jr., p. 405; Morison, p. 34; Rielly, p. 66.
41. Morison, p. 32.
42. *Ibid.*, p. 76.
43. Morison, p. 60; Herring, p. 327.
44. Drury and Clavin, pp. 104, 107, 111, 117, 126, 128, 160; Morison, pp. 68, 70.
45. Morison, p. 72; Drury and Clavin, pp. 99, 135; Karig, p. 100.
46. Drury and Clavin, p. 160.
47. Morison, p. XXV; Drury and Clavin, p. 181.
48. Drury and Clavin, p. 229; Karig, pp. 96–99, 101–102; Breuer, *Retaking the Philippines*, p. 104.
49. Morison, pp. 60, 64, 71.

50. *Ibid.*, p. 82.
51. Drury and Clavin, pp. 158–160.
52. Drury and Clavin, pp. 153, 156–157; Thomas M. DeFrank, *Write It When I'm Gone: Remarkable Off-the-Record Conversations with Gerald Ford* (New York: Berkley Books, 2007), Survey.
53. Drury and Clavin, pp. 57, 60.
54. *Ibid.*, p. 262.
55. *Ibid.*, p. 210.
56. Morison, p. 59; Drury and Clavin, pp. 201, 262, 275.
57. Drury and Clavin, p. 277.
58. Morison, pp. 63, 67; van der Vat, p. 365; Drury and Clavin, pp. 16, 244, 265.
59. Gelzheiser.
60. Breuer, *Devil Boats*, p. 195.
61. *Ibid.*, p. 195.
62. Hart, p. 101; Bulkley, Jr., p. 405; Kalinowski, p. 23; Piotter, pp. 49–50; Rielly, p. 151; Gelzheiser.
63. Young, Jr., p. 2.
64. Bahn, pp. 1–4.
65. Keating, p. 236.
66. Hart, p. 102; Piotter, pp. 49–50; Bulkley, Jr., p. 406; Kalinowski, pp. 23–24; PT Boats, Inc., *World War II PT Boats, Bases, Tenders Memorial: PT Boaters Killed in Action*.
67. Piotter, p. 110.
68. Kalinowski, p. 29.
69. Piotter, p. 51.
70. Hart, p. 103; Piotter, pp. 51–52; Kalinowski, p. 26; Morison, p. 34.
71. Hart, p. 104; Piotter, p. 53; Kalinowski, p. 26; Rock, p. 27.
72. Piotter, p. 53; Hart, p. 104; Kalinowski, p. 27; Morison, p. 34.
73. Bulkley, Jr., p. 406; Piotter, pp. 51–53; Gelzheiser.
74. Rock, p. 28; Smith, pp. 7–8; Gelzheiser.
75. Gelzheiser; Morison, pp. 33, 34–36; Rielly, p. 151; Karig, pp. 127, 129.
76. Morison, pp. 34–36; Piotter, p. 52; Rielly, p. 151; Karig, pp. 127, 129.
77. Rielly, p. 151.
78. Morison, p. 36.
79. Hart, p. 104; Piotter, p. 54; *San Francisco Chronicle*, September 9, 1944.
80. Piotter, p. 54; Rock, p. 27.
81. Hart, p. 105; Kalinowski, p. 26; Piotter, pp. 54–55; Morison, p. 32.
82. Hart, p. 105; Rock, p. 28.
83. Piotter, p. 55.
84. Gelzheiser; Hart: Interview; Morison, p. 43; Smith, p. 8; Breuer, *Devil Boats*, p. 102; Bulkley, Jr., p. 152; West, p. 115.
85. Hart, p. 105; Gelzheiser; Morison, p. 43; Piotter, p. 55.
86. Piotter, pp. 55–56; Kalinowski, p. 29.
87. Hart, p. 106; Piotter, pp. 56–57; Kalinowski, p. 30.
88. Breuer, *Devil Boats*, p. 203; Hart, p. 106.
89. Hart, p. 106; Kalinowski, p. 30; Gelzheiser.
90. Morison, pp. 38–39.
91. Morison, pp. 37–38; Kalinowski, p. 30; Bulkley, Jr., p. 406.
92. Kalinowski, pp. 31–32; Bulkley, Jr., pp. 406–407; Morison, pp. 39–40; Piotter, p. 58; Gelzheiser.
93. Breuer, *Devil Boats*, p. 201; Piotter, pp. 58–60.
94. Hart, p. 107; Morison, pp. 40–42; Piotter, pp. 58–60; Karig, p. 124.
95. Morison, p. 42; Kalinowski, pp. 31–32; Piotter, pp. 58–60; Hart, p. 107; Breuer, *Devil Boats*, pp. 202–203; Young, Jr., p. 3; Karig, p. 124.
96. Bulkley, Jr., p. 407.
97. Morison, p. 41.
98. Gelzheiser; Morison, p. 41; Piotter, p. 60; Young, Jr., p. 3.
99. Bulkley, Jr., p. 408; Morison, p. 41; Kalinowski, p. 32; Piotter, pp. 58–60; Karig, p. 125.
100. Bulkley, Jr., p. 408; Stephen A. Mitchell, *An Encounter: PT 219* (Unpublished account of PT boat experiences by Chief Quartermaster Stephen A. Mitchell); Morison, p. 41; Smith, pp. 8–9.
101. Morison, pp. 41–42; Breuer, p. 203; Kalinowski, pp. 30–31, 34; Karig, pp. 124, 126.
102. Hart, pp. 109–110.
103. Bulkley, Jr., pp. 408–409; Morison, pp. 43–46; Breuer, *Devil Boats*, p. 204; Keating, p. 239; West, p. 376; Karig, pp. 129–131.
104. Keating, p. 240.
105. Bulkley, Jr., pp. 408–409; Morison, pp. 44–45; Breuer, *Devil Boats*, pp. 204–205; Karig, p. 131.
106. Keating, p. 240; Bulkley, Jr., pp. 408–409; Morison, pp. 44–46.
107. Gelzheiser; Paris, pp. 1–2; Breuer, *Devil Boats*, p. 204; Bulkley, Jr., p. 410; Karig, pp. 87, 131; West, p. 377.
108. Hart, pp. 110–112; Piotter, pp. 65–67.
109. Charles B. Jones, *The Orestes* (Unpublished account of PT boat experiences by Motor Machinist's Mate First Class Charles B. Jones), pp. 1–2; Paris, p. 1.
110. Keating, p. 242.
111. Paris, p. 2.
112. USS *Orestes* Deck Log Remarks Sheet, December 31, 1944.
113. Bulkley, Jr., p. 410.
114. Breuer, *Devil Boats*, pp. 204–205; Morison, p. 46; West, p. 377.
115. Bulkley, Jr., pp. 409–410; Morison, pp. 46–47; West, pp. 376–377.
116. Morison, pp. 47–48; Bulkley, Jr., p. 410; Piotter, p. 67.
117. Bulkley, Jr., p. 410; Piotter, p. 67; Morison, pp. 47–48.
118. Gelzheiser; Breuer, *Devil Boats*, p. 205; Bulkley, Jr., p. 410.
119. Morison, pp. 49–50; Smith, p. 9; Karig, pp. 157–158; Gelzheiser.
120. Morison, p. 49–50.
121. Morison, p. 48; Hart: Interview.
122. Morison, p. 50.
123. Morison, p. 189; Piotter, p. 78; Lund, p. 5.
124. Bulkley, Jr., pp. 411–412; Hart, p. 114.
125. Bulkley, Jr., p. 413; Hart, p. 123; Piotter, pp. 76–77.
126. Gelzheiser; Hart, pp. 114–117; Piotter, pp. 72–73.

127. Gelzheiser; Hart, pp. 112–114, 118.
128. Hart, p. 118; Gelzheiser.
129. Hart, p. 122.
130. *Ibid.*
131. Hart, p. 123; Smith, p. 135.
132. Gelzheiser.
133. Bulkley, Jr., pp 415–418; Gelzheiser; Morison, p. 50.
134. Hart, pp. 69, 119–120; Gelzheiser.
135. Piotter, pp. 88, 109.
136. *Ibid.*, pp. 75, 89.
137. Hart, pp. 117, 120–121; Smith, p. 8.
138. Hart, pp. 120–121; Piotter, pp. 78–79.
139. Hart, pp. 121–122; Piotter, pp. 78–80.
140. Piotter, pp. 68–71.
141. Morison, p. 43; Gelzheiser.
142. Gelzheiser.
143. *Ibid.*
144. Piotter, pp. 76–77; Gelzheiser.
145. Gelzheiser; Piotter, pp. 76–77.
146. Piotter, pp. 76–77; Gelzheiser.
147. Keating, pp. 244–245.
148. Keating, p. 244; Karig, pp. 212–213.
149. Morison, p. 192.
150. Bulkley, Jr., pp. 413–414; Hart, pp. 123–124; Piotter, pp. 81–82; Breuer, *Devil Boats*, pp. 244–246; West, p. 382.
151. Gelzheiser.
152. Gelzheiser; Sears, pp. 342–344; Karig, p. 413.
153. Hart, p. 124.
154. *Ibid.*, p. 125.
155. *Ibid.*, pp. 125–126.
156. Piotter, pp. 82–83.
157. *Ibid.*, p. 86.
158. Piotter, p. 86; Gelzheiser.
159. Piotter, p. 89; Gelzheiser.
160. Piotter, pp. 86–88.
161. Bulkley, Jr., p. 436; Morison, p. 265.
162. Piotter, p. 113; Bulkley, Jr., p. 437.
163. Piotter, pp. 90–91.
164. *Ibid.*, pp. 92–96.
165. *Ibid.*, p. 113.
166. *Ibid.*, pp. 96–97.
167. *Ibid.*, pp. 98–103.
168. *Ibid.*, p. 103.
169. *Ibid.*, pp. 103–104.
170. Piotter, pp. 103–104; Bulkley, Jr., p. 442.
171. Piotter, p. 105.
172. *Ibid.*, pp. 105–106.
173. Piotter, p. 106; *Three Came Home*, 1950, film.
174. Piotter, p. 107.
175. *Ibid.*, p. 108.
176. Hart, pp. 127–128; Gelzheiser; Francis Gelzheiser, Military Records; Smith, p. 10.
177. Hart, pp. 127–128; Gelzheiser.
178. Morison, pp. 48, 50–51, 53; MacArthur's General Staff, p. 252.
179. Morison, pp. 50–51; van der Vat, p. 365.
180. Morison, p. 232.
181. Bulkley, Jr., p. 414; Rielly, pp. 73, 86; Morison, p. 157; Lieutenant Commander N. Burt Davis, letter to Captain Selman S. Bowling, January 12, 1945.
182. van der Vat, p. 375.
183. Morison, p. 49.
184. Piotter, p. 77.
185. World War II Data Base; Piotter, p. 72.
186. Hart, p. 121; Piotter, p. 104.
187. Garfield, p. 418.
188. Sears, pp. 198, 244–245.
189. Piotter, p. 109; Gelzheiser.
190. Bulkley, Jr., p. 414; Falk, p. 83.
191. Gelzheiser.

Chapter 9

1. van der Vat, p. 366; Breuer, *Devil Boats*, p. 206; West, pp. 379–380; Karig, p. 205; Breuer, *Retaking the Philippines*, p. 21; Morison, pp. 1, 179, 184, 195–196; Connaughton, Pimlott, Anderson, pp. 100, 186.
2. van der Vat, pp. 364, 366; Sears, p. 256; Morison, pp. 13–14; Breuer, *Devil Boats*, p. 206; Drury, Clavin, p. 73; Rielly, p. 154; Karig, p. 149; Falk, p. 131.
3. Morison, pp. 198–199; Bulkley, Jr., p. 424; Breuer, *Devil Boats*, pp. 209–210; Connelly, *PT Boats in Action*, p. 4; MacArthur's General Staff, pp. 252, 277–279; Breuer, *Retaking the Philippines*, pp. 84, 180, 183, 190, 193, 200, 203–206, 209, 211, 214, 215, 223, 224, 226, 227, 239, 242, 246, 250, 251, 255; Falk, pp. 112, 115; West, p. 384, 385; Karig, pp. 65, 148, 230, 233, 237, 240.
4. Morison, p. 11; Connaughton, Pimlott, Duncan, pp. 72–73; MacArthur's General Staff, p. 271; Falk, p. 103.
5. Connaughton, Pimlott, Duncan, pp. 72–73; MacArthur's General Staff, p. 271; Falk, 103.
6. Stephen B. Oates, Charles J. Errico, *Portrait of America: Eighth Edition: Volume II: From Reconstruction to the Present* (New York: Houghton Mifflin, 2003), pp. 99–111.
7. Connaughton, Pimlott, Anderson, pp. 44, 50.
8. *Ibid.*, p. 44
9. Connaughton, Pimlott, Anderson, pp. 16, 52, 57–58, 68; Breuer, *Retaking the Philippines*, p. 12.
10. Connaughton, Pimlott, Anderson, p. 73.
11. *Ibid.*, pp. 72–73.
12. Connaughton, Pimlott, Anderson, pp. 73, 92; Morison, pp. 196–197.
13. Connaughton, Pimlott, Anderson, pp. 30, 33, 39, 40; Bulkley, Jr., p. 7; van der Vat, p. 367.
14. Connaughton, Pimlott, Anderson, pp. 74, 187–191, 197; Falk, p. 107.
15. Connaughton, Pimlott, Anderson, pp. 100, 186; Morison, pp. 179, 184, 195–196.
16. Connaughton, Pimlott, Anderson, pp. 174, 192; Morison, p. 198; MacArthur's General Staff, p. 191; Karig, p. 217; Falk, p. 108.
17. Connaughton, Pimlott, Anderson, pp. 96, 107, 119, 121, 129, 133.
18. *Ibid.*, pp. 142–143, 181.
19. *Ibid.*, pp. 119–120, 164.
20. *Ibid.*, pp. 70–71, 110, 113; Breuer, *Retaking the Philippines*, p. 253.
21. Connaughton, Pimlott, Anderson, pp. 102–103, 114–116, 122, 144, 164, 172, 194; van der Vat, p. 368.
22. Connaughton, Pimlott, Anderson, pp. 15, 94,

108, 123, 127, 132, 138, 146, 151, 174, 195, 201, 211; Breuer, *Devil Boats*, p. 211; van der Vat, p. 369; Morison, p. 210; Gelzheiser; MacArthur's General Staff, p. 272; Breuer, *Retaking the Philippines*, pp. 43, 259; Falk, pp. 131, 156–157.
 23. Gelzheiser.
 24. Richard "Jim" W. Stanton (Unpublished account of PT boat experiences by Gunner's Mate First Class Richard "Jim" W. Stanton).
 25. PT Boats, Inc., Official Handout; Kalinowski, p. 2; Piotter, p. 118; Gelzheiser; West, p. 389.

Afterword

 1. Grossman, p. 252.
 2. Grossman, pp. XVI, 3, 18, 23–25, 78, 88, 173, 194; Marshall, pp. 50, 54, 71; Keegan, p. 280.
 3. Grossman, p. 43.
 4. *Ibid.*, pp. 161–162.
 5. *Ibid.*, pp. 84, 98, 107, 109.
 6. van der Vat, p. 71; Keegan, p. 71.
 7. Grossman, pp. 11, 107, 144; Marshall, p. 57.
 8. Grossman, pp. 160, 162, 186.
 9. Grossman, pp. 51, 149, 255–256; Keegan, p. 311.
 10. Keegan, pp. 16, 335.
 11. Marshall, pp. 153, 164; Grossman, p. 88.
 12. Keegan, p. 321.
 13. Marshall, p. 140.
 14. Grossman, p. 111.
 15. Marshall, pp. 60, 78; Gelzheiser; Grossman, p. 179.
 16. Keegan, pp. 328–329.
 17. Grossman, pp. 31, 111, 233–235; Gelzheiser.
 18. Marshall, p. 118; Gelzheiser.

Bibliographic Note

PT Boat Odyssey is not a traditional work of history, memoir, or reflection. Instead it is a combination of the three. Numerous primary and secon-dary sources were used to tell this story. Secondary sources include but were not limited to:

At Close Quarters: PT Boats in the United States Navy, by Captain Robert J. Bulkley, Jr. Although this book was first published in 1962, it is still considered the definitive resource on PT Boats in World War II.

History of United States Naval Operations in WWII, by Samuel Eliot Morison. This fifteen volume series is the definitive history of American naval operations in World War II written by one of America's preeminent naval historians.

Devil Boats: The PT War Against Japan, by William Breuer, is a narrative history that focuses on PT Boats in the Pacific by one of our most prolific military historians.

At War with the Wind: The Epic Struggle with Japan's WWII Suicide Bombers, by David Sears. Sears gives a thorough account of the history of the Japanese kamikaze in World War II.

Flyboys: A True Story of Courage, by James Brady. Brady, the son of one of the flag raisers on Iwo Jima (although recently, it has been disputed whether Brady's father was one of the Marines in the iconic photograph), gained acclaim for his first book, *Flags of Our Fathers. Flyboys* is the story of what happened to the men on board the plane piloted by future President George Bush that was shot down by the Japanese on September 2, 1944. Bradley does an excellent job explaining the mindset of the Japanese warrior and why Japan believed that they could win the war despite America's overwhelming production advantage.

PT Boats in Action, by T. Garth Connelly and *PT Boats in Action* by David Doyle. These two books focus on the construction and armaments of the boats and also include numerous and often difficult to find photos of them.

Freedom from Fear: The American People in Depression and War, by David Kennedy, is a volume from the Oxford University Press History of the United States series. Kennedy does an excellent job of giving an overview of America's war against the Japanese.

The Thousand-Mile War: World War II in Alaska and the Aleutians, by Brian Garfield, is an excellent account of the little-known war between the Japanese and Americans in Alaska.

On Killing: The Psychological Cost of Learning to Kill in War and Society, by Lieutenant Colonel Dave Grossman, and *Men Against Fire: The Problem of Battle Command,* by S.L.A. Marshall, are the two most controversial books used. Both authors argue that because killing is unnatural, it is often avoided by men in combat. Some might dispute the statistics used by the authors, but I believe their theses are sound, and their ideas proved very helpful when I examined my father and killing.

Kamikaze Attacks of World War II, by Robin L. Rielly, is an extraordinarily thorough history of Japanese suicide attacks in World War II.

The Battle for Manila, by Richard Connaughton, John Pimlott, and Duncan Anderson, is one of the few books that focuses on the bloody battle for the Philippine capital city.

Dan van der Vat's *The Pacific Campaign: The U.S-Japanese Naval War: 1941-1945* is a thorough survey of the naval war in the Pacific between Japan and the United States.

U.S. Patrol Torpedo Boats in World War II, 1939-1945, by T. Garth Connelly, thoroughly examines the workings of a World War II PT boat, and *Andrew Jackson Higgins and the Boats That Won World War II* by Jerry E. Strahan is an excellent account of the man who built the boats operated by the sailors in PT Boat Squadron 16.

Carnage and Culture: Landmark Battles in the Rise of Western Power, by Victor Davis Hanson, is a personal favorite. Hanson's examination of the Battle of Midway is superb, and he also does an excellent job of explaining why Western societies wage war in such a lethal manner.

Iron Men, Wooden Boats: The Epic Story of American PT Boats in World War II, by Howard E. West, is a fine general history of PT boats in World War II.

Battle Report: Victory in the Pacific, by Captain Walter Karig, is the last volume of a five-volume series written in the years following World War II. Karig's book is thorough, and he includes many first person narratives of America's battle to retake the Philippines. Although written more than 65 years ago, this book series is still one of the most thorough and readable accounts of America's naval operations in World War II.

Finally, in their book *Halsey's Typhoon*, Bob Drury and Tom Clavin give an excellent account of the typhoon that devastated Admiral Halsey's fleet that was protecting the American invasion force in the early days of the Mindoro campaign. Although I used very few internet sources, I did find C. Peter Chen's *World War II Database: Your WWII History Reference Destination* (https://ww2db.com) to be helpful.

The most important primary source used was my father, Francis L. Gelzheiser. One of the difficulties that historians encounter when using firsthand accounts of military history is the reliability of the person providing the information. Although my father waited until late in his life to share his World War II experiences with me, I am confident that his remembrances were very accurate. My father was gifted with a keen memory, and it was not uncommon for him when he was in his eighties to recall information that he had read in a book or been taught while in high school. In addition, when I was a high school history teacher, he came to my classes and told his story on numerous occasions, and the narrative he wove was consistent from year to year. I believe he worked very hard to be accurate, and at no time did I ever believe he was exaggerating or embellishing a story. He also took copious notes of his experiences later in life, and in his final year sat down with me and a video recorder to share his experiences. In addition, I would often encounter descriptions of the events he had experienced in the sources listed above, and there was never an instance when I found a discrepancy between what he said and what was written in these sources. When he died, his long-time friend, Reverend Richard Rush, the retired head pastor at First Church Congregational in Fairfield, Connecticut, said the following: "I say to you that Francis was a *very special* person…. A man of integrity, whose word was not only his "bond," but accurate ... and true." I trust my father's account of his World War II experiences.

In addition, my father had a large collection of material that he had saved from his time in the Navy, and much of this proved useful. This collection included newspaper articles, letters, photographs, and assorted other sources from the war period. I am indebted to Cele Piotter, wife of Squadron 16 member Alfred F. Piotter. In 1972 she interviewed a number of the men from Squadron 16 and compiled *United States Motor Torpedo Boats Squadron 16 History*. This is the kind of primary source material that all students of history covet, and this 162-page document proved to be invaluable in my quest to record my father's Patrol Torpedo Boat Squadron 16 experiences. Tom Hart, my father's shipmate and lifelong friend, also wrote a detailed account of his war experiences titled, *PT Squadron 16: World War II Memories*. I located a copy of this paper early in my research in a file cabinet in the PT boat archives in Battleship Cove, Fall River, MA. Shortly before the completion of *PT Boat Odyssey*, the Hart family published the account. This is an excellent addition to the PT boat library. The pages listed in the endnotes of *PT Boat Odyssey*, correspond to the pages of the unpublished paper and not the published work. There are also numerous other shorter accounts written by the sailors of PT Boat Squadrons 13 and 16 that are used in this book. I met some but not all of the men who wrote these brief histories, and I believe these accounts are accurate. These were all valuable sources. I also used a variety of other primary sources that are detailed in the bibliography.

Students of naval history might note that I generally give the length of ships and not their tonnage, as is the more accepted way to describe a ship's size. I did this because I believe that most readers would better understand a ship's size if they knew its length rather than gross tonnage. I have also written out the rating of enlisted men whenever possible instead of using the traditional abbreviations which are normally placed after the name. I did this because I did not believe that readers would know what many of the abbreviations meant, and I wanted the reader to understand what the skills and duties were of the sailor being discussed. I also wrote out an officer's rank instead of using the traditional abbreviations because I did not think that many readers would know what the abbreviations stood for. If veering away from the traditional way of listing a Navy man's rating and rank bothers any reader, I apologize.

There is also much personal reflection in *PT Boat Odyssey*. Obviously, I have no idea what my father was thinking during the many hours we spent together. However, I know how much he loved life and the great respect he had for all people; and try as he might, I do not believe he was able to keep his memories of the war at bay. In all wars, the survivors eventually come home, but I do not believe they ever completely leave the war. I think this was the case with my father. Experiencing war did not turn my father into a pacifist, but it did make him extremely reluctant to support most military actions; and he was very uncomfortable when those who did not participate in war boisterously used the sacrifices of others as a way to gain support for a political agenda. He quietly loved the United States and cherished her most basic ideals. He realized that it was sometimes necessary to defend these, but he also realized that in doing so, each participant would have to face his or her own Mindoro or Manila. Because he understood war so well, he hated it and did not want to send young men and women into harm's way unless absolutely necessary. I also think he believed that try as we might, those of us who stayed at home could never understand those who went; and for those who went, it would be left to them to come to terms with their war. That is the way with war.

Bibliography

Books

Allen, Thomas B., and Norman Polmar. *World War II: The Encyclopedia of the War Years: 1941–1945*. New York: Random House, 1996.

Anderson, Duncan, Richard Connaughton and John Pimlott. *The Battle for Manila*. London: Presidio, 1995.

Barry, John. *The Great Influenza: The Epic Story of the Deadliest Pandemic in History*. New York: Penguin, 2005.

Bradley, James. *Flags of Our Fathers*. New York: Bantam, 2000.

_____. *Flyboys: A True Story of Courage*. New York: Little, Brown, 2003.

Breuer, William B. *Devil Boats: The PT War Against Japan*. Novato, CA: Presido, 1987.

_____. *Retaking the Philippines: America's Return to Corregidor and Bataan: October, 1944–March, 1945*. New York: St Martin's, 1986.

Bulkley, Captain Robert J., Jr. *At Close Quarters: PT Boats in the United States Navy*. Washington: United States Government Printing Office, Naval History Division, 1962.

Chun, Victor. *American PT Boats in World War II*. Atglen, PA: Schiffer Military/Aviation History, 1997.

Connelly, Garth T. *PT Boats in Action*. Carrollton, TX: Squadron/Signal Publications, 1994.

_____. *U.S. Patrol Torpedo Boats in World War II, 1939–1945*. Ann Arbor, MI: Nimble Books, 2010.

DeFrank, Thomas M. *Write It When I'm Gone: The Remarkable Off-the-Record Conversations with Gerald Ford*. New York: Berkley Books, 2008.

Doyle, David. *PT Boats in Action*. Carrollton, TX: Squadron/Signal Publications, 2010.

Drury, Bob, and Tom Clavin. *Halsey's Typhoon: The True Story of a Fighting Admiral, an Epic Storm, and an Untold Rescue*. New York: Grove Press, 2007.

Duffy, James P. *War at the End of the World: Douglas MacArthur and the Forgotten Fight for New Guinea: 1942–1945*. New York: New American Library, 2016.

Falk, Stanley. *Liberation of the Philippines*. New York: Ballantine Books, 1971.

Garfield, Brian. *The Thousand-Mile War: World War II in Alaska and the Aleutians*. Fairbanks: University of Alaska Press, 1995.

Grossman, Lieutenant Colonel Dave. *On Killing: The Psychological Cost of Learning to Kill in War and Society*. New York: Little, Brown, 1996.

Grun, Bernard. *The Timetables of History: A Horizontal Linkage of People and Events*. New York: Touchstone, 1979.

Hamachek, Russ. *Hot, Straight and True: An Anecdotal View of PT Boats in WWII*. New York: Carlton Press, 1995.

Hanson, Victor Davis. *Carnage and Culture: Landmark Battles in the Rise of Western Power*. New York: Random House, 2002.

Hart, B.H. Liddell. *History of the Second World War*. New York: G.P. Putnam's Sons, 1970.

Herring, George C. *From Colony to Superpower: U.S. Foreign Relations Since 1776*. New York: Oxford University Press, 2008.

Hornfischer, James D. *The Last Stand of the Tin Can Sailors: The Extraordinary World War II Story of the U.S. Navy's Finest Hour*. New York: Bantam, 2005.

_____. *The Fleet at Flood Tide: America at Total War in the Pacific, 1944–1945*. New York: Bantam, 2016.

Karig, Captain Walter. *Battle Report: Victory in the Pacific*. New York: Rinehart, 1949.

Keating, Bern. *The Mosquito Fleet: PT Boats in World War II*. New York: Scholastic, 1963.

Keegan, John. *The Face of Battle*. New York: Penguin, 1976.

Kennedy, David M. *Freedom from Fear: The American People in Depression and War, 1929–1945*. New York: Oxford University Press, 1999.

Manchester, William. *American Caesar: Douglas MacArthur: 1880–1964*. New York: Dell, 1978.

Mann, Charles C. *1493: Uncovering the New World Columbus Made*. New York: Alfred A. Knopf, 2011.

Marshall, Colonel Samuel Lyman Atwood. *Men

Against Fire: The Problem of Command. Norman, OK: University of Oklahoma Press, 1947.

Morison, Samuel Eliot. *History of the United States Naval Operations in World War II: Volume XIII: The Liberation of the Philippines: Luzon, Mindanao, the Visayas: 1944–1945.* Annapolis, MD: Naval Institute Press, 1987.

Norman, Michael, and Elizabeth Norman. *Tears in the Darkness: The Story of the Bataan Death March and Its Aftermath.* New York: Farrar, Straus and Giroux, 2009.

Oates, Stephen, and Charles J. Errico, Eds. *Portrait of America: Volume II: From Reconstruction to the Present.* New York: Houghton Mifflin, 2003.

O'Neill, Richard. *Suicide Squads: The Men and Machines of World War II Special Operations.* London: Salamander, 1999.

Preston, Anthony. *Strike Craft.* Greenwich, CT: Bison, 1982.

Rielly, Robin L. *Kamikaze Attacks of World War II: A Complete History of Japanese Suicide Attacks on American Ships by Aircraft and Other Means.* Jefferson, NC: McFarland, 2010.

Sears, David. *At War with the Wind: The Epic Struggle with Japan's World War II Suicide Bombers.* New York: Kensington, 2008.

Sides, Hampton. *Ghost Soldiers: The Epic Account of World War II's Greatest Rescue Mission.* New York: Random House, 2002.

Strahan, Jerry E. *Andrew Jackson Higgins and the Boats That Won World War II.* Baton Rouge, LA: Louisiana State University Press, 1994.

van der Vat, Dan. *The Pacific Campaign: World War II: The U.S.–Japanese Naval War: 1941–1945.* New York: Touchstone, 1991.

West, Howard F. *Iron Men, Wooden Boats: The Epic Story of American PT Boats in World War II.* Westminster, MD: Heritage, 2005.

Government Publications

Deck Log Remarks Sheet. USS *Orestes*. December 31, 1944.

Gelzheiser, Francis L. Service Records: National Personnel Records Center, St Louis, MO.

General MacArthur's General Staff. *Reports of General MacArthur: The Campaigns of MacArthur in the Pacific: Volume 1.* Library of Congress catalogue card number 66-60005, 1994.

Know Your PT Boat: It Doesn't Mean a Thing if You Don't Have That Sting. World War II PT Boat Manual.

Unpublished Personal Narratives

Bahn, Quartermaster First Class William A. PT Boat Squadron 16. *Account of PT Boat Experiences.* 1945.

Hart, Gunner's Mate First Class Thomas. PT Boat Squadron 16. *World War II Memories.* Please see comment in bibliographic note.

Hindley, Lieutenant Lewis N., Jr. PT Boat Squadron 16. *History of PT Boat Experiences.* 1999.

Howard, Lieutenant Robert V. PT Boat Squadron 16. *Account of PT Boat Experiences.*

Jones, Motor Machinist's Mate Second Class Charlie. PT Boat Squadron 16. *The Orestes.*

Kalinowski, Motor Machinist's Mate Second Class Edmund I. PT Boat Squadron 16. *The Stingers of Some of the Mosquitoes from the Mosquito Fleet, Squadron 16.*

Lund, Carpenter's Mate First Class Philip "Bill." PT Boat Squadron 16. *Account of PT Boat Experiences.*

Mitchell, Chief Quartermaster Stephen H. PT Boat Squadron 16. *An Encounter.*

Paris, Lieutenant Colonel Edward J. (Retired). *The Mangarin Bay Fight.*

Piotter, Cele. Wife of Chief Commissary Steward Alfred F. Piotter. PT Boat Squadron 16. *United States Motor Torpedo Boat Squadron 16 History.* 1972.

Smith, Motor Machinist's Mate First Class Maurice. PT Boat Squadron 13. *Ron 13 As I Remember It.*

Stanton, Gunner's Mate First Class Richard W. PT Boat Squadron 16. *Account of PT Boat Experiences.*

Young, Quartermaster Second Class Oliver H. "Ollie," Jr. PT Boat Squadron 16. *Account of PT Boat Experiences.* 1999.

Miscellaneous Websites, Papers and Publications

All Hands: PT Boats Squadrons, Bases, and Tenders. This is the official publication of WWII PT Boats, Inc. I examined a number of issues to gain general information on WWII PT boats and to confirm what I had learned from other sources.

Avalon Pennsylvania High School Year Book: 1940.

Awards, Citations, and PT Boat Squadron 16 boat and crew list. WWII PT Boats, Inc.

Baseball Reference.

Battleship Cove: America's Fleet Museum, Fall River, MA: Official Handout.

Bowling, Captain Selman S. Note commending the "spirit and guts" of the PT boat sailors on Mindoro.

Captured Diary Entry from Japanese Physician on the island of Attu.

Chen, C. Peter. *World War II Database: Your WWII History Reference Destination.* Lava Development, LLC. https://ww2db.com

Davis, Lieutenant Commander N. Burt. Military Times Hall of Valor.

Davis, Lieutenant Commander N. Burt. Memorandum to Captain Bowling requesting a Naval Unit Citation for PT Boat Task Unit 70.1.4.

Fates of the Boats. WWII PT Boats, Inc.

Gelzheiser, Francis Leo. Electrician's Mate Second Class. PT Boat Squadron 16. Personal collection of lecture notes, notes, photos, and other materials from World War II.

Hall of Valor. Military Times.

Introduction to PT (Patrol Torpedo) Boats. WWII PT Boats, Inc.

Memorial: PT Boaters Killed in Action. WWII PT Boats, Inc.

Moss, Harold. *Beach Mission Preparing for the Mindoro Invasion: December 1944.*

PT Boat Forum 158: Questions and replies from PT boat veterans. Used to corroborate information found in other sources.

PT Information: WWII PT Boats, Inc. 2015.

Rock, Lieutenant Commander James C. Captain of PT Boat *221* Squadron 16. *The Development of the Motor Torpedo Boat.* (This "Short paper No. 2: A Study of World War II" was written after Lieutenant Commander Rock had relinquished his command of PT *221* and was enrolled in the Naval War College Command and Staff Course.)

San Francisco Chronicle, September 9, 1944.

San Francisco News, September 8, 1944.

Stillman, Lieutenant John. Find a Grave Memorial Number 51847236. Record added May 1, 2010.

World War II Patrol Torpedo Boats. WWII PT Boats, Inc.

Interviews

Gaver, Marie. Sister of Francis Gelzheiser. I discussed my father's pre-war experiences with her on numerous occasions.

Gelzheiser, Francis Leo. Electrician's Mate Second Class. PT Boat Squadron 16. Formal interviews conducted: June 1, 1999, May 15, 2000, May 25, 2001, and June 1, 2010. I discussed my father's World War II experiences with him on dozens of other occasions.

Guthrie, Alyce. President WWII PT Boats, Inc., August 2015.

Hart, Thomas and other members of PT Boat Squadron 16. My father remained good friends with many of the men who served in PT Boat Squadron 16. Over the years they attended many reunions together, and my mother and father helped to organize several of these. On numerous occasions, Tom Hart and other members of PT Boat Squadron 16 visited our house. Although I rarely asked them specific questions about their experiences in World War II, I did gain an insight into the kind of men they were, and I do believe this was helpful in writing a book about PT Boat Squadron 16.

Koach, Glenn. Turret Gunner on B-24 Liberator Bomber during World War II. September 2016.

Shannon, Don. PT Boat Curator, PT Boat Museum, Fall River, MA, April 12–14, 2015.

Index

Numbers in *bold italics* indicate pages with illustrations

A-Go 56
Abdill, Capt. Everett Woolman 147
Abeckerle, CMOMM Alfred Gustave "Al" 155, 157
Abukuma 114
Adak Island 57, 61, 62, 63, 66, *67*, 74, 83
Adaman Islands 56
Akagi 59
Alaska 3, 4, 56, 57, 60, 62, 66, 68, 78, 85, 86, 87, 88, 89
Aleut Indians 80
Aleutian Islands 3, 20, 54, 56–58, 59, 61, 62, 63, 66, 73, 76, 79, 85, 86, 87, 109, 232
Allies 121, 124, 126, 128, 133, 135, 137, 190, 208, 222, 227, 229, 230, 240, 243
Allison, CMM Thomas S. 157, 257
Amachi, Takashi 194
Amchitka Island, Alaska 61, 63, 66, 83, 85, *86*
America's Pacific Fleet 56
Amos, RM3 Joseph G. 168
Anderson, QM1 198
Archer-Fish 139, 232
Army Air Corps 63, 103, 156, 179, 224
Army's 7th Division 63
Asagumo 114
Ashigara 184
At Close Quarters: PT Boats in the United States Navy 15
Atka Island, Alaska 74
atomic bombs 124, 140, 227, 229, 243, 255
Attu 3, 54, 59, 60, 61, 62, 63–64, *65*, 66, *67*, *68*, 74, *75*, 76–*77*, *78*–83, 85, 86, 91, 253
Australia 20, 56, 59, 96, 229
Australia HMAS 136
Avalon Annual 12
Avalon High School 12, 258
Axis powers 18, 121, 126

B-17 (Flying Fortress) 20, 56, 57, 122

B-24 (Liberator) 2, 122, 127
B-29 (Superfortress) 122, *123*, *124*, 125–126
Bahn, QM1 William A. 120, 168
Bailey 61
Balboa, Panama 49
Ball, QM2 John W. 168
Bancroft, Dave 9
Baranof Island, Alaska 71–72
base force 32, 71, 86, 181, 202, 206, 213
baseball 3, 6
Basso, SEA1 Albert J. 168
Bataan 119, 269
"Battered Bastards of Bataan" 19
Battleship Cove ix
Battleship Row 18
Beasley, Lt. (jg.) Robert R. 268
Beauregard, FC1 Valamore 169
Beer, QM2 Robert A. 225
Beer Hall Putsh 9
Bell, Lt. (jg.) Chet 71, 89
Bell Labs 25
Benton, Ens. Earl 48
Bering Sea 3, 54, 74, 77, 246, 250
Best, Lt. Cmdr. Richard Halsey "Dick" 59
Bethune, Allyson ix
Biak, New Guinea 95, 109
Big Blue Blanket 144, 146, 148, 149, 162, 174, 232
Bird Cape, Amchika Island, Alaska 83
Bismarck Sea, Battle of the 99
Blankenship, John 164
blue fox 78–*79*, 87
Bohol, Philippines 113
Boise 234
Bomber Squadron 3 59
Boone, GM3 Albert E. 169
Borgnine, Ernest 1
Borneo 56, 224–225, 226, 227, 229, 255
Bougainville 20
Bowers, MOMM2 John R. 169
Bowling, Rear Adm. Selman S. 231
Bozo 12

Bremerton Navy Yard 54, 88, 89, 90
Bremerton, Washington 53, 54, 87, 88, 89, 216
British South Pacific Steamship Company 49
Brokaw, Tom 3
Bronson, Charles 1
Brunei 56
Brunner, MM1 Joseph M. 167–168, 169
Bryant 175
Bulge, Battle of the 1
Bulkeley, Lt. Cmdr. John D. "Buck" 18, 19, 20, 235
Bulkley, Capt. Robert J. 15, 231
The Bureau of Construction and Repair (BCR) 128
Burma 56
Bush 190
Bushido Code 130, 131
Butedale, Canada 69
Butler, Gen. William O. 82

Cabanatuan Prison Camp 145–146
Cabezas, Nicaragua 46–47
Caldwell, Lt. Cmdr. Earl S. 18
Canadian Women's Auxiliary Air Force (WAAF) 69
Cape Calavite 119
"Captain Guts" 219, 220
Carlson, TM1 Robert C. 82, 152, 178
Carlson, CCM Verner P. "Swede" 257
Carney, Roberta 79
Carter, TM1 Don 198
Casco 77, 78
Casco Viejo, Panama City, Panama 52
Cavite Navy Yard, Philippines 19
Cayuco, Cuba 42
Chernofski Harbor, Unalaska, Alaska 74
Chichagof Island, Alaska 72
Chignik Bay, Alaska 73
Chignik Island, Alaska 73
Chilles, MOMM1 George M. 109

287

Church of San Jose 52
Churchill, Winston 56
Cinoman, Susan x
Citrus 81
Clark, GM2 Albert C. 155, 268
Clark Field 18, 133–134
Clougherty, MOMM2 Francis 42, 198, 267, 268
Cocasola, Panama 48
Coghlan 62
Colon, Panama 49
Columbia 48
Colvin, Lt. Cmdr. Almer P. 17, 37, 88, 94, 155, 167, 168, 170, *177*, 182, 220, 250
"Colvin's Railroad" 182
Congressional Medal of Honor 20
Converse 175
Conyndham 220–221
Cope, Barbara 2
Coral Sea, Battle of 59
Corregidor 119, 207, 235, 237
Cortese, GM3 Angelo 169, 170
Cosco Cove 77
Costigan, Lt. (jg.) James 28
Cox, Lt. Gardner F. 268
Cozumel 43
Crawford, RM2 Jack 268
Cristobal, Panama 49
Crosby, Bing 181
"Crouching Dragons" 137
Cuba 38, 39, *40*, *41*, 42, 43, 44
Culion Leper Colony, Philippines 223–224
Curtis Wright Company 14
Cushing 20
Cuyo Island, Philippines 222–223

daihatsus (Japanese coastal barges) 29, 33, 99, *101*, *102*, 103, *104*, 105, 107, 110, 113, 118, 225, 230, 231
Dashiell 147
Davis, Lt. Cmdr. Nathaniel Burt, Jr. 116, *117*, 118, 142, 150, 153, 156, 166, 169, 186, 187, 193, 196, 198, 205, 207, 231, 255, 257, 267; suggested Naval Unit Citation 269–270
Davis's Raiders 116, 117, 166
Delco, Joe 1
Delco, Paul 1, 254
Denny, Lt. James B. 66
the *Dirty Dozen* 1
Disney, Walt 33
Dixie IV *14*
Dobyns, Thurman 2
Donald, MOMM1 James 82, 89, 159
Doolittle, Lt. Col. James "Jimmy" 56
Dotson, William 211, 212
Douglas TBD Devastator bomber 58
Dreese, Richard 2
Duchess 80, 89
Dudas, MOMM2 William L. 168, 169

Dunbar, MOMM Everett A. 109
Dunckel, Brig. Gen. William C. 146, 147, 148, 184, 206
Dusky Shearwaters 85, 232
Dutch East Indies 56
Dutch Harbor, Alaska 57, 59, 60, 63, 66, 73, 85
Dwyer, QM2 George A. 178, 198, 199, 267

Eichelberger, Lt. Gen. Robert L. 110, 118, 206
Eisenhower, Gen. Dwight David 128
Elco PT boats 21, 31, 66
Electric Launch Corporation (Elco) 21
Eleventh Air Force 82
Ellis, QM1 Lester P. 38
English Channel 20
Enterprise 59
Enyeart, SH2 Russel 109
equator crossing ceremony 91, 94
Erickson, Lt (jg.) John R. 158

F6F Hellcat fighter 122
Fairfield, Connecticut 1, 145 257, 258, 282
Fargo, Lt. Cmdr. Alvin W., Jr. 151, 184, 185, 186, 187, 224, 226
Felde, MOMM3 Wallis J. "Red" 89
50th Engineers 64
Filipino guerrillas 33, 105, *117*, 143, 162, 169, 172, 179, 183, 189, 190, 206, 207, 208 211–212, 215, 216, 220, 223, 224, 225, 230, 231, 235, 239, 241, 269
Filipino scouts 166
503rd Parachute Regimental Combat Team 146, 148, 185, 229
Flynn, Errol 85, 86
Fonda, Henry 54
Foot 175
Forbes Field 9
Ford, Lt. (jg.) Gerald "Jerry" 164
Ford, Henry 127
Ford, John 4, 20
Ford Motor Company 127
1493, Uncovering the New World Columbus Created 142
Fourteenth Imperial Army 235
Fowler, MACH1 Ormand O. 39
Francis, Vivian 79
French Indochina 55
Fujita, Capt. 226
Fuller, RD1 John W. 155, 268

Gallagher, Lt. Earl 59
Gansevoort 201, 202, *203*
Gatun Lake, Panama 49
Gaver, Marie, 10, 11, 12
Gelzheiser, Edward L. 13, 257, 258
Gelzheiser, EM2 Francis L.: journey into Manila 243–246; killing Japanese 159–160, 262–265;

Leyte 118; Mindoro 142, 143, *152*, 155, 156, 157, 159, 166, 173, *174*, 176, 180, 186, 194, 203, 204, 205, *209*, 210, 211, 212, 214, *218*, *219*, 221–222, 224, *228*, 255; post World War II 5, 6, 7, 8, 10, 146, 247, 248, *249*, 250, 251, 252, 253, 254, 256, 257, 258, 259; World War II x, 3, *15*, 32, 35, 36, 39, 42–43, 44, 46, 48, 49, 52, 53, 68, 71, 76, *78*, 80, 86, 87, 88, 89, 90, 132, 140, 145; youth 9, 10, *11*, 12, *13*, *14*
Gelzheiser, Janet L. 5, 249, 257, 258, 259
Gelzheiser, Joseph 9–10
Gelzheiser, Josephine 9, 12
Gelzheiser, Lynn A. x
Gelzheiser, Lynn M. 254, 255
Gelzheiser, Robert 36, 48, 78, 80, 81, 85, 86, 87, 88, 89, 94, 104, 145, 157, 160, 171, 180, 204, 211, 217, 219, 232, 233, 246, 247, 248, 249, 252, 254, 255, 256, 258, 262, 264, 265
Germany 57, 127, 132
Gertrude Cove, Alaska 84
Ghost Soldiers 143
Gilbert Islands 56
Goddard, TM1 Billie J. 268
Golden Gate Bridge 90
Great Depression 3, 4, 10, 78, 120, 121, 222, 258
Great Lakes Naval Training Center, North Chicago 14
The Great Producer 129, 130, 132
The Great Raid 145
Greater East Asian Co-Prosperity Sphere 57
The Greatest Generation 3
Griffin, Lt. (jg.) Harry E. 153, 188, 204, 219, 268
Guadalcanal 94
Guam 20, 56
guerrillas see Filipino guerrillas
Gulf of Mexico 17, 36
Guns of Navarone 1
Guthrie, Alyce ix

Half Moon 205
Hall, Lt. (jg.) Thomas C. 268
Hallowell, Lt. Roger H. 223, 224, 226, 267
Halsey, Adm. William Frederick "Bull" 81, 110, 111, 135, 143, 162, 164, 165, 247, 266
Halsey's Typhoon see Typhoon Cobra
Hanson, Victor Davis 58
Hara, Takashi 9
Haraden 147
Harding, Warren 9
Hart, Cecelia 39, 268
Hart, GM1 Tom x, 38–39, 45, 49, 54, 70, 71, 78, 82, 95, 144, 148, 151, 156, 159, 160–161, 166, 167, 170–171, 172, 173, 176, 183, 185, 196–199, 208, 209, 215, 254
Harvest Moon 257

Haughian, Lt. (jg.) Michael A. 221
Hawaii 59
Helme, Lt. (jg.) William B. 216, 268
Henderson, RMT2 MacIntyre E. "Tex" 37–38, 39, 40, 54, 69, 72, 257
Higgins, Andrew Jackson 127–128
Higgins Industries 21, 127–128
"Higgins Men" 23
Hill, Col. Bruce C. 147, 171
Hill Field 171, 172, 179
Hilliard, Ens. Harry 170
Hindley, Lt. (jg.) Lewis 69
Hirohito (Emperor of Japan) 9, 64, 140
Hiryu 59
Hitler, Adolf 9
Hobart Baker 203
Hogan, Col. Robert 1
Hogan's Heroes 1
Holland, Bonnie 79
Hollandia, New Guinea 95
Hollywood Hotel 44
Holmes, MOMM1 Al 155
Holocaust 2
"The Home" *see* Saint Joseph Orphan Asylum
Honduras 44
Hong Kong 55
Hopewell 151
Hopkins, QM2 Robert E. 169
Hornet 56
Howorth 150
Hoyt, Waite 9
Huckins PT boats 21
Huckins Yacht Works 21
Hull 163
Hunnicutt, RM2 Richard L. 267

I Love You 181
Ilin Island, Philippines 154, 155, 186, 187, 270
I'll Be Seeing You 76, 181
Imperial Japanese Army Air Force 133, 135
Imperial Japanese Navy Air Service 55, 114
Imperial Palace 134
Imperial Precepts for the Military 130
Inanudak Bay, Alaska 73
Ingersoll, Capt. Stuart "Slim" 164
Inside Passage 70, *71*, 73
Intracoastal Waterway 37
Ishil, Lt Gen. 226
Iwabuchi, Rear Adm. Sanji 236, 237, 238
Iwo Jima 165, 232

Jackie, BMG2 William "Bill" 232
James H. Breasted 187
Jannotta, Cmdr. Vernon A. 196
Japan 18, 55, 56, 57, 110, 112, 113, 115, 121, 122, 123, 125, 127, 129, 130, 131, 133, 229, 234, 235, 237, 243, 246, 252, 255

Japanese 18, 19, 95, 96, 101, 104, 107, 112, 118, 119, 120, 121, 125, 126, 129, 130, 131, 133, 135, 141, 143, 144, 148, 153, 154, 155, 156, 157, 158, 159, 160, 161, 165, 166, 168, 169, 170, 175, 176, 177, 178, 180, 182, 183, 184, 185, 186, 187, 188, 189, 190, 192, 202, 203, 205, 206, 207, 208, 209, 210, 211, 212, 213, 215, 216, 217, 219, 220, 221, 223, 224, 225, 226, 227, 228, 230, 231, 232, 233, 234, 236, 238, 239, 240, 241, 241, 242, 250, 251, 255, 257, 262, 264
Japanese Army 19, 114, 237
Japanese Empire 122, 156
Japanese High Command 56, 111, 132
Japanese invasion currency **233**
Japanese Navy 19, 56, 99, 110, 112, 113, 114, 133, 135, 231, 232, 237
Japanese planes 19, 117, 118, 119
Japanese prisoners 104, *105*, 107, **108**, *117*, 118
Japanese submarines 105
Japan's Pacific wall ("absolute national defense sphere") 56, 110
Jesselton, Borneo 226
JN 25 (WWII American code breaking team) 58
John Burke 190, **191**
John Clayton 205
Jones, MOMM2 Charles R. 199
Joyner, SC3 Elred 170–171
Juan de Fuca 175, 203
Junyo 60

Kaga 59
Kaitens 138
Kalinowski, MOMM2 Edmund I. 109, 169, 215, 257, 267
Kalinowski, Joseph 2
Kalinowski, Mark Joseph 2, 248–249
kamikazes 3, 23, 33, 115, 118, 119, 122, 132–137, 148, 255, 256, 264, 266; at Luzon 234, 243; attacks on first Mindoro resupply convoy 174–176; attacks on second Mindoro resupply convoy 190–203, **193**; at Mindoro 143, 145, 146, 147, 149, 151, 153, 157–159, 166–167, 168, 172, 173, 204, 205, 213, 229, 230, 232, 263
Keeling, Lt. (jg.) Robert 184
Keith, Agnes Newton 227
Kent, Lt. (jg.) Brian 158
Ketchikan, Alaska 69, 70
Ketsu-Go or "Decisive Operation" 140
Key West, Florida 38
Kiendzior, MOMM1 William 215
Kimura, Rear Adm. Masanori 184, 186, 188
Kincaid, Adm. Thomas C. 111, 113, 143, 220, 231, 234, 235

King Cove, Alaska 66
Kiska, Alaska 57, 59, 60, 61, 62, 63, 66, 83, 84, 85, 232
Kittemath Indian tribe 69
Kiyoshimo 188
Klemanski, F1 John 48, 54, 76
knife (United States Navy) *7*, 15, 160, 250–251, 264, 265
Koach, Glen 2, 254
Kodiak Island, Alaska 72–73
Kofu, Japan 126
Komandorskis, Battle of 61, 62, 63
Kremer, Cmdr. John, Jr. 196
Kruger, Gen. Walter 206
Kublai Khan 133
Kuching garrison 227
Kugimoto, Hobuhide 194
Kuril Islands 57, 64, 75
Kuroshio Current 56

LaCasse, MOMM1 Donald E. "Shorty" 257
La Ceiba, Honduras 44–45
La Fe, Cuba 39, **41**
landing craft **149**
Lardiere, MS Joseph H. 257
Lawson 94
LCIs (landing craft infantry) 207; LCI *621* 205; LCI *624* 192; LCI *1000* 192, 194; LCI *1001* 192; LCI *1005* 192; LCI *1006* 192; LCI *1072* 194; LCI *1076* 190
LCM (landing craft mechanized) 100, 185, 208
LCVP (landing craft vehicle personal) 225
Leeson, Lt. Cmdr. Robert 113
LeMay, Gen. Curtis Emerson 125
Lend Lease Program 21
Lerz, MM2 Francis Xavier 43, 257
Leslie, Lt. Cmdr. Maxwell "Max" 59
Lewis L. Dyche 205, 206
Leyte, Battle of 119, 132, 136, 138, 146
Leyte Gulf, Battle of 94, 113–114, 132, 136, 143, 144, 149, 156, 164, 234; PT boats at *113*–114
Leyte Island, Philippines 3, 111, 112, 113, 114, 115, 116, 118, 119, 143, 144, 145, 147, 149, 156, 160, 174, 176, 183, 184, 190, 191, 192, 193, 207, 234, 235
Lockheed P-38 "Lightning" 122, 146, 167, 169, 172, 174, 176, 177, 179, 188, 194, 197, 213, 215, 224
Loftus, Lt. Joe 148
Long Island Sound 248–249, 252–253, 256–257, 259
The Longest Day 1
Los Negros, New Guinea 94
Lough 220–221
LSTs (landing ship tank): LST *210* 115; LST *460* 175; LST *472* 151, 153, 263; LST *605* 152, 156–157, 158, 159, 263; LST *738* 151, 153, 263, 270; LST *749* 175; LST *750* 192

Luzon, Philippines 3, 111, 114, 119, 138, 139, 144, 145, 146, 148, 149, 156, 157, 158, 162, 165, 170, 177, 183, 184, 186, 190, 203, 205, 206, 207, 215, 216, 220, 223, 229, 230, 231, 232, 233, 234, 235, 237, 239, 243, 269

"Mac, Johnny" 204
MacArthur, Gen. Douglas 18, 19, 20, 21, 35, 96, 97, 101, 103, 109, 110, 111, 112, 119, 143, 146, 148, 149, 162, 225, 231, 232, 234, 235, 238, 241
Macmillan, Cmdr. I.E. 176
Mahoney, TM1 Charles 169
Malaya 56
Mangarin Bay, Philippines 142, 143, 150, 153, *154*, 155, 156, 159, 161, 162, 169, 170, 177, 178, 182, 183, 184, 190, 193, 194, 201, 203, 205, 209, 212, 217, 223, 224, 225
Manhattan Project 123
Manila 3, 118, 119, 156, 189, 212, *242*, 244, 258; battle for 235–243
Manila Bay 119, 189, 234, 235, 237
Manila Herald 234
Manila Naval Defense Force 236, 237
Mann, Charles 143
Manning, Nancy x
Manus Island, New Guinea 94
Marcus Island 150, 160
Marinduque, Philippines 216
Marshall, Gen. George 231
Marshall, Col. Samuel Lyman Atwood 5, 262
Marshall Islands 56
Martin, Ens. Jim 232
Marvin, Lee 1
Massachusetts 5
Massacre Bay, Alaska 61, 66, 76, 80
Mathews, GM3 John G. "Ducky" 257
Mayerhardt, YNSN Jack 42
Mazeroski, Bill 9
McCain, Adm. John Sidney "Slew" "Popeye" 135, 144, 174, 232
McClendon, Lt. (jg.) J.B. 175
McClusky, Lt. Cmdr. Clarence "Wade" 59
McHale, Quinton 1
McHale's Navy 216, 249
McKellar, Lt. Clinton, Jr. 66
McLean, Captain John B. 190, 192, 194, 232
McMorris, Vice Adm. Charles "Soc" 61
Men Against Fire: The Problem of Battle Command 261
Mentz, Capt. George F. 190, 196
Metsch, Wayne 255, 258
Midway, Battle of 56, 57, 58, 60, 113, 129, 132
Midway Island 58, 59

Miegl, GM2 Ladislav 169
Milne Bay, New Guinea 94
Mindanao, Philippines 19, 110, 111, 113, 192
Mindoro 3, 4, 116, 117, 139, 140, 141, 143, 144, 170, *171*, 173, 178, *182*, 189, 204, 205, 206, 208, 209, *210*, 211, 212, 213, *214*, 216, 217, 219, 221, 222, 223, 227, 228, 229, 232, 233, 234, 235, 248, 249, 250, 252, 254, 255, 256, 257, 258, 263–264, 269; battle "score card" 230, 231; defense 156–162, 166, 172, 174, 178; geography 142–143, 210–211, 215; invasion 119, *149*, 142–156, 165; Japanese bombardment 182–189; patrols from 179–181, 297; resupply convoy number one 174–176; resupply convoy number two 190–203
Mindoro Tamarau 215
Mios Woendi, New Guinea 91, *92–93*, 95, 105, 107, 108, 113, *115*
Missouri 120
Mr. Floyd's Motor Club 13
Mitchell, Lt. (jg.) Samuel 368
Mitsubishi A6M1 "Zero" or "Zeke" fighter plane 55, 60, 114, 119, 134, 136, 157, 175, *230*
Mitsubishi G4M "Betty" bomber 55, 138, *150*
Mitsubishi KI-46 "Dinah" reconnaissance aircraft 156, 157
Moale 151
Moen, MOMM1 William C. 267
Mog Pog, Philippines 216, 217
"Moms" 35
Monadnock 206
Monaghan 62, 163
Monterey 164
Morison, Samuel Eliot 203
Morobe Island, New Guinea *97*
"Motor Mac" 24
Motor Torpedo Boat Squadron: (1) 15, 18, 66, 68; (2) 18; (2[2]) 32; (3) 18, 19; (3[2]) 32; (8) 190; (9) ix; (13) 66, *68*, *74*, *75*, 115, 142, 151, 157, 215, 224, 225, 226, 230, 233; (15) 35; (16) ix, x, 3, 4, 8, 15, *16*, *17*, 18, 21, 23, 31, *32*, 95, 107, 108, 110, 127, 140, 231, 246, 249, 250, 257, 258 (awards and citations 267–268; at Borneo 225, 226; at Leyte 115, 116, 118; at Mindoro 119, 142, 144, 148, 150, 153, 157, 161, 162, 166, 167, 173, *174*, 184, 186, 215, 216, 220, 223, 227, 228, 231; "score card" *230*; Unit Citation 233, 269; at war's end 229, 246); (16A) 35, 36, 43, 44, 46, 47, 48, 49, 50, *51*, 88, 89, 91, 94, 95, 109, 228, 250 (in Alaska 68, 69, 71, 72, *73*, *74*, *75*, 76, 79, 81, 82, 85, 86); (16B) 35, 91, 95; (17) 115, 233; (24) 116, 117, 190; (25) 115, 190; (36) 115

Motor Torpedo Boat Squadrons (overview) 31–32
Motor Torpedo Boat Squadrons Training Center, Melville, RI 14–15, 21, 33, 229
Motor Torpedo Boats *see* PT boat
Motor Torpedo Boat fleet 28, 33–*34*, 35, 71, 105, 113, 114, 116, 118, 179, 184, 188, 196, 199, 206, 213, 231, 235
Mount Halcon, Mindoro 142
Mucci, Col. Henry Andrews 145, 146
Mueller, Lt. Kenneth 194
Mukohse, Tadoa 194

Nachi 61, 62
napalm 123, 125, 126
Narragansett Bay 15
Nashville *111*, 146, 147, 171, 263
National Youth Administration 12
Naval Training Center, Sampson, New York 14–15
Navy Unit Citation 233
Negros, Philippines 143
Nehf, Art 9
Neutrality Acts 121
New Caledonia 53, 59, 228
New Georgia 20
New Guinea 3, 4, 20, 29, 55, 88, 89, 91, 94, 95, *96*, 97, *98*, 99, *100*, 101, 103, 105–107, 110, 111, 116, 118, 176, 225, 246, 249
New Mexico 169
New Orleans 15, *16*, 21, *22*, 35, 36, 45, 109, 127, 176, 228
New York Giants 9
New York Navy Yard 18
New York Yankees 9
Newberry, Alyce Foster "Mrs Boats" ix
Newberry, BMC James "Boats" ix
Newcomb 176
Nichols Field 19
Nimitz, Adm. Chester W. 58, 111, 114, 143
19th Infantry Regimental Combat Team 146
Niven, David 1
Noack, MOMM2 Nolan 109
Novak, CTM John A. 44, 155, 268
Nussman, TM2 Everett 167

Oakland 91
O'Brien 151
Ocampo, Lt. Col. Emmanuel V. de 239
O'Driscoll, Martha 85, 86
Ohio River 12, 14, 43
"Ohio River Crawl" 12
Oka (Exploding Cherry Blossom") 138–139, 140, 184, 232, 262
Okinawa, Battle of 135, 137
Omen of the Seas 15, 43, 71, 79, 82, 107, 150, 151, 152, 153, 168, 169, 170, 172, 176, 178, 180, 183, 187,

208, 212, 219, 246; *see also* PT 221
Onishi, Vice Adm. Takijiro 133
Onoda, Second Lt. Hiroo 243
Ooishi, Yutaka 194
Operation Cottage 83
Operation King II 111
Operation Landcrab 63
Operation Olympic 140
Orestes 190, 194, **195, 196, 197**-199, **200, 201**, 203, 204, 256, 270
Ormoc Bay, Leyte 118
Oyodo 184

Pacific Fleet 57, 94, 137
Packard Motor Company 24
Packard PT boat engines *see* PT boat
Pagacz, MOMM1 Frank J. 268
Pagapas Bay, Philippines 215
Palau 115
Palawan, Philippines 145, 147, 148, 222, 223, 225, 233
Palladino, Ben "Dean" x
Panama 3, 17, 35, 37, 47, 48, 49, **50, 51, 52**, 53, 228
Panama Canal 3, 38, 49, 250
Paney, Philippines 145, 160, 233
"Paradise Island," Philippines 217-218
Paramushiro, Japan 57, 61, 64, 84, 85
Patricia Bay, British Columbia 68
Patrol Torpedo Boat Advanced Training Base, Taboga Island, Panama 17
Patton 1
Patton, Gen. George 1
PC 1129 220-221
Peace River, Florida 247-248
Pearl Harbor 9, 14, 15, 18, 53, 55, 56, 57, 60, 81, 101, 120, 121, 129, 132, 237, 246, 261, 263, 264
Peck, Gregory 1
Peckinpaugh, Roger 9
Pecos 206
Penfield Lighthouse 252, 257
Pensacola, Florida 37-38
"Phil" 219, **220**
Philip 202
Philippines 3, 4, 18, 19, 20, 21, 29, 56, 80, 94, 98, 99, 101, 103, 105, 110, 111, 112, 114, 115, 116, 119, 133, 136, 137, 138, 139, 142, 143, 156, 162, 173, 179, 180, 181, 188, 207, 209, 210, 220, 222, 224, 225, 228, 229, 231, 232, 233, 234, 235, 237, 242, 243, 246, 249, 264
Phipps, Tim "Coach" x
Pierman, MOMM1 Andy "Chop Chop" **100**
Pierotti, GMT2 William "Hank" 88, 198
Piotter, CCS Al 153, 159, 257
Pips, Battle of the 84-85
Plage, Lt. Cmdr. Henry Lee 164-165, 254

"Plywood Derbies" 21
Polo Grounds 9
Porcupine 190, 201, **202**
Port Althorp, Alaska 72
Port Hardy, British Columbia 69
Port Lemon, Costa Rica 47
Portuguese Timor 56
Pringle 201
PT boat: (*9*) 20; (*22*) 66; (*23*) 18; (*24*) 66; (*27*) 66; (*28*) 66; (*32*) 19; (*34*) 19, 20; (*35*) 19; (*41*) 19, 20, 110; (*73*) 208; (*74*) 227; (*75*) 162, 203, 208, 215, 216, 225, 227; (*76*) 184; (*77*) 158, 184, 185, 186, 220-221, 223; (*78*) 184, 203, 205, 206; (*79*) 220-221, 223; (*80*) 184, 185, 186, 207; (*81*) 184, 205, 206; (*82*) 186, 207; (*84*) 162, 184, 185-186, 188, 227; (*128*) 100; (*132*) 119; (*134*) 119; (*149*) 207; (*155*) ix; (*167*) 27; (*188*) 28, 207; (*189*) **200**; (*192*) 184, 185; (*219*) 35, 45, 53, 54, 68, 77, 78, 109, 157; (*220*) 35, 53, 54, 68, 76, 81, 172, 177, 203, 208, 225, 226, 227; (*221*) 15, 35, 36, **37**, 38, 39, 40, 43, 48, 49, 50, 53, 54, 89, 90, 108; in Alaska 68, 69, 71, 72, 74, 79, 81, 82, 83, 87, 250, 256 (in Borneo 226; destruction 246; journey to and Battle for Mindoro 144, 148, 150, 151-152, 153, 155, 158, 159, 160, 161, 167, 168, 169, 170, 171, 173, 176, 178, 182, 183, 184, 185, 187, 188, 189, 198, 208, 209, 212, 213, 215, 218, 219, 221, 224, 225; journey to and Battle for New Guinea 88-95, 107-110; on Leyte 118, 119; see also *Omen of the Seas*); (*222*) 35, 53, 54, 68, 69, 80, 81, 88, 89, 90, 172, 177, 178, 198, 215, 216, 219, 220, 221, 223, 225, 226; (*223*) 35, **52**, 53, 68, 71, 90, **91**, 107, 109, 153, 158, 159, 169, 170, 172, 184, 185, 187, 188, 189, 204, 206, 215, 219, 223, 226; (*224*) 35, 48, 53, 68, **90**, 151, 153, 154-155, 161, 169, 203, 223, 225, 226, 227; (*225*) **52**; (*227*) 142, 182, 184, 185, 233, 267; (*230*) 142, 156, 158, 183, 184, 185, 187, 216, 233; (*235*) 223, 226; (*241*) 225, 226; (*242*) 223, 226; (*297*) 154-155, 226; (*298*) 107, 158-159, 199, 206, 215,) 223, 225, 226, 227, 232; (*299*) 107, 226, 227; (*300*) 109, 117, 156,) 167-169, 170, 248, 256; (*301*) 107, 108, 109; (*320*) 118; (*323*) 119; (*332*) 191; (*352*) 192; (*355*) 192, 194; (*523*) 119; (*525*) 119; (*617*) ix; (*796*) ix
PT boat 14, 15, 18, 20, 21, 29, 176; armament *see* PT boat armament; barge patrol 33; battle tactics 33-34, 43, 89, 103; British boats 20; compasses, radar, radios and sonar 25, 53, 66, 68, 76, 89 180; construction 21 **22**; crews 23-24, 32; early boats 20, 21; functions 32-33; Higgins boats ix, 21, **22**, 23-24, 25, **26, 27**; maintenance 25; Packard engines 24, 30, 46, 79; patrol procedures 179-180; repair 213; smoke generators 27; speed 24; torpedoes *see* PT boat torpedos; transmissions, screws, and shafts 24, 116, 157, 188, 246; underway **22, 26**
PT boat armament: death charges 29; 80 mm mortars 31; .50 caliber machine gun 15, **30, 31**, 35, 89, 109, 151, 167, 173, 186, 207, 215, 263; 40 mm "barge buster" cannon 29, 30, 89, 150, 152, 154, 155, 159, 160, 161, 168, 169, 170, 172, 175, 186, 208; Mark 50 rocket launchers 15, 31; 60 mm mortars 89; 37 mm cannon **30**; Thompson machine gun 31, **32**, 103; 20 mm cannon 15, 29, 30, 89, 159, 161, 175, 186
PT Boat Base 8 97
PT Boat Base 17, Babon Point, Samar, Philippines **244, 245**
PT boat gas dump **100**
PT boat gunners 118
PT boat tenders 24, 32, 115, 205
PT boat torpedos, torpedo racks and torpedo tubes 27-30, **28, 29, 40**, 76, 89 188; Mark VIII 28; Mark XIII 28, 53; Mark XIV 28; mechanized mobile 20; Tubes 28, 29
PT Boats, Inc. ix
Puerto Castilla, Honduras 45, 46
Puget Sound 53
Pyle, Ernie 9

Quinn, Anthony 1

Rabaul, New Guinea 55, 101, 110
Rafferty, Ens. Joseph 172, 181, 257
raiders, Allied 33; American 166, 207; Royal Dutch 107
Ralph Talbot 149
Rankin, TM1 Jared 109
The Rat Patrol 1
Rauh, Ens. Walter F., Jr. 198
Records, RM2 Ralph 161
Redfish 139, 184, 232
"Reefer Club" 108
Reitz, GM3 Edward 169
Rock, Lt. (jg.) James C. "Pete" 37, 38, 39, 40, 42-43, **47**, 54, 69, 71, 176-**177**, 257
Rockefort, Cmdr. Joseph J. 58
Rockwell, Vice Adm. Francis W. "Skinny" 35, 83
Rogers, Capt. Bertram 61
Rogers, Sgt. Paul 234
Rommel, Field Marshal Erwin 1
Romulo, Carlos 234
Roosevelt, Franklin D. 19, 20, 110, 120, 121, 214, 221-222, 254
Rosenthal, Ens. Raymond W. 153

Index

Roth, Lt. (jg.) Robert J. 178, 219, 221, 267
Rowe, Lt. Cmdr. George F. 162, 169, 177, 208
Ruddock, Rear Adm. Theodore D. 147
Rum and Cola 213
Russo, MOMM2 Ted 109
Russo-Japanese War 59
Ryujo 60, 139, 232

Saint Joseph Orphan Asylum ("The Home") 10, 11, 12, 222, 254, 258
Saint Lo 136
St. Petersburg, Florida 38
Saipan 20, 139
Salt Lake City 61, 62
Samar Island, Philippines 246
samurai 130
San Francisco 90
San Francisco Chronicle 176
The San Francisco News 23
San Jose, Mindoro 142, 143, 155, 186, 199, 206, 209
San Pedro Bay, Philippines 116
Sand Point, Alaska 73
Sander, QM2 Elmer Clifton "Sandy" 48
Sansapor, New Guinea 109
Santa Cruz, Philippines 218
Santa Isabel 94
Saunders, QM1 Dan G. 82, 257
Sawada, Genji 194
Schuylkill 53
Scott, George C. 1
Scott-Pine 20
Scout Bomber Douglas (SBO) 59
scouts (Allied, Filipino and native) 33, 106, 117, 118, 166, 207, 220, 233
seasickness 71, 76, 220
Seattle 3, 54, 66, 68, 74, 85, 87, 90, 229
Second Striking Force 184
Servicemen's Dependent Allowance Act of 1942 89
Seventh Fleet 220, 231
Seward, Alaska 72
Shannon, Donald ix
Shearwater Canadian Army camp 69
Shenandoah 90
"Sherman carpets" 137
Shiano 138-139, 232
Shinyo or "Ocean Shakers" 138
Shumway, Lt. Dewitt 59
Sicklen, Lt. James H. 268
Sides, Hampton 145
Simon G. Reed 203
Sinatra, Frank 76
Singapore 56
"Singer's Law" 162
Sixth Army 111, 148, 206
Slow Tow Convoy 144, 147, 149, 160
Smith, MOMM1 Maurice 205, 206
Smith, LCDR Russell H. 15, 17

Solomon Islands 20, 56
Song of the Warrior 134
Soryu 59
Spanish American War 20
Specht, Lt. Cmdr. William C. 14, 18, 33
"Specht Tech" 15
Spence 163
spirit warriors 131, 132, 134, 200, 231, 235, 254
Spofford, TM2 Robert, Jr. 170, 268
Springel, Lt. George, Jr. 28
Squadron 16 *see* Motor Torpedo Boat Squadron 16
Squadron VB6 59
Squadron VS6 59
Stalin, Josef 121
Stanley 147
Stellar Cove, Attu, Alaska 83
Stillman, Lt. John 184, 186, 208, 220-221, 223, 267
Stinson, James 257
Street, CRM Robert 216, 218
Struble, Rear Adm. Arthur Dewey 142, 147, 149
Suga, Lt. Col. Tatsuji 227
suicide boats 207, 215, 216, 220, 223, 235
suicide soldiers 137
suicide swimmers 137
Sultan of Ternate 106
Superman 6
Surigao Strait, Philippines 113, 143
Suzuki, Prime Minister Kantaro 140
Swart, Lt. Philip 267
Szczech, GM2 Alexander J. 268

Tabberer 164-165
Taboga Island, Panama 35, 49, **51**
Tacloban, Philippines 118, 243, 244
takayari butai 140
Tampa, Florida 38
Tanah Merah Bay, New Guinea 95
Tarawa, Battle of 132
Task Force 38 143, 144, 145, 146, 148, 157, 162, 163, 164
Task Force 77.11 190
Task Group 77 235
Task Group 78.3.13 175
Task Unit 70.1.4 142, 165, 213, 224, 229, 231, 233, 267
Task Unit 70.1.7 224, 225, 226
Task Unit 93.4.64 226
Taussig 164
Teheran Conference 121
Tenaglia, Doug x
Thailand 55
Theobald, Rear Adm. Robert "Fuzzy" 60
They Were Expendable (book and film) 4, 20
Three Came Home 227
Tojo (pet monkey) 215
Tojo, Prime Minister Hideki 140, 235

Tokyo 124, 126
Tokyo Rose 76, 106, 160, 181, 216, 231
Treasure Island, California 90
Tredinnick, Lt. (jg.) Frank A. 158, 185
Trueblood, Lt. (jg.) Alva C. 268
Truman, Harry 222
Tufi, New Guinea **99**
Turner, Lt. Cmdr. Blaney C. 221
Twelve O'Clock High 1
24th Infantry Division 185
Type 93 torpedo (Long Lance) 55, 137-138
Typhoon Cobra 162-165

Umnak Island, Alaska 61, 73
Umnak Pass, Alaska 74
Unalaska, Alaska 60, 73, 74
unconditional surrender 115, 120
United Fruit Company 45
United States Army Air Force 123
United States Naval Academy 116
United States Naval Training Station, Taboga Island, Panama 17, 35, 49, **50, 51, 52**
United States Navy 21, 32, 35, 36, 46, 55, 56, 58, 76, 84, 85, 88, 89, 94, 109, 110, 111, 114, 116, 127, 128, 136, 162, 173, 176, 186, 222, 232, 233, 246, 258
United States Pacific Fleet 57
University of Pittsburgh 13
Unryu 139, 184, 232
USO Show 79, 128

Vancouver 68, 69
Verde Island Passage, Philippines 119
Versailles Peace Conference 120
Victoria, British Columbia 68
Vigeant, Armand 55
Visayan Attack Force 143, 144, 145, 148
V.J. Day 255

Wainwright, Gen. Jonathan "Skinny" 110, 235
Wake Island 18, 56
Walsh, SC2 George T. 161, 170, 268
Washington Disarmament Conference *see* Washington Naval Conference
Washington Naval Conference 9, 121
Wayne, John 1
Wehrli, Lt. Robert J. 153, 267
Wells, Lt. Herbert H. Pete 107-108, 161
West End Yacht Club 35
West Virginia 147, 160
Westinghouse 25
White, William L. 20
White Christmas 76
William Ahearn 191
William Sharon 191-192

Williams, Arthur 1, 244
"Willie" 211–212
williwaw 57, 76, 81, 82
Willoughby 227
Willow Run factory 127
Wilson 191, 192, 202
Wilson, Woodrow 120, 121
Woodland Regional High School x
Woodruff, Maj. Gen. Roscoe B. 206
Wrangell Narrows, Alaska 70

Yakutat, Alaska 72
Yamamoto, Adm. Isoroku 56, 57, 58, 60–61, 121
Yamasaki, Col. Yasuyo 64
Yamashita, Gen. Tomoyuki 111, 156, 235, 236, 237
Yap, Philippines 111
Yasukuni Shrine 134
YMS *315* (auxiliary [yard] motor minesweeper) 147
Yonai, Ad. Mitsumasa 23, 139
Yorktown 59

You Belong to Me 181
Young, QM2 Oliver H. "Ollie" 108–109, 117, 168
YSD *26* (seaplane wrecking derrick) 78
Yucatan Peninsula 43

Zeithan, Ens. Freddrick A. 199
Zeke *see* Mitsubishi A6M1
Zero *see* Mitsubishi A6M1
Zulick, Ens. John 182

www.ingramcontent.com/pod-product-compliance
Lightning Source LLC
Chambersburg PA
CBHW081541300426
44116CB00015B/2714